CLOSING THE GAP

Lombardi, the Packers Dynasty, and the Pursuit of Excellence

Willie Davis

with Jim Martyka and
Andrea Erickson Davis

TRIUMPH
BOOKS

Library of Congress Cataloging-in-Publication Data

Davis, Willie, 1934–
    Closing the gap : Lombardi, the Packers dynasty, and the pursuit of excellence / Willie Davis with Jim Martyka and Andrea Erickson Davis
        p. cm.
    Summary: "The autobiography of Pro Football Hall of Fame member and Green Bay Packers legend Willie Davis"—Provided by publisher.
    Includes bibliographical references and index.
    ISBN 978-1-60078-726-3 (hardback)
    1. Davis, Willie, 1934– 2. Football players—United States—Biography. 3. Green Bay Packers (Football team) 4. Lombardi, Vince. I. Martyka, Jim. II. Davis, Andrea Erickson. III. Title.
    GV939.D3495A3 2012
    796.332092--dc23
    [B]

                            2012026787

This book is available in quantity at special discounts for your group or organization. For further information, contact:
    Triumph Books LLC
    814 North Franklin Street
    Chicago, Illinois 60610
    Phone: (312) 337-0747
    www.triumphbooks.com

Printed in U.S.A.

ISBN: 978-1-60078-726-3

Design by Amy Carter

Photos courtesy of AP Images unless otherwise indicated

This book is dedicated to my two mentors,
Coach Eddie Robinson, who helped shape everything
I've done in my life, and Coach Vince Lombardi, who still
pushes me toward excellence each and every day

Contents

Commitment to Excellence

"I owe most everything to football in which I have spent the greater part of my life. And I have never lost my respect, my admiration, or my love for what I consider a great game. And each Sunday, after the battle, one group savors victory; another group lives in the bitterness of defeat. The many hurts seem a small price to have paid for having won, and there is no reason at all that is adequate for having lost. To the winner, there is one hundred percent elation, one hundred percent laughter, and one hundred percent fun; and to the loser the only thing left for him is a one hundred percent resolution, one hundred percent determination.

"And it's a game, I think, a great deal like life in that it demands that a man or woman's personal commitment be toward excellence and be toward victory, even though you know that ultimate victory can never be completely won. Yet it must be pursued with all of one's might. And each week there's a new encounter, each year a new challenge. But all of the rings and all of the money and all of the color and all of the display, they linger only in the memory.

"The spirit, the will to win, and the will to excel, these are the things that endure and these are the qualities that are so much more important than any of the events that occasion them. And I'd like to say that the quality of any man's life has got to be a full measure of that man's personal commitment to excellence and to victory, regardless of what field he may be in."

—*Vince Lombardi*

Foreword

There are certain qualities that I believe make up a leader. Both on and off the football field, Willie Davis has shown that he possesses all of them, and that is why he's always been an inspiration.

Commitment. This is especially important if you played for Coach Lombardi. When Willie and I played, one thing I always noticed was his quality of work, the absolute and total commitment to his job from the time he walked on the field to the moment he left. That wasn't something he saved just for the games. Willie was always one of the most committed and hardest-working players at practice, as well. It's one thing to commit to the game. It's something else altogether, a true demonstration of a person's quality and commitment, when they give that same effort in practice, in meetings, or in any other part of the game. Willie was always committed.

Preparation. Willie was someone you could ask to do *anything* because you knew this man had come prepared. You could see it growing in practice as the week went on. He would focus on the game plan, the drills, the strengths and weaknesses of our opponent, how he wanted to play against them. You would see the result of this preparation come game time. I firmly believe this man's performance on the field was a result of his approach to practice during the week.

Discipline. I was raised in a military family and was always thankful for the valuable lessons I learned from that upbringing, especially when it came to discipline. When you have discipline, you can control and do anything. Discipline is an almost immeasurable quality that will get you where you want to go. Willie took his work seriously, both as a football player and later on in his many business ventures. That discipline has led him to unbelievable success. Anything Willie does, he's successful, and discipline is a key factor.

Toughness. There were few players in the league who were as tough as Willie. He was at his best in games in which we struggled. When it was tough, he rose to the top and took our defensive people right along with him. It was a rewarding experience. I loved watching him set the pace. It was also reassuring for the offense. We could always trust our defense would get the job done. Willie made sure of that. He made everyone who worked with him raise their level of expectancy and performance.

Drive. At my first meeting with Coach Lombardi addressing the team, he told us that we were going to relentlessly chase perfection, knowing full well we would never catch it because nothing is perfect. "But in the process," he said, "we will catch excellence." It was that speech that made me realize we were going to win—before we even stepped on the field with him as our coach, I knew we were going to win. We would hear that message throughout his entire time as our coach. It was a special kind of drive that Coach Lombardi felt and noticed in his players. He was not one to point out individuals very often, so if you were acknowledged for good play, it was a big deal. One thing Coach would notice was drive—and he would remind us quite often what a pleasure it was to work with people like Willie Davis.

Humility. Despite all of his success both on and off the field, Willie has been the same great guy. He's been very humble, looking at hard work and success as a responsibility rather than a privilege. That's something I've always respected. He also credited those who worked with him. I think of Dave Robinson, our linebacker who was overlooked too much. Willie made sure everyone knew what an outstanding linebacker Dave was and how much he contributed. Willie was always there to inspire the other players.

Attitude. Next to *God*, I think *attitude* is the strongest word in our vocabulary. You can tell almost everything about a person based on attitude. You will see it reflected in how they go about doing things, how they carry themselves, how they treat others, how they approach their work. Willie has always had a great attitude, and it's constantly on display. You could see it in how he played, how he's worked, how he's lived.

You take all of these qualities and it's no wonder Willie has experienced so much success. Throughout this book, Willie talks about some of these same qualities with a unique perspective on how he developed them and how they helped him succeed. I'm excited that he finally decided to share his story. Anyone reading it will get more than just a sports story—it is a true success story. Others can apply some of these qualities to their own lives to become leaders in whatever they do.

I had the privilege of playing with our defensive captain, a remarkable man who knows better than most what it means to be a leader.

— *Bart Starr*

Preface

I didn't really get to know Willie Davis in his first year or two. To be truthful, our relationship was not active. I had my group of guys on offense that I hung around with, and he was a quiet guy who stayed to himself or hung with the defensive players. For as good of friends as we are now, we didn't have much of a relationship for those first few years.

However, I did quickly develop respect for Willie, mainly because I saw how hard he worked. I saw a lot of similarities between Willie and me in terms of ability and motivation. I think I recognized that Willie, like myself, was adjusting to life in professional football. We were both coming from completely different worlds, but we shared the same goals and challenges of earning both our place on the team and the respect of the coaches and our fellow teammates. And we were both going about it in similar ways by working as hard as we possibly could. Success was critically important for both of us, and I recognized that in Willie.

The first time Willie and I spent any time talking about anything other than a football game was a couple years into our careers while we were in L.A. getting ready for the last leg of our season. Many of the guys were excited because the All-Pro announcements were coming out soon. Willie and I were in the locker room and he approached me.

"Jerry, I think you had a helluva season," he said. "You should make the All-Pro team."

"Well, Willie, you know you ought to be on that team, too."

That opened the gates for us. From that point on, there was always communication. And we soon learned we had a lot in common, especially when it came to our approach to the game and to other players. We judged a guy by his contribution—not by his looks, color, or personality, but by what he did on the field. We had both watched each other, and we both knew we were contributors. There was no question in my mind he was a solid football player—and a solid individual.

I saw his manners and intellect, as well as how he carried himself and how he spoke. I was continually impressed, especially when he spoke to the team. As the defensive captain, he was in front of the group a lot and he always had something to say. You see these guys sometimes and you can't tell whether it's bullshit or banana pudding. Some will give you a smile and just bullshit their way through it. Others are going to show up and do what they're expected to do and do it in a solid manner. That's Willie. In fact, you could say that Willie always gave you more than what was expected. Even in those speeches, you could tell they were something he was working on. He wanted his words to mean something and to inspire. They did.

Your existence in the football world depends on a lot of other guys out there. You naturally judge people by their ability as an athlete and a contributor. What's also critical to me is, what kind of a guy are you and can I depend on you? Can I support you and live and work beside you? With Willie, I knew I could.

As years went on, we drifted closer together. We were both fortunate enough to not make a lot of money. I know that sounds odd, but I'm dead serious. We knew we weren't going to live happily ever after on a football salary. We would have to work. That was fortunate for us because it got us to think of ways to support ourselves after football. I had a few injuries and problems over my career, and I knew I needed something else for when my time in the league was done. I saw Willie going to the University of Chicago and working on his MBA. That was impressive to me because here was a guy thinking about his future, life after football, and planning ahead.

After my roommate, Don Chandler, retired, one of us suggested we room together. It just seemed like the normal thing to do, not a big deal or a big process. We didn't really have any consideration of any bigger significance. We had a lot of similar interests; we had been spending time together thinking of the future, so it just made sense. We were very close friends, and that's what close friends did. Little did we know we were just the second black and white roommates in the league after Gale Sayers and Brian Piccolo in Chicago. Despite our very different backgrounds, the race issue truly wasn't a factor for us. We were just two close friends who shared the same values, and that was enough.

Rooming with Willie was one of the greatest experiences in my time at Green Bay. We became even closer friends, talking about anything and everything. I learned a lot from Wil about friendship and loyalty—especially to the Packers. I remember a particular conversation we were having about the race riots going on around the country at the time. On the road, we had to be in bed with lights out by 11:00 PM, and if you had the TV on, you'd get your ass chewed out. Well, I couldn't sleep, and I was thinking about all the unrest going on around the country—and I wanted to talk about it.

"Hey Wil," I said.

"Yeah, J?"

"You believe in black power?"

"No," Willie said. "I don't believe in black power."

"Hey Wil."

"Yeah, J?"

"You believe in white power?"

"No, I don't believe in white power."

"Well, what the hell do you believe in?" I asked. Willie took a second.

"Green power, J. Green power."

Willie and I have been friends for quite a while now. As you go through life, you'll have maybe a handful of friends who are in it for the long haul. A true testament to their character is how consistent they are throughout that friendship. It doesn't matter if they're making millions or losing millions, or if you are, they are the same fundamentally decent friend. Willie has always been a good friend. When we talk on the phone, even after quite some time, it's just like when we were saying hello to each other in the locker room all those years ago. I'm glad I got to know Willie Davis. Now you have a chance to, as well.

— Jerry Kramer

Acknowledgments

There are simply too many people to thank for their impact, influence, and support in my life. I am truly a blessed man who has met so many incredible people over the years, and each and every one of them has left their mark and helped me become the success I am today. While I couldn't possibly list each individual by name, I hope they know who they are and how much I appreciate them.

I have to give special thanks to my mother, who has always been the most important and influential person in my life. Her strength and eternal love continue to guide me even today, as do the many lessons I've received from my mentors over the years, both in sports and business.

I also have to give a special thanks to my family for their support and for everyone who helped me put this book together, from my co-writers Jim Martyka and Andrea Erickson Davis to our literary agent Tony Seidl, Triumph Books, and everyone who contributed a story or some kind words about their experience with me. This continued support means more to me than you'll ever know.

Thank you all from the bottom of my heart.

Introduction

This book is long overdue.

For years I've been pestered by friends, family, and even business associates to get not just the stories of my life down on paper but also the valuable lessons I've learned along the way. I've been extremely fortunate to have some amazing experiences with some even more amazing people. With age has come the valuable gift of perspective as to what I've accomplished, as well as the life lessons that have led to not just success but the fulfillment of my dreams. Stories and lessons, that's what I want to share in this book. Stories and lessons highlighted to show how I accomplished what I did, and how I got to where I am today in the humble hopes that you can take them and apply them to your own life, dreams, and goals. Because we all have a space that separates us from where we are to where we want to be.

We called it the Gap.

For us, the feared and revered defense of the heralded 1960s Green Bay Packers championship teams, the Gap was the space between where we were positioned and where the running back was looking to cut, the quarterback was looking to drop back, the receivers were looking to break one for the end zone.

We had one job, and we did it well.

Close the Gap.

Figure out the best way, the best angle, to get to where you needed to be to cut the running back's route, pressure the quarterback, or break up the receiver's catch and run. Plan it, see it, feel it—and then execute. Get there and you will make the play; you will succeed. As defenders, we were able to break it down that simply, and it worked. It brought results, a reputation, and ultimately championships.

"Closing the Gap" was an expression I learned playing football under the leadership of Coach Vince Lombardi. Though I'm not sure if he used the term, the concept was at the core of his defensive coaching philosophy. It was a strategy designed to enable us to impose our will on the field, to dominate in the way he not only wanted but expected. For us, it was a never-ending goal, a constant pursuit of the excellence that defined him as a coach and us as a team.

Coach Lombardi brought this hard-nosed philosophy with him from the moment he took over as leader of one of the worst franchises in professional football. At the time of his arrival, the Packers were a laughingstock, a punch line, a place where players were sent to be punished. Coach knew where the organization was, what it had, and what it didn't. He also knew what that football team was capable of. Most important, he knew how to get there. He had the will and a message he preached and pounded time and time again to everyone who put on the Green and Gold.

Here's where we are. Here's where we want to be. Here's how we're going to get there. Here's how we're going to close the Gap.

He would tell us that we could do more, we would do more, and that we would settle for nothing less than championships. He would provide us with the plans, strategies, leadership, motivation, discipline, goals and objectives, and everything else we would need to get there. The rest was up to us. If we followed that philosophy, if we worked hard, if we sacrificed, if we committed and did whatever was required of us to overcome the endless obstacles in our way, we would persevere. Simply put, if we Closed the Gap, we would win. All we had to do was believe and execute.

We did.

The interesting thing was that when Coach spoke of that mission, it rang so true to me. I realized that I had always followed that philosophy on and off the field, whether it was high school, my four years at Grambling, or even in my short stint with the Cleveland Browns.

As a football player, I am proud to say that I quickly developed a reputation as a ferocious and tenacious athlete who never quit. I would find the running back, the receiver, or the quarterback, and I would shut him down. I would plan, play the angles, learn from my mistakes, set goals, and always look to execute better. That was my approach.

In my life, from the time I was a small child growing up poor in Texarkana on the Texas and Arkansas border, I was always a goal-setter. I saw what I wanted, and no matter what it was, I worked to get there. I knew I didn't want to be poor. I knew I wanted to go to college and get a good job. I knew I wanted to play football. I knew I wanted to succeed and be the best at every level. Every time I felt like there was a hole, a gap in my life, I was filled with an immediate urge to overcome it, to conquer it, to do what I had to do to close it.

I have had a truly blessed life. Beyond my success in football, including the thrill of being an integral part of one of sports' true dynasties, I have also celebrated acclaim and financial success as an entrepreneur and business leader for more than 40 years in the beverage industry, radio broadcasting, and with a number of Fortune 500 boards of directors. I have seen the world, developed friendships with some amazing people, and had the honor of speaking with people of all ages about my life, my experiences, and what I've learned.

I am truly humbled by all I have experienced, and I thank God daily for everything I have received. Even more so, I take a respectful pride in all that I have done to get it. I am proud of my achievements, but I am even more proud of the work I have done to earn them.

It's similar in many ways to legendary UCLA basketball coach John Wooden's Pyramid of Success. In his approach, you start with a foundation and simply migrate to the top, encountering both obstacles and opportunities along the way, always keeping your eyes set on what you want to achieve. In essence, that has been the framework of my life and careers both as a professional football player and as a business leader. Two similar philosophies from Coach Vince Lombardi and Coach John Wooden—you could do worse than to follow their advice.

This book will be more than simply an autobiography. That's part of the reason it's taken me so long to write it. Not only have I been trying to figure out exactly what I wanted to say about my experience, I've still been experiencing it! This book, like any other autobiography, will break down my life, from a challenging but supportive upbringing through proud moments at Grambling, enormous success in the NFL, and the good fortune I experienced in building successful business ventures after I retired. It will be filled with tales of struggle, achievements, funny events involving well-known characters, and some behind-the-scenes sneak peeks at what it was like playing with one of the greatest football teams of all time.

Beyond that, it will also encompass a lot of what helped me get to where I am today. I will talk about my personal philosophies and approaches to sports, business, and life in general. I truly believe that there are many different ways to go about achieving whatever goals we set for ourselves. However, I do know that I've learned quite a bit from various mentors along my journey, and with such high stakes as a fulfilling life, every bit of advice helps.

I regularly give speeches to people of all ages, and I can say that one of the greatest honors of my life is when somebody calls, writes, or approaches me to say how I impacted them. I'm hoping that beyond providing a fascinating tale, I can also impart a little wisdom and hopefully even a little inspiration.

Closing the Gap never stops. Whether you're young or old, we all set goals for ourselves, and if we are truly passionate about achieving that goal, we will plan, strategize, and work toward achieving it. Each time we hit one goal, we revel in it briefly and then look to what's next. That's how you succeed.

My old roommate, Jerry Kramer, will call me every once in a while and ask me what's my next mountain to climb. For now, it's this book. This introduction is where we start, where we take that first step to Closing the Gap.

Chapter 1 | The Pursuit Starts Early

I was born determined.

There's a story about me as a little boy, sitting on the curb in Texarkana where I grew up, kicking the dirt, swatting away the flies, and waiting for my stepfather to pick me up in his rusty old pickup truck. I was always a contemplative kid, even at a young age. As I sat there, I would often drift off in my own world, ignoring the sweltering Southern heat and reflecting on what was happening around me, dreaming big dreams of the future.

On this particular day, I paid attention to all the people walking by. I didn't notice their faces, but I sure noticed what they were wearing, how they were dressed for where they were going. Field workers, merchants, teachers, businessmen, you name it. I watched these passing suits and uniforms as they went about doing what they all needed to do to earn a little money, a commodity my family and many other families in that part of the South was always short on. I admired them even at a young age, and I wished I could join the crowd.

One of the passing men, dressed in a sharp charcoal suit and fedora, stopped and looked at me quizzically. I suppose it wasn't common to see such a serious look on the face of a child.

"What are you thinking about, son?" he asked, sincerely curious.

I looked up at him and with a brightness and honesty in my eyes I said, "When I grow up, I want to go to college, get an education so I can get some money and take care of *my* family."

He seemed quite surprised to hear such a proclamation come from the mouth of a child, but perhaps he was even more caught off guard by the determination in my eyes. It wasn't a hope or a dream, it was a declaration. I was aware enough and observant enough to know that life could be better, for me; for my brother and sister; for my mother, who sacrificed so much for us; for the passing suits; for everybody.

I was too young to know *how*. But I wasn't too young to put it out there, to commit to a goal of something more and to start forming the path and strength I would need to always pursue that goal.

Good planning builds success.

Over the years, especially in my time as a business leader, I have become notorious for my attention to detail in planning. I've been fortunate enough to have great co-workers and assistants with me for essentially my entire business career, including one person who's been my aide for the better part of four decades. Several business leaders have said one of the keys to success is surrounding yourself with good people, and I believe that to be absolutely true, especially when it comes to forming, explaining, and executing a plan. I've been lucky to have people who understand my vision, sometimes even before I do. And good planning builds success.

That was one of the first lessons I learned as a young man. I'm sure, like most of what I learned in my formative years, that particular lesson came from my mother. From the moment I made the decision I was going to work, go to school, and do what needed to be done to help my family (a challenging task for a small, poor, black boy in the South), I began searching for ways to make it happen. When I was about 10 years old, I found my first opportunity.

Every day, whether I was with my friends, my siblings, or even at times with my stepfather, I would almost inevitably walk past our town grocery store. It was your average 1940s small-town grocer, wooden and weather-worn on the outside with the week's specials painted in bright colors and outlined with a stark white on the windows. Produce, meats, canned goods, sweets and treats—everything was condensed into one space that always looked much bigger to the eyes of a child. It was a store of habit, never really introducing anything new or exciting to the area, unlike the much larger supermarket that rested on the outskirts of town a mile or two away. Like most stores of the time, this grocer was built for function, to attract repeat customers, and to establish itself as *the* place to go for the community's grocery needs. I would walk by that place every day and often stopped in, being sent there by my mother to pick up an onion, some spices, or whatever else she needed to make dinner.

One particular summer afternoon, I stopped and observed all the people heading into that store, people I'd seen pop in day after day, sometimes more than once. I thought of how many times we stopped in. I thought of all the people who visited that store every day to buy something. I thought of how much money all these people gave to the store owner because he offered something that people needed.

Of course, I was too young to realize such concepts as product costs and net profit (although I think I had a pretty keen understanding of supply and demand). All I saw was a swarm of individuals willing to dish out their hard-earned money to one particular retailer. To me it was an ideal situation, and it helped me realize what I wanted to do to make the money I needed to accomplish my goals.

"I want to have my own business," I told my mother later that evening.

I began hanging around the store more and more, observing and hoping to pick up some secret hints on how to get people to give you their money. The grocer was a sweet, elderly white European man with dark, receding hair and an extremely friendly disposition. He knew everybody in town, as most small town grocers do, and he was always cordial and respectful. You would never catch him trying to push a product; he simply let the customer come in for whatever he or she needed.

He took an immediate liking to me, my curiosity, and my willingness to help. He never once questioned why I was hanging around the store or ever tried to shoo me way. Instead, he put me to work, stocking shelves, moving inventory, taking in boxes, cleaning, hanging signs, whatever needed to be done. He would always tell me how impressed he was with how efficient I was, and he would reward me with some fruit, some vegetables, a treat, or even something bigger to take home to my family to cook.

Pretty soon, he was telling me to come by every day, and on top of the food, he was also giving me about $3, big money for a 10-year-old back then. My mother, who was at first skeptical about why I wanted to hang around the store and why this man was giving me fruit, soon became extremely appreciative of the opportunity and the lessons I could learn helping out. I worked at that little grocery store, my first job, from the time I was 10 to about 17. I developed a very close bond with the elderly grocer, who would often put his arm around me and tell me what a fine man I would turn out to be one day.

In that time, I learned many of my first lessons about not just business but also life. I learned about loyalty, commitment, and compassion while developing a strong work ethic, a sense of community, and an understanding of how to connect with people as customers and human beings. Further, I more strongly and resolutely deepened my desire to one day run my own business, to build a better future for myself and my family by following in the footsteps of my friend and mentor.

In those hot summer days in my small Southern home town or after school in those cool winters, I would run down to the grocer, proud of my job and focused on the money I could earn, the lessons I could learn, and what I thought would be an inevitable future as a local business leader.

In fact, the only thing to ever distract me along the way, the only thing that could catch my eye and slow my run, were those tall billboards promoting the latest soft drink and featuring some of the era's greatest athletes, the titans of the gridiron, professionals in the game of football.

Chapter 2	My Mother Can Whip Your Mother

Appreciate those early influences and what they've done for you.

I initially grew up in a small house on a large plot of land in Friendship, Arkansas, with my parents promising to tend to an owner's cotton and corn crops for a third of the profits. Anyone who thought slavery was dead in the 1930s and 1940s hadn't heard of sharecropping. While my parents had both good and bad years, built some semblance of a decent home, and tended their own fruitful garden that could essentially feed the three of us all on its own, they never saw anything but the bare minimum they needed to survive. My mother told me the most they ever received, in their best year, was about 10 percent—and that was considered generous.

They wracked up enormous debt to their landowner, who they referred to as "the baron." He had several families working on his plot, and he used armed men to help him patrol and monitor his belongings, both the land and the people who tended to it. He was clever in his manipulation, making sure the families that worked for him were always one step behind on the contracts. More deviously, he would provide just enough to the families to keep them on the land and working for him, reminding them, sometimes with more than subtle threats of the debt they were building. He acted as if he was showing mercy even as he created situations that forced naïve workers like my parents into this debt.

While the baron was manipulative and cruel, the men who worked for him were hostile and dangerous. My mother once told me there were often threats made against the families, including them, but she never elaborated on the details, choosing to spare me from the nightmares she had to experience.

But I have one that remains to this day. It was an experience that terrified me and one I realize now could have meant a much different life, or even possibly death, if it had gone wrong.

I have broken, fragmented memories of that little wooden house, the bright white fields of cotton, the white men who always watched us a little too closely, and the late-night talks, tears, and arguing from my parents who were obviously afraid of something. Even at three years old, I was old enough to understand that something wasn't right with my parents, and it scared me almost as much as whatever scared them.

One night, they were up extra late and I heard them talking. Even as I strained to listen, fearful of getting caught, I couldn't understand what they were discussing. All I knew was that the next day my father was gone, having told the baron and his men that he had business off the land that needed tending. The men who came to the door didn't appear to be too happy about that, but they let it go, assuming he wouldn't abandon his wife and child.

The truth of the matter was that it was riskier for my dad to try to escape than it was for us. As a laborer, he was more valuable, and an attempt to escape was not an option due to the contract my parents had. The consequences for such an attempt could essentially be whatever the baron deemed appropriate, even death.

The plan was that my mother and I would follow my father a few days later. Perhaps sensing something wasn't right, the men were back the next day, questioning where my father was with my mother offering the same innocent, vague response.

"He's takin' care of business outta town and will be back later this week," she said. But this time, the baron and his men weren't so sure. They had a sense my father had escaped and that we were planning to leave, as well. They staked a couple of men outside the door to make sure we weren't going anywhere. From what I can remember my mother saying, they also had their dogs with them, tied up but at the ready.

My mother was more scared than I ever saw her in my entire life, and that in turn frightened me more than anything. I cried myself to sleep that night, terrified, worried about my mother, wanting my father, and wondering what was happening.

◆ ◆ ◆

"Willie, Willie, wake up," my mother whispered. Her voice was cracking, and as I slowly wiped the sleep out of my eyes, I could see her eyes were huge. She was sweating and breathing heavily. "Willie, come on, wake up. We're leaving."

"Where?"

"Shh!" she said with a stern look. Now was not the time for questions.

My mother put some clothes on me and grabbed me, securing me in her arms around her waist. We didn't have very many belongings in our place, but I noticed the ones we did have, she was ignoring. There was no time. There was no space. She didn't have enough arms to grab all she wanted. She had mere seconds and could only afford to grab the thing most important to her—me.

My mother had an instinct that tonight would be the one and only chance we would have to escape. As my mother lay in bed with her eyes open, she had begun to hear a deep snoring outside. In fact, she heard two deep snores. The guards had fallen asleep.

It was now or never.

Everything happened so fast from the moment my mother threw me around her waist. We quickly and quietly slipped out the back, my mother simply shooting me a look, begging me to stay quiet no matter what. I knew better. Any noise could startle the guards or their dogs. Then we were running, my mother's breath quickening and the tiniest of moans coming from her as she ran in a state of sheer panic and terror.

I was crying now, bumping up and down against her hip as she ran, feeling the branches and leaves whip against my face as we ran through the woods that surrounded our property. I could feel her heart beating at a rapid pace that scared me even more.

"Momma, what's going on?" I cried.

But again, she just shushed me, saving her breath and exerting everything she could in her running. Eventually, we could hear voices faintly in the distance, back the way we came. They didn't sound happy.

My mother, a former athlete herself, began pushing even harder, running at a full sprint even as I weighed her small frame down. If they found us, who knows what they would have done?

The plan was for my father to find someone willing and ready to pick us up in a truck on a specific road. However, we were supposed to have been there earlier than we were. My mother prayed the truck was still there.

It was.

We were taken back to my grandparents' place in Lisbon. Ironically, they also lived on a farm in a sharecropper situation. However, they had been fortunate enough to find owners who were fair, and we were welcomed. The nightmare was over.

♦ ♦ ♦

When I was in my early teens, there was an incident in the news about something tragic that happened on a sharecropping parcel, and it bothered my mother. I asked her what was wrong and she broke down, crying and telling me the whole story. It was then that I started to put together the pieces of the memory from the night we escaped.

I remember asking her once if she was ever scared after we escaped that the men would come looking for us, and she simply said, "No."

But then again, that was my mother, the woman who dared to grab her child and dash through the woods beyond fear of punishment or worse to a better life, a better opportunity. My mother, Nodie Davis, was and always will be the strongest and most influential person in my life.

She was a small, petite, beautiful woman with the class, grace, and elegance of a lady and the glare, voice, and attitude of a spitfire. She was also extremely competitive, never wanting to lose at anything, a personality trait I inherited. A track star in high school, her real passion was basketball. Despite her height, she was a fast and shifty 5'7" guard and apparently a standout in the sport. She often told us kids that if colleges at the time had offered hoops scholarships to women, she probably could have gotten a full ride. Unfortunately, she never had a chance to go.

Instead she turned her focus to her kids, raising us with that same energy, passion, and competitive spirit. It didn't matter what we were doing, we were told to give it our best. It was what was expected, always. She pushed us to always try harder, to want the best out of our lives, and to always be strong—a lesson she was forced to learn herself when we were all still young.

My father was a tall, slender man, an athlete himself whose passion was the game of baseball. He was a guy who always wanted to provide the support his family needed, but he never really had the means, the education, or the know-how to do it. My father always seemed stressed out, very rarely smiling or happy. He was a frustrated man—frustrated at the cards life had dealt him and at the mistakes he had made.

I was never very close to my father, at least not when I was a child. I eventually reconnected with him much later in life and developed a relationship with him of sorts, though I never considered it a father-son relationship. He was gone so much when I was a child, performing a series of odd jobs, be it on the local farms, the oil fields, or wherever a young black man could find good, honest work. He was typically gone by the time I got up in the morning and came back after I went to sleep.

He had no real hobbies, interests, or friends from what I could see. He was not affectionate, which isn't to say he didn't love his children. He simply didn't show it. The same went with any affection toward my mother. They simply seemed to co-exist, always worried about their living situation, how they were going to possibly stay afloat, and what prospects, if any, the future held.

When I was eight years old, my father had enough. He felt like a failure—miserable, degraded, a loser. He couldn't take it anymore, and somewhere in his mind he thought we would be better without him. So one day he simply walked out, leaving my mother with no job, no financial security, and three kids to feed.

Although my mother was devastated, she chose not to show it. Instead, she simply became stronger and more resolute. As she explained that my father was gone and that we were on our own, she simply stated that nothing would stop us from achieving what was best for our family.

"We will do whatever is necessary," she said. "And we'll be just fine."

Within a few days, my mother had a job. From then on, she worked every single day of her life until I forced her to retire after she was well into old age.

My brother and my sister (who was born just months before my father had left) had no real experience with our father and as such, have no real memories of him. It affected me a little differently, especially as I grew into my teenage years. At eight, I was aware enough to know we were struggling as a family and that losing my father and the little bit of money he did provide for us wouldn't help our situation. I built up quite a bit of bitterness and resentment. Over the years, I grew angry that I never had my father around during the time in my life I needed him the most, those teenage years, when everything is confusing for a young man coming into his own. It also motivated me. I would do better. I would be better. I would find ways to fill the void that he had left behind.

Most important, I would do whatever I could to help my mother, who suddenly found herself struggling on a whole new level.

There was no doubt that my mother was a fighter. As a child, I truly believed she could do it all, mainly because she believed the same. She was not one to take any crap from anyone, white or black. If she felt wronged in any way, she let you know and she would keep the pressure up until you relented and corrected what she claimed was your mistake. If she felt cheated, she had no problems causing a scene. In a time and place when blacks still stayed relatively quiet and discreet, my mother stood up for her rights.

She was a sensitive lady, however, and I know my father's abandonment hurt her deeply. But there was no time for pain and tears. There was only the idea of pushing forward and starting fresh. She was aggressive and determined, and that helped me deal with my father's leaving more than anything. I didn't need to worry about my mother. She would be just fine. We would be just fine.

A few years after my father left, I was out playing basketball with some friends. We were taking a break after some pretty competitive games of hoops, and as boys do, we started trash talking with each other. Even though I was raised right and wasn't much of a curser or bragger, I could still hold my own when I was alone with the boys. I was on a roll, having come off a particularly good couple games on the court, and I was feeling cocky. The trash talk was flying between all of us as we tried to one-up each other. Finally my friend threw a big one at me.

"Well, my dad can whip your dad."

Right after that, another friend said, "He ain't got no daddy," and a few of them laughed.

I couldn't defend it. I didn't know where my dad was. For all practical purposes, I *didn't* have a dad. I looked around at all these boys who had dads to go back home to, and it broke my heart.

Never wanting to show any kind of emotion in front of the guys, I took off and ran home, waiting until I was out of sight before I let the tears start flowing. I ran through the front door in a full-blown crying fit. My mother was right there by my side, ever the worrier, afraid I had gotten hurt. I told her what the boys had said, and as she wiped the tears from my face, without missing a beat, she looked me in the eyes.

"Oh yeah?" she asked. "Well you tell those boys that your mother could whip their mother."

After my father left, my mother became extremely overprotective of me. She needed to know where I was at all times of the day and night. As such, through grade school and high school, I never had much of a life outside the house, where she felt things were the safest. She often called while she was at work to check up on us, and when she got home from work around 8:00 PM, we had to be there. If not, there was hell to pay, even when I was a teenager. She constantly reminded me how much she needed me and my help, how I couldn't let anything happen to myself, and how it would affect the family if something did.

"It's me and you now, and we need to take care of the family."

Being the oldest also meant I had to watch my younger brother and sister. I was often left home to babysit, even at a young age because there were simply no other options. My mother had to go to work, and I had to learn how to watch my siblings. My mother had no choice but to teach me adult-like responsibility when I was a child, and I was eager to learn.

I was willing to do anything to help her out and make her life easier. I learned how to cook (kind of) and did a lot of the cleaning, trying my best to make it possible for her to come home and relax after working a 12-hour day or more. I also wanted to show her that I was different than my father, that I was someone she could count on.

"There's one thing I want you to do," she said. "I want you to go to school, get an education, get a good job, and be a better man than your father."

I heard those words often, and I took them to heart. I would be as determined as her. I would work as much as her. I would be as responsible and aggressive as this woman who was managing to work multiple jobs and raise three kids on her own. I owed her that.

Find your motivation and take on the work.

When all the kids in the neighborhood started to get bicycles, I told my mother I wanted one. At first she laughed it off and told me I was crazy, but when she saw the sadness in my eyes, she hugged me fiercely and told me one day I would own one—just not now. Where most other kids would whine and complain, I let the issue drop, knowing it was a matter of money. I set getting a bicycle as a goal, and I dreamed of the day when I could earn one on my own.

That's where the store helped. By the time I was in my early teen years, I was working there regularly for a little cash and groceries. I also got a job in the mornings, cleaning windows on the local buildings. Later, I joined my mother in working at the town country club.

The country club was a beautiful and prestigious club and golf course that served the wealthier residents. It was an extremely popular and exclusive club that was packed consistently, especially in the summer. My mother took a job there helping to prepare and serve food. It didn't take her long to work her way up to head cook, a position she held proudly for almost 25 years. It was that job that not only gave her the means to raise her family, but also introduced us to some of the best dishes we had ever tasted.

Looking back, I can laugh now, thinking of how we poor black kids from the ghetto probably ate as well as if not better than the white kids across town. My mother was constantly bringing home leftovers from the club; meats, pastas, potato dishes, all kinds of vegetables, and even the occasional dessert—most of which she had prepared. It was through my mother's job at the club that I discovered my love of chicken. My mother could cook, roast, bake, broil, and fry a chicken unlike anyone else. To this day, my favorite dish is a baked chicken smothered in a special blend of herbs and butter that I still have not been able to perfect on my own—and I've tried.

My mother also figured out a way to turn that opportunity into a small side catering business to bring in some extra cash. For the 1940s, my mother was very much ahead of her time. While there were several black women working in food preparation and service industries, there were very few that could call themselves the boss.

I started working at the club with her when I was 12 years old, mostly in the locker room, picking up towels, cleaning, shining shoes, and doing whatever needed to be done. Eventually, as I got into my later teens, I helped serve and worked in the bar, fixing drinks for the regulars who at first referred to me as "Boy" but soon got to know me by name and always appreciated how hard of a worker I was and how respectful.

"Your mother has taught you well," they would say, and I would smile and agree. She certainly did, and her lessons on the benefits of hard work have stuck with me in everything I've done.

For a young man, three jobs, school, and helping raise your siblings is quite a load. But for me it was worth it, not just in terms of the financial rewards it was providing (and would provide even more in the future) but also because it was helping my mother. I got to a point where I didn't want to ask her for things because I knew it hurt her to say no. So I simply went about trying to earn it for myself however I could. My entire life has been characterized by a full plate, and I'm grateful for it.

Chapter 3 | Lessons from the Board of Education

Sometimes we need confrontation to achieve what we want.

I grew up in Texarkana, a traditional blue-collar city split in two that sits restlessly on the Texas-Arkansas border. City officials like to call the two towns partners, but everyone who lives on either side or just visits either side knows better. The towns have changed quite a bit since I called them home, but the general makeup of the city in terms of race (half black, half white), economic makeup (poor to middle class), and civic pride (huge) remains.

When I grew up there, Texarkana shared its addiction to football with other Southern cities. At Booker T. Washington High School, if you were athletic, you played football. Actually, if you grew up anywhere in that part of the country and were male, you played football at least at some point in your life.

But I couldn't play, at least not organized ball, 'cuz my momma wouldn't let me.

I grew up playing football on the playground with my friends from both the Texas and Arkansas side of town. We had a few parks and sandlots just big enough for us to set up a makeshift field. When we did play, I found I had a natural ability. I was a good wide receiver with good hands and a slim, built frame. Of course, when you're a kid, everybody wants to play quarterback or wide receiver. I was a bit of a bigger kid, so I was often moved to be a blocker. But where I truly seemed to shine was on defense.

As we grew up and went to high school, I watched as all my friends joined their teams, taking on the twice-a-day practices in the middle of summer, getting actual uniforms and helmets, and reaping all the rewards that come with being a high school football player in the South. I had to watch from the sideline, though. For two years in high school, even as I grew a bit taller and bigger than most of the other kids my age, even as coaches begged me to play, even as my friends, classmates, and girls ragged me to the point of absolute humiliation, I had to say no.

Afraid I would get hurt, my mother wouldn't give me her permission. It didn't help that a couple years prior a local kid had gotten a serious neck injury playing football. She told me her fears went even further than just an injury. She knew that if I did get hurt, she wouldn't be able to pay for any medical costs. Plus, I was now a provider for the family, and while she wouldn't say it outright, it was clear we couldn't afford a situation where I was unfit to work.

But I was a kid, and I wanted to play. I tried and tried but was always met with the same response. After a last-ditch effort and a surprise visit from the high school coach, I was left with no choice but to confront my mother for the one and only time in my life.

"Momma, I'm going to tell you something," I said to her as she sat in the kitchen. I could feel tears ready to stream down my face. "If you don't let me play football this year, I'm leaving."

Stunned, she began to cry and told me she couldn't believe I would say something like that.

"How could you say you would leave me?" she asked, and suddenly my strong, outspoken mother sounded very small and frail.

"I don't know," I said, and I could feel myself starting to waiver. "It would be tough for me—but I would do it. Playing means that much to me."

She had lost, probably for the first time in her life, in a one-on-one argument, and she knew it. She couldn't fight it anymore. Plus, she loved me, and I think for the first time she could truly see how much it was killing me not playing. She tried one last time to talk me out of it, but I held my ground—just like I would on the football field soon after and for many, many years.

"Alright, if it really means that much to you," she said quietly, finally relenting. "You can play. But if you get hurt, don't you come to me!"

The next day I showed up for practice. The day after that I suited up for my first game. I played briefly in that game—and every game that followed.

Your actions, behaviors, and conduct will show that you are professionals.

If my mother was a woman of strong words, so too was my first football coach. Actually, Nathan "Tricky" Jones was a man of *few* words, but when he spoke, he spoke volumes.

Our varsity football coach, Coach Jones, was a beast of a black man, about 6'5" and 250-plus pounds. He was an All-American in college, and he brought his discipline, stamina, and attention to detail to both the football field and the classroom.

He was as intimidating to all of us as he was popular, both among the men who played for him and the community as a whole because Coach Jones was a winner. In that part of the country, like it or not, winning is more important than anything else in the eyes of the community. He had already been coaching for several years by the time I got there and had established himself as one of the premiere black high school coaches in the entire state. In fact, some said he was *the* best, having won close to a dozen state titles in his entire tenure, two of which came while I played for him.

He was a motivator as a science teacher, mainly because of the almost philosophic approach he took to teaching. He wanted to get his students to think about things differently.

"What constitutes *work*?" he asked us one day in class. Nobody raised their hand.

"Okay, if I told you that I needed my desk moved to the back of the room and you came up here and tried to tug it, push it, pull it, lift it, and it didn't budge, or it only moved part of the way—would that be work?"

We all agreed that yes it would be work because you had to exert some effort even in moving it a little bit.

"No," he said. "It's not work because you didn't accomplish your objective."

"Work is characterized by a result, and if you set out with an intended objective that you don't reach, then you haven't done the work."

He carried that same philosophy to the field, never letting his players end a practice on a poorly executed play. We worked until we got it right—offense and defense—because in order for it to be work, we had to accomplish what we set out to do. He was discipline personified, pushing his team to the brink of exhaustion and then pushing us a little more, showing us what we were capable of and what we could (and would) accomplish. He was fair, holding each and every one of us to the same expectations, and he expected us to be men.

Anybody who wasn't responsible met the Board of Education.

A player met the Board of Education for three things:

1. They were late.
2. They weren't focused.
3. They made an undisciplined mistake.

Coach Jones' players were rarely late, always focused, and didn't make many mistakes—because nobody wanted to meet the Board.

The Board of Education was an enormously large, thick chunk of worn-down pine shaped into a nice flat paddle, complete with handle. The Board of Education never left Coach's side, roaming the practice field with him as he eagerly awaited a violation of one of his rules. In an era where spanking, paddling, and nuns cracking a student's knuckles with a ruler were still widely accepted as proper forms of "getting your attention," Coach Jones didn't use the Board to necessarily enforce the rules. He used it to teach us valuable lessons.

The Board of Education taught me one lesson in particular that I follow to this day.

Midway through our season, we had a practice after school. I got to the locker room a little late from class and didn't dress right away, talking to my friends and just really milling around instead, thinking I had plenty of time to make it to practice. I didn't.

I found myself running to the practice field, and when I turned the corner, I saw Coach waiting for me, paddle in hand.

"Come on, boy," he yelled as the team watched.

I can say without question there was nothing pleasant about getting whacked on the butt, in those tight football pants, with a chunk of pine. I experienced burning well into practice and even later that night as I crawled into bed.

The next day at practice, I showed up on time and told Coach how much that thing really hurt.

"Boy, I know it does," he said in his deep voice. "It's supposed to hurt."

I started to tell him why I was late that day, but he didn't want to hear it. Truthfully, he didn't care.

"Let me tell you, boy," he said, putting his arm around me. "I see you walking into that dressing room a little late and then I see you talkin', having conversations instead of getting dressed. You runnin' around to everyone to say hi and waitin' to the last minute to get ready—and you're not ready. So there you are coming around the corner, running fast to try and make it in time."

That's when he said something that would stay with me through high school, college, the pros (where we all had to adhere to Lombardi Time), and even my business career.

"Boy, listen to me now," he said and smiled.

"An early start beats fast running."

I was never late again—for anything.

The more I played, the more I realized I couldn't get enough of organized football. Coach Jones praised me for my determination, dedication, and passion for the game. As he became more and more of a father figure, I found myself working as hard as I could each and every day, not just for my love of the game but also to impress him.

Coach Jones had me play both offense and defense. At about 215 pounds, I was one of the bigger guys on the team. I was also one of the hardest hitters, which is how I found myself playing linebacker on defense and tackle on offense. For as tall and big as I was, I was also very fast and had good hands, which also earned me some playing time at tight end.

I was also very adept at learning the playbook. In school, I was a good student with about a B average. However, when it came to memorization and repetition, I had a gift. If you showed me how to do something, typically I could duplicate it and do it well. Coach Jones also ran a rather simple offense and defense. The offense featured a good blend of running and passing with a surprise play every now and then. The focus for the offense wasn't on trickery or really even trying to confuse the defense. It was about us executing better than them. The same could be said for our defensive schemes. We weren't going to do anything fancy; we were just going to do what we did better than the opposition.

Coach Jones never let practice end on a poor execution—ever.

"Get back here!" he'd yell in his sharp, gruff voice. "Do it again."

Then, "Let's do it again!"

Then, "Again!"

It didn't matter if it was a defensive drill or an offensive play; we had to end practice by running it flawlessly—a few times. It was often very frustrating for us players, but as with most things Coach Jones did, it paid off when it came time to run those plays in the games themselves.

In my two years of high school football, we only lost a couple games and those were both close losses. One year, we held many of our opponents scoreless. Both years, we went on to win the state championship. Along the way, there were some very memorable games, including tough matches against our rivals. But the one that sticks out the most is the one and only high school game my mother came to see.

She had avoided coming to games because she didn't want to see me get hurt. She finally relented, after some encouragement from friends and neighbors and my nagging, and decided to come to my last home game of my senior year. It didn't go as well as I had hoped.

Our team was doing a fine job of both moving the ball on offense and stopping it on defense. I was also having a decent game, taking advantage of my size, speed, and experience as well as the high I was feeling having my mother in the stands. And maybe that was the problem. I was so intent on impressing her and playing well that I actually did something a bit unusual for me. I tried too hard and lost my focus.

Just before halftime, I got caught. Playing defense, I started to chase down the running back who was sprinting toward the sideline looking to make a cut upfield. As always, I wanted to be the one there to cut him off. I was so intent on making the big play that I didn't check my blind sides. Next thing I knew, I was being pummeled by an offensive lineman who saw an opportunity to impress someone himself. He nailed me in the head, I went down, and my world got a little fuzzy.

It was the first time and, as it turns out, the only time I've ever been knocked out. Everything went black then slowly came into focus as I tried to figure out what had just happened. It started to go fuzzy again, and I panicked. *Is this what it's going to be like the rest of my life?* I finally came to, trying to stand and figure out why everyone was crowded around me.

That's when I heard her voice.

"You can't tell me I can't go out there! That's my son! I'm goin' out there! Now get outta my way!"

I glanced over, trying to figure out where my mother was, and I saw several members of our coaching staff restraining her on the sideline, trying to calm her down and tell her she couldn't go onto the field. I could tell they were a little exhausted by the struggle.

Eventually, the haze cleared completely, and I was able to walk off the field. Upon seeing me get up on my own, my mother calmed down just enough to head back to the stands, but not before shooting the player that hit me and my coaches one of her trademark stares. Thank God for all of them that I got up. I was also thankful this was one of my last games because I knew after that day I would have a hard time ever convincing her to let me play again.

I missed the third quarter, occasionally sneaking a peek up to the stands only to see her watching me the entire time. This was bad. I had to show her that I was okay, so I started to harass the coaching staff until they finally put me back in. I needed to give her the sense that I wasn't completely hurt—even if I was.

"I'm glad I got to see you play, but I don't ever wanna see another one," she said when I got home that night.

"Why not?" I asked with innocent sincerity.

She just looked at me incredulously for a second. "Boy, you scared me to death. I'm just glad this whole football thing's over."

Little did my mother and I know just how wrong she was.

Have an appreciation for achievement at all levels.

My senior year, I earned All-State honors and received a trophy. It was a relatively small trophy, especially compared to some of the world champion trophies I held later in my life, and it was obviously made from cheap wood and plastic with shiny but cracking gloss paint. It was the most glorious thing I had ever seen because it represented the first time in my life I felt I had truly achieved something worthwhile.

I believe that when we achieve something, it pushes us to do more, to want more, to be the best, and that's something that should always be encouraged. Achieving a goal and celebrating that achievement creates drive in an individual.

My high school All-State trophy was the first real tangible thing in my life that I felt I had earned. It showed my energy, passion, effort, and determination. It showed I could excel at something, that I had distinguished myself, that I was one of the best. It was so meaningful for me. It was a true honor and something I knew I would always cherish.

It turned out a few college scouts had been watching my progress in high school, as well.

One of the first schools to take a look at me and a few of my teammates was Arkansas A&M at Pine Bluff. A member of the Southwestern Athletic Conference (SWAC) it was looking to bolster both its offense and defense and saw potential in several of our key players. The school was able to land our quarterback, a defensive tackle, and an offensive lineman. I was the only one who didn't go, and it had nothing to do with the school itself. It was a fine school with a lot to offer. So were many of the other 20-plus schools that recruited me, most coming from the SWAC, including Prairie View A&M and Texas Southern. There were also a number of other predominantly black colleges that made their case, like Bishop College in Texas.

Even more surprising was the initial interest from some of the major universities, including Arizona State and the University of Michigan. For a black player from a tiny black Southern school in an era where black players were just starting to get scholarship opportunities, to even have interest from those schools was both shocking and quite an honor.

However, coming from where I was, the thought of going to such a big school, such a sharp change in environment, was too overwhelming, and I never really pursued those options.

I ended up going to Grambling State because Coach Eddie Robinson was incredibly smart. He knew how to win at everything, including recruiting.

I remember the first time I saw Coach Robinson. Even though it was relatively close to home, I knew absolutely nothing about the school or its coach other than it was one of a large handful of black colleges in the region. After a practice one afternoon, Coach Jones told us we had a visitor who was going to talk to us about college. We had these visitors from time to time, really for the seniors who were contemplating their futures and exploring their options. We sat through a couple of these before and were forced to listen impatiently, eager to either start practice or go home, depending on when the coach showed up.

When Coach Robinson walked in, we were instantly awed. He was dressed in a full suit, a contrast to a lot of the other coaches we had seen, including our own. He was very well put together and extremely professional looking. He called us "gentlemen" and spoke articulately, honestly, and passionately about the importance of college, especially for young black men. We hung on his every word.

I was impressed by Coach Robinson and with everything Grambling State had to offer. It seemed like the right place for me—my mother tried to leave the decision up to me, but a recruiting visit from Coach Robinson to our house (and a promise that he would make me go to church) won her over. I accepted a full scholarship to go play football.

When it finally sank in, my mother was so incredibly proud and I think a little amazed. She also felt a bit bad for all those times she had refused to let me play. From the moment I accepted the scholarship to the moment I left for school, she continually reminded me that the only reason she didn't let me play was that she was afraid of me getting hurt.

A few years later, we had a talk and out of the blue, my mother apologized to me for fighting me on it for so long. It didn't matter, I had been given an opportunity to play, and football was looking like it might become something very important in my life. I wasn't thinking of a pro career (yet), but I knew this opportunity was going to give me something I had never even dreamed of—a college education. I would be one step closer to my business goals.

Chapter 4 | # Coach Eddie Robinson and the Black National Championship

Work to instill the spirit of teamwork.

Going strictly by the numbers, Grambling State coach Eddie Robinson will always be considered one of the greatest college football coaches of all time.

He spent 56 years, from 1941–97, leading young men onto the gridiron at the Northern Louisiana school. (Note: Grambling did not field a team in 1943 and 1944.) In that time, he became one of the winningest coaches in Division I-AA with 408 wins. I'm proud to say that from 1952–55, I took part in 29 of those.

Coach saw more than 200 of his players go on to professional ball in both the AFL and the NFL, including Hall of Famers Buck Buchanan, Willie Brown, and Charlie Joiner, as well as his eventual successor, Super Bowl XXII MVP Doug Williams. Coach is a legend in the sport on any level, and all of us who played for him will always treasure that special honor.

If you look beyond the numbers, to each and every one of us, Coach Robinson was so much more. He was a father figure, a friend, and a disciplinarian who made sure we not only grew up to be men but that we were also ready and able to take on any opportunities that might come our way. Coach Robinson was about preparation both on and off the field. I attribute much of my success to Coach, and I will always be grateful for my time with him at Grambling State.

He was the kind of coach all young men in college should have. I'll never forget that one of the many philosophies he preached to us when we showed up for those first days of practice was *togetherness.* He preached about the value of the team as a whole, a unit where everybody needed to be able to rely on each other, from the coaching staff to the players. Everybody had to do their part. Everybody had to work hard. Everybody had to be willing to sacrifice for each other and carry each other when times got tough.

That sense of togetherness among the players also came in handy in lending each other support when facing Coach Robinson's wrath. He was a tall, well-built, imposing man who demanded your attention when he walked into a room just by his presence alone. A lifelong local, Coach Robinson had played football at the now defunct Leland College in Louisiana where he said he learned the value of competition, hard work, and strict discipline. These were values he was not afraid to share with his young men.

Coach Robinson was a yeller. He was also not afraid to get physical, sometimes offering a little shake of the shoulders or a smack on the helmet if you weren't doing your job. Times were different then, and it wasn't like he ever did anything to hurt any of us. He just wasn't afraid to let us know what exactly we were doing wrong or show us how we could do our jobs better—in his own way. We learned quickly.

Play like you practice.

Coach Robinson was also the first one to really instill in me the value of playing like you practice. For a lot of players, and even coaches for that matter, the impetus is on the games. They value practice, but it is more about the games themselves. The games are where they kick up the energy, the focus, the motivation, the drive. The games are where they look to perform at their best. Coach wanted us to treat each practice just like a game. The theory was that if we could get ourselves in game mode for a practice then come game time that energy, desire, and preparation would automatically amp up a few notches and we would be unstoppable.

"Practice is where it all starts," he said.

He was just as strict and disciplined off the field. Beyond his serving as football coach, he held several other jobs at both the college and the local Grambling High School, including teaching, coaching, and even heading up the cheerleading squad for a while. For as much as he's revered for his success on the field, he equally matched that success in the classroom, holding one of the best graduation rates in the history of college athletics among his players. He was committed to providing us with the tools and lessons to help us grow into adulthood and succeed in our own lives, making good on his recruitment promises. He stressed the values of responsibility and setting a good example. More than anything, he stressed what a privilege it was that all of us were given the opportunity to get a college degree.

"That's what you're here for," he said. "In the end, if you just played football and you don't get that degree, then you denied yourselves one of the best things that a young man could get. If you don't get that degree, then I've failed you and you failed yourselves."

He was constantly checking on us, making sure we were attending class, studying when we had exams, and getting decent grades. I never knew how he could track each of us as well as he did, especially with how busy he was, but there was never getting *anything* by Coach.

I clearly remember getting called in after I had skipped a few classes in a row. I can't even remember why I skipped, but I do remember feeling like I was taking a chance. It was only a matter of time and sure enough, eventually Coach found out. I was sent to his office and just sat down in this little chair across from him as he stared at me silently for several moments. I could feel myself sweating, and I started shifting uncomfortably.

"I understand you haven't been going to class," he finally said in a calm soothing voice, which made me even more nervous. "What's happening with you?"

He waited for a response.

"I don't know, Coach," was all I could muster.

He locked his gaze on me, never shifting, never blinking, just staring at me and speaking too softly.

"Well," he said. "I think you know how I feel about that."

Again, he held his gaze steady for an unbearably long time.

I never missed class again.

For Coach Robinson, part of being an adult was also maturity. That went beyond the responsibility and discipline. It came down to the tiniest of details, like dressing appropriately and speaking with articulation. Coach Robinson was an English major, and he loved to use his skills with dramatic flair. Ever the teacher and coach, he constantly stopped someone he thought was butchering the English language and had them say it correctly.

"Son, that's not right," he said. "What you mean to say is..."

For those of us who weren't exactly top of our class in English, we found it best just to keep our mouths shut and listen to him—and maybe that was the point.

Be both prepared and grateful for opportunities.

More than anything, what I remember about Coach Robinson was how much he was an extreme patriot with an undying love for this country. He always preached to us about how great America was despite the struggles the black community still faced. He was proactive and grateful for what he did have, opportunities he would say that we couldn't find anywhere else in the world. It was an eternal optimism that I admired.

"There is no reason for you not to succeed in America," he said. "It's the land of opportunity. The only question is what are you going to do with your opportunities?"

Coach Robinson took it on himself to prepare each and every one of us for a future career in football, as well. His mindset was, "As long as I'm here, anyone who plays for Grambling will be capable of playing pro football."

He worked on that preparation by expecting perfection in our execution as a team. He tried to expose us to anything and everything we might experience in the pro leagues. Each year in the off-season, he attended professional camps led by some of the pro coaches. He would do what he could to study new techniques, strategies, and game plans in passing, blocking, receiving, defense, you name it. Then he passed those on to us with absolute passion and excitement.

These pro camps were an obsession with him, as was talking with other coaches and doing whatever else he could to keep his players aware of everything the pros were doing. Looking back, I realize now how privileged we all were to be steps ahead of other teams in our conference in terms of the plays we were running, our conditioning, game planning, etc. It was one of the many reasons for our success.

We were privileged in general to have someone like him coaching us through our formative years and as we grew into adulthood.

I can honestly say that I'm glad that I went to a small college where I could get more one-on-one attention. Many colleges out there are so enormous that you get swallowed up, and you're just one of the herd. It's tough for young people to get the support they need there. Grambling was small enough that I had help and guidance from people who wanted me to succeed. Still, my first year at Grambling presented some frustrating challenges.

I had heard what it would be like in college and how different it was, and I thought I was prepared. But I could see quickly that I didn't fully understand or appreciate all the changes that take place. The new environment, just like it is for many kids as they go off to college, was a little unsettling. I would have been at least a little more comfortable if anybody I knew from my school or even anyone I played *against* in high school had gone to Grambling, but I didn't know anyone. I felt alone and overwhelmed, watching as everything in my life was changing so fast in front of my eyes.

It also didn't help that I didn't feel like I was going to get the educational support I had originally desired. In fact, at a place where the dreams of young men and women are supposed to be encouraged, mine were shot down rather quickly.

When I accepted my full-ride scholarship, I truly had no realistic dreams of ever playing professional football. It's so different today, where every high school athlete in the country who finds success and is given an opportunity to move on to college at least keeps the idea of playing pro ball in the back of his mind. For some, there is no other option. They look at the possibility of a pro career as the goal, the ultimate prize, the reason they're even *going* to college.

For a black athlete at an all-black school in the early 1950s, the situation was quite different. There were few blacks even given an opportunity to turn pro, and many of them came from major universities in the power conferences. Nobody who could give me a shot in the pros would even know of me at a school like Grambling. My thought going into my freshman year at Grambling was to keep my scholarship, have fun playing football for the short time I would be able to, and work hard to earn my degree. That meant having to figure out what I wanted to study for my degree. As I soon found out, the counselors thought my options were limited, and business wasn't one of them.

"Business?" my career guidance counselor said as she looked at me like I was crazy. "Why business?"

I shared with her my story about working with the grocer growing up and some of my other experiences and how the world of business had always fascinated me.

"Yeah, but colored people don't get hired in business," she said. "You won't be able to get a job, and it will be impossible to start your own."

Oh, I thought, a little surprised at how quickly my dream was being shattered. She could see by my face that I was disappointed.

"What's most important to you right now?" she asked.

"Well, I want to be able to help take care of my mother and my brother and sister," I said, very honestly.

"Then you want to be able to get a job that can help you with your family, and that means choosing a major that will help you get that job."

"Yeah, but I'm convinced this is what I'd like to do," I said, trying to muster up the courage to at least fight one last time for my dream.

"Willie, let me be honest with you," she said. "This is not what I would suggest. Plus, we don't really have a business curriculum here. It's more of a teacher's program."

"Well, what am I supposed to do then?" I asked.

After talking a little more about what else I liked to do and what subjects I was best at in school, we (or I should say, she) settled on industrial education.

"Hopefully, you can get your degree here and then get the opportunity to coach or teach in high school," she said.

I left the office extremely depressed and frustrated.

To have that conversation so early my freshman year, while I was also struggling with my change of scenery, made things even worse. It was bad enough I was feeling overwhelmed, lonely, and uncomfortable, but now I was feeling unsupported.

In fact, the only place I did feel right was on the football field. While Grambling's facilities, including the field, the stadium, dressing rooms, etc., were nothing compared to most of the major schools around the country, they were still impressive. Even that seemed a little intimidating to me until I put on the pads and lined up against another player. That's when I felt calm, confident, strong, and determined. All those feelings of uncertainty slipped away, and I could simply focus on the task at hand.

Be the bigger man. Win the battle. Do what you know you can do.

Football gave me something comfortable, something I knew I could do and do well, something to hold on to as things changed all around me.

The problem was practice only lasted a couple hours each day. The rest of the time I was on my own. Combine that with my loneliness, discomfort, exhaustion from practicing, and losing my hopes and dreams of one day being a business man, and it was all too much.

Not long after I got to Grambling, I actually tried to leave, but I was talked into staying by Coach. Soon after that, I met a girl, Pearl, who gave me yet another reason to stay and some much-needed comfort as I transitioned. Though he denied it, I always thought that Coach had put her on me—that I met her right after almost leaving always seemed a little suspicious. My life soon became about football practice, classes, and hanging out with Pearl, usually at the student center. With that, college eventually got a little easier each and every day, even as football remained a constant challenge.

Though I was heavily recruited out of high school by Coach Robinson, there were no certainties when it came to college football. I was a dominant player in my two years in high school, often over-matching kids my same age and even those a little older. I was tall and fast, and both of those traits made up for my lack of size. Now I was by no means small, but when I got out of high school, I hadn't fully developed into the "solid" player I would eventually become. I only weighed about 215 pounds or so—not that big for a defensive end or an offensive guard.

Suddenly, I was thrown into the mix with a lot of other much bigger guys who were just as fast and just as hungry. That's one thing any athlete can tell you as they make their way up from high school to college to the minors or even straight to the pros. Just when you feel like you're a dominating player and ready to take on the world, you get to that next level and realize the playing field is all evened out. Everyone there wants it just as much as you do, and often a lot of them have just as much if not more natural talent and ability than you. You find yourself in the position of having to prove yourself once again.

When I got to Grambling, they didn't know where to place me. The coaching staff could see right away I had unique speed and I played bigger than my weight, meaning I could handle guys much bigger than me. On offense, they took advantage of my determination, putting me at offensive guard and tackle. I was one of the smaller linemen, but the coaches assumed that I could hold my own, especially with the type of offense Coach Robinson ran. On defense, they decided to take advantage of my speed and put me in as a linebacker, giving me an opportunity to chase the ball regardless of who had it—quarterback, running back, or receiver.

I found out quickly that chasing the ball was what I loved to do more than anything.

I discovered in college I had a temperament that was designed for defense. It's not that I minded playing offense, but it required a different skill set. On offense, you needed to be more patient, on more of an even keel. You couldn't lose your composure on offense. You had to stay still, worrying about not tipping the play and get ready to execute.

Offense was mechanical. Defense was instinctual.

Defense was just more aggressive. And the football field is where I wanted to release that aggression and energy. On defense, I could be less concerned about my composure, staying calm, or how it looked. I could look at an offense and say, "Here I come."

I could hunt. I could try and read what was happening. I could follow my assignment with determination and use my speed to catch the ball even if it wasn't coming my way. I could do things, whether it was shifting my position, moving around, or even jawing a bit to the linemen to get into their heads and possibly disrupt the play.

Defense also allowed me to hit. Offense was more about bracing yourself for a guy who was going to hit you. Defense was where I could take advantage of my strength. To me, there was nothing more gratifying than making the play, stopping the offense, and hitting the ball carrier.

I loved it.

I developed a reputation at Grambling for consistently breaking the blocking sled. It was an older contraption that had seen plenty of years of work, and its steel frame held some used and abused pads for the defensive players to hit. When we had defensive rookies come into camp, Coach Robinson almost always had them watch me.

"Big Dave, come on over here and hit this," he'd say.

And I would, hitting it with all my might, all my power, all my aggression. Many times, it would break.

"Hell son—you see what I mean?" Coach would say to the new prospects. "You see how he hit that? That's how I want you to hit the damn thing!"

Defense quickly became not only my strength but also my passion. In fact, although I don't believe there are any records of it, I can almost guarantee that in my first game as a freshman at Grambling, I probably led the team in tackles. It wouldn't be the last time.

I developed several techniques in college that lasted throughout my professional playing career—techniques that helped me build a Hall of Fame career. Later, I was praised for being one of the quickest defensive players to get to the ball, a reputation that I proudly carried with me until the day I retired. I would always get to the ball. Even if I made a mistake, I could get back to a good position to get the ball carrier.

Part of that could be attributed to my speed, but the other part had to do with my obsession with defense that started in college.

It's okay to be obsessed with what you love to do.

I couldn't get enough of defensive practice, going over the playbook at night or trying new things. I often lay awake at 2:00 or 3:00 in the morning, focusing on what I had learned that day, how I could approach an opponent, or just visualizing certain plays in my head and how they would go. When sleep would finally come, I found myself once again on defense in my dreams.

I became a student of particular routes I could use from my position to get to the ball carrier, even if he was running away from me. In college, I learned how to play the angles and chase the ball, often meeting the carrier at a point where he either had to run out of bounds or make a choice to push it upfield. I made it clear that running upfield was not his best option.

"Where you goin', boy?" I would yell, and then I would take the choice away from him.

It was at Grambling that I also developed my skills at shedding a blocker. If I found myself matched at the line by an offensive guard or tackle, I developed a strategy that worked for me where I would go inside, getting the blocker to commit. I would then roll out to get past him. It was a method I used many times at defensive end in the pros and one that often helped me get to the quarterback.

I also developed my toughness playing defense for Coach Robinson at Grambling. I always played football with a certain fire in my belly, and defense allowed me to stoke that fire. I lived for those moments, a few seconds before the ball is snapped, when I could line up against another player and know that soon, really soon, he would be trying to knock the hell out of me and I would do what I could to knock the hell out of him. I craved those moments where I could look at him and think that today I would come out on top.

Not today. On another day, against another team, maybe. But not today. No sir. Today, you're going to belong to me.

More than anything, my time playing football for Coach Robinson taught me how to play with distinction. At Grambling, I developed the mentality, a belief that I would always play my best, try my hardest, and do whatever it took to succeed.

Always aim to be a leader.

My determination and my passion to succeed eventually led me to being a captain on the team. That was a significant accomplishment for me and something I was always very proud of.

I believed in the importance of a captain, and I vowed to always set the right example and to lead my teammates by putting forth the most individual effort I could. I always wanted to play with the honor that title deserved. I could always hear Coach Robinson's words echoing through my head, something that Coach Lombardi preached to us in his own way years later.

"You gotta walk off that field today feeling like you just exposed that crowd to one of the best players in the country at that position," he said.

That always made me want to play harder, to lead, to fight, to win.

When it came to football, my four seasons at Grambling were full of ups and downs—mostly ups. During my four years, I developed what I can only call an insatiable desire to walk off the field victorious *always*. I developed focus, a calmness to help me concentrate, and a will that other players found contagious.

On the field, we finished with a winning record each of my four years. We dominated most of the teams we played in the SWAC, taking advantage of Coach's professional offensive and defensive systems. Many teams simply hadn't seen anything like us before, and come game time, they couldn't prepare. Many teams we played walked off that field looking like they never knew what hit them. The games we did lose, we always competed. We convinced ourselves there was nobody more disciplined, hungrier, or better coached than us.

Our best season at Grambling was 1955, my senior year. That season, we finished undefeated, having blown through our conference with hardly a challenge from the other teams. That season was a culmination of a group of young men who had bought into a legendary coach's system and had spent a few years working with each other to develop into an unstoppable force. We were the best team in our conference, and we felt we were among the best programs in the country.

A little taste of success goes a long way when it comes to building self-confidence.

We were given an opportunity to prove just how good we were. At the end of the season, we were set up to play against Florida A&M, another all-black school, in the Orange Blossom Classic at the Orange Bowl in Miami. Florida A&M, who almost always had a great football team, hosted the event every year from 1933–78, taking the other top black schools in the country and setting up a *de facto* championship game. There was no recognized system for declaring a champion among the black colleges, so this game was the closest thing we had. As time passed, it developed a reputation as the mythical Black National Championship game. That year, 1955, was Grambling's first appearance.

Mythical or not, we wanted that title.

Looking back, the game was one of the most exciting I was ever involved in during both my college and pro careers. It went beyond the thrill of traveling out of state with the team or playing in a championship game or the idea of bringing home a trophy. For me personally, that game would lead to a life-changing opportunity, to an almost lucky (albeit hard-earned) break, and a chance for a future in football beyond college.

Mostly, though, what I remember about that game is my brief but memorable "encounter" with Adolphus Cornelius Frazier.

We bussed it to Miami as the college, like most colleges in that time, did anything and everything they could to stretch what little money they had for athletics. It's wasn't like how things are today, with big bucks flowing from boosters and TV contracts into football and the other popular sports programs. Maybe it was at schools like Michigan, Notre Dame, and Florida—but the money certainly wasn't coming into the small black football programs.

As our administrators angled here and there to save a buck, they also had us stop by the Florida A&M campus to have lunch in their cafeteria. I can't imagine a scenario today where a football team would stop by their opponent's campus the day before the big game to eat in their facilities as their opponents ate there, as well!

As we stood there in line, getting our grub, we watched as the Florida A&M team filtered in the room to get in their own line, apparently aware we would be there. We could all feel the tension as two groups of young, excitable men watched each other with hawk eyes, waiting for somebody to do something stupid, something that could start this battle right here and now. It wasn't the mature way to look at the situation, but we were still young men, and we were hungry—not just for the food.

The only thing keeping us from doing something were the serious repercussions we knew would come from our coach. Eventually, both sides stopped glaring at each other, and everybody went back to their meals, content to save it all for the field. Everybody, that is, except Frazier.

Frazier, who went on to play a few seasons in the pros with the Denver Broncos, was a star running back for Florida A&M, along with Willie "The Wisp" Galimore, who played a few solid years with the Chicago Bears. Where Galimore was big and quick, Frazier was a smaller running back who had a reputation for being incredibly elusive and even a little powerful for his size. He also had a reputation for being a trash talker. On this particular day, with his opponent right there in front of him on his home turf, he couldn't help himself.

Though I didn't witness it myself, the story was that Frazier walked right up to our other defensive tackles and gave them a bit of a warning.

"You better touch me now," he said, "cuz' you ain't gonna see me in the game."

With that, he walked away back to his line, with his teammates laughing.

I've always believed the less said the better, especially before a competition. Sure, I've talked my fair share of trash come game time when both sides are in the heat of battle. But I've never understood the compulsion to say things either to or about another team before the game itself. All it ever does is throw a little extra fuel on the fire. It takes the competitiveness that your opponent is already channeling and raises it up a level. It gives your opponent that extra spark, and very little good ever comes from it. It sets you up for a bad situation.

Like what happened to Frazier at the Black National Championship Game.

I was told about the comment by my teammates just minutes before the game started. I remember wondering why they waited so long to tell me, but looking back, I'm sure it was because they knew it was something that would fire me up. I was never one who needed extra motivation come game time, but if it was there, I would take it.

And I did.

That game happened to be one of my best in my four years at Grambling. Not only did we win 28–21 to become national champions, but I was unstoppable, doing my part to help us achieve our goal.

We played in our typical 5-2 defense, which allowed me the flexibility to do what I did best—chase the ball. I could float to the left or the right, depending upon my assignment and my instincts. As such, it felt like every time they ran the ball, I was there to close it down. Pretty soon, after some early scores, their offense became predictable and there was no getting past us. They tried all kinds of plays, relying heavily on a quickly crumbling running game, but the only way they could have broken through would have been through complex reverses—and their team simply wasn't designed to run those kinds of plays. Few teams were at that time.

I played with passion, I was credited with 25 tackles, including a couple of sacks (which were not recognized or recorded at that time). But my performance in that game, my growth at Grambling, and my eventual career in pro football really came down to one defining play.

As the game was still close, Florida A&M had the ball. By this point I recognized their offensive positioning, and I knew a running play was coming and that Frazier would get the ball. I wasn't sure yet whether it would be to the right or the left, but I had a hunch. Sure enough, it went to the right, and I jumped. However, I quickly saw that side clogging up, filling with our defensive linemen. Frazier had a decent game, but it was frustrating for someone like him. He was used to bigger runs, and I could see that he was at the point of taking more and more risks, trying to generate a big play on his own. I knew he was going to cut back, and he did.

I was there waiting. I had read it perfectly, and as he tried to cut upfield past me, I remembered what was said, how badly we needed to stop this run, and how close we were to being champions. I hit Frazier with all my force, enough to make sure he would not gain another inch on that play. I wanted him to think twice about running at me again. As I used to say, "I was gonna see if I couldn't put a memory on him."

The impact was one of the harder ones I experienced. I give Frazier credit. He didn't back away from the impact, taking it with all of his weight and determination, as well, trying to get that extra yard, trying to carry his team on his back like a winner does.

But not today.

After the hit, I looked over and there, sitting on the ground, were both of Frazier's shoes. I hit him so hard, that he literally slipped right out of both of them. He was lying next to them, trying to catch his breath and figure out what exactly had hit him. Meanwhile, my defensive tackles, the same guys Frazier had so coolly approached the day before with his warning, were helping me up and slapping me on the back. It was something that made for good storytelling on that glorious bus ride home.

That play set the tone, and we were able to tough out a victory. We had played like the champions we were, doing what we had to do to win. We followed Coach's advice and left that field knowing the crowd had seen a distinguished team that day.

Little did I know who was sitting in the crowd.

While we were still riding high in the days following our victory in the Classic and our declaration as national champions, we began to hear rumors of some rather important people who might have seen the game. At Grambling, we weren't used to any kind of coverage from anyone other than the local press. Coverage of college football as a whole was still just a fraction of what it is today, and there was really no attention being paid to the black colleges. With our victory, we all expected or at least hoped for a small mention somewhere—and we got it.

Even more important than press, we began to hear rumors that some representatives from professional football, scouts and whatnot, were there in attendance—including legendary coach Paul Brown of the Cleveland Browns. We had never dreamed of that kind of exposure to anyone in the pros, not for a bunch of black players at a small black college. It was thrilling to know we had played and dominated in front of such a prestigious coach. A few days later, I saw a local newspaper article that confirmed Coach Brown was there. Even more exciting, he was quoted as saying that he had come to the game to check out both Frazier and Galimore from Florida A&M, but he left the game talking about Willie Davis.

I had certainly picked a good day to have a good game.

"You know, Willie, you might get drafted," a teammate suggested after the article came out.

That was really the first time I ever had a serious thought about playing professional football. Sure, I had fantasized about what it would be like, but I had never let that dream get too far. I thought the odds were stacked too far against me. I knew I was a good player, but I didn't think I had anything extra special to offer on that level. Still, I thought back to what Coach Robinson had told us time and time again.

"If you play well, they'll find ya."

Unbelievably, based mostly on my performance in that game, I was taken by the Cleveland Browns in the 15th round of the 1956 NFL Draft, the 181st pick in a solid draft filled with what would become some key professional players and future Hall of Famers, including future teammates Forrest Gregg and Bart Starr.

The day after the draft, I got a phone call from a representative from the Browns organization giving me the official word, congratulating me on this privilege and opportunity, telling me the details of reporting to camp, and what kind of contract the team was offering me. There were no negotiations. It was a take-it-or-leave-it offer.

One year for $6,800.

I had made it. Just like that, completely unexpected, I was a professional football player.

Chapter 5 | Learning the Hard Way in Cleveland

If you work hard, you will eventually be given a chance.

I wasn't really in the Cleveland Browns training camp long enough to make a difference. My opportunity to make a name for myself would have to wait because I got drafted almost immediately after reporting to my first preseason camp and had to serve in the military for two years.

After bouncing around from base to base and playing football for the army, I left the military a stronger, more focused, and mature man. I learned independence, responsibility, accountability, resolve, and the ability to make tough decisions. I would need all those things when I finally returned to Cleveland.

The military had also turned me into a much bigger player physically. After a year and a half of constant conditioning, physical labor, routine, and an army diet, I went from 220 lbs. to about 245—all muscle. I was already fast, and I believe my time in the army (and all the running we were expected to do) made me faster. When I reported to training camp a couple years prior, I had been intimidated and overwhelmed by the experience, as short-lived as it was for me.

Now, after my time in the military, my attitude had changed. I was still intimidated as I showed up for camp before the 1958 season on a small college campus about 40 miles south of Cleveland that was full of thousands of eager fans hoping to catch a glimpse of a team expected to compete for a championship. It was hard not to be nervous when you had all those eyes on you and all you wanted was to leave the right impression with one of the game's most prominent coaches. Plus, I was worried at what my time away from football might have done to my skills. I was playing in the military, but it wasn't the same as training every day with a professional football team.

In the eyes of the coaches, I was still a "tweener." Even with the added muscle, many of the coaches still thought I was still a little small to be playing on the defensive line—or the offensive line for that matter. Compared with some of the other monster athletes they had in camp, I couldn't argue. Despite my speed, I was also considered too big to play linebacker. I was on the bubble, somewhere in the middle, and so the coaches kept shuffling me around in camp, trying to decide where I could best fit in.

In fact, I think my speed might have been the only thing that kept me there. While the coaching staff was impressed by my added muscle and my ever-increasing determination, it was my speed that attracted them and convinced them I could contribute. The league was starting to shift a bit in the late 1950s, and more teams emphasized speed over size. Some of the positions were shrinking in terms of the size of the average player, but quickness was definitely becoming a hot commodity.

When I came back to Browns training camp in 1958, the organization had recovered from a dismal 1956 season that was its first without Otto Graham under center, followed by a surprise 1957 season that featured the team playing for a championship, thanks mainly to a star fullback they had drafted out of Syracuse by the name of Jim Brown. Unfortunately, they had been routed 59–14 by the Detroit Lions in a game that many experts thought the Browns would win.

The feeling in camp before the 1958 season was one of high hopes and expectations, a commitment and determination to get rid of the bad taste the players had from the championship game and once again re-establish themselves as the game's elite team. There was a focus, a drive—and the feeling wasn't lost on me.

Here I was competing with guys I had been reading about in the paper every Sunday or Monday, and now I needed to try my best to take their starting positions from them. These were some great players, and my instinct was to treat them like stars. But I couldn't—not if I wanted to succeed. I knew that if I wanted to make my mark with the Cleveland Browns and the NFL, then I was going to have to treat them like equals. I was going to have to look at them as my peers and nothing else. I was going to have to compete and know that I could be better than them, that I would be better than them. Fortunately, I was working with a legendary coach who would give me all the drive and motivation I would ever need.

There are men who have coached in both college and the pros that are so good at what they do, so accomplished, that they have awards, trophies, and sometimes even stadiums named after them. There are very few who are so distinguished that they have an entire franchise named after them. In the professional ranks, there is only one: Coach Paul Eugene Brown.

When I first reported to camp upon being drafted in 1956, Coach Brown was an intimidating presence. He was almost a mythical figure who had redefined success for coaching. He was never satisfied with winning, always looking to the next challenge, the next task, the next opportunity for him and his team to prove their greatness. His expectations were high from the outset. Coach Brown, a man who always had a hard, serious look on his face, reminded us in his caustic way that playing on this team would never be easy.

When I came back almost two years later, very little had changed. Coach Brown did not accept failure, and he vowed that this season the Browns would do all they could to avenge the previous season's loss. He expected us to push ourselves to our absolute limits. He also reminded us that nobody's job was safe and that all positions were up for grabs. Whoever worked hardest and showed the most tenacity and grit would be the one starting.

I liked that approach. It gave me a chance.

It was true—camp before the 1958 season was one of the most challenging camps I ever found myself in. Time-wise, we seldom practiced more than an hour and a half, but that time was as intense as the players could handle, if not more so. Coach Brown believed in repetition, drills, and conditioning, and he pushed us to the max in all three. We became masters at various calisthenics routines, pushing our muscles to their thresholds. We worked as a team, with everyone taking part in the same regimen. When it was time to break down into individual and group assignments, the pushing continued with tackling and blocking drills designed to test our stamina, strength, and endurance. The practices were run at a pace that was supposed to be even more intense than the games themselves, getting us ready physically and mentally for our opponents. Coach Brown's philosophy was the harder and more intense we practiced, the easier execution would be come game time.

Nobody broke execution down to a science like Coach Brown. His obsession with the precision of running a play to maximize its effectiveness helped to redefine both offense and defense. Coach Brown truly believed in football being a game of inches. He wouldn't just create and run plays; he would analyze every aspect of how each player lined up and positioned himself to execute the play.

He became notorious for continually stopping practice to shift guys into their positions. If a defensive end had trouble breaking through to the quarterback, Coach Brown would walk up to the player and physically move him over about 6" and have him run the play again—usually with more success. If a lineman was having problems blocking, Coach Brown would shift his shoulders or move him an inch or two to the right or left to give him a better starting position, and it would make all the difference in the world. Coach Brown observed everything and believed in the details. He preached precision, believing that those few inches would mean the difference between winning and losing.

It was a big change for me, coming from a place where I just went out and played. In high school and college, the game of football was very simple. Coach Brown made things a bit more complicated, and it took some time to adjust. Of course, when I did adjust, I saw the effectiveness of his strategy. Once we found the exact positioning that worked, he made sure you worked it long enough to get comfortable with it and to memorize it. At that point, he made it clear that it was up to you.

"We can teach you and we can show, but we can't do it for you."

That was his favorite expression and one that we received loud and clear. He coached us, showed us the play, and showed us how we could be the most effective at executing that play. What we did after that was up to us, and it meant the difference between playing and sitting on the bench. Coach Brown was quick to pull a player who forgot that message. In one game my rookie year after I had failed to make a couple plays in a row, Coach Brown called me to the sideline to deliver a specific message.

"Willie, what did I tell you about that play?" he yelled. "Now we can teach you, but we can't do it for you. And if you can't do it, that's when we start to look."

I knew exactly what he meant.

One of the key reasons for his success was his recruiting. He covered the entire Great Lakes region and was able to find some talent in that part of the country, including Otto Graham. In a time when many owners still shyed away from it, he also actively and openly recruited black players, including future Hall of Famers Marion Motley and Bill Willis. The subject of race was something that simply didn't come up with Paul Brown. When we were in camp, we all felt we had an equal chance. We were all treated the same, and we were all told we could make the team. We believed it.

He was not making a stand for what was right. He was not trying to start a controversy. He was a coach focused on winning, and he would do what it took to win, including using black players if they were the best.

Coach Brown also used extensive classroom lecturing and testing to determine a player's mental strength and intelligence.

That's how I got to be called Univac.

Paul Brown's intelligence tests were feared among the players. They were all based on his playbook, which was also one of the most extensive in the game at the time. A frontrunner of what eventually became the West Coast offense, Coach Brown had a long list of both running and passing plays that changed with each formation, including the assignments for the linemen. His defense was just as difficult, featuring a number of different packages to defend against the run and the pass.

We were given these plays and asked where certain players were supposed to go and when. We sat in class and marked up these sheets with how the plays should run, testing our memory and instincts as players. What made them challenging, beyond the sheer number of plays, was that we were all expected to know all of them—meaning defensive players had to know the offense and vice versa.

By this point in camp, the coaches had decided to keep me mostly in the defense, and I was starting to get comfortable. I was terrified of these tests. I was always a decent student and I had improved dramatically in college, but it was still a lot of information.

The test was on a Sunday, and I spent that entire weekend studying. After practice, we were given time off, and most of the guys used it to relax or go out. I never once left the complex, spending all my time literally pouring over each and every play and trying my best to come up with both the offensive and defensive assignments for each one. I knew a lot of them, and for the ones I didn't, I guessed based on other plays and what I had seen in practice. I also relied heavily on my instincts on where players could go to be the most effective.

The test came and went and I had no idea how I had done, but I figured by the amount of grumbling I heard among the other players that I had done better than some. That next weekend, I was called in to see Coach Brown.

"Sit down, Willie," Coach said, and my heart started racing. "What did you think of the test?"

"It was fine, coach," I responded, not knowing what to say.

He studied me for a second and then looked over what I assumed was my test sheet again.

"Willie, we're going to start working you into a little offense as well as defense," he said. "We'll see if we can't find a couple positions that you can help us with."

It turns out I had gotten the second-highest score on Paul Brown's test and the highest by far of any defensive player. From that next practice on, I started playing offensive guard more regularly as well as defensive end and linebacker. When I told the other players, they gave me my nickname. I'm not sure who it was, but somebody started calling me Univac, the name of one of the first computers around that time.

"Hey, where are you supposed to go on this play?!"

"I don't know," someone would respond. "Ask Univac."

It wouldn't be my only nickname through the years.

Throughout that camp, I began to find a place on the team. I felt like taking part in both offense and defense would better my odds at getting playing time, so I was eager and excited to work the extra duty. I also began to feel a sense of belonging with the team among the players. I developed close bonds with some, but none closer, much to my pleasure (and Coach Brown's annoyance) than the one I had with the legendary Jim Brown.

There is a lot you can learn by watching the greatest.

In my opinion, Jim Brown is the greatest running back of all time. I don't say that lightly as I also played alongside Jim Taylor, who in short yardage situations was almost always guaranteed to get you the yards you needed *when* you needed them most. In a goal-line situation or a third-and-3, Jim Taylor was as tough as they come.

I've also witnessed the amazing talent of Gale Sayers firsthand. Even though he had a short career that ended too soon because of injuries, in his prime, nobody could touch Sayers. He could evade and outmaneuver his own shadow. He was awesome to watch and dangerous to play against. Whenever he got the ball, I was always looking for help in catching him and bringing him down.

But there was nobody like Jim Brown. A combination of strength, skill, speed, attitude, and determination, Jim was the ultimate back. One need only look at his stats and records. From 1957–65 in nine seasons, he made the Pro Bowl each year, and he was named MVP of the game four of those years. He was also an All-Pro selection every season, being named First Team All-Pro for eight of those seasons. As gifted a receiver as he was a rusher, Brown still holds the record for total seasons (five) leading the NFL in all-purpose yards. He is also the only rusher in NFL history to average more than 100 yards per game for a career. When he retired, at the young age of 29, he was the record holder for single-season rushing and career rushing, as well as rushing touchdowns, total touchdowns, and all-purpose yards.

He was just amazing. And the stats don't show his toughness.

It started mentally. Jim was definitely a team player, but he was not someone I would call a "rah-rah" guy. He wasn't one to get the team fired up or to make big speeches. He was individualistic in many ways and often kept to himself. He was always focused, always centered, always aware of what his job was and what was required to do it. He was slow and methodical, always calculating, until he had the ball in his hands. Then you had a problem because Jim Brown didn't take any crap from anyone.

He was quick, but he was by no means the speediest of runners at the time. He was, however, the baddest. Jim did not go down easily, often shaking off tacklers who dared to get in his path. He was built like a truck and often ran like one, barreling over anyone who got in his way, including his own blockers! When he hit you, he told me once, he wanted you to remember that hit. He wanted you to think twice about trying to stop him. Jim Brown did not believe in running out of bounds. As such, he was one of the most dangerous offensive weapons a team could have. He was a true football player and a measuring stick for anyone wanting to show their toughness and earn their place in the league.

If you could make a play on Jim Brown, you could make a play on anyone.

Find the opportunity to leave an impression.

In those first few weeks of training camp, while the coaches were still trying to decide where to put me on defense, they lined me up as a linebacker in a scrimmage. I knew at some point I was going to have my shot at Jim. He was going to run my way, and I'd have to stop him. This was my chance to make my mark and open some eyes to my ability.

And it was—at a cost.

During a drill they gave Jim the ball on a designed running play and he broke to my side, getting past the linemen and heading straight toward me. I broke a little to the left to meet him head on and hit him with as much force as I could muster just as he lowered his shoulder and threw his body into me. To this day I can remember the sound of our pads and helmets hitting and the floating sensation I had as I hit the ground, feeling like I had just been run over by a cement truck.

There was a hush that came over the practice field as I looked over at Jim Brown, who had also fallen. He was getting up slowly, a trademark of his, but this time he looked like he had felt the hit. He had been stopped, and everyone knew it. For as much pain that he was in (if any), my body was screaming for mercy. I don't think I had ever been hit that hard, and everything in me instantly ached. For the sake of pride, I hoisted myself up, even as my body begged me to lie back down. All eyes were on me and Jim, then he gave me a quick look before heading back to the huddle. There was no expression on his face, but that quick look was all the acknowledgment that I needed. Yep, he had felt it alright.

I would have plenty of opportunities over the next two years in Cleveland to prove my toughness to Jim Brown, both on and off the field. In the off-season and even during the season, many of the Browns players would shoot hoops at the local rec center to help stay in shape. Just like in the game of football, Jim Brown was one of the best and also one of the toughest. Never afraid of a challenge, he was notorious on the court for his rebounding ability, mainly because of how quickly and fiercely he swung those gigantic elbows of his.

I got put on the other team for a pick-up game, and we established a steady flow rather quickly. I was hitting my shots, having a particularly good day, and Jim was getting his points and his rebounds, as well. He and I struggled against each other, fighting for position just as we did time after time in football practice. Then, on one particular play, he and I went up at the same time and he came down with his elbows right above my eye, causing a nasty gash that instantly sent blood streaming down my face. Not one to apologize for hard work and hustle, Jim gave me a nod as others made sure I was okay. I was and I'll tell you what, I wasn't coming out of that game. With each drop of blood, I became more determined.

Probably because of my toughness, Jim and I formed a friendship. He quickly took a liking to me and my style of play.

"Willie Davis," he'd say. "Willie Davis will hit ya."

That was a test of manhood for Jim Brown, and he respected those who didn't back down from a fight. I was in awe to be close with him, a big-time player from Syracuse who was already building a legacy in the NFL. He was admired by a lot of the other players, including me, and I was a little overwhelmed that he even knew who I was. As time went on, we developed a friendship based on mutual respect, one that we maintain to this day.

In fact, we even roomed together for a while, having fun and running around town. Jim and I were both young, single guys who were ready to take on the Cleveland night life—and we did for a short while. Jim, who was an established superstar, had no fear of breaking the team rules. I, on the other hand, was still struggling to find my place and playing time. When the coaches caught me falling asleep in a team meeting after a night out, let's just say they expressed their displeasure. In fact, they called my mother and told her they were worried I wasn't focused enough on my career in the league! That was all I needed to hear. I moved out, found me a girl, settled down, and focused on finding my place with the Cleveland Browns.

On the field, Jim was always there to lend a hand, offering me guidance and support with even the occasional compliment. Mostly, he offered tips about a play or a player. As a rather reserved individual, this wasn't something he did with just anybody and I was certainly grateful for it, especially when I went toe-to-toe with Big Daddy Lipscomb, a mountain of a defensive lineman for the Baltimore Colts. At the time, Big Daddy, who I swear looked like he was almost 7' tall and more than 300 pounds, was one of the biggest defenders in the game. He was a professional wrestler in the off-season, and he clearly brought a lot of what he learned to his football game. I don't want to say that he was a dirty player, but he had a couple of questionable signature moves, including head slapping.

I started this particular game against the Colts as defensive end, but our offensive tackle got hurt early, which meant I was going to pull double duty. I lined up against Big Daddy just awed by the man's presence.

He was huge. I was no small man, but this guy was a giant! And he played like one, pushing and slapping me around on every play. I couldn't provide any kind of protection for our quarterback or create any kind of a gap for Jim to break through. On the sideline, I went to Jim, exhausted, and told him I thought this guy was impossible to block.

"I'll tell you what," Jim said calmly. "Next time around, block down on him. Get your feet under you and block him a little lower, and I'll do the rest."

Jim Brown just needed the defender to be slightly off balance. It didn't matter how big Lipscomb was, Jim was too tough. Once I started blocking down, it was just enough to throw off Big Daddy's balance, and Jim was able to run over and past him—again and again and again. Jim Brown ran for more than 200 yards and scored five touchdowns that day. But the thing I'll remember most about that day is the ferocious Big Daddy yelling and swearing at me, saying I was blocking him wrong and threatening the both of us. That was the kind of impact Jim Brown could have.

Brown was not well liked by many defenders. He also had a tendency to ruffle the feathers of some of his own teammates and even some of the coaching staff, none more so than Coach Brown himself.

It wasn't like they fought very often. They absolutely had a mutual respect and admiration for each other. But Jim was always ready to take this team on his back, and that didn't always necessarily fit in with Coach Brown's game plan. There were many times they simply didn't see eye to eye both on and off the field. With as much talent as Jim Brown had and with how smart of a coach Paul Brown was, it was always interesting to see who was going to win. The clashing would mostly come up during the games themselves.

During one important division game, Jim wanted Coach to call a specific play we named Flip to the Flex. Essentially, we lined up Jim Brown in the backfield off to the side of the quarterback, and when the ball was snapped, it was pitched to Brown. Depending upon the defense and where we were blocking, he had the option to follow his momentum to the outside and cut up field or find a gap and make his cut sooner. It was a highly successful play we used a lot that enabled Jim to use his talents: strength, speed, and making decisions with the ball.

Jim got to the huddle as I was leaving for a substitution and told me to tell Coach to run the play, which I did. I knew it was a mistake as soon as the request left my mouth.

"What?!" yelled Coach. "You tell Jim Brown that I make the damn decisions!"

I decided there would be no more recommendations from me. The next time I went to the huddle, I very quickly and matter-of-factly told Mr. Jim Brown that Mr. Paul Brown was not willing to answer his request at this time. That didn't sit well with Jim.

As the first half continued, our running game was rather stagnant, as was the score. We all waited anxiously for Coach Brown to call the play, knowing in our hearts that he was holding off on it now to teach Jim (and probably any of us who were questioning him) a lesson. Finally, right before halftime, he called it.

Jim Brown ran the play for about 30 yards and a score. The last 10 yards of that run, he slowed his stride and seemed to look to our sideline, almost as if to say, "See what I told ya?" At halftime, Coach Brown gave us a speech about how he called the plays and nobody else.

"And the reason I call the plays is because I know when a play is ready to be run!" he said to a silent locker room. Nobody dared speak, not even Jim, who I'm sure was smiling on the inside. "I knew that play wasn't ready to be run 'til that moment. That's why we ran it then!"

With that, he looked right at Jim Brown, who just stared right back, continuing what could only be called a silently tumultuous relationship that led to some very great things.

Savor every first moment.

We opened the 1958 season, my first real season as a professional football player, against the Los Angeles Rams on September 28. We spent a couple days before that game practicing at the Rose Bowl in Pasadena, a grand spectacle for me. I was equally impressed with the size of the L.A. Coliseum where we played the game itself.

Walking into these two stadiums served as an instant reminder that now I was playing a game on a much grander stage. In just a few years, I had gone from begging my mother to let me play for a small high school in Texarkana to running onto the field of an enormous stadium with one of the league's premiere teams and coaches. If I had ever stopped to think about it, I would have been overwhelmed.

I never expected to make the final cut with the Cleveland Browns, if I'm being honest. But now that I was there, I wanted more. I told myself that everything beyond this was a privilege, but the competitive player inside me wanted more. I knew I would be happy sitting on the sideline for only so long. I wanted to play.

Other than the feeling of coming out onto the field for the first time as an actual professional football player, I have very few other memories of that first game, mainly because I never saw a snap. We won 30–27, mostly on the back (and legs) of Jim Brown, and the win kicked off a five-game winning streak that helped us set the pace for reaching the title game. As for my part, I spent it as an awed spectator, eager to get in on the action. I wondered if I would ever get a chance to play. I fought off those feelings of anxiety and sadness and did the only thing I could do—work hard and get prepared for next week in case I got the call.

I eventually did.

We went up to Pittsburgh to face the Steelers in a game that Coach Brown thought was essential to our momentum. If we could get home to Cleveland having won our first two games in a row, we would be in good shape.

Knowing how big this game was and since I hadn't been used the previous week, I once again didn't expect to play. However, I learned enough about Coach Brown to know that anything was possible—especially with his itchy trigger finger. He was an amazing coach, but he was also a bit volatile, especially come game time. Coach Brown was nervous early, which meant if you weren't playing the way he thought you should, he would often make a snap decision and pull you. Each and every one of us had to be ready.

On the third play of the game, Coach Brown pulled our starting defensive end Paul Wiggin, saying he didn't like how Wiggin was maneuvering around the offensive line. I was sent in. As soon as my name got called, I ran out onto that field as quickly as I possibly could. It happened so fast, I didn't have a chance to think about it. I couldn't afford to take the time to let it all soak in or it would have been over way too quick. I had a job to do, and I was focused on one thing and one thing only—not messing up and getting called back to the sideline before I had a chance to leave an impression. I told myself that I had to do something in the first couple plays to show Coach Brown he had made the right choice in putting me in. If he had little to no patience for a seasoned veteran, Coach Brown would have even less with a rookie.

My first play was one that set the tone for the rest of that game and helped me earn a spot on the field for the first part of the season. Once the ball was snapped, I rushed after the quarterback with such ferocity, such speed, such determination that I was not going to be stopped. Had he not attempted a quick pass, I would have gotten him. I would have sacked him. As it was, I broke though quick enough to force him to get rid of the ball early.

That moment actually hit me. On my first play, I saw I could compete. I knew I had a chance to affect the game. These guys might have been more experienced, but I was hungry and determined. I belonged here.

Wow, I gotta keep pushing. If I do, I'll get to him.

Then I got close again. And again. I think I benefited from the Steelers having no idea of how to play me. I wasn't someone they had seen before, therefore they had no idea how to prepare for my speed. I was not the strongest guy on the field, but on our defense, I was one of the quickest and that gave me an advantage. Eventually, as our defense continued to pound their tired line, I was able to get to the quarterback. The league didn't record sacks back then, but I had a couple en route to a 45–12 whipping.

It was enough to get a pat on the back by Coach Brown and an opportunity to keep playing at defensive end (along with the occasional snap at offensive tackle) for the next seven games, rotating back and forth with other players.

Unfortunately, I was still a rookie and even though I had tremendous talent and speed, I was still learning the professional game. I was still developing my skills and my ability to execute Coach Brown's game plan.

Plus, I was still a tweener. Other teams put up bigger players on offense, and the coaching staff still thought I might be too small for the defensive end position. I was also competing with veterans who knew the pace of the game a little better. That constant struggle defined my two years of playing in Cleveland.

My first year we went 9–3 and lost to the Giants in a tiebreaker play-off game. My second year we went 7–5. I did enjoy my brief time in Cleveland, and I fell in love with the city. In my personal life, I met my first wife, Ann, with whom I had my two children, Duane and Lori. I also started doing some teaching and took an active role in the community.

On the field, however, I constantly fought for playing time, always worrying if I would get news of being cut or traded. After my second year, I got that call.

Chapter 6 | Headed to Siberia of the North

Sometimes the best opportunities are tough to see at first.

The Cleveland Browns traded me to the Green Bay Packers at the end of the 1959 season for A.D. Williams, a young offensive end from the University of the Pacific. A.D. had played one year for the Packers, catching one pass for 11 yards. The trade is considered by many NFL historians to be one of the best in Packers history.

What was interesting is that right before I got the call, I signed a new contract with the Browns. I was told coming into the 1960 season that I would eventually be the starting left offensive tackle, replacing veteran and future Hall of Famer Lou Groza, who had been with the Browns since the team's inception. I wasn't given any guarantees or timetables, but it was made clear to me that I would be rewarded for my efforts.

A few weeks later, I found out I was traded—on the radio.

Driving home from my substitute teaching job in Cleveland, I heard on a local sports talk show that I had just been traded to the Packers. Needless to say, I was dumbfounded. I was shaking off the remainder of the rough season we had, focusing on working in the off-season and doing what I had to do to prepare for my next chance with the Browns. Now all of it was gone.

This must be a joke, or at least a mistake.

Green Bay was nothing to joke about. With the Browns, I was lining up to start on one of the most respected teams in professional football, playing for a legendary coach in a town that loved football and their Browns. I had money in my pocket, a good wife, another job that I could at least tolerate, and the beginnings of a life built around playing football. I had everything that I wanted. When I heard the words "Green Bay," I feared the worst. Green Bay was nothing more than a threat our coaches used on rookies and veterans alike during practice.

"If you don't like it or you can't do it, then we can always ship you off to Green Bay!"

It wasn't just *our* coaches. Everybody looked at Green Bay as a last resort, a place of desperation, horrible weather, and even worse—bad football. It was dubbed the "Siberia of the North" by players, coaches, owners, and even analysts. It didn't feel like a true NFL team, and more than a decade of losing seasons did little to change that perception. I knew very little about Green Bay, the small town, the team, the players, or their new coach, a former Giants assistant by the name of Vince Lombardi. What I did know didn't appeal to me—or anybody for that matter. Nobody wanted to go to Green Bay.

I was terrified, especially when I got home and saw there were a few messages from Jack Vainisi, the Packers' top scout and the man in charge of player personnel, asking me to call him back so he could go over the logistics of getting me into the Packers system.

This was real.

I'd like to say that I felt mixed emotions, but I can't. I was scared, angry, and even hurt. As I look back on it with age and experience, I can see that it was simply a good business move and nothing personal against me. In fact, it may have even been for my benefit.

Although there was talk of me taking over for Groza in Cleveland, he was a veteran and a good one at that. He had a good lock on the position, and fighting him for it might have been tough. I also had some flexibility at the guard position, but that year the Browns drafted Dick Schafrath out of Ohio State and the coaches were incredibly impressed with his ability. Besides, Coach Brown knew I loved defense and that my mentality was built for defense. Unfortunately, what he needed were people dedicated to offense. If he could get someone like that for a utility player like me, he would have to make the move.

At the time, I felt slightly betrayed. I felt the organization didn't care much about me, like I was being thrown away. I also panicked, wondering what this would mean for my future. I absolutely *did not* want to play in Green Bay. In fact, I was so turned off by the idea that my first thought was about retiring.

But being a professional, I thought I at least owed it to Jack to return his call and see what he had to say. After telling him what I thought, he had one simple request.

"Coach Lombardi will be back soon. Just wait until you chat with him."

Jack knew more about Coach Lombardi than I did. I would soon learn.

While it's good to be skeptical, also be open.

"Willie," said the man on the other end of the phone. "This is Coach Lombardi. I hear you're thinking about things, and I want to help you with that. Willie—you're going to come to Green Bay, and you're going to play for the Packers."

That was my first experience with Coach Lombardi. I had heard of him before that phone call but knew little more than that he had helped Green Bay to its first winning record in years in 1959, which had earned him some accolades around the league. But that was it. I knew nothing of his personality, his demeanor, or his approach to coaching. I soon learned my first lesson. Coach Lombardi was the most authoritatively convincing man I had ever met.

"Well Coach, I do have some things I've been thinking about," I responded, caught off guard.

"Willie, you're going to come up here, and you're going to play left end for us," he said again. "I want you to know that we are the ones who made this trade because we believe you can come up and help us solve some of our defensive problems."

Admittedly, that made me feel a little better about the whole trade situation; at least it satisfied my ego. I think Coach Lombardi knew it would have that effect. I'm sure he was able to understand why the trade had affected me and that some of these thoughts of retiring or leaving for

Canada were coming out of hurt and frustration. When he told me the Packers pushed the deal because they wanted me for a specific purpose, it helped to ease the soreness. It also piqued my interest.

He explained how the Packers had lost veteran defensive end Nate Borden to the Dallas Cowboys in that year's expansion draft and were looking to fill a specific hole.

"I think you have all the abilities we're looking for to fill that position," he said. Coach Lombardi told me what he thought made a successful lineman, a philosophy that he was quoted on many times in the next few years. He told me that a good lineman must have speed, agility, and size. "You give me someone with two of those, and they'll do okay. If you have all three, you can be great. Willie, I think you have all three."

He went on to describe a play that I made against the Giants when he was a coach there that he had watched over and over again on film. It was a sweep the Giants ran that tricked me at first. When the ball was snapped, I immediately started to break to the inside, thinking that's where the running back was going to make his move. I quickly realized they were running him to the outside and I was able to throw off the blocker, switch direction, and sprint to the outside in enough time to make the play. Coach thought the play was so impressive that he called in the rest of his staff to come see it.

"That's when we knew we wanted you to come here," he said. "And Willie, I know you've been playing both offense and defense at Cleveland. I want you to know that as of right now, it would not be our intention to have you play offensive tackle. We want you to focus solely on defensive end."

I was getting more excited.

"Jack will give you all the details as far as when to report," he said, fully aware that he had grabbed my attention. "Willie, I want you to tell me one thing."

"Yeah, Coach?"

"Tell me you're going to come," he said. "Tell me that you'll be at camp."

Even though I was excited about what he was saying, I was still confused. I didn't know what to think, and I wasn't sure I was ready to make any kind of commitment. This morning I had gone to my substitute teaching job like any other day, and now I was faced with some major life decisions. I was trying to gather my thoughts.

"Well, Coach," I said. "I'd like to think about it."

"No, Willie, you tell me right now," he said, and that's when I knew he was a closer—and a winner. "We want you up here. We'd be a good fit for you. I want to feel like when I hang up this phone, I know that you're coming to play for the Green Bay Packers."

"Yeah, Coach," I said, getting my first taste of the power and magic of Coach Lombardi. "I'll be there."

"Well you made my day, Willie," he said, and he actually sounded clearly relieved. I began to realize he wasn't just saying these things to make me feel better. He really, truly wanted me in Green Bay.

I still had doubts and concerns. This was the Siberia of the North after all, and even if they had a winning record the previous year, they still had a reputation as being one of the doormats of the league. At that point, that organization was little more than a punch line, and I was afraid of going from greatness to mediocrity or worse.

"I don't know if you followed the Packers at all last year, but we made some improvements," he said. "Willie, I can tell you—we're going to win. You hear me? We're going to win."

| # My Mentor, My Colleagues, and Life in Green Bay

Learn from your mentors and pass on their words and influence.

There has been so much written and said about Coach Vince Lombardi, so much that is both known and unknown, underappreciated and exaggerated about the coach and the man. That's how it is with legends. All these years later, he still represents the pinnacle of sporting accomplishment, praise and glory, the definition of excellence, and the model for what we should all strive for, no matter what we do with our lives. Decades after he achieved greatness, he is still quoted by everyone from coaches to sports fans, business leaders to priests, motivational speakers, counselors, anyone looking to lead someone to something greater—and rightfully so. Coach Lombardi was more than football. He was something much greater, and those of us who played for him were given a rare privilege.

Coach Vince Lombardi was also the single most influential person in my adult life. He was responsible for my success both on the football field and throughout the course of my life after football as a successful business leader. He is still the single most influential person in my life today. If you ask those who played for him during those Green Bay Packer glory years, I think you would be hard-pressed to find a different answer from anyone, even those who didn't always see eye to eye with him. And yes, there were some.

He built his legacy with fire and energy, a need to control, inspiring speeches, grueling practices, dedication to those things most important in life, a temper, fire, passion, and love for his Green Bay Packers. He changed the game of football, carrying the future of not just the franchise, but eventually the league on his back and into glory. He did so with moments of fear and vulnerability as well as moments of unrelenting strength. We all loved him in our own way, and we loved playing for him, fully aware we were part of something special because of this man. Coach Lombardi pushed me and taught me more than anyone, turning me into a Hall of Fame player and a business leader who has always reached for something more, something greater, something that would make him proud.

The first thing I noticed after meeting him in person was his obsession with the game of football. Coach Lombardi was a man who often shared his principles on life and his feelings about certain things he felt were important, but inevitably, everything always came back to football. It was on his mind constantly, and if you played for him, he expected it to be on your mind, as well. To Coach Lombardi, football was more than just a game; it was a way of life.

"Gentlemen, there is something about how you play this game of football," he told us once during one of the many speeches I was privileged enough to witness.

"How you play this game is a reflection of how you will live the rest of your life."

We learned that everything we put into preparing, working, and executing in each meeting, practice, and game was a microcosm of how we would live our lives. That's why it was so important to him that we always work hard, that we succeed. He truly believed the game of football was something more, and that passion and devotion to the game was something he passed along to all of his players.

I also quickly saw there was nobody in control of the team other than Coach Lombardi. He gained a reputation over his years of coaching for being a dominating personality who very rarely sought the advice or guidance of others. He also was not one to tolerate conflict or disagreement with his outlook and manner of coaching. This was Coach

Lombardi's team, and it would always be his team. If you didn't like it, Green Bay probably wasn't the place for you.

It was a reputation that he earned right away, coming in before that 1959 season and either trading or cutting some players who had been around the organization for a while and bringing in a new crop of veterans and rookies. While he preached that the changes came from a need to reinvigorate the organization, there were always rumors that some of the people were let go because they didn't see eye to eye with Coach and he was afraid they might cause trouble by not buying into his approach.

One trade that was particularly surprising was when Coach Lombardi traded the team's top receiver, Billy Howton. There was never really a reason given, but the rumor was that Billy tried to tell Coach Lombardi about certain cliques and groups on the team and how things were done in Green Bay, offering him advice on how to coach the team. Not only would Coach Lombardi not tolerate anyone telling him how to run his team, he also wouldn't tolerate any kind of division, a message he still preached a year later when I joined the team.

"There are problems that this team has had in the past, and I can guarantee you that those problems are going to go away," he said. "We are going to have the best players we can have, working as a team and doing what we have to do to succeed."

That started with forming the right habits. The emphasis on good habits is something that I learned from Coach Lombardi and have preached to myself over my years as a business leader. You draw a straight line from A to B, and that line represents the path to success. No matter who you are, what you want to accomplish, what your goals are, your situation in life, circumstances, etc., you will inevitably see another line deviating off that straight line as you go down the road of your life.

My sense has always been that if you pick up bad habits, they will drive you along that second line, whether you're talking professionally or in your personal life. It's the whole concept of the straight and narrow and doing what you need to do to stay on that path. It's so tempting for all of us to drift away from that line. We can deceive ourselves by thinking that having a clear goal in mind is enough to keep us on track, but it's not. We must develop good habits to keep on the path.

"Good or bad, habits will soon become the natural thing to do."

Good habits included individual responsibility, accountability, self-discipline, commitment, focus, and hard work. There is nothing new and revolutionary in this philosophy. We all know what kind of results these kinds of good habits can bring. But what Coach did better than anyone was constantly remind us of those habits, help us develop them individually and as a team, and show us exactly what kind of results we could get if we stuck to them.

He did that with positive reinforcement, acknowledging good play, and celebrating team success, reminding us of what we were capable of achieving. He also made it clear he would not tolerate the bad habits, especially those that came from a lack of focus or a lack of self-discipline.

Coach Lombardi loved the game so much that he couldn't understand those who didn't feel as passionately as he did. He couldn't understand how a player could lose his focus or concentration on a play, and as such, he didn't tolerate it. Nothing invoked his wrath more than a lazy player, or even a committed, focused, and great player losing his concentration even just for a play.

He also didn't understand those players who couldn't show self-control or self-discipline. Not only was he a devout Catholic, he also respected the game so much that he would never put himself in a position to lessen his impact or commitment to it. He couldn't understand those who would jeopardize what we were trying to build in Green Bay by doing things like letting themselves go physically, staying out late at night, showing up unprepared, and worst of all, drinking. Coach Lombardi was okay with the men on the team drinking or really doing anything, until it showed the slightest negative effect on the player—or more importantly, the team as a whole. Then it became intolerable, something he was quick to tell us each and every week.

Throughout my years there, some players came and went, and I can honestly say that a few of them were released because they couldn't get control of their bad habits.

Being on time was one of the most important habits, and it was the one that built his notoriety. Even today, you hear people talk about Lombardi Time, which meant showing up at least 15 minutes early for anything. What's so interesting is that it really grew out of Coach Lombardi's impatience more than anything.

If Coach Lombardi called a 5:00 PM meeting and a majority of the room was full at 4:45, he'd simply start the meeting, unaware he was starting early. Inevitably, we had players walking in with confused expressions on their faces, having just popped by the local bar for a quick beer after practice, checking their watches to verify that they were still early. Regardless of the time, Coach Lombardi would stare them down or even say something. The message was clear: the meeting starts when Coach says it starts, and you better be here.

Nobody wanted to be on his bad side, which meant now we had to always be there early, just to be safe. We wanted to make sure that he saw we were there early, ready to listen, and not one of those players whose cleats you could hear click-clacking down the hall as they ran to pop in at the last possible minute. Eventually, it became so ingrained that the players policed ourselves on Lombardi Time more than he did. If somebody showed up "on time" at 10:00 AM for a 10:00 AM meeting, they'd catch hell from the other players.

"Hey man, you need to reset your watch!"

I still show up at least 15 minutes early for everything. I still judge myself, my actions, and even my habits, by how Coach Lombardi would have judged them. His influence is still that strong over me. I make sure that what I'm doing with my life is helping me stay on that path to success, always, and I gauge that by what Coach Lombardi would have thought.

"Success is not a gift, it's earned."

He was the strictest of disciplinarians, focusing on the importance of hard work and consistency in everything we did as individuals and as a team. Just as there was no tolerance for bad habits, there was no acceptance of anyone not pushing themselves 150 percent or executing at a perfect level.

"Fatigue makes cowards," he said. His team would not be afraid. His team would own the gridiron. His team would dictate how the game was played and the outcome. His team would accomplish what they set out to accomplish. One of the strengths for me individually and for the team as a whole over the course of his tenure there was domination in the fourth quarter of games. We were often in better shape, mentally and physically, than our opponents, and that was because of how hard Coach Lombardi pushed us in practice. As time went on and we experienced more and more success, we gained more confidence in his approach, embracing the work.

In many games, I would walk up to that line in the fourth quarter and stare at my opponent, watching as his breathing got deeper and heavier, as the sweat poured down his face, and as he moved just slightly slower off the ball. I was not tired. I was not fatigued. I was just as focused and strong as I was in the first quarter because I had been conditioned to be that way. I would stare at my opponent and feel a lift.

Oh yeah, I got this guy now.

The good habits, self-discipline, and hard work ethic also helped to create a winning reputation that Coach Lombardi thought could also lead to a winning mentality. As soon as he got to the Packers, he changed how the team was both perceived and how the players perceived themselves. He emphasized that his taking over as coach reflected a new start for the failing organization, that the past decade no longer mattered, and that the team had an opportunity to start fresh.

He brought in new equipment, new ways for the team to travel, and new requirements for how to dress when we traveled or showed up for games. He preached how image was important to building a team's reputation as well as their self-confidence. We would practice like winners. We would play like winners. We would look like winners. Then we would become winners.

He was our leader—and as our leader, he wanted us to think he was invincible. There is nobody I have ever met in my life before or since who could rally a team and motivate us the way Coach Lombardi could. We were willing to fight for him, to suffer and struggle for him, always. He brought an unmatched intensity to the game and he used it to push us, to focus us, to make us hungry for everything victory and success could bring. He made us crave winning and winning alone.

For me, Coach Lombardi proved to be exactly what I needed to push my game to the next level. Coach Lombardi took all of my potential, my natural abilities, technique, training, and experience, and he added more motivation than I thought possible. He pushed me to rise above what I thought I could be to what he knew I could be. He yelled, he rallied, he charmed, he yelled some more. He did whatever he had to do to push each and every one of us to reach for something more, something we never thought possible, and that's why we were so dominant. We weren't suppressed by our own limitations. We were heightened by his expectations.

"You work hard, you stay disciplined, and you deserve this win," he'd say before a game. "Now go out there, put it together, and do it!"

He was a man who always thought he could make a difference, and he was right.

And if there is one thing he taught the NFL, it's how to win a championship—and keep winning.

There is often a simple formula to building a winning team.

You start with a group of players with immense talent and even greater potential. You teach them how to work together, how to believe in a single philosophy, a single purpose. You guide them along their way, pushing them to achieve greatness, celebrating the goal when it's accomplished and getting them hungry to do it again.

That formula starts with the players themselves, and it might be one area where Coach Lombardi was underappreciated. He was an amazing coach with the Packers, but he was an equally impressive general manager. The moves he made when he took over the team laid the groundwork for our success, giving him the foundation he needed to shape a winning team. He found veterans eager to earn a shot at glory as the twilight of their careers rapidly approached. He found established players who just needed a bit more extra guidance and attention to reach their potential. He found rookies who would be eager to impress. He found utility players who would fill in the gaps. In each and every one of his players, he found people who would be open to his coaching philosophy and his alone.

As a former offensive coordinator, that started with the offense—more specifically, the big three of Bart Starr, Paul Hornung, and Jim Taylor.

Bart Starr is one of the most special guys I have ever met, both in football and beyond. On the Packers, he was a competitor, a leader, and a true teammate who looked at everyone equally, regardless of playing time, position, financial status, or even race. Like Coach Lombardi, he was someone you didn't want to let down because he was simply too nice of a guy and he believed in everyone so much. He was and still is a true gentleman, a model of a man, and a leader.

Bart spent his first few years in the league working as a backup on a terrible Packers team. Even when Coach Lombardi came in and saw Starr's potential, Bart still had to fight for the job that led him to four Pro Bowl selections, the first two Super Bowl MVPs, five championships, and entry into the Hall of Fame. When Coach Lombardi came in, he liked Bart's eagerness to buy into his system. Bart loved Coach Lombardi and thrived on what Coach taught him, which in turn built a unique trust that Coach placed in his quarterback.

Starr was a quick learner, a disciplined player who loved practices, meetings, study sessions, etc. The son of a military father, Bart always believed he had something to prove, and those were the kind of players Coach Lombardi liked the most. Still, Coach had his doubts about Starr, mainly because of his politeness of all things. Coach Lombardi wondered if he was too nice to be the tough, vocal quarterback needed to lead the team. So in his first year in Green Bay, Coach Lombardi brought in seasoned quarterback Lamar McHan to play the position.

Never one to complain, Bart continued working at becoming the starter and got his chance when McHan went down with a knee injury in 1959. Everybody on the team loved Bart as a person. Coach Lombardi had affection for him, as well, but Coach continued to wonder if the well-mannered Bart would ever grow into the fiery leader he wanted. He often called Bart out in front of the other players, something that would bother those of us Bart had reached out to, but Bart just hung his head and kept silent—at first.

After one particular loss, Coach Lombardi got into what I call "chew-ass" mode, where he pointed us out for sloppy, unfocused, and undisciplined play. He scanned the room, making sure to comment on each player he thought didn't perform to his standards, to Green Bay Packers standards. When Coach got into chew-ass mode, we all spent a lot of time with our heads down, studying our shoe shine not wanting to make eye contact and incur his wrath even more. He saved Bart for last.

It was one of the few times in my career I actually felt my blood boil in regards to Coach Lombardi. He laid into Bart, who looked beaten and depressed that he had let down Coach and the team. When Coach asked him a question, he would reply in a soft-spoken voice that was overmatched by Lombardi's yelling. In that moment, I felt something ball up inside of me, wanting to get out. I looked around and could see it on the faces of a few other players, as well. I wanted to yell out, "God damn, Bart, don't take that shit!"

He was our leader on the field, and during my time at Green Bay, as he and the team achieved success, Starr became more vocal off the field, as well, even eventually standing up to Coach Lombardi. In rare moments, he even admonished Coach for criticizing players in front of each other, saying it did little for morale. Coach, in turn, learned to trust Bart more and more with each and every game and respected Bart as the leader he had the potential to be.

Paul Hornung was the team's Golden Boy and was almost a second son to Coach Lombardi. Coach treated everyone on the team equally, but it was obvious that he always had a special affection for Hornung, mainly because Paul was a true worker who gave it his all and continually produced.

The No. 1 pick overall out of Notre Dame, the "Horn" could play almost every position but found his niche as a one-man offensive arsenal, playing quarterback, halfback, and place kicker, continually leading the league in overall scoring year after year.

It didn't take long for the Horn, with his All-American Boy image and charismatic charm, to become a national star. As our team grew more and more successful, and Paul put up larger numbers each and every year, he cemented not just his place as one of the league's leading players but also as one of the faces of the league. He was someone who loved the spotlight, loved the attention. He was our generation's Peyton Manning in that regard, doing a number of commercial endorsements and making himself visible and accessible to the public. He was one of those rare athletes who comes into a sport with a lot of hype and not only lives up to it but relishes everything that comes with it.

He was also a notorious party boy. Along with a few other Packers players, Paul was always breaking curfew and any other rules Coach Lombardi decided to hand out, especially when we were on the road. He was a young, good-looking, famous football player who women loved and men adored, and he wanted to soak it all in. He would often be seen sneaking out late at night and coming back to the hotel early in the morning. He never paid attention to Coach's drinking restrictions, and he was often seen with a variety of women. He was one of the few players on the team who didn't really fear Coach Lombardi because he knew how much Coach loved him for what he brought to the team. It didn't excuse his breaking the rules in Coach's eyes, but Paul Hornung knew he wasn't going anywhere. Other players on the team might have had a problem with that if Paul hadn't been such a hard worker. He became my biggest influence in how to conduct myself in practice and at the game.

He was one of the most impressive workers I have ever seen. It didn't matter if it was practice, drills, a scrimmage, or the game itself—Paul always gave 110 percent regardless of how he had spent the evening before. He was always on time, always prepared, and always willing to work on the field, even during Coach's grueling practices. While we all suffered through some of those practices, Paul seemed to relish in them, working more vigorously than anyone else on the field.

A perfect example is when we practiced some of our running plays, working just on the execution without full contact. Coach would have the offense run certain plays just to show us all how they worked and where the running back would go on each specific play. Although it was purely meant as an instructional tool, every time Paul was given the ball, he'd run full speed, sprinting about 40 to 50 extra yards downfield before coming back to run it again.

He was someone we all respected because of his work ethic. Plus, he was someone we could look to in terms of how to handle ourselves with Coach Lombardi's tirades. Contradictory to the attitude and personalities of many star athletes today who think they're more important than the goals of the team, Paul was actually very humble. He thought of himself as just one of the boys. That meant he never once (vocally anyway) sought special treatment. In fact, just the opposite, Paul was more of a target for Coach Lombardi because of how important he was to the team and how much Coach loved him. Paul could take it. He could take the yelling by simply working that much harder every time he was singled out. That made us all a bit more comfortable, helping us realize that even the superstars weren't immune to Coach's wrath.

If Paul Hornung was the team's flashy, pretty-boy runner, Jim Taylor was his rough-and-ready, hard-nosed opposite. He was a man who loved to hit and get hit. He was punishing in how he ran, typically straight forward and over his opponent. Paul was more of a finesse runner who looked for the open holes, bobbing and weaving. Jim Taylor didn't care if there was someone in his way. He knew where he was going, and he was determined to get there at all costs. Jim Taylor was the team's workhorse.

Taylor still holds a number of Packers record, including career rushing yards, touchdowns, and single-season touchdowns. He had an insatiable appetite for running the ball. Jim was also one of the more vocal players on our team, at least when he was on the field. It didn't matter if he was talking to an opponent or even one of his own teammates, he loved to boast about the long runs, the heavy hits, the scoring, the big plays. It wasn't cockiness or arrogance—it was just an excitement about the game that he had to share. It was something that often rallied the offense.

But one topic he didn't want to talk about was my former teammate, Jim Brown. Though he wouldn't admit it, Jim Taylor was obsessed with Jim Brown and compared himself to the Cleveland star. Every Monday morning, Jim would grab the sports section of the local paper and check the box scores to see what kind of numbers Brown had put up. He often asked me about playing with Brown and what I thought Brown would do on a particular play we were running. In those stretches when Jim Brown had put up some of his monster numbers, Jim Taylor was visibly frustrated. A man with a quick temper, he could switch quickly from being quiet and focused to arrogant and aggressive if he overheard people talking about Jim Brown.

Tough, aggressive, determined—with a bit of a grudge and an edge—that's what Coach Lombardi wanted in his fullback, and he got that with Jim Taylor, our team's Thunder to Hornung's Lightning.

As Coach Lombardi developed his three big offensive weapons, he surrounded them with players who were no less equal in importance to the powerful offensive attack Coach Lombardi demanded. Some of those vital pieces he actually brought in himself. For the others who were already in Green Bay, Coach helped them focus on their positions or found other areas where they could help both themselves and the team as a whole.

A perfect example is Boyd Dowler. Coach Lombardi brought in Boyd from Colorado in the third round of the 1959 draft. A multi-talented player, Boyd could have played any position on offense and probably many on defense. As No. 86 to my No. 87, I spent my entire Packers career with my locker next to Boyd's in the dressing room. There are few players on the team I knew as well as Boyd. Not only was he one of the kindest and most open-minded individuals I ever came to meet in my time in the league, he was also one of the best conversationalists. Originally from Wyoming, Boyd probably hadn't had much experience with black people, but you never would have guessed it by the way he treated me when I first arrived. In fact, I often wondered if Boyd even knew I was black!

As a player, I never met a guy who was more prepared than Boyd. He had such a knowledge of the offense that he could have been thrust into any position and done well. He was just as physically gifted as some of the other players on the team, but his mental acumen set him above and beyond. With Coach Lombardi recognizing his versatility, he knew he could utilize Boyd as a target for Bart Starr. Boyd was a strong rookie receiver to compliment the veteran Max McGee who had been with the

Packers since 1954 (minus a two-year hiatus serving as a pilot in the U.S. Air Force). Max had been one of their top players, putting up solid offensive numbers even as the team struggled.

Upon first impression, Max looked like little more than the team jokester. There was very little he seemed to take seriously, including Coach Lombardi's team rules. A notorious partier, Max *always* broke curfew. He also drank a lot, showing up to meetings, practices, and even some of our most memorable games still feeling the effects of a previous night on the town. He was one of those rare players who could handle it. I never knew how somebody could survive one of Coach Lombardi's practices with a hangover, but he managed, even when Coach had a feeling Max was dragging a bit and pushed him harder.

Max was a bit of a mystery to some of us. He seemed like the kind of player Coach Lombardi wouldn't want on his team, somebody who had been there a while, was used to his own way of doing things, and Max didn't seem to have much respect for this new coach's controlling authority. It wasn't that Max was defiant. He was just more aloof than Coach Lombardi would have liked. But it did help at times with team morale. Max was truly one of the funniest people I've ever met in my life, and he was always ready with a joke.

"A martini is like a woman's breast—one's not enough, but three's too many."

"Hummingbirds hum because they don't know the words."

"The difference between a wife and a mistress is 30 pounds."

"Asphalt is actually a rectal problem."

"Did you know that Captain Hook actually died of jock itch?"

I think there might even have been a time or two when I saw Coach crack a smile at Max. He knew players like Max, despite their defiance of certain rules, were good for the team's overall attitude and makeup, especially if they could produce. And Max could produce. When I came into the league, Max was notorious for making the big catch. Every team needs a clutch receiver, and Max was ours.

While Starr had his two weapons to throw to, the real key to our success was that Thunder and Lightning running game that Coach put together with the help of a new system of blocking, what's now called *zone blocking.* Coach Lombardi often doesn't receive enough credit for his contributions to a style that changed up running attacks and in effect, defensive schemes. Previously, most running attacks featured linemen blocking other linemen one on one. However, Coach Lombardi introduced a system to us where the linemen blocked as a unit, each with designated assignments of where they were supposed to go, opening up holes and gaps in the defense for the running backs to break through. It was his "running to daylight" offense, a scheme that relied on key players working together unselfishly and methodically to give us the best chance to move the football.

This line led us with the now infamous Packer Sweep, Coach Lombardi's signature design that would be copied throughout the years, even today, but never run as effectively as our offense did it. Put simply, the Sweep relied on the linemen pulling themselves out of their positions and shifting quickly to one side to block downfield for a running back trailing behind them, coming around the end. When we debuted it, the Sweep was something that nobody in the league had ever seen, and we were able to catch defenses off guard because of both its trickery and because of the discipline and strength of the men who led the way.

It started with our center Jim Ringo, truly one of the toughest guys I've met in my life. Jim had been with the organization since 1953 when he was drafted out of Syracuse, suffering through some of the lowest points in Packers history, playing for three different coaches before Coach Lombardi. It made him bitter and angry, and Jim Ringo was a mean mother. A loyal and devoted player, he had a short temper, even with his teammates. It was not unusual to see Jim in a tussle with someone in practice. We all knew not to turn our back on Jim. He was a small lineman, just more than 210 pounds, but what he lacked in size he made up in grit and competitiveness, developing into one of the game's best centers.

Jim's toughness set the tone for our offensive line. Our two guards were newer additions to the team when I joined. Fuzzy Thurston was a star who was drafted out of Valparaiso and played the 1958 season with the Baltimore Colts before coming to Green Bay in a trade. Coach Lombardi brought in Fuzz for a few reasons. First of all, he had experienced winning a championship with the Colts the previous year and Coach thought inserting a player who had achieved that kind of success would help boost the team. Plus, Fuzz was a vocal, rah-rah kind of guy, one who believed in trying to pump up the team and get them ready. Every team needs at least a couple players willing to take on that role.

Many football experts, historians, analysts, former players, and coaches consider Jerry Kramer to be the single greatest player in NFL history not to be inducted into the Hall of Fame. A five-time NFL champion, two-time Super Bowl champion with three Pro Bowl selections, five First Team All-Pro selections, and a member of the NFL's 1960s All-Decade team and 50th Anniversary Team, Jerry Kramer is one of the best guards the game has ever seen.

A big lineman (for the time), Jerry was drafted by the Packers out of Idaho and became a starter in his rookie season in 1958. When Coach Lombardi came in the next year and introduced his blocking schemes, Jerry flourished, especially with the Packer Sweep. Jerry was a man who liked the more focused offense, eager to match up not just with a single man but an entire line. He was edgy, hard-nosed, fiery, and just as competitive as Fuzzy. The two of them were very close as teammates, but there was also that competitiveness boiling under the surface between the two of them. Coach Lombardi helped them hone that feeling and unleash it on their competitors.

Off the field, Jerry was one of the nicest and most accepting individuals I ever met. Over the course of my time there, he and I formed a tight bond. When I first arrived, all I knew of him was that he was not someone who would let a defender through. He was someone who would open up holes—and if you weren't careful, he would knock you on your ass.

So, too, would our tackles, starting with Bob Skoronski. Bob was a very caring individual and still is, even today. As the Packers hold team functions for their former players over the years, if by some chance I miss one, I'll still get a call from Bob making sure I'm okay. He's a dear friend who cared for each and every one of his teammates, showing an unmatched loyalty.

He was also someone who believed in boosting morale. He was always quick to congratulate teammates on a good play, offer encouragement, and even bring us some gifts. At least a couple of times a season, Bob shipped in Polish sausage, bratwurst, kielbasa, or some other kind of meat from his hometown of Ansonia, Connecticut, and passed it out to the players. Bob was an extremely dedicated lineman who took every assignment seriously. He was also an emotional player who felt the peaks and valleys of the game. Bob gave his all in every game, leaving nothing on the field. His looked at his role as a team leader to make sure the other players were doing the same. He was a player we could rally around.

Our other tackle was my good friend Forrest Gregg, a friendly face from my military days that I was happy to see when I joined the team. Forrest had been drafted by the Packers the same year as me and was establishing himself as one of the offensive leaders, as well. He completely bought into Coach Lombardi's system, and in turn, it brought him (and us) unparalleled success. A true warrior, Forrest played in 188 consecutive games from 1956–71, earning nine trips to the Pro Bowl and something even more valuable, a declaration from Coach Lombardi that Forrest was "the finest player I ever coached" in Lombardi's book *Run to Daylight*.

If I was going to be in a foxhole, I would want to be there with Forrest. He was trustworthy, someone you could lean on and someone who jumped up eagerly to fight alongside you. On the field, he was fierce, unforgiving, and someone just tough and mean enough to have a win-at-all-costs attitude. He wasn't a dirty player, but Forrest would take advantage of certain opportunities that presented themselves. We could have just come out of the locker room, having a pleasant chat about world affairs, laughing, smiling, joking. But once that helmet went on, if I beat him in a drill, I knew I would have to watch next time for a potential hold, chop block, pull, or whatever he could do to make sure I didn't beat him again. If I was winning, I knew I had to be careful with Forrest.

There is no other player who helped me become a Hall of Famer more than Forrest. We lined up in front of each other, squaring off in one-on-one battles against each other for 10 years, and we pushed each other to new limits. We respected each other so much that we never went easy on each other, even if we noticed the other was tired. We battled and battled each and every day and it got us ready to excel come game time.

Even during the games, we continued to help each other, studying our opponents and offering tips to each other on how to play them.

Find someone to help you where you're weakest.

Coach Lombardi was an offensive-minded guy. For as much as he liked to control every aspect of the game and his team, however, he was as aware as anybody that in order to accomplish what he thought this team could accomplish, he needed the right man at the helm of his defense.

He needed somebody who first and foremost bought into his system. He needed somebody who could lead the team but remain loyal to him and his plan, never once questioning the overall leader, the man in charge. He needed a brilliant coordinator who was just as crafty and progressive as he was when it came to scheming his defenses. He also needed someone who could give the team some balance in terms of style of coaching; he needed someone cool, calm, and collected to even out his fired-up temper and passion.

That man was Phil Bengtson.

Coach Lombardi brought over Phil from San Francisco. Phil became yet another example of Coach Lombardi's insight and brilliance when it came to choosing personnel. It wouldn't take long for Phil to prove himself as one of the best defensive coordinators in the league, especially when it came to figuring out multiple offensive schemes and preparing his players for whatever any team threw at us.

It was almost as if he had a sixth sense about how other teams were strategizing against us, like he was one step ahead of everyone else. He was one of the most methodical and analytical coaches I had ever seen. Phil was able to break down every aspect of an opponent's offense to the point where things became predictable, and then he took the time to explain not just the plays to watch for but the theories behind them. He was able to prepare us in many instances to the point that we saw few surprises on the field. He often sniffed out any kind of trick play from the opponent, giving us a head's up in case an opposing coach wanted to try to catch us off guard. It was his job to prepare us for both the expected and the unexpected, and he developed defensive schemes to do just that.

In the early 1960s, more and more offenses were toying with the concept of putting their players in motion to confuse opposing defenses. There was no team better at this than the Dallas Cowboys. They built a reputation for opening up their offense by running their players all over the field behind the line of scrimmage and crossing up defensive ends and linebackers who were trying to stay with them without running into their own teammates. It was a system built on confusion, and it worked.

In one of my first games against the Cowboys, we played them differently. Phil boldly decided we wouldn't play into their style, deciding instead to simplify the situation to keep us from scrambling to catch up. A mindset borrowed directly from Coach Lombardi, we were going to make them play our game, not the other way around.

Phil developed a simple three-color defensive system that we could switch and convert to based on whatever offense they showed. We were each assigned lanes on the field as opposed to following a particular player. When we saw the offense line up with the running back off to the strong side, where the tight end was lined up, we called that Blue. If the running back lined up on the weak side, that was Brown. If they had both the running back and fullback on each side, that was Red. We'd start our defense based on whatever they showed us when they got to the line. Then if they shifted from a Red to a Blue, we simply called out the formation and switched responsibilities. We didn't move from our base defense other than to shift forward or drop back, trusting that no matter where the ball went, somebody would get him. If we stayed in our lanes, committed to our responsibilities, and trusted in each other, we'd be able to stop anyone.

It was a defense built around the idea that everybody on the team would be equally strong. We would have no holes, no weak points for an offense to exploit. Every player didn't necessarily have to play every position, but they had to be prepared to cover all portions of the field. Three of the stronger pieces of our defense that the coaches brought in were Dan Currie, Bill Quinlan, and Henry Jordan.

Dan was actually more or less inherited, having been the Packers' first-round draft pick out of Michigan State in 1958, but he was molded into a key cog in the Packers' defensive machine by Coach Bengtson. Dan was one of the smartest players I ever lined up alongside. He was meticulous in his preparation, studying his opposition to the point that he felt he could be prepared for every play. In fact, he was so prepared, that he often predicted what the other team was running. Right before they snapped the ball, he'd start yelling out their play based on something he saw in their formation. He'd tell you exactly what they were going to run and where, and he was right many times. He was also very frustrated when he was wrong.

Bill Quinlan was our run stopper, and he reveled in it. I played with Bill at Cleveland for a season before he left for Green Bay in Coach Lombardi's first year, along with Henry Jordan and our utility player Lew Carpenter. Yet another stand-out defensive player from Michigan State, Bill was a tough-as-nails athlete who liked to hit and hit hard.

Coach Lombardi and Coach Bengtson made it very clear that hitting the running back was Bill's main responsibility. Bill was inserted into spots on the defense where he could quickly plug any kind of holes their line created. He was a big, speedy guy who was crafty at finding those holes and not letting anything slip through. While any great defensive player, he had a sense of where the play was going and where he needed to be to make the stop. Combined with Phil's defensive formations, Bill became the team's heavy hitter against the run, allowing other defenders such as Henry Jordan to focus on rushing the passer.

Henry was a fifth-round 1957 draft pick out of Virginia who showed potential at Cleveland. Coach Lombardi also brought over Henry in his first year, seeing something in the undersized defensive tackle that he knew hadn't been unleashed yet. With Phil's help, they turned Henry into a four-time Pro Bowler with a reputation for being lightning quick. Going up against bigger players, Henry relied on his speed to put him in the right position to make the plays, often eluding blockers and finding ways to get around them to the quarterback. Once he got there, he was able to hit just as hard as men twice his size. Henry was also an intelligent player, which became a staple of Phil's defenses. He was a player who could quickly find a weakness in an opponent and exploit it over the course of a game.

Henry was also one of the team jokesters and one of my favorite players. He still to this day has perhaps the greatest quote about Coach Lombardi. When somebody from the press interviewed Henry about how tough Coach Lombardi was and how fair he was as a coach, Henry had a great response.

"Coach Lombardi's very fair," he said. "He treats us *all* like dogs!"

With Coach Lombardi more offense-oriented, he pretty much left most of the defensive responsibilities to Coach Bengtson. The only time Coach Lombardi would really get involved is when we weren't playing well and he thought we needed a kick in the ass. During a game or even a practice, we would go a while without hearing from Coach Lombardi and then suddenly he was in our face.

"What the hell are you guys doing out there?! You're not playing with passion. You're not playing with aggression. Get in there and stop somebody!"

Phil was much more even-keeled. He looked at us as paid professionals who had a job to do, and he expected us to do it. He provided us with the necessary tools, and the rest was up to us. He was not one to yell, to get angry, or to even really get frustrated. He spoke in a quiet, monotone voice, encouraging us to forget about the mistake we made or the good play they made and focus on what was coming next.

We all loved and respected both coaches. We wanted to play our best for both of them. One we worked hard for out of fear and devotion. The other we worked for out of love and respect. Both types of motivation worked. They complimented each other—and as such, the defense excelled.

Be careful in making assumptions.

When I came to the Packers in 1960, they already had some of their pieces in place. Coach Lombardi and Coach Bengtson made it clear I was going to be yet another piece of the puzzle. Between the offensive weapons I saw that the Packers had assembled, the solid young defense that would only get better, the methodical defensive coach, and the brilliant, motivating head coach, I quickly began to see potential in the Siberia of the North. I was suddenly excited to be part of it, even if it was going to be a major cultural change for me.

When I joined the Green Bay Packers for training camp in 1960, I was one of just three black players on the team.

There was Paul Winslow, a little-used back-up running back who was a quiet but nice guy, a good teammate who did his job and worked hard in practice. Paul, unfortunately, joined the team when we had both Taylor and Hornung, so his chances to acquire any kind of playing time were slim to none.

There was also Emlen Tunnell, the veteran defensive back out of the University of Iowa. He had been in the league since 1948, joining as the first black to play for the New York Giants where he got to know Coach Lombardi when Lombardi was an assistant there. Coach brought Emlen over to the Packers in 1959 to bring some veteran leadership to the team. Although he was entering the final stages of his career, Emlen was still one of the most effective backs in the league, having racked up more than 75 interceptions in his decade-plus and showing no signs of slowing down. He knew Lombardi's coaching methods, and he used his experience to help make the transition a little smoother for some of the other Packers players.

"Boy am I glad to see you!" he said to me the first day I met him.

For the first part of training camp, it was just us three, but we were soon joined by a fourth black player—Willie Wood out of USC. Willie's journey to the Packers was an interesting story, especially for a player who would soon become one of the greatest defensive players in Packers history.

After standing out as a quarterback with USC, Willie essentially had to beg for an opportunity to try out for a team. He was overlooked in the 1960 draft even as a half-dozen other USC players went ahead of him. Despite Willie's success at the quarterback position, NFL teams were worried about his lack of size. He was about 5'10" and no more than 175 pounds, small for any position in the league, even back then. He was a guy general managers wouldn't necessarily have picked to compete in the league just based on his appearance. Critics also had issues with his arm strength as quarterback. Knowing he wasn't going to have a chance to play at that position, Willie decided to switch his position to defense.

After the draft came and went, he sent out letters to each team, describing how he felt he could contribute. Coach Lombardi noticed and decided to give him a shot to join his rebuilding effort in Green Bay. As the last player to join the team in 1960, Willie excelled.

He showed right away that despite his small stature, he was fearless. On his first play from scrimmage, he showed speed running down a pass like I had never seen—and then he hit the intended receiver with all the force of a lineman. Willie was one of our team's best tacklers and a determined athlete who felt like he always had to prove himself, even years later as he racked up eight consecutive Pro Bowl appearances and five first team All-Pro selections. He was also a hard worker who became extremely nervous before games, even to the point of making himself sick. It actually helped him stay calm and focused on the field. He was also a bit of a character, a man who was comfortable in his own skin despite playing in a league with such a small percentage of black players. He was always quick to tease someone on the team, white or black, and he also wasn't afraid to do his own bit of trash talking. Willie could back it up.

♦　♦　♦

There were four of us black players, which was more than several other teams in the league had in their organizations.

I would say that nobody had more impact in creating diversity in the NFL than Coach Lombardi. It was partly because he took a new approach, almost playing ignorant to any kind of racial tension in the league. He didn't buy into debates or arguments about his drafting, trading (or in the case of Willie Wood) letting black players walk on. Right from the start, he treated us as equals, just players competing for a spot on the team. He chose not to see color in an era where most coaches chose to look the other way in terms of blacks. It was as if he felt the best way to fix the problem of segregation and racism in the league was to actually pretend it didn't exist—at least to us.

The other impact he had on the issue stemmed from his success. Coach Lombardi stayed true to his belief that the best players would earn the starting positions on his Green Bay Packers team and that was final.

It didn't matter what school you came from, how successful you were in college or the pros in previous years, your time and experience in the league, or your race. If you were the best man and gave Coach the best chance to succeed, you would earn the starting spot. With the field wide open like that, those blacks who were on the team were truly given an opportunity to let it all out and work hard. As such, many of us became contributing players during the next few years.

And we won.

It would be interesting to have seen how the issue of blacks in the league would have faired if we didn't have as much success as we did. Our success probably helped diversity in the league more than anything. Coach Lombardi and the Green Bay Packers had so much success during the next eight years—adding more and more black players each season—that the rest of the league knew they had to keep up. It was as if the owners took a look at Coach Lombardi's formula and said, "Hey, I gotta get some of those!" Pretty soon, all the teams opened up shop, allowing all positions on their teams to be earned by the best competitors.

Coach Lombardi never really talked to any of us about his true feelings on the issue of black players, but he gave us enough to know how he felt about it. We never really understood why he was so open while other coaches and managers weren't, but we thought part of it might have to do with him being a tremendously dark-skinned Italian. He had experienced his own forms of prejudice, or so we heard, especially when arriving in Green Bay, a town that wasn't used to blacks, Italians, or really anyone other than Polish, German, and some Scandinavian. It wasn't aggressive prejudice by any means, but when he first arrived, Coach Lombardi was not a popular choice to take over the franchise and he received some backlash. Sometimes in the world of sports that backlash can get ugly. At first, the fans were more inclined to run him out of town, and sometimes there are fans who get a little too involved and their actions and words go too far.

I knew that I was going to have a fair shot in Green Bay, which eased a fear I had in coming over from Cleveland. In Cleveland, diversity wasn't much of a problem. It was a city that was fairly integrated with a professional football team that was also fairly integrated for its time. Plus, our best player, and arguably the best player in the league, was Jim Brown. Race wasn't an issue.

I was worried that wouldn't be the case with the Packers. That being said, I can say with all honesty that I was never insulted or called any kind of name by anyone in the Packers organization—relating to my race at least! There were some players that I could tell were a little more uncomfortable at first than others, players who worked with you in practice and then went their separate ways once the pads came off, but they kept quiet. Then there were players like Bart Starr who went above and beyond to make the black players feel comfortable, to feel like we were part of the team. During the next couple of years, that approach became the norm in Green Bay.

That was partially because of Coach Lombardi's philosophy of fairness. It was partially because nothing brings a team together more than winning. It was also partially because of our environment—the city of Green Bay and its people, the greatest fans on the planet.

I feel awful saying it now, but I expected my experience to be bad. There wasn't a booming black population in the Siberia of the North. I heard that there were literally a small handful of black residents in the city of Green Bay, probably numbering less than 100. That constituted less that 1 percent of the city's entire population. Its reputation was that of a small town with a redneck population that was just fine staying behind in the times. One of the jokes floating around the league at the time said it all.

"Green Bay? Well, you know you can put shit on your shoes and still go to the formal."

That's what people thought of a town they knew nothing about. And for us black players, we assumed the reason there was such a small black population was because they simply didn't want us there. That's the only reason, I thought, that African Americans wouldn't settle there. Other Midwestern cities, including Cleveland, were experiencing significant growth in pockets of blacks. There was still a great deal of segregation in these cities, like Chicago, Minneapolis, and even Milwaukee, but there were at least communities where local black residents could feel comfortable. I assumed, as did the other three black players, that if the black population hadn't made it in Green Bay, there must be a significant reason. I feared that we four black players, who somebody joked made up 4/5 of the black population in the city, would not be welcomed.

I was dead wrong.

With the exception of a couple of incidents of guys being guys at the bar, there was no other trouble. To say I was surprised is an understatement. At a glance, Green Bay was very similar to many of the cities I had seen in the South where not just segregation, but blatant racism, still ran rampant. It was the state of the small town back in the early 1960s. There were indications that times were changing, but not rapidly, and not in small towns. As I said, I expected the worst, and instead what I experienced most was curiosity.

There was some hesitation among the residents to approach me or any of the other black players. We were always met with stares and whispering. But there was something unusual about it. It didn't feel cold or malicious. It felt more like trepidation. I began to realize that a lot of these folks *did* want to talk to us, but they were uncomfortable. They didn't know how to approach us.

I was told by many residents, usually after having to gently nudge them into a conversation, that I was not only the first black person they had ever talked to, but I was also the first they had ever *seen* in real life. As we talked, they would stare at me from head to toe, fascinated by how different I looked compared to the pale white population of the North. I could tell they didn't want to be too obvious about their curiosity, but they often failed miserably. I swear there were times I almost expected them to ask if they could touch me!

They had no idea about black people except for what they saw on TV, which at that time was typically even more negative in its representation of the black community. They had no real life experience with black people out here, and they were perplexed and fascinated by us. They were also innocently naïve.

"Maybe all those things I heard about you people aren't true," was a rather common phrase I heard in the beginning.

It wasn't something I was upset about or even took the wrong way because as I soon found out, beyond their shyness and inexperience, the residents of Green Bay were some of the nicest people in the country.

The longer I stayed there and got out in the community, the more comfortable the residents got in talking with me. Not only were they fascinated by me and the other black players, they all wanted to be our best friends. I can't tell you how many times I had a beer bought for me or how many times bar or restaurant patrons argued to see who could sit next to me. I also had dinner invites to their homes on almost a daily basis. Many times, I accepted.

The race issue actually led to more humorous moments than anything. In a long-standing tradition, as Green Bay East prepares to face off against Green Bay West in one of the oldest high school football rivalries in the country, they will invite the captains of the Packers team to give a speech. They call it their "color day" because all the players wore their uniforms and all the students wore the team colors. It was yet another example of a community that valued its traditions, and I was glad to take part along with Bob Skoronski, the offensive captain.

As we were introduced, I was met with extra long stares and even some whispering mixed in with the applause. When I told the crowd, "It's a real pleasure for me to be here for your color day," the whispering turned to polite laughter and the cheering got louder. In fact, the crowd went nuts. It didn't hit me why right away, and then Bob told me what I said and how this innocent crowd probably took it. All I could do was smile and laugh along with them, another chapter in what would be (and still is) a long-standing love affair with Green Bay fans of all ages.

Be proactive, especially when it comes to relationships.

As I fell in love with the city and its people, I decided I was going to be an ambassador for the black community as a whole. I looked at my time there as a possibility for some two-way learning. I saw how much I could learn to love about the city and its residents. At the same time, I knew they all had questions about us that they wanted to ask. They wanted to get to know us and our community. They just didn't know how to approach us. I would feel it every time I left practice, went out to run errands, walked down the street, hung out at a bar, went to dinner, etc. I could feel them staring at me, wanting to approach, wanting to connect. I decided that I was going to make it easy for them.

I took it as my own personal obligation to make the residents feel as comfortable as possible. I was going to be friendly, patient, and most of all approachable, and in turn I knew that they would give me more than respect and acceptance. They would give me friendship. I found myself taking the lead. If people were looking like they wanted to approach, I'd go talk to them or I'd invite them to come join me.

"Hey there, how you doin'?" was all I would have to say, and that opened the door.

"I know you're a Packer, but which one are you again?" which I thought was funny since there were only four of us who were black.

"My name's Willie Davis," I'd say with a smile. "Nice to meet you."

And we'd go from there. We'd talk football, life in the small town, what it was like living and playing in Cleveland, the best bars and restaurants in town, and inevitably the topic of how I was the first black person they had ever talked to would come up. More than anything, what I found these people wanted to talk about was their love for the Green Bay Packers. They have always been and always will be the most loyal and wonderful fans in the world.

When I was traded to Green Bay, I dreaded the move. It was the last place I would have chosen to play. A decade later, there was no other place I would have wanted to be.

Chapter 8 | Luck Is When Preparation Meets Opportunity

A leader must have a clear mission, inspiration, and rules.

Coach Lombardi gave the same speech at the beginning of every season he was involved with the Green Bay Packers, and it never once lost its power or impact.

It always took place at 6:00 PM on a Sunday night in that first week of training camp in a meeting room at St. Norbert's campus, where we trained. The room was full of all the players—the players who would eventually lead the team on the field, those that would unfortunately get cut, and everyone in between.

He would stroll in right on time, Lombardi Time, and stand tall and proud in front of all his men. He was instantly so authoritative, demanding, and commanding, grabbing our attention and not letting it go until we were ready to follow him into battle. He was like this each and every time he spoke. He would lead. You would follow. It would start right here.

After the obligatory welcomes and introductions, he got right down to business.

"Gentlemen, some of you have heard this before, and some of you are hearing it for the first time. Regardless, I want you to hear me unmistakably loud and clear. If you are going to be a member of the Green Bay Packers organization, you are going to adhere to the following things."

No matter what year it was, the room would go quiet—not just out of respect for Coach but out of awe in watching him speak. This first night is when he began the work of building within us the belief we could succeed, that we would succeed, no matter what. He told us about how we were going to continue to build a winning tradition in the city of Green Bay, and we believed him. We would do it for him.

He told us about how practices would run, about his style of coaching. He went over other teams in the league and our pending season and how we were poised for success. He went over his rules of conduct and what would happen if those rules were broken. He told us that we needed to commit 100 percent, and there was no room for anybody giving any less.

"Let me tell you up front that the individuals who make up this team will be the best football players we can find among you, regardless of experience. You will all compete for your positions, and you will work hard to earn that position. Then you will succeed at that position. These are the things you need to do to be a Green Bay Packer. So gentlemen, you need to each make up your minds right now on whether or not you can live with these things. If not, well, then I'm not sure we can get along."

With that, he flashed that charming smile of his and relieved some of the tension in the room for just a second, just enough time for him to drive home his main point. The wording would change from year to year, but the point was always the same and it was always just as powerful.

"You need to know that over the next six months, you need to be prepared to dedicate yourself to this organization. You will work hard, stay disciplined, and do what must be done to succeed. You will be dedicated to each other, to the team. You need to know that for the next six months, there are three things that should be most important to your life: your family, your religion, and the Green Bay Packers."

What wasn't said but rather implied was, "And not necessarily in that order."

Coach Lombardi never would have put a football team, even his beloved Packers, in front of God and family—at least not out loud. But if you asked anyone there, they would have said they got the message loud and clear. In order for us to not only make the team but also succeed, we had to make the Packers organization our top priority. We had to literally bleed Green and Gold, and Coach was letting us know that was going to happen.

I heard that speech eight times, and it never once lost its impact. In fact, it meant more and more each year, especially after we experienced success. Each and every year, that speech marked the beginning of our pursuit of excellence and the path to glory.

The success of the Green Bay Packers started with Coach Lombardi's inspiring words and came to life with rules and regulations and his grueling practices.

Rules included an 11:00 PM curfew, all players riding the bus together to and from practice, eating meals at the regulated times, and making sure we were all watching our weight. Breaking any rules would result in not just a scolding by Coach but also in heavy financial fines. It started each year in training camp and carried through all the way to the end of the season, including championship games. There were rules for a reason, he told us, and they were non-negotiable.

Then there was practice. In my entire tenure with Coach Lombardi, he ran each practice essentially the same way, changing only the plays we ran based on what we needed to prepare for next week's opponent. Game-planning was always the focal point of each practice, preparing for our approach and our opponent. But all these years later, what I remember most about practice isn't the plays, the scrimmaging, or the preparation. What I remember is the discipline, the drills, the exercising, the sheer exhaustion, and the push to make us more than men, to make us invincible machines.

He told us time and time again how we would stand taller at the end of every game. We would walk off that football field spent but ready to fight again. We would terrify the other teams in the league with how mighty we were, how determined. Nothing would stop us.

"That starts right here in this practice," he said.

Coach Lombardi, like Coach Brown, believed in precisely timed practices. He ran them to the minute, shifting from one station to the next with few breaks. We'd often start by running around the field a few times as a warm-up. Stretching was something we were expected to do on our own, once again making sure to follow Lombardi Time and get there early enough to get it in. If you didn't have time, Coach wasn't going to wait for you, and you would pay for it. From there, we'd shift to a heavy calisthenics regimen before taking on a series of intense drills. After drills, we tackled the plays, both offensive and defensive, and scrimmaged before ending the day with more running.

All in all, each practice took only about an hour and a half, but it was the longest hour and a half of your life. He was strict about making the most effective use of our time, running practice at such a tempo that there was no way a player could do it without being in shape. As it was with most things under Coach Lombardi, there was work we each had to do on our own, a trust he put in his players that they would make the right decisions, the adult decisions to meet his expectations. In this case, it was up to us to make sure we worked to keep ourselves in shape, both during the season and in the off-season. We had to keep ourselves in shape simply to handle Lombardi's practices, and if we didn't, then we knew exactly where we would end up.

"There are plenty of planes and trains leaving Green Bay every day."

The drills were the toughest, especially in preseason. They were what Coach used to determine who wanted it most. The more you pushed yourself in those drills, the more you impressed him. The most punishing was his Grass Drill.

The Grass Drill went a long way in helping to make up an individual's mind on whether or not he wanted to be there, and Coach knew it. The Grass Drill was designed to be brutal. Coach Lombardi made no attempt to hide it.

"If you want to be ready to play this game, you have to be prepared to do all the little things, gentlemen," he said. "And you will be ready to play this game."

The Grass Drill started with each of us running in place, chopping our feet with an intense fury. There would be no jogging or simply stepping. We were to pump our legs as if we were priming ourselves for takeoff. Eventually, when he felt ready, Coach yelled, "Hit it!" and we dropped to the ground—without using our hands to brace ourselves. We had to hit that ground gut first, taking the full impact with our stomach muscles, before hopping right back up and continuing to run in place. This went on for several minutes, more if Coach thought we had a bad practice or game. At the end, regardless of duration, you were wiped.

I eventually learned the key to the Grass Drill was subtle pacing. You had to work hard at the drill but pace yourself and allow yourself just the slightest of breaks in those half seconds Coach wasn't looking your way. In my first practice, my first experience with the Grass Drill, I was still young and eager to impress. When we started, I was determined to show Coach just how fit I was and how well I could handle such a drill. I pumped my legs harder and faster than anyone else on that field as those who had played under him the previous year watched with amused concern. I went through about 15–20 of the hit-its with an unmatched intensity—before throwing up all over the field.

I can't be sure, but I think Coach may have been the only one doing this drill at the time. Like most things Coach Lombardi did, it was soon adopted into other systems in some form, but at the time, that was a Green Bay Packers drill. We could tell by the looks on the faces of players we drafted or traded for from other teams as they experienced the drill for the first time. It was a man killer. We feared the Grass Drill, and knowing that we would have to push ourselves longer in the drill after a bad performance pushed us to set higher expectations for ourselves. We didn't want to face what we could call his get-even punishment. A good performance meant less of the Grass Drill, and he knew fear worked.

For as tough as the Grass Drill was, the true test of manhood came with the Nutcracker Drill. This was where a young unknown like me could make an impression.

The Nutcracker Drill took three players—a running back, an offensive lineman, and a defensive lineman or linebacker. Two tackling dummies were set up on the ground five yards apart to give us warriors a small arena. The objective was simple. The offense had to run the ball successfully past the defensive player within the confined space. The defensive player had to make sure that didn't happen.

Although he was offensive minded, Coach Lombardi loved the battles that took place in the trenches, the point of attack where everything started. He wanted his linemen on both sides of the ball to be able to impose their will. He loved watching the struggle between two men exhausting themselves to gain each and every inch. The Nutcracker Drill was, in Coach Lombardi's mind, the origin of any football play—man verses man to see who could be stronger.

Both sides had a unique advantage. The defensive player obviously knew it was a running play, but the offense knew the snap count and used that to get an early jump. For the defensive player, it was not only about forcing the blocker off his mark to open up space to get to the runner, it was also about taking up as much space as possible to limit where the runner could go.

The Nutcracker Drill is where I started to earn both my reputation as a defender and my opportunity to play with the Green Bay Packers. I loved the drill. I loved the opportunity to go toe-to-toe with anyone. I used that drill to not just showcase my strength and speed but also to observe, study, and look for tactical advantages that I could use. I watched where Jim Taylor or Paul Hornung liked to make their first move. I studied how the linemen would shift or pull once the play started. I tried different approaches to see how I could best take advantage of my personal strengths against each and every player.

My two coaches acknowledged my readiness, my intensity, my need to excel at not just that drill but every drill, every play, every moment. I discovered quickly I wasn't alone. Because of the coaching, the team in general quickly developed a mentality of discipline and a hunger I had never seen before. It would be more clearly defined later in a famous speech where we heard our coach utter the phrase, "Winning isn't everything; it's the only thing." But that need, that push, started within the first few practices of training camp. It had actually started the year before when Coach arrived, but even he was growing more intense in his philosophy of pushing us to be the men he expected us to be, the team that would settle for nothing but championships and excellence.

That expectation carried from the very start of practice to the very end when we ran sprints—at full speed after a full practice. Coach Lombardi used sprinting at the end of every practice (except maybe on Fridays) to see how intense we were, how ready. It was brutal, but there was no dogging it. The more any player dogged it, the more we ran. It was that simple. It was common to see a group of us panting and jogging, gasping for air, looking to Coach, begging him with our eyes to call a stop, but he would be focused on one or two of us he felt had yet to push themselves.

"Well, I guess some people don't want to run yet, so we'll do another one and we'll keep doing them until they do."

At that point, you were ready to have a talk with whoever was dogging it.

The tough part was that Coach Lombardi was so detail-oriented and observant that he quickly realized how each and every one of us should be performing if we were sprinting full speed. He observed how we each finished and how fast we could be, and he used that to gauge whether or not we were giving a full effort. I was by far the fastest of the interior linemen and had showed him so early on in practice. Therefore, I always had to finish ahead of the other linemen, without exception. If we didn't finish where he thought we were supposed to, it would be another lap—and so on and so on. There was no escape. He seemed to notice everything, always.

Perhaps the worst incident I can remember of the sprints might have been after one of our worst practices. We were coming off a loss, and Coach was already displeased with how the team was performing that day. During the week when we ran sprints, Coach seemed to cut it off at about five or six or so, getting us a little comfortable with that number (and mentally giving us a goal to look forward to as we pushed ourselves).

I can't remember now who said it, but I do remember that whoever it was incurred the wrath of the entire team. As we approached our fifth lap, somebody from the back yelled out, "Okay, let's make this last one a good one."

My heart sank as soon as I heard it because I knew what was coming next.

"Who the hell said that?!" yelled the voice. "I will tell you when you're finished! I will tell you when it's the last one! Now pick up the pace!"

We ran six or seven more laps after that, and nobody on the team ever made a mistake like that again.

It wasn't the last time we incurred Coach Lombardi's wrath. At this point, the rage that he could muster and express when we weren't focused has been well documented. His reputation as a fiery Italian with little to no patience for poor play or a lack of discipline is the stuff of legend, and as someone who observed it for almost a decade, I can say it's all true. He would yell; he would scream. His face would get red, his eyes would get wild, and his body would shake. He was small in stature, but he was terrifying to everyone, rookie or veteran, superstar or backup player, white or black, big or small.

For as much as he screamed and yelled and pushed and pulled, we appreciated it because he made it clear why he was doing it. We didn't necessarily like it at times, but we knew it was never out of anger or disrespect or any kind of selfish reasons. Coach yelled and pushed because he believed in us, in our abilities, our potential. He saw something in the Green Bay Packers, to a man, that made him believe that we were something greater, and he felt it was his responsibility to help us achieve that. While we often lived in fear of upsetting the old man, we also knew he was right and his tough love was used for a reason. It was going to make us better than we ever thought we could be. It was going to bring us together as a team. It was going to make us strong, focused, disciplined, and champions—and that was something we could buy into and believe in.

"Practice will make us as close to perfect as we can be."

Part of that also included running our plays over and over again. One of the more unique aspects of Coach Lombardi's method was the simplistic approach to his plays. While Coach Bengtson handled the defense for the most part, Coach Lombardi's approach was made very clear. Every man would be equally strong, and we would force the offense to adjust to us rather than us adjusting to the offense. We would hold our ground, not getting caught up in shifts and misdirection. The defensive packages would be simple and effective, utilizing our strength and discipline as a team.

The same applied to offense. Not only was it vital for Coach Lombardi to find the right players to fit into his system, he also wanted to develop the right system for the players he had, taking advantage of their individual strengths and talents. From an offensive standpoint, Coach

Lombardi's playbook was unusually simple and easy to remember. Further, Coach took the time in practice to explain the philosophy behind each play, how it would work, why it would work, and what the offense needed to do to make it work. He also explained it to the defense at times, giving us an advantage in defending against it in practice. The idea was to give us the head start to ensure that the only way the offense would run the play successfully would be if they ran it to perfection.

Practice is where our offense perfected the Packer Sweep.

When we ran that play in games, I almost felt sorry for the opposing defenses, mainly because I felt their pain. We ran that play over and over and over again in practice after practice, perfecting it beyond the point of perfection—at the expense of the defense. When we scrimmaged or ran plays, defending against the Packer Sweep was our defense's true test. The frustrating thing was knowing it was coming but still failing to prevent a gain. There were times when we did in fact do our job and break up the Sweep—and when that happened, you would never see Coach Lombardi more angry. His thought, being an offensive guy, was that he had designed the play perfectly and if it failed, it was on the offensive players not being focused, or being sloppy. Watching Coach scold the offense was a minor victory for us, especially considering how many times in practice they ran that play well.

That play led our team to victory time and time again. However, what wasn't as obvious was how our practice defending against that play made us one of the best defensive teams in the league. That was the secret to Coach Lombardi's approach to practice in general. He was always one step ahead of everyone else, thinking of advantages that most of us couldn't see until later. Everything he did, everything he made us do, was meant for one reason and one reason only—to make us the best that we could be in every aspect of the game.

A team of focused, like-minded individuals is unstoppable.

There is nothing like fighting in a war together to bring a group of men closer. And there is nothing like taking the lead and working harder than everyone else to earn individual respect. We all strove to work harder than each other and to push each other to our limits. The result was a close-knit team that had a singular mentality.

If you attack one of us, you attack us all.

We were quickly becoming, even in 1960, the kind of team you didn't want to attack. That push to make each other better was what really helped us achieve our success. Sure, the coaching was the major part of it, the thing that triggered us. Coach Lombardi was a brilliant coach who knew how to motivate, terrify, love, and push us. But no matter what, coaching will only ever go so far. The rest is up to the players. And we were all fortunate to be on a team of like-minded individuals who wanted the same thing—championships.

Unfortunately, for as close as I was getting to my teammates, especially my fellow defenders, I also knew that I had to be better than them to earn a spot. That was the irony. Coach Lombardi and some of the other coaches and veterans on the team were preaching togetherness while also encouraging fierce competition between us. What it created were strong competitors with unbreakable bonds forged out of respect and dedication.

I was determined to become a starting defensive end for the Green Bay Packers from the moment I first met Coach Lombardi. I also thought the position was mine to lose. That may have been bold of me, but Coach had made the move to trade for me and I assumed that meant he wanted me in the position of defensive end. It was up to me to show him he was right in his assessment that I wasn't being used properly in Cleveland and that I was capable of so much more. Each and every practice was a test, and I was dedicated to being better than anyone else, especially at that position.

Still, I was one of the newer members on the team and relatively young and inexperienced, which meant I had to play the dreaded special teams. If you ask any player and they're being truthful, nobody likes to play special teams. Not really. I played on kickoffs and found that special teams provided the most opportunities for big hits, potential mistakes, and reasons for the coaches to chew you out. I liked tackling and I liked hunting people with the ball, but the faster you're running on a straight line downfield, the better chance there is for some blocker to put a huge hit on you. There is also a better chance for a ball carrier to get past you for a big play. Very rarely, even today, are special teams players acknowledged for doing all the little things that come with covering that kind of territory and making a big play. However, each and every mistake leads to the chance to end up in the dog house. I tried to find the positive in playing special teams as an opportunity to earn some more respect, but truthfully, I didn't like it.

Luckily, I got my opportunity to play defensive end a lot sooner than I would have thought. I was brought in to replace Nate Borden, who had been traded to Dallas. However, the Packers also had a big guy out of the University of Wisconsin named Jim Temp who had been with the team the last three years and was expected to compete for the position. The problem with Jim (and a possible reason why Coach brought me in) was that he had suffered a shoulder injury the previous season that required an operation, and the coaching staff wasn't sure how well he would recover.

In my second practice, our first scrimmage, Jim went in for a play and after making a hit, and he came to the sideline in some pain.

"Willie, get in there," Coach Lombardi yelled.

I was nervous, feeling the pressure of the moment as I always did on big plays. It was something that I felt many times over the course of my career, but I thrived on it. I loved the big plays because the big plays were what defined big players. I wanted to be a big player, especially in those first few practices.

Ask yourself, what if this is the *only* shot I get?

On my first play, I guessed it was going to be a running play to my side; perhaps the coaches wanted to test my instincts. As soon as the ball was snapped, I jumped, swung my big frame to the right, and found a gap to the inside, getting close to our quarterback as he handed off the ball before getting a hand on the runner and helping to stop the play for no gain. It was the best result for a first play that I could have asked for, and the coaches noticed. I did it again on the next play, and suddenly people were aware of where Willie Davis was lined up.

I stayed in as defensive end for the rest of our scrimmage that day and the next. In fact, from that moment on, I started as defensive end every single practice and game until the day I retired. Unfortunately, I worked so hard at special teams that they decided I was valuable there, as well—so I played both. Thus started my career with the Green Bay Packers.

Chapter 9 | The Most Important Vow of My Life

Don't let a bumpy start throw you off course.

At the start of the 1960 season, the rest of the teams in the league still didn't know what to make of us. Green Bay, under Coach Lombardi's first year, had barely finished above .500. It was still a team with a low reputation, and a group of players that for the most part were unknowns or past their prime. Many pundits thought this would once again be a transition year for the team. In 1959, the team had earned at least a little respect, as opponents would actually game plan for us now, but we still weren't seen as much of a threat. The sense was that we were the kind of team that might cause problems for a quarter or two before fading away to more experienced and talented players toward the end of the game. That's simply what losing teams did, and for years the Packers were that losing team.

We got off to a bumpy start. We opened the season at home against the Chicago Bears. Just as I remember the first time I got on the field at home in Cleveland, I will never forget that feeling of playing in front of the crowd at what was then City Stadium, which would eventually be renamed Lambeau Field. At the time, it was a newer facility, having opened in 1957. It was (and still is) breathtakingly beautiful, a true football field meant for one thing and one thing only—Packers football. The passion of the crowd filled the stadium with a buzz and energy that grew with each big play, each win, and each championship. There has truly never been another football venue like it, and I can't imagine there ever will be.

I marveled at it and took in as much as I could in that first game against the Packers' longtime rival, but I was focused on my opponent. That's just how I played the game. I appreciated my experiences in the league, but nothing would distract me from my purpose. Focus is the key to everything. Since this was my first game, I needed to stay focused on accomplishing my mission on each and every snap.

There are a few plays I can remember from that first game all those years ago, but one in particular that stands out was one of those rare moments in a football stadium that every player experiences at least once or twice. It doesn't matter how deafening a place can be in terms of the fans cheering, there is almost always that one moment where it goes eerily quiet. City Stadium was no exception. The fans at every game I ever played, watched, or attended since were extremely loud and passionate, never letting up in their cheering on of our team or their harassment of the Bears. It was my first glance at just how heated this rivalry was and always would be. But there was one moment late in the first half as we lead by a couple of scores that the place went quiet. The Bears had the ball and were starting to drive. We had shut them out thus far in the game, and they were looking to add more of a passing attack to make up for their failures on the ground. As the crowd went quiet, which was a little unnerving to us players, I waited for the ball to be snapped. A split second before they started the play, I heard a voice booming from the sideline.

"Get in there, Willie!"

I heard him. The Bears heard him. The entire stadium heard him. That's when I knew I had only seen a fraction of Coach Lombardi's passion and power. It was like the voice of God calling from the heavens, and there was no ignoring that. Without hesitation, I went and got the quarterback, stopping the play and the Bears' momentum for at least that one drive.

In the second half, however, we struggled on defense. After leading 14–0 for the majority of the game, we gave up 17 points in the fourth quarter, losing the game in front of a disappointed crowd who went home wondering if they were in for yet another disappointing season. Maybe last year was really just the fluke that many sportswriters had called it. For as disappointed as we all were, it was nothing compared to how furious Coach Lombardi was with us. I had seen him angry, disappointed, and mad. I realized after that first game that I had never experienced his true wrath.

Rivals should make you step up your game. We all need rivals.

The scolding after the Bears loss and the pressure we felt to rebound led to two wins in a row before a Week 4 bye. Both home games, we were able to win back the confidence of our fans with a 28–9 victory over the Detroit Lions and a 35–21 win over the Baltimore Colts, who proved early and often to be one of our biggest challenges year after year.

The Colts were always a tough game for us, no matter where we both were in terms of record. Whenever we played the Colts, we knew we were in for a long day. As a defensive back, I always had my hands full with their offensive weaponry, including tight end Raymond Berry, halfback Lenny Moore, and the legend himself—one of the best quarterbacks I ever saw play the game and a good friend—Johnny Unitas. Johnny had a fluidity about him and a toughness at quarterback that was unmatched by many others. He was a competitor in every regard, and through the years I looked forward to playing him because I knew I would have to bring my A game. Often standing in my way was Big Jim Parker, a burly lineman who let very little get through.

In our first meeting, the Colts were heavy favorites. After demolishing the Lions, the experts said the Colts would be our first real test as a team. Paul Hornung and Jim Taylor both had great games that day, and I was eager to take part in my first difference-making play with the Packers.

Up 21–14, we had the Colts backed up near their own goal line with Unitas dropping back to pass. I had gone to the right side of the linemen most of the day with little success, so on this play I decided to fake right, go in past the left lineman, and try to get to Johnny. It worked and I caught him with a huge hit, knocking the ball out of his hands. Ken Beck recovered, and we went up 28–14, never giving up the lead.

We finished strong in that game, pulling off the upset. That was the intention, the reason for the intensity in practice. For too long, the Packers had been known as an organization that collapsed late in the game. Not anymore. Although we opened the season with a fourth-quarter collapse, we were told it would never happen again. Coach Lombardi wouldn't let it. We needed time to adapt as a team, and the win against the Colts showed that not only would we not fade in the fourth quarter, we would dominate it.

After the bye week, we won our next two games, a 41–14 blowout against the 49ers and a close last-minute 19–13 win against the Steelers in Pittsburgh, to jump to 4–1 in the league. Suddenly, we were getting noticed. These teams that had grown accustomed to beating up on the Packers year after year were being caught off guard. That truly helped us a bit my first year, no question. We were able to surprise some teams; and often if we got a lead, we wouldn't let them catch up. We introduced them to a new Packers team.

There would be no more looking back, not for us and not for our opponents. It was about moving forward, no time for relaxation or celebration. We had goals to accomplish each week, new challenges. We were going to show them all, each team, what we were about. When we hit them, we were going to hit them as the new Packers.

Just as we built our confidence, we hit our mid-season slump. With the exception of a blowout win versus the brand new expansion team Dallas Cowboys, we lost our next three games to the Colts, Lions, and Los Angeles Rams. In all three, the defense gave up too many points. Suddenly, we had gone from a contender to 5–4 with just three games left, and we needed a miracle to reach the championship. We were frustrated, but we also weren't ready to give up. We had an opportunity to right the ship and get some revenge in early December when we traveled to Chicago to play the Bears once again.

The Bears also found themselves struggling during the season, something out of the ordinary for a team coached by George Halas. "Papa Bear" Halas was someone I always greatly admired. In fact, I can't think of anyone associated with the game, even those of us who played against him, who doesn't have a certain amount of respect for what Coach Halas did for the game of football. An owner of 63 years, a six-time champion as a coach, and the man often credited as the Father of the National

Football League, George Halas was often bigger than the game, and his presence made the Bears one of the biggest and baddest teams in the league.

During my career, I had many battles with George Halas and his team. Like Coach Lombardi, he was also of the mindset of accepting nothing short of excellence. Coach Halas looked for an edge in every way, shape, or form imaginable. Sometimes that even meant in the off-season. Many players and coaches would take part in banquets and events put on by the league or teams in the off-season. Coach Halas attended many of these, and we often ran into each other. Each and every time, especially after I started to earn accolades for my performance on the field, Coach Halas would drop jokes about my coming to join Chicago. It was always presented with a wink and smile, but I knew that below the surface was a fiery competitor who only needed me to say yes. Instead, I'd just smile, shake his hand, and tell him, "See you next season, Coach."

There was another time when I went to the Pro Bowl that Papa Bear hoped to steal an advantage. I arrived late, having played in the Championship Game. Coach Halas was coaching the Pro Bowl team and was using an offensive and defensive system that mirrored ours. He kept looking to me and other Packers players for advice on running the system. While we couldn't be sure, it certainly seemed like the whole thing was set up for us to help him understand more completely how our systems were run.

On the field, he was worse for opponents. He spent entire games yelling at the top of his lungs. It was often quite a spectacle when the Bears and Packers put on a close game, listening to Coach Lombardi and Coach Halas compete as to who could yell the loudest. When they played against each other, it was clear they both would have liked to put on pads and go toe-to-toe. Coach Halas heckled the opponents, taunting certain players and trying to distract us ("Hey No. 87—Willie—you're offsides!"), or running outside the coach's box on the sideline and getting in the faces of the referees who were trying to contain him. Coach Lombardi would then yell at him, "Get back in the box and leave my players the hell alone." He would turn to us and tell us to kick the Bears' ass, shut him up, and get him back in the box where he belonged.

"I don't want to see him walking that sideline!"

They respected each other, but they absolutely did not like each other, especially when we started winning. Coach Halas and Coach Lombardi always had good things to say about each other, but when the game started, their true feelings came out. In those games, with bragging rights on the line, there was no choice but victory. I played some of my best games against Chicago because if you didn't play well, you were going to hear about it. And God help us when we didn't win!

In that rematch late in 1960, we were at a crucial point in our season. We needed a win badly. We were frustrated because we knew we were better than our record indicated. We were also feeling emotional because we had recently lost Jack Vainisi, our talent scout who had helped Coach Lombardi put together this team. Just 33 years old, Vainisi was well known around the league and later gained respect as the man who brought Lombardi and his team to Green Bay. He was close with several of the players, so close that Hornung vowed the Packers would beat the Bears for Jack.

With all of that on the line, we went out and played a determined Bears team at Wrigley Field that kept it close until halftime. Coach Lombardi's speech was brief but powerful, reminding us how important this game was and asking us if we were contenders or not. I think it was an honest question. We had to come out in the second half and do the things necessary to impose our will on the Bears.

And we did, playing the best game of our season and beating the Bears 41–13 in front of a stunned crowd. It was one of the biggest margins of victory in the history of the rivalry. It also provided one of the most exciting plays in my entire career.

With the Bears at their own 20-yard line, we forced them to punt. As they lined up, I made the decision to charge hard and see if I could find a crease, a lane to the punter. I'm not sure if somebody missed an assignment or if I simply blew past them fast enough, but I had a clear shot, so I stuck out my hands and blocked the punt, picking up the ball and taking it into the end zone for a touchdown. It was a rewarding moment and actually a surreal one for me. I wasn't often provided with the opportunity to score and didn't really know what to do with it. Luckily, I was surrounded instantly by my teammates, congratulating me and ushering me off the field.

Our win all but slammed the door on the Bears' season. With a little help from some other teams in the league, it also opened the door for us to still win the division. The following week we went to San Francisco and shut out the 49ers 13–0, our best defensive performance of the season. That set the stage for a big game in Los Angeles against the Rams at the Coliseum in front of more than 53,000 people. We needed a win or a tie to take the crown. Back then, there were no playoffs, no wild card, nothing but a division winner with a chance to play for a championship. We wanted that chance.

A back-and-forth game that started with a Rams touchdown didn't go as expected—at least in terms of Packer strategy. On the offensive side we had built our success on running the ball, relying on Taylor and Hornung to carry us to victory. Paul had an amazing season, scoring a record 176 points with both touchdowns and field goals. He was adding to his reputation as one of the league's best runners, and he was expected to get a majority of the plays against the Rams.

Instead, we worked our air attack with Bart throwing a touchdown pass to Boyd Dowler and Hornung using his arm (and a little trickery) to throw a touchdown pass to Max McGee. The defense also did its job, blocking a punt in the end zone once again for a touchdown. We jumped to a 28–7 lead and never let up, winning 35–21.

In my first year with Green Bay, we were going to the Championship Game. I didn't know what to think. I had come to Green Bay expecting very little in terms of team success and now, 12 games later, we had a chance to win the whole thing. Only Philadelphia stood in the way of us calling ourselves champions!

Being the favorite to win rarely means anything.

We had gone from league laughingstock to the team favored to win the league's title despite the fact we were playing against a Philadelphia Eagles team with a better record (10–2) at their stadium, Franklin Field.

We played the championship on a Monday, the day after Christmas, at noon as the stadium didn't have any lights. There were more than 67,000 people there, and it was one of the largest crowds in professional post-season history. I had experienced the hype and buzz of a championship game before with Cleveland, but it was nothing quite like this.

On paper, we were equally matched with the Eagles, but we had two completely different playing styles. We were a disciplined team that looked to overwhelm our opponents and outlast them with our conditioning and our relentless attack. The Eagles were a much looser team with more diversity in their playbook, strong, multi-faceted athletes and a veteran quarterback in Norm Van Brocklin to lead the charge. It was also a surprise matchup, considering neither team had been close to the championship game since the 1940s.

Both teams wanted this win.

Leading up to the game, there was very little said by Coach Lombardi. If there was one person who had expected us to be here, it was him. This was why he came to Green Bay, to turn this team into a contender. It was his job, and so he did it. Also, for Coach Lombardi, just getting here wasn't enough. That was his only message. We would not be pleased to just be playing. We would win, and we would win by playing Green Bay Packers football.

For the first part of the game, that's exactly what we did. Defensively, we came out with a vengeance, stopping their running game, frustrating Van Brocklin, and creating turnovers. We were able to read what they were doing and impose our will on the blockers. They didn't have an easy play as we continued to dominate, and eventually they cracked. Bill Quinlan intercepted deep in their territory, giving us the ball and a chance to score. A short time later, we forced and recovered a fumble that set us up in field-goal range and gave us a 3–0 lead.

The problem was that the Eagles defense came to play, as well. Wanting to be aggressive, Coach Lombardi twice went for it on fourth down in Eagles territory instead of kicking the field goal, and both times we came up empty. The defense kept creating opportunities for the offense, but we kept getting stuffed, especially our running game. Led by Bobby Freeman, the Eagles made this a defensive battle. In the second quarter, Van Brocklin was able to connect on a long pass to Tommy McDonald for a touchdown. They quickly followed with a field goal, and we found ourselves going into halftime down 10–6.

There was no memorable halftime speech, especially for the defense since Coach thought we were playing at a high level. His frustration was saved for the offense despite the last couple of scores we allowed before the half. He also had some fear over how our offense would work in the second half because we had lost Hornung earlier in the game with a pinched nerve in his neck. The staff was unsure if he would be able to return. In the next few years we witnessed some of the most passionate halftime speeches in the history of sports. But today wasn't one of those days. Today's speech was about offensive strategy. For the defense, it was about holding on just a little longer.

The third quarter opened to a rowdy Philly crowd who tasted blood. They had wanted this not just for the city but also for Van Brocklin, who was extremely popular. Having arrived in Philadelphia a few years prior from the Los Angeles Rams, the Dutchman had already built a Hall of Fame career and brought a championship to one city and was looking for the icing on the cake, a return to glory. We weren't as eager to give it to him.

The third quarter continued much the same way with both defenses digging in and refusing to budge, even when one caused a turnover. But in the fourth, Max McGee took a bold chance that—lucky for him— paid off.

Backed up at our own 19-yard line and stopped once again on third down, Max was sent in to punt with very clear instructions to kick the ball and to not take any chances. Max told us later that was exactly what he intended to do. Down 10–6, we were still very much in the game and each possession was proving to be vital. He didn't want to make a blunder this deep in our territory to cost us some much-needed field position. But when the ball was snapped to him, he took a split second to look up field and saw there was nobody in front of him. We were not a team known for trickery, and nobody on the Eagles thought we would take any kind of chance this deep and this late in the game, so they all dropped back into punt coverage.

After the game, Max said that his instincts simply took over. He saw open field and he tucked the ball and ran—for 35 yards and a first down. His teammates both on the field and on the bench were just as surprised as the Eagles. We had been preparing our defense to go back in and get another stop, but suddenly there was Max running. Nobody was more surprised than Coach Lombardi, who didn't quite know how to respond. We joked that Max was very fortunate to have picked up the first down as there was no telling what Coach Lombardi would have done if he had missed. Max put the exclamation point on the play a short time later by catching a touchdown pass from Bart that put us up 13–10.

With how we were playing on defense, this should have been the end of it, but we made two mistakes—one on the ensuing kickoff and one on a drive that I personally made that may have cost us the game. The mistake on the kickoff was something that still happens often today on punt and kickoff return teams, and it's something that I have used as a talking point in speeches to teams and businesses for the past 40 years on the importance of every single player on the team doing his job.

A team is only as strong as *every* individual component.

Since the invention of special teams the positions have often been used for non-starters, players good enough to earn a spot on the team but looking to make an impression and bump up their playing time on either offense or defense. As I had mentioned, it is not a position that most players want to find themselves in as it lacks glory and leaves a lot of room for error. It's also difficult to come off a bench when you've been sitting for the better part of a half hour and be warmed up and expected to make a play. There is an inevitable lack of focus and concentration that can occur all too easily—and special teams is not a place where anyone can afford to lose that focus. As is seen time and time again in football, special teams is where the big momentum plays happen, as it did with us in that Championship Game.

As we celebrated on the sideline and congratulated Max, who was making sure to stay far away from Coach Lombardi, unsure how Coach was going to react to his ignoring the Old Man's orders and faking the punt, we heard the crown erupt in a cheer. We turned to look just in time to see Ted Dean busting through an open lane and carrying the kickoff deep into our territory, automatically putting them in scoring range.

On kickoffs, we were coached to play lanes. It's tough as any defender's instinct is to go after the ball. It's almost primal. You see a man with the ball, and you hunt him. On special teams, that doesn't always work. The blockers have an advantage because they have the entire field to work with in terms of blocking, and the returners are swift enough to make dazzling plays, cutting and switching direction before you can even get your head turned. If you play lanes—each man covering a section of the field—there should be a wall that would be challenging for anyone to get past.

All it takes is one man to come out of their lane to provide the opening the ball carrier needs. That's what happened on that kickoff. One of our little-used players, a solid athlete who had struggled to find regular playing time, came out of his lane, looking to take a different angle. It created the hole in the wall that allowed Dean to bust through. It was a lack of discipline, something uncharacteristic of a Lombardi team. As the defense jogged onto the field, I could hear the coaching staff hollering at this player (who I'm choosing not to name) about leaving his lane. All but sealing up any chance he would have at a career with the Packers, he argued that he wasn't aware of the importance of playing the lanes.

I realized during the coming years in both sports and business that any organization is only as strong as the one who is considered the "last" person in that organization. Everybody has a job, and when it comes right down to it, every single job is vital to the survival and success of a group. Everybody has to do what's expected of them. Everybody has to feel like they're part of the team, and everybody has to know their importance, even if they're not in the position they'd prefer. If this player had been more clear on the importance of his job on that particular play, his role in the overall strategy of the moment, and the approach of the team, there may not have been the lack of concentration, the instinct to go elsewhere. Instead, there would have been focus, discipline, and an appreciation for the bigger picture.

That's a business fundamental that I learned—one of many that would translate from sports. I would make it my goal as a business leader to make sure every person in my organization not only felt respected and appreciated, but also that they knew the goals of the organization and, most important, how they played a significant part in achieving those goals.

That following drive also taught me another hard lesson, this one about dedication and regret.

Never give up on a moment because it may be the crucial moment.

The Packer defense trotted out onto the field once more, worried about where they were starting but fired up that we were now playing with the lead. We were exhausted but still determined, and we could see that despite the burst of energy they got from the kickoff, the Eagles' offense was looking fatigued, as well. This would be a test of wills.

For the first couple of plays, we held them in check, knowing they would look for a touchdown and not a field goal. We felt good about our positioning and our continued ability to frustrate Van Brocklin. Now it was third and long, and we knew that if we held them here, they would be in serious trouble.

We expected a passing play but lined up in a basic defensive package that would allow us to come up and also play the run. We dug in, each of us taking our spots. Van Brocklin came up to the line and scanned the defense for just a quick couple of seconds. I knew instantly it was going to be a running play. I was at right defensive end, and I had an instinct the ball was coming my way. I was going to jump the snap and gain an advantage, pushing past the blocker and stuffing the ball carrier in the backfield.

When Van Brocklin snapped it, I knew instantly I had made the wrong guess. He quickly handed the ball to Billy Barnes—not their fastest running back, but a shifty one who could quickly turn it upfield. I was able to recover and started working my way back down the line toward the ball carrier, but I could tell he was out of my reach. Plus we had other guys on that side who would be able to stop him.

So for the first and last time in my career, I gave up on the play.

To this day, I'm not sure why I did. I had already built a reputation for myself as a tenacious defender who often took a gamble because I was able to recover so quickly and still chase down the ball. In fact, that signature move was the whole reason Coach Lombardi had brought me here in the first place. It was a play I had made several times before and one that I could have made again. Barnes was well out of my range and we did have other players there to pick up the tackle, but if I had fought my way over there, if I had taken the right angle, I could have helped bottle him up and contain him or at least caused him to second guess where he was going.

Instead, I watched as Barnes broke through the left end and turned it up field for a huge gain and a first down. It instantly hit me like a bolt of lightning.

I had missed my opportunity to make a big play.

I hadn't missed the tackle necessarily, but I had missed the opportunity—and for a competitor like me, that was unacceptable. As a result, a few plays later the Eagles were able to hand the ball to Dean for a touchdown, putting them up 17–13 with little time left.

After both teams exchanged punts, we found ourselves with the ball and just more than a minute to play. We had a chance, but all I could do was watch from the sideline and hope. Bart led a methodical drive down field with short passing plays and effective use of our patented sweep. After a pass play to Gary Knafelc that got us to the 22-yard line as the seconds continued to count down, we found ourselves with time for only one more play.

It was going to go to our workhorse, Jim Taylor. As the ball was snapped, Bart dumped a little pass to Jim who just had to cut back over center, which he did, instantly finding the hole. Out of nowhere came a young player for the Eagles by the name of Bobby Jackson who made perhaps the biggest hit of his career, stopping Jim at about the 10-yard line. We glanced up at the clock, wondering if there was any chance for one more play. Then we watched in horror as veteran Charlie Bednarik thrust himself on the pile, not allowing Jim to get up and run another play. Charlie sat on Jim until the clock hit zero, even as Jim screamed the most vile of vulgarities at him from beneath the pile. As soon as the game ended, legend has it that Charlie stood up, looked at Jim, who was still sprawled out on the field, and said, "Now you can get up."

Afterward, on the field, both teams congratulated each other on a well-fought game, and we walked off the field with our heads held high, but there was heaviness in our hearts. We knew we could have won this game, that we *should* have won this game. Worst of all, we knew we had let down Coach Lombardi, and that was tough for us. All the yelling, the fear, the explosions, the pushing, the hard work, all the things that we took issue with Coach for over the season had gotten us here. As the season went on, we realized that and accepted it more and more. We knew that he could carry us to great things. The proof was in the fact that we were playing in the title game. We wanted this win for him more than ourselves, and we just couldn't do it.

We were so close that Coach wouldn't even really admit defeat, using one of his famous lines: "Time didn't permit us to win." He even said it to the press, if we had had a few more moments at the end of the game, we would have won.

In the locker room, he was as quiet and somber as the rest of us. We didn't quite know how he was going to respond. Surprisingly to all of us, he was remarkably positive. He told us he was proud of how we had fought. He told us to keep our heads up and reminded us we would be back. He told us we should celebrate a strong season. And then he said the most poignant thing of all.

"Remember this feeling because this will never happen again," he said. "We will be back here again, and we will win. You will never lose another championship."

We never did.

That moment, that speech, set the stage for our performance in future title games from then on. We never wanted to experience that feeling of getting so close and failing ever again. It was too hard, too painful after all the hard work that we had put in. For me personally, I made an even deeper vow.

I would never again give up on a play.

For the entire off-season, I couldn't shake my memory of that sweep to the left that put Philadelphia in position to score a touchdown. It kept me up at night, and for the few weeks immediately following the game I woke up with that thought every morning. What if I had guessed the other way? What if I had switched direction and pursued like I always did? What if I had even just caused a little more of an obstruction on that side? Would they have gotten the first down? Would they have scored? Would we have won?

Football, as in life, almost always comes down to single moments that define success or failure. That moment may not have meant anything. There was a possibility that I never would have gotten to him and he would have ran for that yardage regardless. Yes, there was a chance. But I would never know, so all I could do was assume that my giving up on the play had influenced it.

How are we to know which moments will make all the difference? Sometimes they're obvious, and sometimes they come when we least expect them. The only thing we can do is be prepared to pursue each moment with as much heart and passion and effort as we can muster. That ensures our best chance at success. It was what Coach told us often in practice.

"How you play this game is reflective of how you will live the rest of your life."

This was one of those moments where I took a break and neglected an opportunity. I vowed that from that moment on, I would try my best to never again do that on the field or off. I had let my teammates down. I had let my coach down. I had let myself down. I couldn't change that now, but what I could do was make sure I never did it again. That's the wonderful thing about life. We are all given chances, and we all make mistakes and blow an opportunity or two along the way. But inevitably, in some way, another opportunity will present itself and we once again have the chance to prove that we are ready, that we can take it, and that we will succeed. That moment propelled me to become the best defensive end I could, never forgetting the feeling of that loss and the promise I made to give it my all—always.

Chapter 10 | Redemption

Replace missing pieces to help you achieve even more.

Our appearance in the 1960 Championship Game finally established the Packers as a contender. Even before the season began, we received national attention with fans all over the country looking to support the small-market team and sportswriters eagerly following our story, hopping on the Vince Lombardi bandwagon. His mythology was already growing, and people everywhere were getting to know the players, the coach, and the story of the Green Bay Packers.

So was the rest of the league.

There were still some people who thought our appearance in the Championship Game might have been a fluke. But teams were a lot less willing to take the chance. We were a surprise team, and a surprise team is always difficult to figure out. They either burn brightly for a while and then fade away, or they grab a foothold and hang on tightly, establishing their place among the elite. We couldn't fly under the radar anymore. The rest of the league was watching us closely, waiting to see what we were going to do next.

The bitter taste of that championship defeat, of getting so close only to see it all slip away, was still there for those of us who played. Many of us had come to the Packers with little to no expectations, but now that we had gotten so close, now that we had realized our potential, we wanted it all. Just getting there wouldn't suffice—and there was no doubt in our minds we could get there again. In fact, there was little doubt that we *would* get there. We were ready. We wanted to take care of business.

First we needed to add a few more pieces. Willie Wood took over the full-time starting duties at safety. We also utilized a little-used bull of a player by the name of Ron Kramer. Ron was a beast, about 6'3", close to 240. At the time, that was big for a player at the tight end position. He became integral in the blocking scheme of some of our sweeps as well as option plays. Not only that, the first-round draft pick out of the University of Michigan could catch, giving us yet another offensive weapon.

He helped round out an offensive lineup that was almost as scary as our defense with Boyd Dowler and Max McGee catching passes from Bart Starr and the running attack of Taylor, Hornung, and a new running back that we added to the rotation, another black player and future Packers Hall of Famer Elijah Pitts.

Elijah was an interesting player. He had all the confidence in the world, but he also feared he wouldn't make the team. He had total faith in his abilities, but he always felt like he had something to prove. It partially came from the lack of black players in Green Bay and his getting used to the idea that on this team we were all treated equally. It also came from the fact we already had two proven star running backs, and he knew he would have to fight for playing time. And he knew that amidst these star college players, he was from a small school called Philander Smith. People used to joke with him about it when he first got there.

"So, are you Elijah Pitts from Philander Smith or Philander Smith from Elijah Pitts?"

Elijah took it in stride, laughing along and keeping his Southern gentleman attitude. ("Yes sir," "No sir.") I quickly made friends with Elijah, feeling that as another young black player, he could use some guidance on how things worked in Green Bay.

We all approached camp with a single attitude: "Whatever's necessary." We were ready to work harder than ever before. We could still taste defeat, and we didn't like it. We were closer to each other than the year before, having battled with each other, united in our pursuit. There was a love and respect, a brotherhood unlike any other. We could feel it all coming together even before that season started. We had the talent, we had the depth, we had the leadership, and now we had the bond. We were focused. We were going to win. We couldn't wait for the season to start.

And again, we lost our first game.

The Lions beat us at home 17–13 in one of the season's more frustrating games. We were so ready, so excited after a solid training camp and preseason. Maybe that was the problem. The Lions, along with the Bears and the Colts, always played us hard. The division opponents were always a tougher game, especially when we had to open the season against them. It didn't matter if it was at home or away, those opening games were often the toughest ones we'd play all season, and despite our yearly successes, it was interesting that we often came out on the losing end in those opening games.

It wasn't the coaching. It wasn't the talent. It wasn't a lack of preparation or focus. It was tough to see what exactly the problem was at the time, but I think we just came in a little too fired up. There is a balance, and at the start of many seasons we found ourselves tipping the scales for a game or two before settling in and playing Green Bay Packers football.

One year when we were gearing ourselves up for a big game against the Bears, in the week leading up to the game we studied that team more than ever. We broke down everything they did, practicing against simulated Bears offenses and defenses, focusing less on where we were dominant and more on shutting down their strengths. We talked constantly about nothing but the Bears. We ate, drank, breathed, and dreamed Bears, Bears, Bears. We even went as far as to surround ourselves with Bears logos, paraphernalia, anything that could get us ready. By the time the game came around, we were exhausted and we got killed. Sometimes there is something to be said about being so overly excited about something that you lose control. That's how we started the 1961 season against the Lions.

In typical Packers fashion, we rebounded quickly by whipping the San Francisco 49ers 30–10 the following week thanks to the amazing kickoff returns of our little warrior, Willie Wood, who was establishing himself already as a league leader on special teams, and our Golden Boy, Paul Hornung, who scored 18 points himself in the game with his running and kicking.

The following week, we decided to exact a little revenge from the Lions game on another division opponent, the Bears. As always, we wanted this game badly and there was nothing that could put a season back on track more quickly than beating the Bears. In front of a raucous home crowd, we dismantled them at every turn, with Jim Taylor bullying over them for huge gains and Willie Wood again sneaking by on returns. The Bears players, coaches, and Papa Bear himself spent a majority of that game complaining to the referees and watching our backs as we passed them by time and time again. When all was said and done, we won the game 24–0, the first time we had shut them out since 1935.

It was the game we needed, the one that we knew would set the tone for the rest of the season. This was the team that we knew we could be and the type of performance we knew we could give each and every week. It also caught the attention of the league. After the Lions game, there was talk that we might have been a fluke as far as our appearance in last season's Championship Game. But now, after a dominating performance like this against another of the league's elite teams, we were fully legitimate. We commanded respect and we knew that from this point on, we were going to get everyone's best shot. It didn't matter, though—we had too much momentum on our side.

In our next game we completely dismantled yet another rival, beating the Colts 45–7 in a contest that saw yet another amazing return by Willie Wood and witnessed Hornung put up an astounding 33 points himself. It was also a game where we used the Packer Sweep with amazing precision and showed the rest of the league we had a play so amazing in its design and run so disciplined and precisely by some of the most talented players in the league that it didn't matter what they did. They couldn't stop it. In this day of wildcat formations, rushing quarterbacks, and complicated option-running games, that simple sweep is still the most effective running play I have ever seen.

There is nothing wrong about seeking redemption.

A 3–1 record took us on the road for the first time that season and set us up for the game that I personally circled on the calendar. October 15 was my first trip back to the team that got rid of me, the team that sent me to the Siberia of the North. On October 15, we went to play in Cleveland.

I was determined to win this game. I wasn't alone. The other three former Browns—Bill Quinlan, Henry Jordan, and Lew Carpenter—also wanted to make a statement. This is what you were going to get for trading us. Look at where we are now and what we're doing. We needed to win this game to show them they had underestimated not only the Green Bay Packers and Coach Lombardi but also what we could accomplish as individuals on a team with a common goal.

I never once regretted my time in Cleveland. I loved playing in that city with my teammates and for that organization. But by the time I returned home to face the Cleveland Browns for the first time, I was a full-fledged Packer. We were able to get the entire team to rally behind us. They all saw that there was a bit of extra meaning in this game. Bart, Paul, and other members of the offense would come over to us former Browns and pat us on the back.

"Hey Willie, we're gonna win this one for you!"

My fellow defenders, my brothers on the field, talked nonstop strategy for stopping Jim Brown, who was still proving himself to be the all-time dominant running back in the history of the league, and the potent Browns offensive passing game.

"As soon as we see Jim Brown get the ball, let's make sure we got a lot of folks there to greet him!"

"Let's not let [Milt] Plum get any time in that pocket. Let's show him a pass rush like he ain't ever seen before!"

For my part, I did anything and everything I could to prepare myself and the team. I pushed as hard as possible in my preparation that week, trying to be perfect. I pushed my teammates to go that extra mile, setting the stage for a future role as defensive captain. I spent extra time with the coaching staff on both offense and defense to give them a breakdown of each and every player I had played alongside during my time in Cleveland. I had no problems pointing out what I thought were their strengths and weaknesses and spots where we could take advantage of opportunities and impose our will. I was ready to do anything to help us win. When it came to game time, I didn't need Coach to give us a speech on the importance of this game to keep us in the race. I thought to myself, *Just give me the game plan, Coach, and I'll go kick some booty!*

Running onto that field in front of 75,000 fans who used to cheer for me and now gave me mild applause was surreal to say the least. I found myself shaking, a little nervous, and pent up with almost uncontrollable energy. It was an emotional game, as it was each and every time we played the Browns. I looked over at my former teammates, my former coaches, my former sideline, and I felt ready to take care of business. I had nothing against them, but just like any other opponent we played, there was no time for feelings on the field. I could reminisce, exchange pleasantries, or whatever I needed to do after the game. I wanted to soak up the experience, but I couldn't afford to let it linger. We needed this game as a team, and individually, and it was time to get to work.

The Pack Attack wasted no time in establishing themselves, with Taylor trying his best to show up his longtime rival, Jim Brown. Taylor was a man possessed during that game, and we were able to ride his anger and determination. Taylor broke one early in the game, barreling over the Browns defensive line for a 26-yard touchdown run. He later followed that up with another long run that set up another touchdown for the Bull. At halftime, the score was 21–3. When Taylor scored yet another touchdown after halftime to make it 28–3, the game was essentially over.

Still, the offense was only part of the game. We had to step up on defense, and we did just that. I personally had one of my best games ever, shutting down runs that came my way from Jim Brown and chasing Milt Plum all over the field, catching him for a couple of sacks. The rest of the defense was right there with me, creating havoc and never giving up more than a few yards at a time.

One moment from this game sticks out in my mind and helps me remember exactly what set us apart from other teams in that era of dominance. It was a cold, dreary day on the lakefront, and puddles and mud littered the field. Although we were winning by a lot at this point, Jim Brown was having yet another of his typically great days, racking up runs of 20 yards or more thanks to his signature combination of strength and agility. With the game well in hand, we still fought hard on each play, and so did Jim. He gained another 20 yards on a running play and got tackled by a few of us out of bounds right by Coach Lombardi, who helped pick up Jim.

"Great run, Jimmy, great run," Lombardi said with the enthusiasm of a man who simply loved the game of football. When he was with the Giants, Coach Lombardi had gotten to know Jim as the teams played each other quite a bit, and he loved his toughness. With a smile on his face, Coach patted Jim, our opponent, on the back and sent him back onto the field. And in a flash, he turned to me with that Italian anger and screamed, "Damn it, Willie, too much yardage, that's too much yardage. You gotta stop it in the backfield!"

For many other teams, there would have been a moment that both the coaches and the players would have taken the foot off the gas. Not Coach Lombardi and not us.

After back-to-back wins against the upstart Vikings, we experienced a 45–21 loss to the Colts in a game where our defense couldn't find a way to shut down Unitas and the deadly Colts offense. But again we rebounded, beating the Bears 31–28 the next week.

We played with a sense of urgency in this game, not just because it was against a rival, a road game, and a chance for us to pull ahead by a couple of games in the division, but also because we knew we were going to face losses to personnel at any moment. Unfortunately, that happened sooner rather than later.

A few weeks earlier, about two dozen players from the league who were active military reservists got called to report for duty. Teams all over the league suddenly had to deal with the potential loss of key players as they approached the second half of the season, the time when the men separated themselves from the boys in league play. There had been rumors this was a possibility, especially with the construction of the Berlin Wall and some concerns the Department of Defense had about Europe at the time. As a country, we weren't that far removed from our last major military conflict, and nerves were frayed on a worldwide level. Still, the call came as a bit of surprise as did the names that were on the list of players being called up.

The Packers were going to lose three players: little-used but rising star Ray Nitschke; our solid No. 2 receiver Boyd Dowler; and the biggest blow of them all—the Golden Boy himself, Paul Hornung. By midseason, Paul was already putting up numbers worthy of an MVP Award. Losing him, losing all three actually, in a year when we were already dealing with injuries and the bitter taste of last year's defeat, was a deadly blow. We had so much momentum carrying us through the season, but once the call came in, we now found ourselves facing the possibility of losing some key components and one of the cornerstones of our offense.

Paul was to report for duty in mid-November, right after the Bears game. Coach Lombardi was torn about the situation, as were we all. Many players around the league, including myself, had military experience and understood the importance of the obligation of serving your country. It was something to be proud of, something with honor, and we had a great appreciation for anyone who wanted to serve. That was especially true for Coach Lombardi, who served as a coach at West Point for the U.S. military. Yet the coach in him knew what this could mean for our team.

There was some wheeling and dealing that went on both behind the scenes and out in the open in terms of trying to get our players deferments or at least allow them to report at later in the year, after the season. Local congressional leaders openly asked the government for deferments, and there were even rumors that Coach Lombardi tried calling a few government officials he had gotten to know, asking for help.

Hornung was crushed. While he was willing to serve, he felt as if his leaving would let down the team. All we could do was remind him that we understood and appreciated the obligation. Lucky for us, we had plenty of weapons to replace the three we lost. The defense was stacked, and while we would miss Ray, he wasn't yet the star or the starter that he would become the following season. Boyd would be missed, but Bart had plenty of other receivers to throw to, outlet and backup receivers who would be the top dogs on most other teams. Replacing Paul would be difficult of course, but we still had Jim Taylor, one of the most feared backs in the league. We also had Elijah Pitts and Tom Moore, and Tom was ready to step up.

Be patient and be ready when the time comes.

Tom Moore was our running back reservist out of Vanderbilt. He joined the Packers in 1960 with little to no hope of getting the starting running back position anytime soon, following Thunder and Lightning. But I never once heard him complain. He was a quiet guy who came in and did his job every day. He worked hard in practice, studied, helped his teammates, including those who were ahead of him on the depth chart, and he got ready to take advantage of any and every opportunity that came his way, even if it was just the occasional carry.

When Coach Lombardi asked him to step up, to start contributing, and to fill the Golden Boy's shoes, Moore was ready and he didn't disappoint. He finished that season with about 60 carries for a little more than 300 yards, averaging five yards per carry. He put up those numbers while constantly being shuffled in and out of the lineup. Paul had to miss the game against the Rams, which we won 35–17, but then he was flown back from Fort Riley in Kansas for a 17–9 Thanksgiving Day win over the Lions. That's how it would be for the remainder of the season, but again, Tom never complained. He simply stepped up when needed.

His efforts were a great lesson in patience and preparation for me at a young age. I think of him as a prime example of how to conduct yourself within any organization. It's very easy to see yourself at the bottom of the food chain and see a bleak future with little room for advancement. That can suck the drive and motivation out of anyone, especially when you have superstars in their prime in front of you. Complacency can set in as you ponder what to do with your lot in life.

Tom Moore taught me that you should use that opportunity to prepare, learn, train, and work as hard as possible to get yourself ready in case an opportunity arises. Why? Inevitably, an opportunity *will* come up. Something will happen. You will be given a chance, and it may only be *one* chance. Then it will be up to you to see what you can do with it, to see if you can change where you are and move to the next level. If you're lamenting your situation, you won't be ready and that chance will pass you by. If you're prepared and working hard, you will get your shot and you will succeed. Tom Moore put up great numbers when Paul had to report to duty. He impressed everyone, and his preparation paid off. For the remainder of that year, even after Paul came back, Tom got carries—same with the following season and for the rest of his career. He went from being the backup to a couple of superstars to becoming a key part of our offense—all because he was prepared.

With our wins against the Rams and Lions, we pretty much had the division sewn up. We took on the New York Giants at home, needing a win or a tie to clinch a trip to the championship to play—the New York Giants! During the preview game (and a chance for both teams to get an up close and personal look at each other), we both fought hard in a defensive battle with us pulling out a 20–17 win and a trip to the promised land.

Our last two games didn't even matter at this point. We were going to play once again for the title, this time against a team that had been there three times in the past five years. This was a personal game for Coach Lombardi, facing his old team. This was a personal game for all of us who had lost to the Eagles the year before. The rest of the league and all of the pundits loved this matchup. They loved the offensive firepower of both teams. They loved the brutal stubbornness of the two defenses. They loved the coaching. They all thought this was going to be one of the hardest fought and most evenly matched championship games in the history of the league.

They were wrong.

Chapter 11	# How to Play the Perfect Game

Relish in perfection.

The 1961 Championship Game was a culmination of everything we had worked for, everything we had learned, everything Coach Vince Lombardi had instilled in us, the philosophy, the schemes, the drills, the practices, the belief that we could and would be world champions—that we would be perfect.

It was a reflection of how Lombardi's Packers would be recognized thereafter—as one of the greatest teams in sports history. It served as the ultimate example of what teams to come should strive for and what they could accomplish. Beyond that, for the Green Bay Packers, from this day forward, it would now be expected.

It was the true beginning of Titletown U.S.A., something more than just a moniker that was given to us by our fans that stuck with the national media. It became a name and a legacy that spanned generations and captured not just the hearts of local fans obsessed with their men of winter but also new fans young and old across the country and later the world, who gained an appreciation and a love for this small-market team, its players, and their dedication, heart, strength, will, and success.

The Championship Game encapsulated the great coach's words, "Winning isn't everything; it's the only thing" better than any that followed. It laid the foundation for what was to come. It made all of us fully aware of what winning (and winning so decisively) could do, and it made us want so much more. It was a game in which the outcome was never in doubt, even as the stakes were at their highest. It was redemption for a coach, a prize for a dedicated team, and the launching of a dynasty that would forever be associated with a city and its franchise.

In the 1961 Championship Game, we defeated the New York Giants by a score of 37–0.

Despite all the hype, all the excitement, all the newspapers predicting a Giants win in a "Goliath crushes David" scenario, we remained calm, cool, and intensely focused. We knew what was at stake, not just for a coach who would have given anything to take away a title from his old team, but also for the reputation and respect of our team, the loyalty of our city and its fans, and the future of the NFL as a whole. This was a game that we knew would help shape the future of the league, offering proof that anybody could beat anybody on any given day regardless of size, stature, and prominence. We wanted to prove that this was a league of equals, but we were the best. We also knew all too well what a loss would mean. The Giants could beat us any other day—but not this day.

We didn't read the newspapers. We didn't listen to what everybody was saying about the big-city Giants and the small-town Packers. We refused to get caught up in the hype of championship week, the outside distractions and the buzz that a championship football game caused. We spent our time practicing and focusing more than we ever had before for a game. We ran the extra laps in practice, and we pushed a little harder in the drills. We studied our game plans and the tendencies of the Giants. We communicated, we listened, we kept our eyes on what we wanted to achieve, and we made sure we were ready to execute.

I had always taken every game I ever played in with respect, but up to that point I don't know if I had ever been so serious about a game. I didn't put myself in any position during that week leading up to the game to do anything that would prevent me from being my best. I played out the entire game in my mind before I even stepped onto the field. I knew what I wanted to make happen and what could happen. I had enough humility to know that regardless of the size of the game, where it was played, who was playing and for what, that the other team had just as much to both lose and gain as we did. I knew they were approaching things the same way we were and that we had to be ready for anything, especially from such a huge, respected organization.

Coach Lombardi heard some rumors that members of the Giants staff were speaking negatively about the Packers organization, the city of Green Bay, and the coach himself. The sense was that the Giants were looking at this game as a should-win for them, despite the fact that it was a home game for us and we had beaten them earlier in the year (albeit by a slim margin). That didn't sit well with Coach. There was a sense, at least in how it was portrayed in the media and around the league, that the Giants felt like they had an obligation to come in and show us who was king, that although we had a "cute" story in the small town in Northern Wisconsin, this was a game for the big boys from New York.

Coach was mostly quiet during the week leading up to the game, only occasionally yelling at us. We didn't need the motivation. He had taught us well, and we were well aware of what was at stake. We motivated ourselves.

We also knew we could win. All the ingredients were there. We knew their style of play. We knew how to beat teams like them. We were playing on our field in front of our fans. We also reveled in the fact that we were being underestimated. We all felt it. We were going to shock the world.

The game itself was the first million-dollar game in the history of the league. About 40,000 people packed the stands at City Stadium to see it live, paying $10 a ticket. Plus there was more than $600,000 in TV revenue generated by the game as it was broadcast to an estimated 50 million viewers on New Year's Eve. These were all big numbers in 1961.

In typical Green Bay fashion, the weather was going to play its role. The field was covered with a tarp to help with its preparation, but during the week it had been covered with more than a foot of snow that froze when the temperature later plummeted. Luckily on game day it was a balmy 20 degrees, but that still didn't help the field, which after a week of rough conditions still contained quite a few iced-over spots, reaffirming the field's reputation as the frozen tundra. Right before the game started, we had to switch from cleats, which weren't going to dig into the ground, to regular sneakers, which meant slipping and sliding but also more speed—in theory. It was uncomfortable. It was cold, frozen, harsh, and annoying. It was just the way we liked it.

The matchup between the two teams was an interesting one. We had the highest-rated offense in the league, relying mainly on our running game and the precision passing of Bart Starr. The Giants, led by Coach of the Year Allie Sherman, had the No. 2 offense in the league thanks mostly to their veteran quarterback, Y.A. Tittle, and his two offensive weapons, fullback bruiser Alex Webster and split end Del Shofner. Those were the three we knew we had to shut down to keep this game close.

We had confidence in our defense, which was ranked No. 2 in the league behind only the New York Giants. They had a terrifying defense with five Pro Bowlers: Andy Robustelli and Jim Katcavage at defensive end, Sam Huff at linebacker, Erich Barnes at cornerback, and safety Jimmy Patton. They were tough, ruthless, and unrelenting, and they gave up fewer points than anyone in the league that year. Our offense assumed it was going to be a struggle to put up each and every point.

Plus our offense was still nicked up. Jerry Kramer was still recovering from his ankle injury. Jim Taylor had been banged up all season, and he wasn't at 100 percent. Bart was dealing with stomach issues that were making him weak. There were other guys on the line who had experienced some minor injuries throughout the year that always seemed a little worse at the end of the season. There was also a concern about whether or not we were going to get our military boys back. Ray, Boyd, and Paul were three integral parts of our team, and having them would have been a huge blow against a team that was already favored to beat us. When we first learned we had made it to the Championship Game, that question was on everyone's mind, especially with Paul.

Is the Golden Boy going to play?

First reports were that the military had strict rules about service time, and they couldn't make an exception for professional athletes. But something happened.

Few people know for sure, but the rumor was that Coach Lombardi called in a favor with new friend President John F. Kennedy. A huge football fan, President Kennedy was an admirer of Coach Lombardi and the two had talked, even going as far as to try and arrange a visit when they were both in the same city. The rumor is that Coach Lombardi wrote to the president explaining the dilemma, and the president called for a special leave of absence for all three Packers players. We weren't sure exactly what had happened, but we didn't care. They were a welcome sight.

We had our weapons back, we had the strategy, and we had the hunger. We were ready to play. Game time couldn't come fast enough. We were nervous, we were excited, and we definitely felt the pressure. Even our locker room clown, the guy we relied on to loosen us up, Max McGee, was relatively silent. He stared at the floor of the locker room, concentrating, taking his moment to determine what he was going to do today. We tried to hold our emotions in check.

On the defense, we only needed to exchange looks with each other to know that we were all on the same page. There were few words, at least to each other. There were plenty for the Giants offense, even from me.

"On some other day, buddy, maybe. But not today. Today I own you. I flat-out own you!" I said, using the same lines I once called out to college opponents.

Up and down the line, similar things could be heard coming from the Packers defense, but we did more than talk. We worked, and we showed them how things were going to go. This was a Green Bay Packers day.

The Giants never had a chance. For all the build-up, all the hype, all the time and preparation that went into this game, it flew by. There was no scoring in the first quarter as both teams tried to assess each other's strategies, neither wanting to make the big mistake. Our defense held firm, gaining confidence with every play. We were imposing our will, and that pumped up our offense.

After a nice drive, Hornung ran in for a 6-yard touchdown to put us up 7–0, and we saw that we could move against this highly regarded defense. Boyd then caught a 13-yard pass from Bart to put us up 14–0, followed by Kramer catching one from 14 yards to make it 21–0. Paul tacked on a field goal before the half, and we went up 24–0, completely stunning the nation and shocking the Giants into nothing more than a slow pulse.

At halftime, we knew we could make a statement. We wanted to keep applying the pressure, crush this team, and create a story that Packers fans could talk about for generations. We wanted to cement a champion's legacy with a dominant performance.

For my part, I played one of my best games, sacking Y.A. Tittle a couple of times, causing a fumble, and applying the pressure time and again. I spent more time in the Giants' backfield than I did in any game before. I was always in Y.A.'s face, so much so that years later he said that every time he looked up, he saw me coming.

"He was always coming at you, coming all the time," Tittle said.

He also said that my hands were like two giant toilet seats slamming down on him! It was my personal goal to be in his face all day, and I made that happen. I gave absolutely everything I had to give. I made that promise to myself after the Philadelphia game, after looking back and realizing that I hadn't given it my all—that was not the case here. I walked off the field exhausted and victorious.

The offense and defense helped each other all day. As Forrest ran off the field, I pointed out things about their defense that I had noticed and he did the same for me with their offense. We saw pockets, places for Bart to throw against them in the first half and beyond, and we told him. We worked as one on both sides of the ball.

The second half saw Paul add two more field goals and Ron Kramer take another touchdown pass from Bart for a final score of 37–0 in one of the worst defeats in NFL championship history. As it got close to the end, Coach Lombardi pulled the starters to well-earned standing ovations. When the final gun sounded, he was hoisted on the team's shoulders as the fans swarmed the field.

The locker room after the game was one of my most joyful memories of being a Green Bay Packer. I think even Coach Lombardi was amazed at not only what we had accomplished but the manner in which we did it. He went around hugging each and every one of us, telling us that we could now call ourselves champions.

"You are the greatest team in the NFL today. I mean it," he said to cheers that must have reverberated to what I assume was a quiet and solemn Giants locker room.

Coach Lombardi was more ecstatic on that day than I had ever seen before or anytime after. There was a sense of relief about him, a pride of what his boys had done and a pleasure in the fact that it was against his old team, against all the critics, against anyone who doubted him or the

Green Bay Packers. This was our time. This was the game that built the Green Bay Packers.

I left that game exhausted, satisfied, redeemed, and aware of what had just happened. I didn't stick around for any postgame celebration, driving back home to Chicago with my wife to avoid the madness that was sure to follow in the city of Green Bay. I celebrated with my teammates and my coach for a while, but I really wanted to take in the full impact of what I had just experienced alone. I wanted it to sit there, to take over. I wanted to feel what it was like to be champion—and it felt good.

It was a perfect game, a perfect moment, the end of a near-perfect season. We were the champions. We were no longer a cute story but the title-holders. We were the team everyone would be gunning for, the one that would have to fight hardest, that would have to become even more dedicated, more focused, and more disciplined. We were the team that would have to get better because now there was only one thing left to do as we approached 1962. Only one thing would satisfy us.

We had to win it all again.

| **The Rise of Titletown U.S.A.**

There are many different kinds of toughness, and they all have a benefit.

I was an NFL champion, a rising star in the league who analysts were starting to notice and predict good things about in the near future, playing for a team that had recently claimed a spot in the heart of the American public. In today's game of football, I would have been completely set financially.

But not in 1962.

Salaries wouldn't really start spiking until a couple years later in the decade, when the rival AFL and NFL started bidding against each other to recruit top college prospects. They wouldn't jump to unthinkable numbers until many years later. In 1962, this was still considered just a game, at least for the players. The teams and their owners were starting to see just how lucrative professional football could be with television contracts, increased ticket sales (and prices), and so on. For many of the players, including some of the league's best and most marketable athletes, this could barely be considered a job at all but rather a hobby that paid a little cash. Almost all of us had to find off-season jobs.

That's how I found myself playing basketball as a member of the Green Bay Pachyderms.

I was living in Chicago with my wife, Ann, and our two-year-old, Duane, in the off-season, doing some substitute teaching, trying to save what little I could from my meager NFL salary and from what Ann was making as a teacher. We needed money, and like other guys on the team, we knew that we could make some off our names and newfound recognition as NFL champions—and we could have fun doing it.

The Green Bay Pachyderms was an amateur basketball team made up of a few members of the football team and some other guys we knew, friends of teammates who helped us round out the roster. We spent a portion of the off-season traveling around small towns and cities in Wisconsin, playing scrimmages against each other and pick-up games against local teams and leagues made up of fathers, sons, cousins, uncles— almost all Packers fans who were just excited to meet the players in real life and have a chance to compete against them. We'd play once a week and earn a couple hundred extra bucks for our appearance. It was my first taste of using the title "celebrity" to my advantage.

I was clearly one of the worst players on the team, but I could hold my own. I had a jump shot and could pick out passing lanes with a kind of ease. And as I had proven when I played pick-up games with the Browns in the off-season and had to go toe-to-toe with Jim Brown, I could get physical. But I was playing with and sometimes even against guys with collegiate and maybe even semi-professional basketball experience. Some days I would show up in Sheboygan, Beloit, or another community in the state expecting to pick up an easy paycheck only to find myself competing as hard as I did on the football field.

It was also, believe it or not, a little dangerous. More often than not, we'd go into a pick-up game with guys fired up enough to want to whoop our booties. Half the time these guys would come out with the specific intent to somehow say they got their lick in. While they cheered their hearts out for us when we were on the football field, on the court they wanted a story they could tell (or show) their friends and families.

When it came to the physical challenges from our opponents, there was no one I worried about more on my basketball or football team than Ray Nitschke.

For the early part of his career, just as I was getting to know him, Ray had an immense temper. He was a big man for the time and one who never shied away from any kind of challenge. In fact, his temper often created a challenge out of even the most innocent of situations. On the basketball court, he was fun to watch. He was immensely talented, one of the best on our team, and the guy we could count on to entertain the crowd with crazy stunts like half-court shots. But I used to dread playing against a group of guys who decided to get physical against us. I knew that I could handle it, pushing back just enough to compete. But I had to watch and worry about the moment one of them would bump Ray. It would inevitably happen and sure enough, there was Ray slamming his massive frame into the guy, talking trash, and taking the confrontation to the next level. It was usually up to me to grab him.

"Come on, Ray," I would say as I pulled him away from his victim. "You can't do that."

"Well, did you see what he tried to do to me?" he would ask as the guy half his size checked himself for injury, shaking off the cobwebs.

On the field, that temper worked to Ray's advantage and eventually gave him the reputation as one of the hardest-hitting, toughest, meanest, and most feared linebackers in the history of the league.

I say eventually because for the first few years of his career, Ray didn't see as much playing time. It was something that the outspoken Nitschke, who people called the Judge, had no problem voicing his displeasure about.

"Why do they call you the Judge?"

"Because I'm always sitting on the bench!" he yelled.

Beyond our depth, Ray's temper, aggressiveness, and excitement, the same qualities that helped him to earn his reputation later in his career, initially kept him in a utility position. Coach Lombardi expressed his concerns about Ray's initial lack of discipline, as if he were a wild stallion that needed to be tamed just enough without breaking his passion. On the defense, we loved the spark that Ray gave us when he came into the game. As his playing time increased, Coach Lombardi learned to love it, as well. Ray eventually became the spirited leader of our defense. He was the guy who pumped us up after we had given up a few scores or some big plays. He helped us get back on track and remember who we were on defense.

We just had to make sure we didn't tell him anything secret. For all of his tremendous qualities as a defender, Ray was someone you couldn't tell anything. He was simply too excited and if you gave him a secret or something you read from the opposition in the game, you could almost always count on the fact that in his excitement, he was going to blow it.

We played a tough game against the St Louis Cardinals, and we were trying to determine if we should take advantage of a signal we picked up from the Cardinals' offensive line. This was always part of the chess match that occurs in a professional football game. Along with all the early preparation and study, there is a constant observation of your opponent in the moment. Every team comes to the game with surprises, and if you can get a clue, a piece of information, you can often find a huge tactical advantage. We had tremendous scouts, but some days we were lucky to pick something up.

With the Cardinals, one of our scouts noticed that in previous games the guards shifted their blocking patterns when the quarterback called, "60." The center blocked to the left and the left guard pulled to the right, causing a cross block up the middle, very similar to a blocking scheme we ran on offense, which meant we knew how to defend against it. Coach Bengtson debated how to use what we had picked up, but being the conservative (and smart) defensive coordinator that he was, he feared that the Cardinals might purposely be leaking information in the hopes we picked up on it and got caught making a mistake that would lead to a big play. Still, he knew that if we were fortunate enough to make the discovery on our own, it could lead to some successful blitzing. He compromised and told us that only the linebackers should take advantage of this info. The defensive line should hold true to their original formation.

That was all Ray needed to hear. From the start, Ray bolted onto the field, eager to bust through, just waiting for the moment he heard them call "60." It came a few plays later and Ray went ballistic before the ball was even snapped, waving his arms and screaming at all of us.

"What are we gonna do?! Tell 'em. What are we gonna do?!"

Sometimes we were as confused as the offense as to what the hell he was talking about. Ray could barely contain himself, knowing he was going to hit the hole as soon as the ball was snapped. On blitzing plays, I often compared him to a big tractor with a motor revving up or a dog waiting to be unleashed. I swear sometimes I even thought I heard him growl.

He was that eager at this moment. However, we failed to inform Ray that if the Cardinals sensed blitz, they would probably call off the cross block.

They sensed it. Ray didn't. They snapped the ball and Ray bolted to the center only to be laid out by their strong center Bob DeMarco.

Confused, Ray jumped up onto his feet and yelled, unbelievably, at DeMarco.

"Hey Bob, don't you even know your own plays?!" he yelled.

We couldn't believe what we were hearing.

"Ray, you just let them know that we were on to them!"

The thought never crossed his mind. Ray just never thought about things like that, so we had to be careful what we shared. But he'd get upset when he found out we would occasionally hold back information from him. Sometimes we just had to. He was so emotional, going on instinct alone. That became obvious with how many times he needed one of us to tell him where he was going on certain plays. We'd see him looking at our sideline, confused by the play that was being called in by Coach Bengtson and we'd tell him where to line up. It wasn't that he wasn't smart enough to remember, he was just too excited.

That excitement, passion, and heart was also what earned him a starting linebacker position in 1962. He had shown growth and sparks of greatness the season before, even after having to deal with being shipped off to the military midseason. Coach Lombardi knew that with the pressure of repeating and the target on our back, we needed fiery leaders like Ray to keep us motivated and hungry.

Ray had such a reputation for toughness that once during practice, a metal tower on our practice field fell unexpectedly and landed right on Ray. Coach Lombardi heard that it had hit one of his players and in a state of panic ran over to see the victim. Once he saw it was Ray, he sighed and turned back to all of us, yelling, "He'll be fine. Get back to work." The tower had actually pierced a spike through Ray's helmet, but sure enough, he got up without any injury as he did many times in his career.

Those early championship years also saw another one of our veterans step up and take on a key role. Hank Gremminger had been with the Packers since 1956 and had always been a key contributor. But he was often lost in the shadows of the other dominating personalities we had on the Packers defense. Hank was just as good, just as solid, but he either wasn't as flashy, as hard-nosed, or as vocal as some of the other characters we had on the defensive squad. As such, he seemed to play more of a supporting role, and a utility role as a defensive back, cornerback, and safety.

But in 1961 and 1962, he stepped up in a big-time way, becoming more of a player who led by example. Off the field, he surprised me when I met him. Hank was a good ol' boy from Texas, someone who had been in the league for a while and could still clearly remember the days when black players were few and far between. I incorrectly assumed that Hank, being from a state that wasn't exactly tolerant of blacks, might be the kind of guy who would cause some problems for me. I couldn't have been more wrong. Hank wanted nothing to do with cliques, with discrimination, with anything other than being a team player. He went out of his way to connect with all players on the team, black or white.

On the field, he was a key cog in Coach Lombardi's defense, the guy we could rely on to fill any position. He had experience and covered the field—and he did it for us game after game. It was a great example of how everybody on the team became a dominant player at his position. We had the established superstars and the young up-and-comers, but even the veterans, the reserves, and the special teams guys stepped up in a big way.

Don't let success kill your hunger to do more.

Coach Lombardi said later that the 1962 team was one of if not *the* best Packers teams ever. Coming into the 1962 season, as much as other teams were starting to hate us, we were the envy of the league. Beyond being more motivated then ever, we were also deeper. Just one look at our running back corps—Hornung, Taylor, Moore, and Pitts—showed four guys capable of being the top ball carrier on most other teams in the league. Wide receiver was the same. Our offensive line was quickly gaining a reputation as one of the most bruising in the league and had several capable backups ready to step in should anyone go down. Our defense was filled with current and future All-Pros, and we seemed to get better with each game, each practice, and each play.

Coming into the season, we felt like we were exactly where we wanted to be. We were riding high off last year's championship, and while we knew we had teams gunning for us, we looked at ourselves and could appreciate what we had in Green Bay. We were the Packers, and we were going to start 1962 the right way by showing our dominance and how hungry we were to win again.

We opened the season at home in front of a raucous crowd that was still high off of last year's championship celebration—when the Packers win, the partying never really stops in Green Bay or the state of Wisconsin for that matter. We played against the Vikings, and we went into the game very aware of our record in season openers the last few years. We did not want to start off this season on the wrong foot, and with the exception of Paul Hornung tweaking his knee (which bothered him off and on for the remainder of the season), we accomplished our goal, beating Minnesota 34–7 in a very lopsided affair. The week after, we took care of the St. Louis Cardinals 17–0.

But our real opener and the game that often defined how our season would go, always seemed to fall against one of our rivals. Those early games set the tone for the season, and while Coach Lombardi trained us to never look ahead and to always focus on the game we were playing that week, on our personal calendars, rivalry games were the ones we circled.

In Week 3 of the 1962 season, we played against the Bears at home. The Bears had started off 2–0 like us and were eager for a shot at the champs. They were also acutely aware of how we had dismantled the Giants the previous season and that we had established a dominating reputation—like the one that the Bears had enjoyed over the Packers for far too long. Momentum in that relationship had changed in recent years, and the Bears wanted it back.

We dismantled the Bears. We destroyed them, killed them, whipped them, however you want to say it. We handed the Bears the worst defeat ever in their long history, and it felt good.

After a scoreless first quarter where we saw Paul Hornung hurt his ankle again, we opened up our offense and exploded. Taylor scored a couple of touchdowns with his typical hard running. Starr was the definition of accuracy with passing scores to Ron Kramer, Elijah Pitts, and even running one into the end zone himself. The defense played with an unbelievable ferocity, rushing and sacking Billy Wade and Rudy Bukich, who were both heard yelling at their exhausted offensive line. We got five picks off the Bears' quarterbacks, including one that was run back for a touchdown.

We left Bears bodies all over the field. They talked earlier in the week about what they were going to do to the champs and how this would once again be their season. They started right but then ran into a team more possessed and powerful than they could have possibly imagined. When it was all over, we defeated Papa Bear Halas' team by an embarrassing 49–0 score. Worse than the Giants defeat. Worse than the ones from last season. Worse than ever. It set the tone for the Bears that season, sucking the fight out of them. They were expected to compete for the crown and instead finished a very average 9–5 on the season. It came down to that game and the doubt we put, or rather buried, into their heads.

It was funny to think that just a few years ago a win like this would have meant everything to this organization. To defeat our rival in such a dominating fashion would have equaled a successful season. But we were a different team now. We were champions with a lust for success. This was just a game, just a step on the path. We had to look forward because our next game was against the Lions.

Be willing to give an unknown a break.

If there was a team in the league that could equal the strength and fortitude of our team, it was the Lions. They were also considered a contender and came into our Week 4 game undefeated, as well. They would not take us so lightly. There was very little talk from the Lions that week as they witnessed what we had done to the Bears. They stayed relatively quiet, focused under Coach George Wilson. They knew they could match up with us, but they did give us the respect as champions (in public anyway). They wanted to do their talking on the field.

The Lions were a scary team, especially on defense. Led by their beastly defensive tackles Roger Brown and Alex Karras, they also featured a punishing linebacking crew with Joe Schmidt and a secondary that was one of the best in the league, led by Yale Lary. They were hard-hitting, dirty, and hungry for the ball. They refused to budge and didn't like anyone trying to push them around.

Neither did we. Both teams knew coming into this game that it would be a defensive struggle. We both had high-powered offenses, but the style of play from both teams and the game-planning called for a defensive chess match. We were able to jump out to a quick 3–0 lead on a Hornung field goal that we were able to hold for the first quarter and into the second.

However, we found that we could hardly move the ball after that. Their defense bore down on us, stuffing the run and filling the passing lanes. We experienced more three-and-outs in that game than we had in recent memory, and Coach Lombardi and the offense were clearly frustrated. On defense we held strong, chasing quarterback Milt Plum all over the field. For most of the first half, the Lions couldn't move the ball. They only had one solid drive that half and really for the entire game. Unfortunately, they were able to score on that drive, taking a 7–3 lead.

After the break, we continued to challenge each other back and forth, Detroit relenting only once to give us another field goal. Time was not on our side. We found ourselves down 7–6 with less than a minute left, and the Lions had the ball. We had timeouts remaining, but all they really had to do was run the ball to run out the clock and the game would have been over.

Instead, inexplicably, they decided to pass. The cost them the game and perhaps the season. It enraged fans and even Lions players who questioned whether the call had come from the coaches or from Plum himself. It was indescribable for those watching it, and yet maybe it was fate. Whatever it was, on the play, Plum dropped back to pass a quick out to his flanker who slipped. A little-used player on our team, Herb

Adderley, snatched the ball midair for a critical pick and set us up in Lions territory. Two running plays later, we kicked a field goal on the last play of the game for a 9–7 victory.

The game helped us continue our season of dominance and again did just enough to rattle the Lions to an overall record of 11–3. For Adderley, it essentially gave him the starting cornerback position, one that he played to five Pro Bowl selections, cementing his place as one of the greatest Packers defenders of all time.

Herb was drafted by the Packers in 1961 as a halfback. Coach Lombardi wanted him as a backup but eventually switched him to defense because of the depth we already had at that position. While some people struggle with such a drastic shift, Adderley was a natural on defense. Over the course of his career, he recorded 48 interceptions (39 with the Packers and nine with the Cowboys), including seven returned for touchdowns. He played sparingly in 1961, still getting used to the defense, and then he made an impact in a few of the early 1962 games. He was incredibly fast, something he didn't mind reminding us about at every opportunity. He was also a tough competitor who was ready to play his part and ready to take on whoever the opponent's top receiver was at any time. And could he talk, especially to those receivers.

"Hey boy, I'm just telling you, I'm gonna kill you if you catch that ball, man!"

Between him and Nitschke, there wasn't much need for the rest of us to say anything. Off the field, Herb was an incredibly warm guy. He was someone I got close to, eventually sharing an apartment with him and Elijah Pitts. Herb had come from a big college, Michigan State, and while he was a heralded athlete, he did not have a great experience there. He felt like he hadn't had the kind of support, leadership, and sense of community that he had hoped for, unlike those of us who went to smaller schools. He carried a bit of a grudge with him to Green Bay, hoping to find a family.

He wasn't alone. Lots of guys arrived here feeling the same. I'm proud to say that all of us found what we were looking for in Green Bay. We created that family atmosphere, that blending of all personalities, and it paid off for us in the end. In 1962, we welcomed Herb to the family, and he thanked us by building up an already unstoppable defense into something even greater.

By the time we faced the Bears again in Week 8, we were well aware of the streak we were on. Coach Lombardi had never placed much of an emphasis on streaks, not in professional sports. He had his superstitions and his habits, but he didn't like to talk about streaks, feeling they could end just as quickly as they began.

Still, it was hard for us not to notice. After our destruction of the Bears in our first meeting and our skin-of-the-teeth victory against the Lions the following week, we rattled off three more impressive wins in a row, a 48–21 shootout against the Vikings in Minnesota, a 31–13 dismantling of San Francisco at home, and a gutsy 17–6 win against the Colts in Baltimore. Coming into our second meeting against the Bears, we were 7–0 and the pundits were already talking repeat. Even more so, they were talking that we might not only be one of the greatest Packers teams of all time but one of the NFL's greatest teams.

Don't let success go to your head—stay focused!

It was difficult to ignore that kind of hype, especially for younger professional athletes. That's why I always feel so bad when I see a young prospect come out of college in this day and age of extensive social media, television coverage, and fast-paced news. There is so much hype and build-up for these kids that the pressure quickly mounts. Some of them can handle it. In fact, some thrive on it, finding comfort in all the attention. However, as we've seen a majority of the time, the pressure often gets to be too much, the expectations too high. There is little room left for development. Once the attention is on them, everyone from coaches, teammates, fans, press, and management, expects them to live up to ridiculous hype. Often they fail. Just take a look at the majority of first-round draft picks over the last decade in not just football but any sport. Many of them, kids who once graced the front pages and covers of sports magazines and appeared regularly on ESPN highlight reels, are long gone and long forgotten, at least in terms of professional sports.

Starting our season 7–0 got everyone talking—except our coaches. And if our coaches didn't talk about it, neither did we. They had their reasons. It wasn't because they didn't want us to focus on the streak. They had confidence that we could handle the pressure as we had proven time and time again. They knew we wouldn't get rattled or distracted by the attention, at least not enough to forget the mission or stray from the plan. We were too well trained. They didn't even fear that all the talk would get to us and we would slip up. Coach Lombardi believed in the power of pressure and expectations. He thought they worked hand-in-hand to build winners. That's actually why we didn't talk about the streak.

To Coach Lombardi, the streak just wasn't that important. It wasn't special. It wasn't any kind of unbelievable pressure. It was expected.

"I will never coach a team that accepts defeat," he told us. "I won't accept players who plan on doing anything other than win each and every time they take the field."

It wasn't that he just didn't accept losing. Coach Lombardi didn't *understand* it. To win seven games in a row, to finish the season undefeated, to never lose another game in the history of the Packers organization was not really an accomplishment. It was simply us doing our jobs. Where other coaches dream of an undefeated season, we were expected to do that each and every year. Every win wasn't an accomplishment. Rather, every loss was a failure. There were no streaks. There was just consistency.

That was passed on to each of us from the moment we joined the team, and it carried through the start of the 1962 season. We ignored what was being said and focused on the opponent each week. We looked at games one by one, truly buying into the take-it-one-game-at-a-time approach that so many coaches and players espouse in interviews. It's not a cliché. It's a way to thrive in your sport. We proved that.

Still, we knew we were winning and that we were leaving an impression on the league. We didn't really care about going undefeated. We cared about scaring the hell out of our opponents. So we did what we could individually to make sure we didn't curse the streak. Some players prayed, others carried good luck charms. And some of us ate at Chili John's.

I'm not exactly sure when that started, but I'm almost certain it was during this streak. A few of us black players discovered the chili restaurant one day walking around in Green Bay. Being such a small community, there weren't very many restaurants to choose from, and we were surprised to find one that we hadn't eaten at before. We just happened to pop in on a Tuesday afternoon and got to talking with the owner, a huge Packers fan who was more than thrilled to serve players from his team. To this day, that is some of the best chili I have ever had. It had the right mixture of spices and ingredients with just enough of a kick. We ate bowl after bowl, thanked our fan and headed out, already missing his chili. Next Tuesday, we found ourselves back there with more members of the team. The following Tuesday even more joined us and so on.

Somehow it just got be our thing to do during the season. The owner recognized that it was becoming a superstition and was always ready for us each and every Tuesday. We needed that chili every Tuesday. If we missed it, we didn't feel right. Something was off. There is a lot to be said about routine. Chili John's became an official Packers spot. Of course, we didn't let Coach Lombardi know that the dominance, focus, and consistent play of his Packers rested solely on one man's bowl of chili.

We entered Week 8, bellies full of chili, ready to once again prove to the Bears that we controlled the rivalry. They were still hurting from the last game. In fact, according to the reports, some of them were more than frustrated, they were angry. Some of them even commented on the fact that they thought we had unnecessarily run up the score. We weren't interested in getting into that argument and wanted to focus only on this game and not the past. We knew that this time the Bears wouldn't be surprised. They would come out with a fire and a fury, and we would have to be ready, especially since it was being played in Chicago.

Motivation and determination can go a long way, but we had more of it.

After an early back-and-forth battle with Jim Taylor continuing to rack up the running yards in his record season, our defense was able to break down the Bears. Tied 7–7, I got a solid pass rush on their quarterback, Billy Wade, forcing him to throw a pick to Nitschke that set up a field goal from Jerry Kramer, who was kicking in the place of the injured Hornung. Not long after, we forced a fumble that led to a touchdown.

We then forced another fumble when I knocked the ball out of Wade's hands and Bill Quinlan recovered. With the defense stepping up, the offense was able to take advantage and soon the score was 38–7 in front of a booing home crowd.

The streak continued, and the Bears' season was effectively over—always a point of pride for any Green Bay Packer.

We didn't have time to savor the victory, not that we ever really did. Our next opponent was going to be a big game for us. More than that, it was personal. Coach didn't mind personal grudges. In fact, he found them useful in getting his players fired up. But he also stressed that no one opponent was more or less important, or more or less dangerous, than another one. He didn't want us looking ahead to games because that set us up for failure when we met the teams in front of them. He insisted that our concentration and focus stay zeroed in on who we were playing each week.

Still, we all knew when were going to play the Eagles.

Many of us from the loss in the 1960 Championship Game were still on the team, and those who had joined us since understood how important that game was for the organization. We had come so close in 1960, and the pain was still there. Granted, the destruction of the Giants in the last Championship Game had helped ease it, but it wasn't gone. We had something to prove to the team that had actually beaten us, the team that had proven itself to be better than us. We couldn't wait to show them how much we resented that loss.

The Eagles never had a chance.

Our team came in at almost full strength, with everyone wanting to suit up and play at the scene of our last great loss. Even Paul, who was still reeling from his injury, got in on the action, not wanting to miss out on what was essentially a bloodbath. It all happened so fast that I'm not sure we were even aware of what was happening. I know the Eagles weren't. I could see the bewilderment in their eyes. How could this have happened? What was going on? Who were these guys?

It was beautiful.

Bart Starr was at his sharpest, completing both short passes and long bombs with absolute precision. Our defense refused to budge. Most impressive of all, our running game of Taylor, Hornung, and Moore was simply unstoppable. The scoring quickly piled up:

Touchdown, Moore: 7–0

Touchdown, Taylor: 14–0

Touchdown, Moore: 21–0

Touchdown, Moore pass to Dowler: 28–0

Touchdown, Taylor: 35–0

Touchdown, Taylor: 42–0

Touchdown, Taylor: 49–0

That's what redemption tastes like.

It would never taste as sweet as a win in that Championship Game would have, of course, but it was pretty darn close. For that season, a blowout of those proportions against that kind of team would have to do. Besides, we had more games in front of us and higher goals that went beyond redemption and streaks—goals that would make people forget about the 1960 Championship Game altogether. There were still some other teams in our way.

We were 9–0, and we knew it. That's not to say we were cocky or overly self-assured or obsessed with going undefeated. But we were a dominant team with closers, big-time players who could and would get the job done at all costs. Those who played us saw it. In 1962, the Green Bay Packers really became a fourth-quarter team. Coach had preached the philosophy of finishing strong since he had gotten there, and he had worked us so hard physically in practice that we were ready to apply that approach, more so that year than in years past. We would hang around with a team (if we didn't blow them out right away), and then we would out-will them in the fourth.

With each win, the pressure mounted. It would not have been surprising if the team experienced a bit of a letdown after our back-to-back demolition of the Bears and the Eagles. But we won our next game, a tight one against the Colts that really exemplified the fact there was very little that could rattle us that year—especially on defense. There were two sequences in that game that proved to the rest of the league just how good we could be, if holding the Bears and Eagles to a combined seven points wasn't enough.

Early in the game, the Colts drove the field and set up a fake field goal that took the ball to our 1-yard line. We got back to the huddle, frustrated at how they had not only moved but also deceived us. They were not going to score. We yelled at each other, each man committing to stopping them no matter what.

On first down, the Colts tried a run with their halfback up the middle and we sniffed it out, all converging our massive frames up the gut to block the hole. No gain. On second down, they tried a run to the left, but Willie Wood, Bill Forester, and Jesse Whittenton were right there to contain their back for a short loss. Third down brought another run up the middle and another loss of down with no gain. Frustrated, the Colts decided to go for it on fourth down, rolling Unitas out for an option run/pass. Forester was right there in his face and dropped Unitas for a 13-yard loss.

Later in the game, after we went up 17–13, the Colts had one more chance manufactured by a fake pass and a run by the ever-elusive Unitas, taking the ball all the way down to our 7-yard line with little time left on the clock. Again, first and second down went nowhere. On third down, Ray Nitschke dropped the runner at the 2-yard line. On fourth down—their last attempt to score—Ken Iman blocked a pass from Unitas, and that was the game.

The Packers were 10–0 with four games left. We felt good about where we were and what we were looking to do. And then Thanksgiving happened.

It wasn't that we thought we were that much better than the Lions or that we could beat them easily. After all, we all remembered the only reason we had come out victorious the first time was because of a fluke pass picked off by Herb. No, we weren't looking past them. We weren't tired. We weren't under-prepared. We weren't even buying into the hype about our team. Honestly, I don't know what we were.

Except dominated.

By the start of the fourth quarter, we were trailing 26–0 in a stunner. We were angry and frustrated. The offense was confused and tired from being chased by the Lions defense. Coach Lombardi was dumbfounded. Was this even the same team? It became apparent that this one had gotten away, so we tried our best to relax. Rumor has it that Max McGee even went into the offensive huddle and told Bart Starr to throw an interception so nobody got hurt, which made them all quietly laugh for fear that Coach would see them.

The game was an embarrassment, but at the very least we didn't have to worry about the streak anymore. We could now focus 100 percent on the prize. The Lions game was a setback, but we quickly rebounded with three wins in a row to end the season 13–1, earning another trip to the Championship Game, this time as the favorite against a team that would be eager to face us—the New York Giants.

Study your competition, know them inside and out, and you will have an advantage.

This time, we were the clear favorites.

It actually had very little to do with the hurting we put on the Giants the previous season in the Championship Game. Each season is a new season, each team is a new team. The Giants had a good one with eight players who reached the Pro Bowl that year, an experienced coach, and a 12–2 record that included a nine-game winning streak. Plus, they still had some players, including their gunslinger Y.A. Tittle, who could taste the embarrassing loss we had handed them last year and were looking for a little revenge.

We were almost everyone's pick to win. In that season, we outscored our opponents 415–148, a combination of sheer dominance by our defense and precision by our offense. We also picked up some awards along the way with Bart Starr leading the league in passing percentage (62.5%), Willie Wood leading in interceptions (9), and a major accomplishment that meant everything to Jim Taylor, the single-season rushing yards award (1,474) and touchdowns scored (19). At the time, he was the only player in NFL history to lead the league in individual rushing and scoring. Even more satisfying for Jim was that it was the one year that he actually beat out Jim Brown in those categories, proving to himself and to any doubters that he could compete with any running back in the league. On the defensive side of the ball, we were just as strong. Our linebackers, safeties, and cornerbacks were considered among the game's elite, and our line was quickly developing a menacing reputation of aggressive pursuit, patience, and a hold-steady approach to stopping the ball carrier. As we dominated as a unit, some of us started to gain attention from the league and the media, including me.

I was in my third year with the Packers and had finally gotten extremely comfortable with Coach Lombardi's and Coach Bengtson's systems. At this point, I knew I would be a regular starter as long as I played my game, so I didn't have the extra pressure of worrying about going back to the bench. I just had to show up and do my job, and there was no doubt that was exactly what I would do each and every week. I also felt like I was a veteran on the team and could be more vocal in my leadership. I had always tried my best to lead by example, but now I could do my part in getting us together to accomplish the task at hand. These leadership skills helped me go far later in life and in the business world. They were developed on the practice fields, in meetings, huddles, and locker rooms in Green Bay.

I worked on my personal approach to defense, all within the system, of course. I was an aggressive player and a reactive player and always had been. Coach always said I played with a "reckless abandon" that was fueled by powerful instincts. Those instincts often proved right, and even when they didn't, I was so aggressive about them that I typically did something to disrupt or disorganize the play, giving some of the other players on our team an opportunity to make a key play.

But I wanted to do more. I wanted to get inside their minds. I wanted to know what they were going to do, not just take my best guess. I wanted to sort it all out in advance and be ready. I studied the films and watched for patterns in opposing offenses and anything else that would tip their hands. It continued on the field, especially for the first part of the game. I analyzed everything the guy across from me did, how the offensive line set up or shifted when certain plays were called, where the quarterback liked to look first in a passing play, and how the running back took the ball on a handoff. I watched the eyes, the gestures, and the movements. I listened and observed. I trained myself to know more than they wanted me to know.

I also made damn sure they couldn't read me. I knew that for every player I watched, someone on their team was watching me. I wanted to make sure they could never get a full read on what I was doing. I constantly changed my approach over the course of a game. If I thought they expected me to go inside, I would do it once or twice and then go outside. As soon as they got comfortable with that, I went back in. I changed the point where I charged in. Sometimes I would be a little more patient, and sometimes I would come barreling in. I also talked to them, doing whatever I could to not only learn a little info but distract them from analyzing me.

For a good part of my career, the Colts had an offensive lineman, George Preas, who was a solid player and also a student of the game. I always felt like he was analyzing me just as much as I was analyzing him, and we would call each other out on it, talking to each other the entire game, trying to throw each other off.

"Hey man, I noticed you did this on that last play!"

"You didn't notice nuthin'!"

"Here's where I'm comin' for ya on the next play!"

"Stop wasting your breath, you ain't gonna do nuthin'!"

I became a man obsessed with the role of defensive end. Each week's opponent, each week's matchup became the most important thing in the world to me. I would lay in bed all week, thinking about my opponent and the ways that I would go about beating him head-to-head. I relived the training, the study, the planned attack over and over again until it truly became second nature. I took my performance from the previous game, reveled in it only slightly, and then set my sights on who was next. I built off that victory, studying on Monday and Tuesday, pushing myself Wednesday and Thursday, and finding that calm and the plan on Friday. Saturday we traveled, and it was about staying focused, determined, and hungry. When Sunday came around, there was no doubt. I already knew what the result would be before we even stepped onto the field. I had seen it, felt it, and determined it. Now all I had to do was execute.

That type of dedication and preparation was not unique to me. Coach Lombardi had us all focused, all pushing ourselves to be better, all looking to do the extra little things that could mean the difference between glory or defeat, which explained why we were a dominant team in 1962 and why we were favored. We were the best team in the league. Now it was up to us to finish it, to take home the crown yet again.

For as confident as we were, we were also dinged up. Paul Hornung had a sore knee that continued to aggravate him, and Jim Taylor started dropping weight from an illness. Several other offensive weapons were also nursing injuries. The defense was holding steady, but it had been a long season yet again, and it had taken its toll on all of us. Still, there wasn't one person on this team who wasn't ready to play.

The same was true for the Giants and the 64,000 fans that had packed into Yankee Stadium. The players were ready and eager to get their shot at redemption. We were littered with boos when we took the field, and signs all around the stadium being hoisted by fans in thick coats let us know exactly what they wanted: "Okay Y.A., Make Green Bay Pay!"

The Giants players were just as fired up, talking to us during warm-ups and all the way up to game time and then some.

"Hey man, I know you did this and that to so-and-so, but you ain't gonna do that shit to me!"

"Today is our day."

"You shouldn't even have bothered comin'!"

We expected nothing less. We had embarrassed them completely the year before, and they were mad. Just as we were mad earlier in the season coming into the Eagles game. We knew what they were feeling, what they wanted, and we knew we would not have the benefit of them underestimating us again. We blocked it all out, the taunts, the fans, the pressure of the moment, and we focused.

We were ready for everything except the cold. The game-time temperature was around 18 degrees, but there was a fierce wind blowing off the bay that dropped it 20 degrees if not more. I played in the famous Ice Bowl a few years later and several other cold games in Green Bay, but I swear this Championship Game in New York was one of the worst.

The turf was basically a skating rink and so frozen there was absolutely no way anyone could get any traction. We all switched to rubber shoes, as if we were playing the game on a basketball court. It didn't help.

What did help at least a little was a new innovation that teams had started using during games in cold climates. The 1962 season saw the start of big heaters on the sideline to help keep the players warm. On a day like this, they were a blessing. The only problem was we weren't quite used to them or the technology, and we kept burning our frozen hands by keeping them in front of the heaters for too long.

Despite the cold, we kept our composure. We huddled in the locker room for one last moment, no speech needed by our great leader. We had been working for this all season, and now it was time to go to work.

The Giants expected us to come out strong with a heavy passing game supported by our triple-threat running attack. Starr had been a precision passer all season and defenses feared him, meaning they had to always respect his arm and play back just enough to let our running backs get the room they needed to run. It was an incredibly efficient offense that managed to open up both pieces of our attack, making us virtually unstoppable. Coach Lombardi knew that the Giants would be prepared for our offense to pass first.

So he decided to have us pound the ball with our running game of Hornung, Taylor, and Moore. The Giants defense was notorious for its ability to stop the run, but we were hoping to catch them off guard, put them back on their heels, and confuse their game plan. And though Coach wouldn't admit it, we also thought it might have been Coach Lombardi's way of imposing his will. We would beat them where they were strongest, and they would have no fight left in them. We opened with a long, slow, punishing drive that resulted in a Jerry Kramer field goal to put us up 3–0.

Then it was the defense's turn. Both coaches had emphasized how important our defense was going to be in this game. We knew this Giants team would probably be able to slow down and even stop our offense at times. It was up to us to hold them at bay, to get the ball back so we could continue to pound it down their throats. Our offense reminded us what we had done to the Giants last year, and they asked for a repeat performance. We were willing to do our part.

"We will not be bullied today," was all I had to say to my defensive teammates as we took the field for the first time. My fellow combatants just nodded.

But on the Giants' first possession, Tittle and the Giants surprised us with a short passing attack, completing several 5–10 yard passes in a row, confusing us on where to line up for a time. We quickly recovered. After a few completions, Y.A. threw a pass that Ray Nitschke deflected and Dan Currie picked off, running for a return that could have possibly gone for a touchdown if Dan hadn't slipped. The Giants held us on that possession but not long after, on another Giants' drive, Dan made Phil King fumble. This time it was Ray's turn to recover the ball, giving us possession at the Giants' 28-yard line.

The defense was already frustrating Y.A. and quieting the crowd. We blitzed more than we had ever blitzed before, and it was throwing him off his game. We were in constant pursuit, hands raised high to the sky to not let anything past. I know I got him a couple times, but Ray was an absolute monster, chasing, blocking, and tackling whatever came his way. Ray was playing like a man possessed, like a man with something to prove. He had been on the bench for too long, and he would not be returning to it. I knew the feeling.

On that offensive possession, we kept handing the ball to Taylor, who found himself used and abused by the Giants defense, especially by future Hall of Famer Sam Huff. Jim said later that Sam and other players on the defense were scratching, pushing, kneeing him in the groin, doing whatever they could to slow him down. At one point, Huff hit Jim in the helmet so hard that Jim bit his tongue and spent a portion of the game swallowing his own blood. Needless to say he didn't exchange the kindest words with the Giants' defense. At one point, when he thought he saw Huff's exposed calf after a tackle, he bit—hard. It was only when he heard the yell and the swearing that he realized that leg actually belonged to Dick Modzelewski.

Jim was eventually able to struggle his way in for a satisfying and well-deserved touchdown to put us up 10–0. At that point, the temperature seemed to drop and the wind picked up, making everyone uncomfortable. As such, the play got a little sloppy and erratic. It felt like the kind of game that would be determined by the team that could take advantage of mistakes—and we made the next one.

After being stopped deep in our own territory, Erich Barnes blocked Max McGee's punt and it was recovered in our end zone by Jim Collier to make it a ball game at 10–7. Max got a good snap and went through his normal motion of punting, but they got a good rush and found a hole to the kicker. Just like that, the Giants were back in business.

Luckily, they returned the favor. After forcing us to punt again, the Giants botched the return and Ray, who was flying down field, was able to recover the ball, setting up Jerry Kramer's second field goal and putting us up 13–7. Kramer added one more on a later possession to make it 16–7. After that, the cold and the defenses joined forces to do their job on both offenses. Neither team moved the ball.

We watched the clock move achingly slow, ticking down unwillingly to 00:00. Finally, it relented, and we were champions once again. We rushed the field congratulating each other and our coaches. Amidst the jubilation that comes with a culmination of all the hard work, hours, blood, sweat, and tears, I did catch a sad image, one that is always tough to see—the picture of the person or the team that came up short.

As my teammates celebrated around me and we walked off the field to carry the party into the locker room, there was Y.A. Tittle, one of the greatest quarterbacks of our generation, kneeling on the ground, exhausted from being chased all game long, and banging his fists into the frozen field in utter frustration. We had beaten him again, this time at home. For as sweet as redemption tastes, there is nothing more bitter than failing to get your revenge.

The championship win got us thinking of something we didn't even dare talk about throughout the season—the possibility of a three-peat. It was relatively unheard of at the time, not just in football but all sports (with maybe the exception of the New York Yankees). There was so much parity in the league even back then and it was such a brutal game that the idea of a team going the distance three times in a row was tough to fathom. Yet we had done it twice, and most of our team was returning—a team comprised of several All-Pros, including myself.

It was a tremendous honor for me to be recognized for my efforts by the league. Just a few years ago I was a bench player lost in Cleveland, and now I was an All-Pro defensive end for the champions. It made me want to push harder, to accomplish more. It made me want to be a leader and hold on to this title, this honor.

I didn't make the Pro Bowl that year, despite predictions that I would, and I have to admit that I was extremely disappointed. I felt like I had earned it. Coach Bengtson thought I had as well, but his words made me feel better.

"You just need to realize that this thing just happens this way some-times," he said. "I can tell you that there's nobody going to the Pro Bowl that's better than you, and if you keep it up, your time will come."

I believed him, and the All-Pro honors helped. It proved I was going in the right direction just as the team was, and there was something very satisfying I found about winning. I wanted to do it for a third time.

| Chapter 13 | **Back to College—and Beer** |

Take calculated risks, even when you don't necessarily need to.

Throughout my life, whether on the field or off in my various careers, I have prided myself on taking chances and taking advantage of opportunities that came my way.

It may seem like common sense, but in order to be successful in any kind of venture, these two approaches are an absolute must. It doesn't matter if you're talking about sports, business, or just life in general. There needs to be a willingness to take calculated risks—and I can't emphasize the word *calculated* enough—and an openness to certain opportunities that come your way—because they will.

Now that's not to say that there won't be some opportunities that come along that will simply be missed, but truly successful people learn even from those missed opportunities and they gain a sense of what to look for in the future or how to accept new challenges. Life has a funny way of putting those opportunities right in front of us, testing whether or not we have the insight, strength, and desire to pursue them. It's up to us to say yes. Successful people learn to say yes because they know it's the only way to take those steps on the path to success. Taking risks and taking advantage of opportunities that arise along the way are truly the only ways to accomplish our goals and fulfill our dreams.

Those opportunities aren't always clear right away. They may take time to develop and, as such, uncertainty can come into play—and patience. After the 1962 season, I took advantage of an opportunity that came my way, one I initially accepted to help me make a few extra bucks. I had no idea that summer job would eventually lead me to become a highly successful player in the business world, an industry leader, and a director working on some of the biggest and most important boards of directors in the country.

When I still played for the Browns, I happened to attend a banquet in Cleveland where I ran into a guy who was the regional manager for a Pittsburgh-based brewery named Duquesne Brewing Company. "The Duke," as it was referred to by the trade, was a popular beer in the Ohio/Michigan/Pennsylvania region of the country, and they were looking to expand to the Cleveland market. Duquesne, which would shut down less than a decade later, was peaking and looking to take full advantage of its place in the local market.

We got into a conversation, chatting about football and the event, when he asked me how I was spending my time in the off-season. I told him about teaching, and he could tell it wasn't exactly a job I was passionate about.

"Have you ever thought about going into the beer business?" he asked.

I hadn't. And if I had told him no, that could have ended the conversation right there. Instead, I decided to open up about my childhood dream of owning a business. I proceeded to tell him all about the rejection I faced coming out of high school and how I had settled for pursuing a teaching degree. I told him how I hadn't lost my zeal, my desire to work in business, to study and eventually make a name for myself in the business community. I'm not real sure why, but I found myself opening up more with this stranger about that dream than I had with anyone in a long time—and I apparently made a compelling case.

"If you really want to pursue something in business, you should consider the beer business," he said.

I told him I would, shook his hand, and we went our separate ways. A week later, I got a call from him saying that he and his people at The Duke wanted me to work for them. I became a special regional representative for the company, using my status and appeal as a professional football player to make appearances, do promotions, and work with the sales reps to help them potentially sign new customers. It was a part-time gig that I could do mainly during the off-season, and it paid better than the substitute teaching job.

At the time, I didn't have any grand hopes or expectations as to where such a job could take me, but I did recognize it as an opportunity to get my foot in the door of the business world, even if it was on the bottom rung of the ladder. I jumped at the chance and spent the next couple years working for Duquesne.

It wasn't the toughest job. Many times I found myself sitting at a display, signing autographs, shaking hands, and talking with customers. Other times I made sales calls and did what I could to influence potential store owners to carry the brand. The company realized the public's fascination with professional athletes, and although I was nothing more than a role player in Cleveland, they were still taking full advantage. I was aware of it and enjoyed it.

I've always enjoyed talking with people, and I realized this opportunity was a way for me to get some firsthand training and experience and gain some perspective on how a business works. I was hungry for more, but this was a good start. Like I've done with everything I've pursued, I worked as hard as I possibly could. I started thinking to myself that if I did this the right way, it could possibly expand into something bigger down the road.

Not long after I arrived in Green Bay, that opportunity presented itself.

I attended a state wholesaler convention in Wisconsin and met a man by the name of Ben Barkin. Ben went on to help found the Great Circus Parade, an immensely popular tradition in Milwaukee, an old-fashioned celebration of the excitement caused when the circus came to town. Ben became one of the most influential people in my business career, someone who guided me, mentored me, and pushed me to success. At the time I met him, he was working as a public relations representative for the Joseph Schlitz Brewing Company, the highly successful distributor of "the beer that made Milwaukee famous."

Ben heard from reps at Duquesne about how good I was at my job and was eager to put me in touch with executives at Schlitz. Now spending a majority of my time in Wisconsin and in my new home in Chicago, it made more sense for me to work with a local distributor. I had experienced some great success with the Packers in my first few years, and the executives from Schlitz saw how that, combined with my passion for business and my hard work ethic, could benefit the company. Once they heard I was interested in working for the company, I was hired.

I essentially did the same kind of work for Schlitz that I did with Duquesne, but now that I had some experience under my belt, I felt I could be a little more aggressive in my pursuit of a business career. I still only worked part-time during the season, but I very quickly worked my way to full-time in the off-season. I also began to pitch ideas to company leaders in terms of how we could run promotions, how we could reach difficult markets, and how I could be more effectively utilized.

They listened. The company, already established in the industry, seemed to be growing. I began to see how this profession could be something much bigger for my future. This was not just a job, this was a possible career. I let them know I eventually wanted to be more than just the promotions guy. I wanted to learn the business. I wanted to work in as many facets of the company as possible. I told them that I was committed to growing in the company, doing what I had to do to go forward. I was told to have patience and do my job just as well as I had in Duquesne and I would have the opportunity. I committed to doing even better than that, and I made sure that I did whatever was required to impress them and give myself that chance.

That, I learned, is what successful people do with opportunities.

The off-season between 1962 and 1963 marked the beginning of a second lifetime for me, a career that has led me to succeed in much more than just football. But back then, I was just getting started, the path definitely moving forward but still unclear. Plus I had other priorities, as well. My football team was a two-time defending champion looking for a third championship, and it was time to focus on football.

There will always be interesting characters in your life.

If the Green Bay Packers had been on everybody's radar the previous year, in 1963 we were the top target. We suddenly became the team *everybody* circled on their calendar. We knew the days of underestimating the Packers were long behind us. Lucky for us almost everybody from our championship team was returning along with two huge new weapons to bolster an already powerful defense.

At cornerback we saw the emergence of Bob Jeter, a second-round pick out of the University of Iowa in the 1960 draft. Bob was a halfback with the Hawkeyes where he broke school records and won an MVP Award in the 1959 Rose Bowl for a performance in which he ran for 194 yards on just nine carries! Unfortunately for Bob, he was coming to a team loaded with All-Pro running backs and was never going to get a chance to really compete at that position. Determined to play, he worked on his defense, utilizing his speed at the cornerback position and finally receiving his chance in 1963.

With Bob alongside Herb Adderley, we had the best cornerback duo in football. They were fast, smart, and willing to hit. They also both had great hands and scared most quarterbacks into throwing short passes for fear of being picked off. They were also extremely competitive. During my tenure with the Packers, our defense was known as a group that played hard from the first to last snap, and those two guys epitomized that approach. Adding Bob completely changed how offenses planned to play against us and truly left them with few options in moving the football.

Up front, we also added another defensive end, our team's mystery man, Lionel Aldridge. A late-round pick out of Utah State, Lionel surpassed expectations and landed a spot on our roster, and soon after, a starting role on the line. He was quick, ferocious, and determined—and he showed all three traits all the time, whether it was in practice or in the game.

He was also a tough guy to read. I never quite understood Lionel. I'm not saying he was a bad guy or a bad teammate. He was just someone who seemed to have a lot of pent-up anger. As such, many of my teammates and I had trouble communicating with him. He also had an extreme temper. Even in practice, if somebody managed to block him during a drill or scrimmage, he seethed. Forrest Gregg, Bob Skoronski—none of the offensive linemen knew how to deal with him. By this point, other players, especially on the defense, were looking to me to reach out to new players, so I tried with Lionel. Most of the time, it was like talking to a wall.

I always felt his anger might have come from the fact that while he had been such a dominant player in college, he had to struggle to earn a spot on our team. It's not that uncommon. I experienced it when I first came up, and I tried sharing that with Lionel, but he didn't really seem to listen. I also got the impression he had some jealousy toward me. I was beginning to peak in my career. I had paid my dues and worked hard to get where I was, which brought some recognition around the league and with the media. Lionel didn't see it that way. He never had a real good relationship with the press, and there were a couple times I heard him scolding them after a game.

"You don't want to talk to me, you want to talk to Willie," he barked. "He's the one you write about anyway!"

I even tried to befriend him by praising his skills and reminding him how valuable he was to our team. After one particular game where we both had a couple of sacks, I went up to him afterward to congratulate him and he just scoffed at me.

"Bullshit," he said. "You're the one who gets the credit."

I always had the impression he thought my success somehow denied him his own success. He was very sensitive around me, and I had to treat him with kid gloves. Some days he was a great teammate, even a leader who was ready to do whatever he could for the Green and Gold. But there were too many days where we just couldn't figure out how to approach him and after a while, many of us stopped trying.

We found out after he retired from the game that Lionel suffered from paranoid schizophrenia, and that always made me feel bad. None of us knew at the time, and if we had, we probably could have done more, or at least we could have been more understanding of his struggles. Much later in his life, he wound up homeless, but I was very happy to hear through the grapevine that later in life he found some stability, rebuilding a life for himself and even helping other homeless and mentally ill people in need.

For as strained as our relationship was, nobody could take away Lionel's impact on the field. As we came into the 1963 season, our defense was as solid as ever.

On offense, we also found a new offensive weapon in Marv Fleming. He was 6'4" and about 230 pounds, a strong tight end and competitor with the squeakiest voice I've ever heard on a man. It's hard to compare it to anything other than to say that if you talked to him on the phone, you never would have guessed the voice on the other end belonged to a professional football player.

An 11th-round pick out of the University of Utah, Marv really became a more involved part of the offense a few years down the road, but even as early as 1963, he was a big play guy averaging almost 20 yards per reception and providing some key blocking for our running game. He was a dedicated teammate who instantly bought into Coach Lombardi's system and showed a willingness to play his part, even if it wasn't always the most glorious. He was also an extremely excitable guy who could be a little gullible at times, which made him a target.

Marv also had a tendency to find himself in unpleasant and unfortunate circumstances, and I typically had to be the guy to talk to him about it. I developed a leadership role on the team, especially among the other black players. Coach came to me to talk about any issues that were going on with those members. It was an honor for me and a job that I took seriously. I knew it was a sign that he trusted me, and it laid the groundwork for me being more involved with the team in the future.

One day Coach called me into his office and told me I had to talk to Marv. Coach had apparently received a phone call from a Wisconsin farmer who said there was some young black guy on the team who was trying to date his daughter, and if he didn't knock it off, he was going to shoot him. Nowadays that might seem a little far-fetched, but back in the early 1960s in a rural area like the Dairyland, a threat like that had to be taken seriously.

We both knew right away it was Marv. He was a young kid, a free spirit who liked to party. He was the youngest guy on the team, and he frequented the bars and clubs that would serve him. He also liked to talk about his partying and the girls he had met. I told Coach I would take care of it.

"Say Marv," I said to him as we got ready for practice. "I need to talk to you."

"Yeah," he said in that little voice. "Whatchoo want?"

We huddled up a bit, and I put my arm around him.

"Let me tell you, some guy just called Coach and said you were trying to date his daughter," I said.

"Who?" he asked.

"Some farmer," I said, and I saw the recognition in his eyes. "Yeah, he called Coach and said if you don't stop, he's gonna shoot ya."

His eyes got really big for a second, and then he looked right at me.

"You think he's serious?" he asked.

"You're a black man up here, and this guy's a white farmer who hasn't seen many black people and he's saying he don't want you seeing his daughter," I said. "You wanna test it?"

As far as I know, Marv never saw her again.

For as much as we picked on Marv, we all respected his talent, dedication, and willingness to accomplish the task at hand. He was yet another vital cog in the Packers machine, and his good nature and the fact that he was a good sport and a team player came in handy, especially as we got some news that rocked the team and put an enormous strain on our plans to repeat as champions.

Adversity is inevitable, especially with continued success.

A couple of months before training camp was set to begin, our Golden Boy, Paul Hornung, was suspended indefinitely from the NFL for betting on professional football games.

We knew a lot of gambling had gone on in the league for quite some time. It was just something a lot of the guys did in their spare time, even betting on football games. The commissioner's office had caught wind of it and enforced even stricter rules prohibiting that kind of activity. The bets seemed, for the most part, to die off. For as wild as Paul could be, he was incredibly intelligent and extremely dedicated to the Packers. It shocked us that he still took this kind of gamble, literally, and that he would jeopardize his career and the team's chances at success. To say we were disappointed was an understatement.

Coach Lombardi was more shocked than anyone. Coach had a very close relationship with Paul, almost treating him like a son at times. He had no idea that Paul was involved with gambling and didn't even know about the investigation. He appeared poised, in control, and even a little defiant in the public eye, saying that Paul had let down his teammates and the Packers would simply prepare to play without him. He also said Paul's return to the Packers depended upon how the team did without him and whether or not his teammates wanted him back.

We all knew that those harsh words coming from Coach meant he felt hurt and betrayed. Paul had let his gambling stand in the way of the things that Coach held most dear, namely the Packers organization. Yet at the same time, he tried his best behind closed doors to defend Paul's actions, saying he believed there was no way Paul would have continued to gamble if he had any idea there was even a chance of him getting caught.

The fans and the football community were just as surprised. Gambling around the league dried up quickly after that. If the commissioner was trying to make a point, it was well received. Players didn't want to mess with the rules if they were facing "suspended indefinitely" as a possible punishment. The fact that the league did this with one of its superstars proved to many lesser-known players that they could get the same or worse.

As Paul's teammates, we did what we could to rally behind him. We told him we supported him and that he would be welcomed back if and when he returned. But typical of a Coach Lombardi team, we weren't allowed to focus on Paul and his problems. We had a season to get ready for— a season that had just gotten a whole lot harder now that we were missing one of our top offensive weapons. Luckily we had great reserve running backs, and Tom Moore and Elijah Pitts were prepared to get a lot more carries. Jerry Kramer was a fantastic kicker, so he took over those responsibilities. Physically we were deep enough to cover the void left by one of our stars.

We did miss his leadership. We had plenty of leaders on that team, but there was something special about Paul. He had a way of getting us ready, getting us confident. He was a player who led by example and rallied the other players. It was up to other guys on the team to fill those shoes. Bart Starr, Forrest Gregg, Bob Skoronski, myself—several of us all put in extra time, got extra vocal, and pushed extra hard to cover for Paul. We got the team together to focus on the task at hand.

Inexplicably, we still came out looking unprepared, undisciplined, and unmotivated in our opener at home against the Bears, losing 10–3. It was a shocking loss despite the fact the Bears had loaded up on talent in the off-season, determined to best us after a few years of dominance on our part. Papa Bear Halas had quite enough of losing to the Packers, and he was prepared to make the deals the Bears needed to compete for a title against their rivals to the North.

At this point, we were worried as was Coach. It was too easy to blame the lack of focus, the lack of offensive movement, and the loss itself on the fact we were missing a key offensive weapon. But that wasn't the case. There was no way we should ever score only three points against *any* team.

There was a sense of uneasiness because nobody could figure out what was wrong. We were all working just as hard. Coach was pushing us to our fullest potential. Practices were running as smoothly as they could, and all of the players looked ready. Commitment was absolutely not the problem and never would be on a Vince Lombardi team. We were all extremely hungry to hang on to our championship trophy. We were doing every single thing we had done the previous two years when we were successful. So what was wrong? More importantly, what could we do to fix it?

Sometimes there's a solution. Sometimes you need to look a little deeper to find out what's causing the problems. Sometimes a string of failures requires introspection, examination, and ultimately change. Other times it requires patience, discipline, and staying on track. It requires trust that things will all come together through faith in each other and in the plan.

Sometimes fixing a problem means staying the course.

After the loss to the Bears, we won our next eight games in a row, all by convincing margins. The defense held teams to 7, 10, or 20 points, and the offense put up huge numbers, averaging in the 30s. We became unstoppable, the best offense in the league combined with the best defense. We started playing at a championship level.

There was no solution, no answer to our sudden success. It had been there the whole time, and it ultimately came down to execution. We were not a team to make excuses—the Old Man wouldn't allow it. We stuck together, kept our faith in each other and our leader, worked hard at our game plan, and committed to ourselves and to each other to do better.

During that streak, we had different players step up in each and every game. Sometimes it was the defense. In a 42–10 victory over the Rams, the defense put quarterback Roman Gabriel on the ground the entire game, blitzing and rushing, including a personal highlight for myself when I sacked him in the end zone for a safety. In a 31–10 win over the Lions, Boyd Dowler looked ready to step up and take the leading receiver torch from the aging Max McGee. In a 31–20 win against the Colts, Tom Moore showed he was looking more and more comfortable as a starting rusher, running the Packer Sweep with power and fluidity.

Unfortunately, during that streak we also had a scare in Week 6 when Bart broke his wrist in a 30–7 win over the Cardinals. With Hornung gone, we relied even more heavily on Bart's arm. He had been so dependable, including playing through bumps and bruises, that his back-ups hadn't gotten a lot of experience. Coach brought in veteran Zeke Bratkowski from the Rams to replace Bart. Zeke played for us for the next five years, often serving as an efficient backup for the times Bart got hurt. Zeke became a critical backup player, mainly because of the good friendship he established with Bart. The two were inseparable. On most teams, the quarterbacks were always looking to compete with each other, so there was some distance. With the Lombardi Packers, everyone knew their role and accepted it, trying to do the best he could. Nearing the end of his career, Zeke accepted that he was the backup quarterback and made sure he was always ready so that when his chance did come, we didn't really experience any kind of drop off in performance.

Upon his arrival in 1963, he couldn't get acclimated to the system in time. Instead, we went the next five games primarily with John Roach as our quarterback. A journeyman quarterback out of Southern Methodist

University, John wasn't going to win any MVP awards that season, completing less than half of his attempted passes and throwing a few more interceptions than touchdowns. But he had a leader's mentality, and he knew Coach Lombardi's system. With Roach in place and the other weapons we had, we were able to cruise into Chicago with an 8–1 record for a rematch with the Bears, who had the same record.

If there's one thing more frustrating than losing to your rival in a big game during a season, it's losing twice. We were simply outplayed. Their offense moved the ball on us at will, scoring 26 points. Their defense choked us off at every turn, allowing us to score only seven points. They looked like the better team.

We went into the game confident and looking for revenge. But they were even more fired up, and we just got pounded. It had been a while since the team was handled like that, and for the first time in a long time, we lost our composure, yelling at each other on the sideline and in huddles, taking out our frustrations at coming up short against the Bears yet again. Coach was beside himself, fuming and furious. We played our hearts out, but we were overmatched and the final gun couldn't come quick enough. Not only was this loss demoralizing to our team, it also put the Bears ahead in the standings with a two-win advantage over us, which meant we were probably going to need to win out the rest of our games and hope they lost one or possibly two games.

We weren't thrilled about the punishment we thought we were going to have to endure at practice the coming week, but all of that took a back seat on November 22, 1963, when we received the news that President John F. Kennedy had been assassinated.

Have perspective on what's truly important.

We were practicing in Milwaukee for our next game against the 49ers. I can still see Lee Remmel, the legendary *Green Bay Gazette* sportswriter and historian who covered the team (and later worked for us), hustling across the practice field to Coach, who was in a huddle with the offense, talking to them about a play. We all knew something was up because Lee was smart enough to never disturb practice unless it was an absolute emergency. I watched across the field as Lee whispered something to Coach, and his reaction frightened me. He looked as if he had just taken a bullet himself. His face got pale, and he seemed visibly stunned. He put his head down for a second, lost in thought, and then he called the entire team over to tell us the news.

Like everyone else in the country, we asked ourselves, "Could this really be happening?"

It hit me hard. It's impossible to predict how you're going to react to news like that, whether it's news that affects you personally or on a broader social scale. We all like to think we have the strength and fortitude to handle whatever life throws our way, and sometimes we do. But then there are those other times that can move you in ways you never thought possible, that can truly hurt you at your soul, those times that impact you forever. When Coach told us about President Kennedy's assassination, I forgot all about football. I felt like somebody had just beaten out every bit of energy and concern I had about the game in that moment. I had so much love and hope for our president and what he was trying to do with this country. As it's been documented many times before, President Kennedy was a man of power who appeared to be making a positive difference in terms of uniting our nation and its many cultures. He did so much for black people and really for all Americans, and there was just a sense this tragedy meant the momentum might stop or at least slow down. He was a great man who most people in the country could connect to in some way or another. One look at the faces in the Green Bay Packers huddle, with both black and white players from cities and small towns all over the country, said all that needed to be said about his impact on our nation. Nobody could speak.

Coach could have called practice right then and nobody would have cared. Instead, he spent a few moments telling us how important President Kennedy was to him personally. Then he got us back to work, fully aware that our concentration might not be what he typically expected. I don't think he wanted to continue with practice either, preferring to mourn the loss of his new friend and a man he truly admired. But he also knew what going back to work could do for us in terms of coping and as a distraction.

For the rest of that practice and the week, Coach was as soft as I had ever seen him. There was no hollering or screaming, which was highly unusual for him, no matter the circumstances. Practices and meetings were subdued, very low key, and shorter than normal as we all waited to hear if we would even play on Sunday or if the game would be canceled. On Friday we learned that there would be a game.

It was one of the most surreal games I was ever involved in. It actually didn't even feel like a real game at all. Unsure of what to do under these types of circumstances, the league made some adjustments, for better or worse, to cut down on the normal celebratory feel of the games. There was no starting lineup announced, no halftime band, and no television coverage. The game was just about two teams showing up to play for 60 minutes to record it in the books.

It was the one and only game in my life that I didn't feel like playing. I walked onto that field and just couldn't generate the excitement I normally had. The assassination had taken the heart out of me and pretty much everybody. If they had taken a vote, my guess would be that the players would have agreed to not play. As a result, it was a slow, sloppy game we still managed to win 28–10. There was no celebration.

The next week we played in our traditional Thanksgiving Day game against the Lions. With time came a bit more healing and actually, some of us felt a lot better when Coach started yelling at us again in practice. We were looking for a bit of a return to normalcy, and hard practices were the perfect cure.

We were also excited because Bart was going to come back to play. As he typically did when he returned from his injuries during his career, he played masterfully, showing no signs of rust in a 13–13 tie against a Lions team that didn't have a good record but came out and played some inspired football at home.

We were obviously disappointed with the tie, but we were even more frustrated when Ray Nitschke broke his arm in that game. We had dealt with our fair share of injuries that year, and this was just another one to add to the pile. Luckily, we still had enough depth to compensate for the loss. We couldn't focus on injuries. We were keeping pace with the Bears and had to focus on winning our last two games to have a shot at the championship game. It was still within our grasp, despite all the injuries, distractions, and other baggage that seemed to come up that season. We could still play for a third title. We believed we would.

We came out and played two great games in a row, against the Rams and the 49ers, winning both and finishing with an 11-2-1 record. In most seasons, this would have been enough. Unfortunately, in 1963, the Bears compiled a record of 11-1-2, including two wins against us. We had blown it for ourselves. We had lost twice to our rival, and that ended up being the difference. Even if we had just split those two games, we still would have had the better record. We would have gone to play the Giants yet again. Instead, we found ourselves in the Playoff Bowl against Cleveland, a game that neither team got fired up about. We won that game 40-23, but nobody cared.

We were not a team that could accept defeat. It started with our Coach and trickled down. We had faced adversity from the outset of the season and all the way through, but that was no excuse. Every team faces adversity, and the great ones find a way to push through. We hadn't accomplished the task at hand. We had a unique opportunity to be the first team in the modern era to win three titles in a row, and we let it slip through our fingers. We didn't even get a shot, and that was the hardest fact of all.

It was the first time in three years that I watched the Championship Game from home, and it didn't sit well with me. I made a personal vow to not let that happen again. It would be different next season.

The pain I felt from our team coming up short that season was slightly offset by a personal honor, one I treasured very much. After a tremendous season for me statistically and leadership-wise, I was bestowed with the honor of my first trip to the NFL Pro Bowl. I would have traded that individual honor for a chance for my team to compete for that third title in a row, but the prestige of being placed among the league's best that season was a bit of vindication and yet another piece of proof suggesting that if I set a goal and worked hard, I could achieve what I wanted and be rewarded for it.

And that's what sent me back to school.

It's never too late to pursue your real passion.

We all knew football wasn't going to last forever. The longevity of the average football player was less than ten years, and that meant there were many men who were jobless with little financial security by the time they were in their early 30s. That was a scary prospect. I wanted to make sure I didn't fall into that category. I knew I was still just at the beginning of my career, but I needed to keep an eye on the future and make sure I was covered if and when my football abilities started to slow.

I had my promotional/sales work with Schlitz Brewing, which was proving to be very interesting in terms of the opportunities I saw there. I made sure I worked as often as possible, which meant weekends and sometimes even weekdays around practice during the season. I paid attention and showed them how eager I was to learn. Any task that was given to me, however menial, I pursued and accomplished beyond expectations. I wasn't sure what the future held for me at Schlitz, but as long as I saw potential for a future, I was going to be ready to seize any opportunity that came my way.

Working for Schlitz also reignited my interest in my old dream of working in business. I always regretted letting my counselor talk me out of my pursuit of a business degree. It was something I looked at as a challenge that I didn't take on, and that wasn't like me. I had wanted to pursue a career in the business world since I was a small child, and that dream hadn't gone away.

I thought now might be the time to take on that challenge.

Following the 1963 season, I enrolled at the University of Chicago's Graduate School of Business to earn my MBA with a focus on marketing. In many ways, it proved to be one of the most challenging opportunities I ever pursued. I hadn't been in school for a while, so my academic skills were a little rusty and I'd never taken any real business courses. I knew very little about the school and the program other than it was a prestigious business school headed by renowned economist (and future secretary of the treasury and secretary of state) George P. Shultz, who became an invaluable mentor.

I also had an extremely full plate. Beyond my commitment to the Packers organization, I wanted to keep working at Schlitz as much as possible. I also started to take on a number of local speaking engagements, and I even continued to play in the occasional basketball game. Plus I had family obligations that included our four-year-old son.

But the idea of schedule overload never crossed my mind. It never has.

That's what being driven is all about. People who have the drive to succeed want to keep doing more. They crave opportunities. They aren't settled unless they're working on a variety of projects. They need to know how to balance their lives and prioritize everything they have going on, but they're not afraid to take on more. I have always been the kind of person who wants to say yes to opportunities. It helps when it's something you're passionate about, as it was with football and business. Because I played football, I knew I couldn't take a full course load during the season, so I took the occasional class and then took a majority of my courses in the winter and spring quarters.

I accepted the fact that I had to work extra hard to keep up with my course load. I needed more time than others to study the material and prepare for exams. I had to read more, re-read more, and seek help when I needed it. I was fine with that. That was the price I was willing to pay to get this degree. My dream was worth it.

I lived in the South Shore area of Chicago and drove to campus every day, getting there before 8:00 AM to get a parking spot. I spent almost my entire day at Harper Library, pouring over the books. Each course had its own collection of books, but to get all the info we needed, we had to check out others at the library. I spent so much time in that library, especially my first few semesters, that I earned a new nickname—Stacks Davis.

"Cuz you're always in the stacks!"

It wouldn't be the only harassment I'd get over my enrollment. Many of my teammates, especially the other black players like Willie Wood, gave me a ton of grief about being a student again. Several of the white players, like Hornung, Dowler, and my good friend Jerry Kramer, also joined in. I can't be sure, but I think this is where the nickname "Doctor" first started.

"Oh look everybody, here comes the Doctor! What you studying now, Doc? When do you get out of school?"

"Doctor" applied to several other stories. Some of my teammates started calling me Dr. Feelgood because I was always laughing and upbeat at practices. That turned into Doctor or Doc for short. I also had a habit of checking in with my teammates, especially later in my career when I was in a leadership role, and one of the first questions I would ask was, "How you feelin'?" There were some other stories, as well, but I think it really all started, especially among the other black players, when I went back to school. I never took their ribbing personally because I knew they all supported me.

Plus it was unusual for an athlete to pursue a degree in the middle of his playing career. Nobody else on our team was going for their Masters, and I would say less than 10 percent of the players in the league had post-grad ambitions in terms of furthering their education. Sadly, that number is even less with athletes today in a society where these young men are empowered with an abundance of money whether they play or not. In the current state of athletics, many athletes will never earn their degree. They have no incentive to do so. They are rewarded financially for their athletic prowess, earning more than a comfortable income whether they're a superstar or just a backup player. There is and always will be a debate on the worth of an athlete, whether or not they deserve the riches that are bestowed on them. Regardless of opinion, a sad truth is that the sharp rise in player salaries has pushed many young men to skip college and thus lose out on the education, development, and life skills learned there.

If there was one player on the team who truly appreciated my pursuit of a degree, it was Bart Starr. Bart, as kind as he was, never once took part in giving me grief. Instead, he talked to me about the struggles of school and encouraged me to stick with it, telling me that what I was doing was inspirational. I was scared but also excited. Going back to school made me feel like a winner, like I might be able to achieve my dream after all.

Chapter 14	Our Last Year in the S--- Bowl

Sometimes things simply don't go the way they should.

It's true for everyone, even a team as talented as ours. Of all the seasons I played with the Green Bay Packers, 1964 was the most inexplicable.

There were a number of factors that contributed to what can only be called a down year. Some thought there was still a bit of a hangover from the previous season, a bitterness for having missed the Championship Game for the first time in three years despite an impressive record. Some speculated teams were just more ready for us. Some pointed to the injuries and how it affected team chemistry. Some suggested that we had peaked as an organization, that we had players who were perhaps past their prime.

Coach Lombardi didn't care to hear any of those excuses, and he didn't believe any of them. The 1964 season was the most frustrating of his illustrious career, as it was for most of us. To this day, I still can't quite figure out what went wrong with the Packers that year. But we felt it week after week—the frustration, the inability to execute, the wrath of our coach, the disappointment, and the fear that maybe we weren't as good as we thought. Something happened in 1964, and it was something we never, ever wanted to experience again.

The season started with us losing a valuable member of our offense and adding two more pieces on defense, two guys who helped set us up for future championships.

A big loss for us was our veteran center and perennial Pro Bowl attendee Jim Ringo. Coaches often say center is truly the key position on any offensive line, the anchor that connects the line to the offensive arsenal. Also, as many coaches have discovered through the years, an All-Star center is tough to find. We had one that had been with the organization in good times and bad, someone who not only knew our system and coaches but had also developed key relationships with our quarterback, running attack, and the other members of the line both new and old. Jim Ringo was a leader, a dedicated Packer who played 126 consecutive games for the Green and Gold in 10 seasons, making seven Pro Bowl appearances.

The reasons behind his departure are still a mystery, something of Lombardi Legend. The rumor (that many of us believed) was that Coach Lombardi had been trying to get Jim to sign a contract extension in the off-season but was unable to reach him. After several failed attempts, Coach finally got Jim in for a meeting. Jim brought an agent.

Back then, Jim was the only person I knew who had an agent. Having somebody else manage your business affairs was a new concept, and in most cases owners didn't know how to deal with them. Previously, owners dictated contract terms. There was very little negotiation, especially before the AFL came along. We were valued at a certain price, we knew what that price was, and we got what we expected—and not a penny more.

Jim supposedly came in with his agent and demanded more money than what Coach and the Packers were offering. We heard Coach was furious both insulted by the presence of the agent and that one of his players was making a demand of *him*. He apparently excused himself into a separate room, made a phone call, and came back five minutes later to tell Jim he had been traded to the Eagles.

It was the shining example of how Coach controlled the team, how what he said was law no matter what. If you didn't like it, you'd be gone. Nobody was bigger than the team, Coach would have no problem making an example out of anyone, including one of our best players. We all heard the Jim Ringo story, and we got the message.

We found out much later that Jim's trade didn't exactly go down that way. While he did want more money and tried to have an agent negotiate the deal, Jim admitted he had mentioned to Coach how he wanted to go to Philadelphia to be closer to his family. Coach had little time, patience, or understanding for anyone who didn't feel 100 percent committed to the Packers, and I'm sure from the moment they had that conversation, Coach was at least open to trade options. In fact, it came out later that Coach had already been thinking of Jim as a bargaining chip for a linebacker from the Eagles by the name of Lee Roy Caffey.

Lee Roy was a late-round draft pick out of Texas A&M who had blossomed early, winning All-Rookie honors in 1963. He was an extremely talented running back who had been converted to linebacker, and he brought his speed with him. Lee Roy had a unique approach to his position in that he typically waited a few seconds after the ball was snapped to determine where he was going to go, partly because of the faith he had in his speed. Lee Roy knew he was faster than most of the players on the field, and he could catch up to just about anyone. He wanted to see the play develop in front of him so he could figure out the best path to the play. He looked to see where there was an opening, and that's where he would go. Sometimes he would be dead wrong, and that's when we got to see Lee Roy's other talent—his ability to talk—a lot.

"Who's guy was that?" he'd yell when he came back into the huddle. "Ray, you gotta cover that guy!"

"Lee Roy, I'm telling you that's your guy!" Nitschke would fire back, but Lee Roy would just shake his head.

"No, no, no, you got that hole, that's your man. Now let's go! Let's get 'em this time!"

Most of the time, Ray was right. For as talented as Lee Roy was (and he was an unbelievable blitzing defender), he also had problems focusing. I swear in all the years he and I played in Green Bay, he never once completely learned the defense, often faking his way and relying on his instincts. I think Coach Bengtson knew, as we all did, but with Lee Roy, it was tough to get a word in.

"Awwright boys, let's go!" he'd yell in the huddle, and then as we broke, he'd come over to me for a quick second. "Willie, who do I get this time? Where am I supposed to go?"

I'd tell him and he'd break away, still jawing.

"Awwright, let's go now!"

That year also brought us Dave Robinson. A standout player for Penn State, Dave had the distinction of being drafted by three different organizations in the same year. He was drafted by the Packers in the first round. In the AFL, he was drafted by the San Diego Chargers in the third round, who planned to offer his rights to the Buffalo Bills. He also got an offer from the Montreal Alouettes of the Canadian Football League. Dave chose to come to Green Bay because of what we had already achieved and our potential to go even farther. He also got "the talk" from Coach Lombardi. The Packers wanted Dave so bad they offered a large contract to lure him in; two years for $45,000 with a $15,000 signing bonus. Big money!

Dave converted from his natural position as tight end on offense and spent his first year in Green Bay learning and backing up Dan Currie at linebacker before taking over in 1964. If Lee Roy leaned more toward winging the game plan, Dave went to the other extreme. He might have actually known too much! Having received an engineering degree and academic honors from Penn State, Dave was an incredibly intelligent player who spent a lot of time analyzing every nuance of his opponent and learning all possibilities on every play. He was constantly trying to point out things to us like patterns in the offense, clues to what they were going to run, even his thoughts on who was fatigued, unfocused, hurt, etc. And if there was one thing he shared with Lee Roy, it was his ability to talk—especially to our opponents.

"Hey man, we know what you doin'. You can't be running that. Don't even try it now."

When Lee Roy and Dave started flanking me on both sides, I never played in a quiet game. Also like Lee Roy, Dave was a huge playmaker, someone we could trust to get the job done when the game was on the line. During his time in Green Bay, Dave put up unbelievable numbers in tackles and even interceptions. He was a three-time Pro Bowler, including one Pro Bowl MVP and a member of the 1960s All-Decade Team. Unbelievably, he has not been asked to join the Pro Football Hall of Fame.

With Lee Roy, Dave, and Ray Nitschke, we had arguably the best linebacker trio in the history of the game. Bolstering our defense brought us a good deal of confidence heading into the new season. So, too, did the reinstatement of our Golden Boy, Paul Hornung.

When Paul was suspended "indefinitely," there was no indication of when or if he would be able to come back. The commissioner made it clear that Hornung's return would be at his discretion. Apparently, Paul showed just the right amount of contrition, and in early March 1964, he was told he could rejoin the team. Paul had a lot of making up to do in Coach Lombardi's eyes. We all heard about how angry the Old Man was, and rumor was that he explored trading Paul Hornung or cutting him. But Coach loved Paul and what Paul could do for the Packers, and we knew Coach would stick with him.

Paul joined the team and reported back to camp to work out early with Bart Starr and Boyd Dowler. His return to us was as quiet as his departure. There were no special meetings, no apologies, nothing other than the usual greetings. We all appreciated the delicacy of an ugly situation and that he had been through enough. We knew Paul well enough to know he felt bad about letting down the team. We also knew he was not one to apologize. Rather, he showed how much this team meant to him by going out there and doing what he always did, working hard on every single play from practice to game time. He was a leader and would regain our trust and respect by leading us.

In terms of Packers football, there isn't much to write about in the season of 1964. I was excited to make my second consecutive Pro Bowl appearance that year, but Lombardi's Packers based their success on one thing and one thing alone—winning. That was something we just didn't do enough of in 1964.

We had a number of problems. We found ourselves dealing with injuries to key positions. Bart Starr found himself in and out of the lineup with minor injuries. Each week, someone from the defense seemed to go down with some kind of ailment. Also the offensive line was dinged up all season, which meant protection for our quarterback and running backs wasn't as solid as it had been in the past.

One of the scarier injuries sidelined Jerry Kramer for most of the season. Jerry had been complaining about stomach pains for some time, excruciating pain that periodically sidelined him. It got so bad that there was talk the injury might even be something untreatable like a form of stomach cancer. When it started to get worse, we seriously worried about the life of our teammate. After a series of tests and X-rays, doctors discovered a huge splinter of wood had lodged itself in Jerry's midsection, infecting his stomach. He had gotten the injury as a child when he hit a wooden post while chasing a calf on his family farm. Somehow over the years, the injury (and the piece of wood) had gone unnoticed until 1964 when it started to flare up. To see the size of the chunk of wood is a marvel in itself, and how he didn't notice it sooner is a mystery.

With Jerry out (and Jim Ringo traded), our line was softer. Plus Jerry was our backup kicker to Paul Hornung, and with the exception of the first game, Paul struggled in his first year back, missing a remarkable 26-of-38 field-goal attempts. Those missed field goals and extra points came back to haunt us in several games, including our Week 2 loss to the Colts. Paul muffed an extra point, and we lost the game 21–20.

Being a leader means sometimes taking one for the team.

We had experienced so much success in the past few seasons, we found ourselves getting more and more frustrated with each other and with our play. There was less focus among the players and more yelling and squabbling. The more the losses and/or close wins mounted, the more the tension and frustration grew. The same could be said about Coach Lombardi's anger.

He never handled losing well. He never would. Coach hadn't experienced a team that was less successful in a long time. After a Week 4 loss to the lowly Vikings put us at 2–2, Coach came into the locker room with a fury that needed a place to be unleashed. He had vented his frustrations on the offense the first few weeks and knew at this point his screaming may be falling on deaf ears. It was the defense's turn, and allowing a late drive by Fran Tarkenton that resulted in a field goal to give the Vikings the win gave Coach his reason.

Coach stormed into the locker room before practice a couple days after the game. He scanned the room and pointed to some of the defenders, calling us out by name.

"Lionel Aldrich, Ron Kostelnik, Henry Jordan, and Willie Davis, all of you stand up!" he bellowed.

We were all a little confused and frightened by how he used our full names. It wasn't uncommon to see Coach single out players for certain mistakes, but he never had people stand up. We got up slowly, and I made sure not to look Coach in the eye.

"You didn't show up against Minnesota," he said. "This defense did not do its job, and I want you all to apologize to your teammates!"

He let that hang in the air, and the entire locker room was stunned. I looked around at the other players, both offense and defense, and they didn't know whether to laugh or take this seriously. When my eyes met his, there was no doubt.

The timing seemed strange. Sure the defense had given up a late drive, but we had held solid for most of the game. The final score was 24–23, and once again, the reason it wasn't tied was because we had an extra point blocked. But we listened to Coach, always. We all quietly apologized and sat back down, waiting for Coach to finish his practice notes. Once he left, there were plenty of laughs at our expense, especially from the offensive linemen.

After the practice was done, Coach called me into his office as he often did during my time there. My locker was close to the entrance, and he often peeked his head around the corner, telling me in hushed tones to come see him before I left. On this particular day, he could tell I was angry about what he had done but that I would never admit it.

"Willie, I want you to know that you weren't that bad in the Vikings game," he said. "But the defense as a whole—well, you guys were awful."

He went on to explain how we were a unit and how if one or two failed, we all failed. It was something I understood from playing with Coach Robinson and Coach Brown and from my time in the military. Plus it was a lesson Coach Lombardi engrained in us from the moment we arrived. In a season of frustrations, Coach found it necessary to re-emphasize some of those basic lessons, fearing we were getting away from playing Green Bay Packers football. He knew being singled out would bother us and motivate us to work harder. In any other season, it would have worked.

After a win against the 49ers, we lost back-to-back games to the Colts and the Rams, putting us at 3–4, a losing record for the first time in years. In the loss to the Rams, I experienced one of my more frustrating games, finding myself unable to get around the Rams offensive line, especially Charlie Cowan. I swear it seemed like the Rams had schemed specifically to keep me out of the backfield. I heard Cowan actually received a game ball for his blocking effort against me. I vowed it would be the last time that happened.

During the next two games against the Vikings and Lions, the defense enacted its revenge. In a 42–13 victory against the Vikings, we blitzed Tarkenton all day, including a sack by Henry Jordan that led to a fumble I recovered. We also imposed our will against the Lions, holding them to just seven points while our offense put up 30.

Unfortunately, the following week, we lost our focus against a team that became a bit of a nemesis for the next two seasons. We inexplicably lost to the 49ers 24–14. We seemed to have all the momentum back on our side. Plus we had the extra motivation of knowing we had to win out the rest of our games that season in order to make the Championship Game.

Somehow we still came out flat. After the San Francisco loss, we knew it was going to take a miracle to help us reach the Championship Game. We could have folded, but that wasn't something Coach would ever allow. It wasn't in our team DNA. We didn't know how to quit. Even if we weren't playing for anything other than pride, it was enough. He worked us hard in practice, setting us up for victory each and every week. We didn't know if there would be an opportunity to play for a title this year, but if it should happen, we would put ourselves in position to make a run.

It didn't, but the last stretch of games in 1964 helped us build momentum going into the next season. In a 28–21 win against the Browns, the team that ultimately won the title that year, we found ourselves more determined than ever on defense, busting through the line and holding their mighty offense. In a 45–21 win against the Cowboys, the defense caused a series of turnovers while the offense got rolling. In a 17–3 victory over the Bears, we established our dominant role in the rivalry and sent a message to teams for next year. The Pack would be back.

Our season ended by playing the St. Louis Cardinals in Miami for the Playoff Bowl. We lost 24–17, but nobody cared. We had no interest in playing a game for anything less than the title. We were already looking to next year, promising each other things would be different. The attitude was reflected in Coach Lombardi's postgame speech to us.

"The Playoff Bowl is a shit game in a shit city played by two shit teams," he said. "We will never play in this game again."

No, we wouldn't.

| Chapter 15 | # Winning Isn't Everything; It's the Only Thing |

Achieving success rarely comes easily.

There are so many factors involved, so many things that need to go right, so much preparation and commitment that at times success will seem like an impossible goal. Coach Lombardi's famous words about success not being a gift but something earned still ring in my ears today. I have never found success easily. It has always been a process with obstacles and challenges, whether in football, in business, or in my personal life.

There are steps involved and traits and requirements that will help a person or a team of people succeed. There is a blueprint, which means that anybody can achieve success. I truly believe that. Everyone is capable of greatness if they do what greatness requires.

It starts with a hunger, a passion for a goal, and then comes finding a path that will lead to accomplishing that goal and embracing the journey heart, mind, body, and soul. There needs to be a willingness to put in the work, knowing none of it will come easy. That's where tenacity, toughness, and courage come in. There will be a series of obstacles and setbacks, and they will have to be faced. Lastly, there needs to be belief in both the dream and one's ability to succeed. The belief will often inspire the rest.

Despite two seasons in a row of missing the Championship Game, the Green Bay Packers believed we would be back. We were ready to do whatever was required. We would let the coaches guide us down the right path, with each player making the commitment. We would work harder than ever before, being strong and courageous and focused on both the task at hand and the ultimate prize.

We already had everything we needed in place with arguably the greatest coaching staff in all of professional football, and we had more combined talent than any other team in the league. We didn't want to focus on 1964 any longer. It was done, in the past. We were ready to move on. As Coach Lombardi said, "No more bullshit."

From the moment the season ended, we vowed second place would no longer cut it. There would be no reflecting on the past and no excuses for the future. We were focused on one thing and one thing only—to be champions once again.

Coming into 1965, Coach Lombardi was satisfied with the personnel and the makeup of our defense. Despite a mediocre year, we were a league leader in several defensive categories and needed little more than a refocusing to make sure we were ready for the upcoming season. Our two problems left over from the previous year were more offensive weapons and a better kicking game.

The year prior, Coach drafted Bob Long out of Wichita State. A speedster who instantly dedicated himself to the Packers cause, Bob never became a superstar for any of the teams he played for, but he was always regarded as a decent receiver, a reliable option who took some of the pressure off the top guys. He'd also go down as one of the luckiest of Green Bay Packers, staying with the team for three championship seasons before moving on.

While Bob was a solid second or third option, Carroll Dale was our deep threat and a player who made an instant impact. We got Carroll from the Rams in a trade that involved our linebacker, Dan Currie. Carroll was always a decent receiver and one who burned our defense for long passes a few times during the previous four years. Like many other players who came to Green Bay, he peaked once he put on the Green and Gold and became a Packers Hall of Famer, giving Bart Starr yet another option when he decided to go long.

Another instant contributor was tight end Bill Anderson. Bill played six solid seasons with the Washington Redskins before retiring and joining the University of Tennessee as an assistant coach. Feeling he still had some good years left, Coach Lombardi reached out to Bill and convinced him to give it one more shot for the title that had thus far eluded him. Bill came to the Packers and thrived under the tutelage of Coach Lombardi, becoming a tough blocker for our running game and a surprise passing option in short-yardage situations.

The biggest pickup for us in the off-season had to be Don Chandler. The struggles of our kicking game (and the wins it might have cost us) still burned Coach Lombardi. It became apparent that Paul Hornung was no longer the answer, and Jerry's season off due to his stomach infection made Coach nervous, as well. He didn't want to have to worry about a kicking game, looking to focus elsewhere. He wanted someone he knew, someone reliable that could take those concerns out of his hands.

Coach worked with Don for three seasons in New York and knew Don had a talented leg. Don was the kind of player who could be more than just a reliable option, he could be an offensive weapon. After nine seasons, Don, who was friends with Jerry Kramer and respected the hell out of Coach Lombardi, said goodbye to the Giants and came to Green Bay where he spent our next three championship seasons squashing any fears we might have had about our kicking game.

When you have the chance to step up and lead, do it!

On defense, we only had one real change—but for me personally, it was a major one, as it was for Coach Lombardi, the Packers organization, and professional football as a whole. In 1965, I received the high honor of becoming the Packers' first-ever black defensive captain.

I honed my strengths, instincts, and everything the coaches gave me in terms of training, and in turn I was now regarded as one of the fiercest defenders in the league. I was a two-time champion who could now be considered a Pro Bowl regular, a perennial All-Pro who also won several AP Defensive Player of the Week awards.

I don't take all the credit. I know my discipline, hunger to succeed, and work ethic only accounted for part of my accomplishments. I know and appreciate the value of having the coaches I did, as well as my teammates, both on offense and defense. Nobody on this team was a superstar without each other. Nobody would have put up the numbers they did without the supporting cast we had. I was a better football player because I was a Green Bay Packer.

With my individual success, I found an even deeper appreciation for the ebb and flow of the game of professional football, and that helped me find a comfort zone while playing. I trusted myself more. I believed in what we could accomplish as a team. I wasn't afraid to be more vocal with other players on our team, especially the younger guys. I made a concerted effort to show my teammates a strong work ethic and a positive attitude. I knew I had ever-growing responsibilities, and I even felt comfortable with those. I was becoming a leader, and Coach Lombardi noticed.

Leading into the 1965 season, Coach began to push for me to be defensive captain. He started by saying things about my individual play, something Coach rarely did. Not wanting to make anyone feel they were ever more important than the team, Coach didn't really believe in glorifying players or plays. When you got a compliment from Coach, especially in the media, you knew it was special.

"There aren't many who are a better example of how to play as far as practice, in the game and in every aspect of what the game is about than Willie," Lombardi said.

And then after one of my better games, "It was a great game, but that's the kind of game Willie gives you every week."

Coach's words meant a lot to me. So did the rare moments he personally opened up to me. It didn't happen often, but when it did, it was special, including one meeting in particular.

"Come on in, Willie," he said, and I saw he was sitting behind his desk, looking *heavy*, as if he were contemplating something extremely important. I took a seat across from him and asked what he wanted to see me about. He just stared at me for a second before getting a sly grin on his face.

"I know why you have to play the game the way you do," he said, letting his words hang in the air. I was taken aback, not really sure how to respond, so I just did what came natural and asked him to tell me why.

"You have a helluva lot to prove. You have to prove to me, the other players, fans, and everyone else how important this all is to you," he said. "You play hard and you work at it because you want to convince people that they've just seen the greatest defensive end in the league. You want the world to recognize you for what you're doing."

I had never thought about it before, but I knew the moment he said it that he was absolutely right. He still is today. It doesn't matter what my endeavor, from football to business and everything in between, I have always felt a need to prove I could be the best. I've always had it, and I'm grateful I do. I'm also grateful Coach recognized it in me.

"You want to make a statement," Coach said, and he took a deep breath. "Willie, let me tell you something. I understand it. I face the same challenge. There is no other coach who wants to win more than me. That's why I have to coach the way I do. I *need* to succeed. I waited around a long time for my opportunity. It took me forever to get here. I was overlooked or not even considered for jobs I was qualified for, and I want to show them that they made a mistake in looking past me."

At this point, I could tell he was getting emotional. This had been weighing on his mind, as well, and he needed to get it off his chest.

"Willie, I just can't leave this all to chance," he said. "I have to make sure that we do well. This thing has to be done in a way that people realize I was one of the great coaches. I can leave no doubt as to what kind of coach I am, just like you can leave no doubt as to what kind of player you are."

Nothing about being a defensive captain was discussed in the conversation, but Coach opening up showed me a new level of respect and faith he had not just in my abilities but in my personality as a player. I was someone he trusted, and my desire to win for him soared to even greater heights. That talk gave me a new perspective on how I played the game of football as well as the game of life, and I was grateful to see how I had something in common with this man I respected so much.

Typically, the players work with the coaches to elect a team captain on both sides of the ball. For example, the previous year, the team had all voted to name Bob Skoronski the offensive captain. We expected the same with the defense, but Coach opted not to do it this way. Instead he gathered his coaching staff and a couple of key players and got their opinions before making the call himself. I've often wondered why Coach decided to do it this way, but I think there were probably a couple of reasons.

One reason was control. He had to have his hand in all decisions, and for something as important as this, he wanted to make sure he had a guy in the position who he could trust and that his players could trust, someone who could work as an intermediary between him and his team, someone who could be honest about the team's concerns but also be respectful and understanding of what Coach was trying to accomplish.

He also didn't want any controversy on the team. In the years since he arrived in Green Bay, Coach, the team, and even the community had made several strides in terms of relations between black and white players. As the league grew in diversity, so did Green Bay. There was more of an acceptance and mutual respect among all of us on the team, created mainly by Coach's zero tolerance of anything but total dedication to each other. There was also a respect in the community for these black players that folks there hadn't come in contact with before. It was comfortable to be a black player in Green Bay.

That being said, the organization had *never* had a black team captain, and I think Coach was worried that leaving it to a vote could have split the team or singled out some players. He never wanted anything to chip away at the foundation he spent grueling hours building. It wasn't about animosity or even racism because we were all brothers on this team. We all got along. It was more about old attitudes that were still fairly prevalent in certain parts of the country where some of the players were from. There were some guys who still may have had a problem with a black man in a leadership position. Coach didn't want any distractions.

Yet he knew naming a black defensive captain was also probably a good step forward for the organization and the league. And he felt I was the right person for the job. With more experience under my belt, I had shifted to helping others focus on improving their game as well as my own, and I was blessed enough to have other players actually credit me for helping them become better defenders and even blockers. Even before Coach named me captain, I took it upon myself to push others to meet the challenge. I also wanted to show any and all players they had the support they needed to succeed. Support and leadership were values I took seriously and Coach knew it.

Coach made it his decision, knowing nobody would question it. It was his way of showing us like always that all we had to worry about was playing football and he would take care of the rest. We all believed in him so much, we accepted whatever he told us, including naming a black captain.

"Well, if that's what Coach says is best, that's what we're doing."

The response I received I think surprised even him. After a practice right before the season began, he huddled us up and unceremoniously named me captain. There were no headshakes, no gasps, no mumbling. After Bob Skoronski was named offensive captain once again, I was named defensive captain with rousing applause and pats on the back. It was overwhelmingly positive, and I felt honored that I had not only the respect, support, and trust of my coaches but also of my fellow players.

Being defensive captain helped focus my discipline—another trait that served me well in the business world. I was already a rather disciplined player in terms of effort, efficiency, timeliness, patience, and other areas in which Coach preached. However, now that I was captain, I took it upon myself to practice even more, accepting the responsibility that came with the position and giving it the maturity I thought it deserved.

I vowed to never do anything to jeopardize my position with the team or my participation. I vowed to be more vocal, to lead by example. I vowed to show support to my teammates while encouraging them to reach for more—and to listen to their advice on how I could get better. I vowed to act like a captain and make sure nobody ever had any doubts about my being the first black team captain in Packers history.

When Coach told me a few years later that naming me captain was one of the easiest decisions he ever made and one he was proud of, I knew I had done my job, which ultimately was to help him win.

"Winning isn't everything; it's the only thing."

We heard Coach Lombardi use those famous words a few times in my career in Green Bay. The legendary quote given by the legendary man came to define his approach to the game and his beloved Packers, and it has served as the mantra for people who want to succeed, people who believe they are destined for something greater. It is the philosophy of winners.

Each and every time Coach said those words, it moved whoever heard them. What's interesting is that despite popular belief, Coach Lombardi did not come up with the quote. It actually was first attributed to UCLA Bruins football coach Red Sanders back in the early 1950s. How and where Coach first heard it is a mystery, but like so many other famous and inspiring quotes, he ingrained it into his team's approach to the game and to life in general.

Unfortunately, as time has passed, there has been quite a bit of mis-understanding and confusion about what exactly Coach meant when he used the phrase. Even back at the height of the team's dominance during Coach Lombardi's reign, those words caused a stir. Some people thought the words sent the wrong message to competitors. There is a belief that the importance of sports should be the participation or the effort as well as *how* one competes. Coach Lombardi's quote has been criticized for im-ploring a win-at-all-costs mentality, a focus on being successful versus doing your best.

I've never understood why some people had a problem with the quote. What's wrong with the desire to succeed? As successful people will tell you—not a damn thing!

Coach himself claimed at one point that the quote was taken the wrong way. He said what he meant was that while winning wasn't every-thing, the *will* to win was the only important thing. He wanted to stress to his players how crucial it was to always possess that will to win, to push and do what was required to succeed. For those of us who heard him speak, there was no confusion or controversy. Coach wanted us to win because winning was the only thing worth shooting for. It was about working our hardest and doing our best, not cheating or playing dirty but rather striving to do the best we could. He knew we could win and he knew that total effort and commitment would be our path to victory.

One of the more memorable times I heard the quote was after a crucial game in Green Bay. The week before, we had gotten our butts whipped, and Coach was unhappy. After a proper ass-chewing and a week of hell-ish practice, our team woke up and we won big the following game. In the locker room after the game, Coach came in to see us all laughing, slapping each other on the backs, bragging about plays, and talking about how excited we were for the next game. As he took it all in, he smiled and called us over.

"You see, gentleman, winning is the only thing," he said. "It's the only thing that can make you feel like this. *This* feeling, this is what winning does, nothing else."

For me, that's what the quote always symbolized, and I think it was the same for the other members of the Packers, as well. There was and is no fun in losing—ever. There's no enjoyment, no celebration, no pay-off. Winning is what successful people crave because winning is the only thing that makes the effort worthwhile. It's the only thing that will make us truly happy, fulfilled, and excited. Of course, there is always a lesson to be learned or experience to be gained in fighting hard and coming up short. But winning, there's nothing like it.

As we opened the 1965 season, winning was the only thing on our minds. Yet, inexplicably, we still struggled—again—in our opening game against the Pittsburgh Steelers. This was before the Steelers earned their reputation as one of the most successful franchises in all of football. That wouldn't come until the 1970s. In 1965, they finished 2–12, and it was almost 3–11.

The defense did its part, setting the stage that defined us as a unit all season. We played aggressively, blitzing and overpowering front lines. We were also willing to hit hard. We wanted to establish in each and every game that we were in charge and that we would dictate how the afternoon would go. We bruised opponents on the line and in the back-field, relying on our speed at the corners and at free safety to neutralize any passing attack. We were not willing to give up touchdowns.

The Steelers were only able to score three field goals in the first half of the opener. Unfortunately, our offense hadn't scored anything, and the only reason we had any points at all was thanks to Herb Adderley's pick for a touchdown.

Here we were again, clearly the dominant team but struggling to put it all together at the season opener. We could tell Coach was furious about it. His halftime speech offered little encouragement. Instead he spent the entire time railing the offense for not living up to the defense. This was not the tone we were looking for to start the year. This did little to ease the doubters who looked at us as an overly talented team that sometimes underachieved. This was not Lombardi football. This was not Packers football. The season, it seemed, was in doubt after just one half of football.

Then the second half started.

We scored 34 unanswered points on a beautiful blend of passing and running. The defense, already stingy in the first half, tightened up even more, allowing absolutely nothing. By the time we heard the final gun, everybody had forgotten about the first half and instead immediately looked forward to the following week in Baltimore against our old rivals, Johnny Unitas and the Colts.

Despite having been in the league for almost a decade, Unitas was peaking in the mid-1960s, as was the Colts team. A few years later, they would be in the Super Bowl, but for now they were a scary opponent who always played us hard. True to form, the Colts hit us and hit us hard in Week 2, especially our offense. Jim Taylor got injured and had to come out. Paul Hornung hurt his neck on a play, and he had to sit, as well. Boyd Dowler was hit hard on an incomplete pass, and he was forced out. Worst of all, Bart Starr twisted his ankle on a sack that put him out of the game. Four of our top offensive weapons were down again.

But this is where we could all tell that the 1965 season would be different. Injuries had plagued the Packers the last two seasons and we had paid the price, watching as two other teams played for the title we coveted. This year, we had the depth and the experience. We had guys to cover any injury, players like Elijah Pitts and Bob Long that would start on most other teams. These were extremely talented athletes who believed in the greater good by doing their jobs, making sure they were prepared for any opportunity, and focusing on the grand prize of an NFL title.

A great example was Zeke Bratkowski, our backup quarterback who proved more than useful several times during the season. Against the Colts, while the defense struggled to just keep the game close, Zeke took control and led the team downfield for a final-minutes touchdown pass to Max McGee to clinch a 20–17 win.

After cruising through our next two opponents, the Bears and the 49ers, we found ourselves at 4–0 and looking to the Lions, a team that had grown to hate the Packers and our success. As such, those games were typically a major struggle. This game was no different. Perhaps we had gotten too far ahead of ourselves, or maybe we weren't prepared for what the Lions were going to bring. Regardless, we found ourselves down 21–3 at halftime with players from the Lions actually taunting us from the field and the sideline. We entered the locker room steaming, breaking into our separate corners, offensively and defensively, to talk about what was happening, what we had done, and what we needed to do to fix it. There was a lot of yelling, especially on the defensive side, as we had given up more points in that half than we had in any other game so far in that season.

Suddenly, we heard the voice.

"Gentleman, pay attention!" Coach yelled over the locker room noise. Here it comes, I thought. If there was somebody who was going to be truly enraged about our first-half performance, it would be Coach. As I turned to listen to what he had to say, I saw him smiling.

Coach went over the adjustments he wanted, and then he told us how we could beat this team. Finally, he took a minute to look at each of us, and it looked like he was about to tear up.

"Gentleman, I just want you to know that win, lose, or draw, you're my football team."

Once that pressure was gone, we were ready to get back to playing Packers football.

Being a great coach or leader also requires having a very special skill—awareness.

There are times a team will need leadership. There will be times they need discipline, and there will be times they need encouragement. Then there will be times when it's best to let them take care of any problems themselves. A leader must see and trust that the members are committed, that they have learned and accepted the mission. At that point, as a good leader, the responsibility is to help relieve the pressure and let them know they have support and belief in them.

After Coach's surprising halftime speech, we went out and destroyed the Lions. The defense didn't give up any more points and forced a couple key turnovers, including an interception by me on a pass into the secondary after I had dropped back. On the offensive side of the ball, Bart threw for 225 yards and three touchdowns in the third quarter alone. We carried the 31–21 victory and 5–0 record back home for a game against Dallas. We had shown our talent, depth, leadership, focus, and our desire to win. Now, against Dallas, we would show the final thing we needed to be a championship team—the ability to fix any mistakes.

We were eager to play the Cowboys because for the first time since the team's inception, they had beaten us in our annual preseason game 21–12. Although the Cowboys were no longer the league punching bag, we still knew we were better and we wanted to show it. The defense pressured Don Meredith and the Cowboys all game long, making sure they stayed uncomfortable. We hit hard, making sure we sent a message on each and every play. The Cowboys were barely able to squeeze out three points. I personally had a couple of sacks and a fumble recovery that helped us seal up the game. More important, I made sure they could feel me and my presence on each and every down.

While our offense still sputtered, we were able to get what we needed to win, showing that the Packers were putting together all the elements they needed, including the ability to overcome adversity.

A great team will both face and overcome adversity.

It seems that with most championship teams, the last piece of the puzzle is to see how that team deals with struggles. At some point in the season, even the best of teams will find themselves facing a particular challenge or set of obstacles that will make them (and everyone else) question whether they have what it takes to make the push to be champions. At this point, some teams fold or fade away. Others find solutions and use those challenges as the cornerstones of success. They also fix them quickly. The ability to do so is what truly sets apart the professionals.

After starting 6–0, we were about to hit a major mid-season slump that put our title hopes in jeopardy. We worked just as hard, prepared just as much, and fought our hearts out, but things just stopped clicking.

We started off by getting creamed 31–10 by the Bears, a team hungry for a win. We followed up with a loss at home against the Lions who were still smarting from their early season matchup with us. The game featured a lot of taunting, especially between Alex Karras and Ray Nitschke, who always had a word or two for our opponents. There was also a lot of heavy hitting by both sides, and Starr found himself on the ground more than usual. A couple of key mistakes gave the Lions a 12–7 win.

Trying to right the ship, we were eager to play the following week in Milwaukee against the 1–7 Los Angeles Rams. We never took any opponent for granted, but we felt confident we could use a team like the hapless Rams to help us rebuild our confidence and get back on track. The players were as frustrated as Coach, who looked ready to blow a fuse. The worst part of it all was we couldn't figure out exactly what we were doing wrong. We were simply playing bad football. We made a promise that wouldn't be the case against the Rams. Unfortunately, the Rams had a different idea.

On the defensive side of the ball, we could not have played any better. Bill Munson and the Rams' passing attack were inefficient at best. The running game wasn't much better. We consistently broke through the offensive line, not allowing any of the Rams' plays to ever truly develop and making sure the quarterback was aware of our presence.

But our offense got stuck for the third straight week. We couldn't run the ball, and our receivers couldn't get open. Bart looked off and ended up making some costly turnovers. For the first time in years, he was benched for a backup. While Coach Lombardi assured both Bart and the local media after the game that the Packers didn't have a quarterback controversy and that Bart was still the starter, the move went a long way in showing the offensive-minded coach's frustration with our inability to put points on the board.

We scored 10 against the Bears, seven on the Lions, and in this game between Bart and Zeke, the offense only managed three points until the very end when our defense caused a fumble at their 20-yard line with less than a minute to play. The play resulted in a game-winning field goal to actually give us the 6–3 edge in a game that never should have been that close. We had some major problems, and we were starting to worry about how they were going to get fixed.

Our young offensive tackle Steve Wright didn't help things.

On the Tuesday following the game, we were all back home in our locker room, waiting for a team meeting with the coaches. It wasn't uncommon to see guys joking and laughing with each other before this first meeting of the week, coming back from Monday off. It was our last moment to shake off the last game, win or lose, and to relax before the meeting and before all the preparation for the next game began.

We waited as the coaches met in the adjoining room to talk over their notes. This week's "festivities" were a little less jovial as we all pondered where the team was headed, especially the veterans. Each week, the pre-meeting chitchat inevitably turned to the previous game. Last week's was both a sore subject and a hot topic. The veterans preferred to move on, and the young guys were about to learn why.

As Steve, a promising young tackle out of the University of Alabama, joked with some of the other linemen, he didn't notice Coach come into the locker room. Coach snuck in sometimes, hoping to catch his players in candid conversation to see if there was anything he should know. Listening in on locker room talk could provide some valuable information. Today, however, he wasn't in the mood.

"6–3, can you believe it?" Steve said with a smile on his face. "Batter up!"

As a few of the linemen laughed at his baseball joke, they slowly realized Coach was in the locker room. We all looked up, feeling his presence and quickly falling silent. At first, Coach didn't say anything, just looked at Steve and the linemen as his face turned red and then purple. Coach had done everything in his power to hold in his frustrations over the past few weeks, but to walk in to see some of his players laughing about the team's struggles—that was too much. He didn't contain his anger any longer. Before he even started, I looked down at my feet, thinking it might be a good idea to spend the next several minutes examining my shoe shine. I did that a lot with Coach Lombardi.

Coach started his tirade by punting a garbage can for what I'm sure would have been about a 30-yard field goal if it had not been stopped by the locker room wall. When we saw him limp away later, we knew just how hard he had really kicked it. That was just the start.

"How the hell can you be laughing and joking and happy playing the way you're playing?!" he screamed. "How can you be celebrating? How can you be pleased at all with your performance?! Huh?!"

Nobody said a word, and Steve tried as hard as he could to disappear. It wasn't going to happen. Coach yelled at us for several minutes, making sure to aim several of his comments directly at Steve, who from this point on would always make sure to check over his shoulder before making a joke. We listened without anyone making the slightest noise. Any movement, comment, or even a misplaced breath was met with the full force of Coach's rage. We needed to let him get this out of his system. Plus we needed to save our energy for what was certainly going to be a difficult week of practice. When he was done, he was in a full sweat. He ordered us out onto the field, and we all knew there was no way we could lose the next game. Steve was the most determined of us all.

Coach pushed us the following week to a 38–13 destruction of the Minnesota Vikings. We took a while to get going in that game, even trailing after three quarters. The offense awoke with a vengeance in the fourth quarter, tying a record by scoring 28 points. In the game, the defense also made its contributions. Herb Adderley made a key interception, and our line caused two fumbles, including one for a touchdown.

It was the kind of game we needed, and after a week of frustration and intense practicing, the win provided relief more than anything. We congratulated each other in the locker room, laughing and talking excitedly about what we had just done to another of our rivals. Then Coach walked in, and we all fell deadly silent.

"Gentlemen, you go ahead and celebrate this one," he said, beaming with his trademark grin, one we rarely saw mid-season. He told us to laugh, to congratulate ourselves, and to revel in what we had accomplished. We had worked hard, and we had seen the results. We had earned the right to celebrate. "What you're witnessing here is why winning is the only thing. It is the only thing that will make you feel like this, make you experience what you're feeling right now. It is the only thing that creates this kind of environment, this atmosphere. Nothing will ever come close to making you feel the way you do right now other than winning. Now I want you to remember this feeling as we finish out the season."

If there had been any reporters with us for that speech, there never would have been any controversy about what Coach meant by, "Winning is the only thing." There would have been even less doubt about whether or not his team believed in it.

We felt confident about our destruction of the Vikings, especially given how we had played the fourth quarter. In sports, they often talk about a light being switched on when a team finally clicks and starts playing together as a unit. We thought we were clicking on all cylinders, and we were eager to head to Los Angeles and take on the 1–9 Rams. Although we had won the first time, the low score was a source of embarrassment and we looked at it as a revenge game—which made our 21–10 loss completely inexplicable.

Once again, we had no offense. The defense faltered. We gave up too many big plays while committing a ridiculous number of mistakes. We were unfocused, undisciplined, and we played without any heart, a reminder that just as quickly as the light gets switched on, somebody can come along and turn it right off.

"I am the only one here who gives a damn about winning and losing!" Coach screamed at us at the meeting before our Tuesday practice, a complete reversal from just a week prior. We showed up somber, frustrated, but mostly confused. "Nobody here wants to pay the price! Nobody here wants to win!"

He had stormed into the locker room and didn't even bother asking us to huddle around him. It didn't matter where we were sitting, we were going to hear him. We sat and just silently listened, taking it all in and waiting for Coach to exhaust himself so we could get to practice.

Well, most of us were.

"I am the only one who puts any heart into the game! Don't you guys care?"

That was all Forrest Gregg could take. Out of nowhere, he yelled back at Coach at the top of his lungs, a rare confrontation that could only come from extreme frustration.

I was born determined. Even as a young man growing up in Texarkana, I had my sights set on being successful at whatever I did. (Photo courtesy of the author)

I graduated from high school completely unaware of where my life was headed, especially that it would include a Hall of Fame career in the NFL! (Photo courtesy of the author)

I was the 181st pick in the 1956 NFL Draft and was selected by the Cleveland Browns, starting what would become an illustrious 12-year career. But in those first two years, I was just trying to avoid being cut!
(Photo courtesy of the author)

We didn't get paid what today's players make, so we had to work in the off-season. Here I am substitute teaching during my brief stint in Cleveland. (Photo courtesy of the author)

In back to back Championship Game victories, we gave Y.A. Tittle and the New York Giants all they could take. In both games (1961 and 1962), our defense was tenacious. (AP Photo)

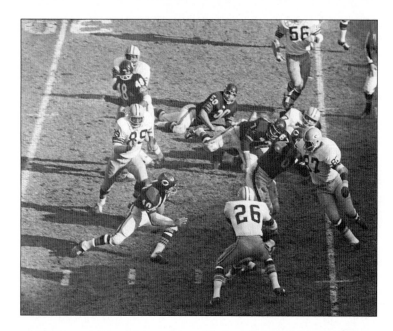

The Chicago Bears have always been a big rival. Dave Robinson (89), Herb Adderley (26), and I trap the great Bears running back Gale Sayers. (AP Photo/Larry Stoddard)

Even toward the end of my career, I had the speed and strength to close the gap, as shown here chasing down Detroit Lions running back Nick Eddy in 1969. (AP Photo/ NFL Photos)

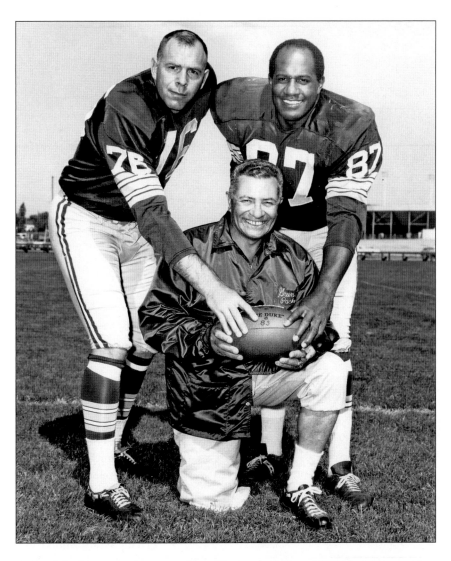

One of the greatest honors of my life is when Coach Lombardi named me defensive captain along with offensive captain Bob Skoronski.
(AP Photo/NFL Photos)

My mother, my father, and I at my Hall of Fame induction in 1981. "Mom, you know it's a long way from Texarkana." (Photo courtesy of the author)

When football's been your passion for so long, it's tough to leave, which is why many athletes go into broadcasting when they retire. I worked briefly as an analyst for NBC alongside the great Ross Porter. (Photo courtesy of the author)

My business mentor, Bob Uihlein of Schlitz Brewing Co., helped me pursue my other passion after football...a business career. I eventually took over the South Central Los Angeles distributorship of Schlitz. In just one year I turned it from worst to first. (Photo courtesy of the author)

My newest passion turned out to be the radio business. I formed All Pro Broadcasting in 1976 and have loved every minute of working in this exciting field. (Photo courtesy of the author)

I am and always will be a Green Bay Packer. (Photo courtesy of the author)

"God dammit, Coach, I want to win!" he yelled. "It makes me sick to hear you say that. We lay our ass on the line for you every Sunday. We live and die the same way you do, and it hurts. It tears my heart out when we lose, but don't say we're not trying!"

I looked over at him and couldn't believe the amount of red in his face. Even more stunning, Gregg looked like he was ready to take a swing at the Old Man. I think Coach saw it too because he fell silent, letting Gregg get it off his chest. As a couple other players stepped in to make sure Gregg didn't make a mistake he would regret, Bob Skoronski, who was sitting between Forrest and I, decided to speak up, as well. He was just as red.

"That's right Coach," he said. "Don't tell us we don't care about winning. We do care. We care about it every bit as much as you!"

Bob was a bit more reserved in his confrontation, looking less like he wanted to take down Coach and more like a team captain trying to rally his troops. Coach recognized it, and you could tell he appreciated it. He wasn't losing control of his team. In fact, just the opposite, he was getting validation that his approach to winning, his need to win, was affecting his players. They were just as frustrated as he was, and that's where these outbursts were coming from.

"Alright! That's the kind of attitude I want to see! Who else feels that way?"

I don't know if it was the tension of the situation, hearing Coach's voice, hearing someone confront Coach, a pure accident, or divine intervention sent down to relieve the situation. Whatever it was, the moment Coach asked who was on board with him, the chair I was leaning back on fell out from under me.

I almost tumbled backward into my own locker. Another half a second and that's exactly where I would have been. But my reflexes kicked in and I hopped up, standing right next to Bob. The whole locker room, including Coach, stopped what they were doing and turned to look. I froze, unsure of what to do and decided to just say the first thing that came to my mind.

"Uhh, yeah—Coach—me too—I wanna win!"

I tried to put on my meanest, most determined, angriest face, which was incredibly unnatural for me. But it was too late. I don't know how any of the other players stopped themselves from laughing. It was so contrived and awkward. Granted, I meant what I said, but it sounded so false and ridiculous. I could even see the smallest trace of a grin on Coach's face as he turned away from me. He looked at the rest of his players and suddenly the locker room came to life, everyone cheering and making their pledge about how they wanted to win—and even more important, how they *would* win.

"Alright then, gentlemen!" Coach yelled over the roar. "Let's get the hell out of here and have a good practice."

For the second time in a row, after a season low moment, we bounced back against the Vikings, this time winning 24–19. The significant footnote about this game was that we played without Paul Hornung, who had been benched for the first time in his career without an injury. Paul was entering the twilight of his glorious career, and it was starting to show. The Golden Boy, who at one time was the most prolific scorer, ball carrier, and all-around offensive weapon on the team, had only scored three times in 11 games during the season. Plus he had three single-digit rushing games.

It was a poignant move for Coach Lombardi, who still loved Paul as a second son. It showed that nobody was more important than the Green Bay Packers as a whole. If you couldn't contribute, no matter what you had done in the past, you would be replaced with someone who could. Coach would say he pulled Paul because Pitts and Moore gave us a better chance to win, but we also knew it was a message to us to make sure we played as determined as possible. It was also a message to Paul, telling him that if he was going to get any last mileage out of his body in the game of football, the time was now.

Paul heard Coach loud and clear. In Week 13, we played our most important game of the season to that point. Coming into the game, we were a game ahead of the Bears and a half game behind the Colts to see who would go to the championship. A win against the Colts, who we beat earlier in the season, would give us the edge with just one week left to go.

We played in Baltimore, a hostile environment with a thick fog covering the field, meaning low visibility. Every play would be crucial. As it is with most games where weather is a factor, we knew there would be a lot of mistakes and the potential for turnovers. But we were determined to come out ahead in that battle.

True to form for such sloppy conditions, we gave up two fumbles and an interception that lead to a total of 13 Colts points. However, we got three picks ourselves that led to two touchdowns. One advantage we had was that the Colts were playing with their third-string quarterback. Unitas had been hurt earlier in the season and had to sit out and early in the game, our defense knocked out backup quarterback Gary Cuozzo on a huge hit in the backfield. That left the Colts relying on Tom Matte, a utility player who also spent time as a receiver and running back.

Our defense was able to pressure Tom all game long, continually rushing his throws and sacking him. Still, for a third-string quarterback, he made a valiant effort, showing a lot of heart and keeping the Colts in it for the duration. He led two drives for touchdowns, giving the Colts a total of 27 points. Unfortunately for the Colts, our offense couldn't be stopped. Bart Starr showed his short-game passing strength, taking advantage of a Colts defense that respected our ability to make long plays. Jim Taylor had one of his best games of the season, bullying anyone who got in his way, including one run where he broke eight tackles by himself.

However, the man of the hour, one last time, was the Golden Boy. Paul had been bothered by Coach benching him the previous week. Ever the competitor, Paul didn't complain to the press, who barraged him with questions; to teammates; or to Coach Lombardi himself. Instead, Paul made sure he arrived early for each practice that week and stayed late. He brought a new energy to practice and even cut down on his "extracurricular activities" during the week. He was determined to not only get back in the game but perform better than he had in some time.

That's exactly what he did, rushing for more than 60 yards and scoring five touchdowns, three on runs and two on passes. He was also a vocal leader on the sideline, yelling encouragement to the defense that could be heard even over the increasingly frustrated crowd. Perhaps Paul's biggest play of the game was a desperation tackle on Bobby Boyd, who had scooped up a Jim Taylor fumble and was looking to score minutes before halftime. If Paul hadn't made the play, the Colts would have gone up 20–14 at the half. Instead, the stop forced the struggling Colts offense back onto the field and two plays later, Dave Robinson picked off a Matte pass and ran it in for a touchdown to give us a 21–13 halftime lead. We never looked back.

We won 42–27 and put ourselves in the driver's seat in the division. All we had to do was win our last game against the San Francisco 49ers and we would be playing for the title. However, the frustrating 49ers put a wrench in our plans.

We were a better team than San Francisco. There was no doubt. We knew what we had to do, and yet we were distracted—both before and during the game.

Our task was to beat San Francisco, but there were still a number of other scenarios in play. If we lost and the Colts won, they would get the division. If we both won, we would get it because we beat Baltimore twice. If we both lost, there was still a chance Chicago could sweep in and get the division. If we tied, Chicago would be out and we would play Baltimore in a playoff. With how hard the Colts played us each and every time, a playoff was inevitable.

Coach tried to get us to focus, but we couldn't help thinking about the different scenarios. During the game, the coaches received updates on how the Colts were doing, and despite Lombardi's wishes, the information trickled down to the players on the sideline. Admittedly, we were probably a little too focused on what the Colts were doing and less intent on our own game.

We overlooked a team priding itself on playing the role of spoiler, and we paid for it. Because of our talent and depth, we were able to take a 21–17 lead deep into the fourth quarter. As the 49ers rallied for a drive, their Pro Bowl quarterback, John Brodie, threw a pick to Willie Wood that eventually led to a field goal and a 24–17 lead. Then we just got sucker punched.

Brodie and the 49ers took the ball on a steady drive upfield with a crowd looking for a satisfying result on the last game of the season. As we got word that the Colts had won, the pressure mounted. Suddenly, the 49ers were in our territory, and a little-used tight end by the name of Vern Burke lined up on the right side. We hadn't scouted him and didn't know if he was part of the passing attack or just a decoy. We found out soon enough as he ran a standard out pattern to the end zone, catching the game-tying touchdown pass with less than a minute left. We had it in our grasp, and we lost it. Well actually we didn't lose it, but the tie meant we would get Baltimore one more time this season for a playoff game to decide who would play Cleveland in the championship.

Success requires you to keep working even as the work piles itself on.

This time, Coach didn't say anything negative to us. He didn't need to, we were frustrated enough. We had once again let ourselves down, and now there was no choice but to fix it. There wasn't any time to grieve or pout. We were about to play in a playoff game that suddenly meant everything. The entire season came down to one more game against our old rival. It was one of many iconic games that I played in and one I'll always remember.

We had the benefit of having just played Baltimore, so we still had the experience fresh in our minds. We knew exactly who we were facing and how hard they would play us. They still had to rely on Matte under center because Unitas and Cuozzo were still out with injuries. What we had learned last time about Matte was that he didn't have the strongest arm or the best accuracy. But he was very moveable, a quarterback who looked to roll out of the pocket. Also he had a ton of heart and determination. Despite the fact Matte was the third-stringer, we were going to make sure we didn't take him for granted.

We also had the benefit of having our leader, Bart Starr, back at full strength—for one play.

We started with the ball, and as our offense took the field, the roar from the home crowd was nothing short of deafening. We spoiled them a few years ago, and they enjoyed the taste of victory. Then, just as quickly, we let it get away from us and the fans were eager to see us in the championship once again.

Before any of them could even take their seats, we lost Bart on the worst first play from scrimmage we could possibly conceive. Bart dropped back and dumped a short pass to tight end Bill Anderson, who turned upfield with room to run. However, Bill was quickly blind-sided by a couple of Colts defenders and the ball popped out. Colts linebacker Don Shinnick scooped it up and broke for the end zone with only Starr in front of him, trying desperately to stop the play. As Bart went in for the tackle (and Don went in for the score), he was blocked hard in the back. Watching from the sideline, we looked from the Colts players celebrating in the end zone to Starr who was taking too much time to get back up.

"Uh-oh," I heard a few players on the sideline whisper as the crowd fell silent. Sure enough, the trainers went to get Bart, who came up holding his back by his ribcage. They signaled instantly that he was done.

As I took the field for the first time, already trailing, I saw a lot of celebration on the Colts sideline. I don't think it was because Bart was hurt, but then again, we had put out their last quarterback, and they knew we were stronger with Bart. I knew this game had just gotten a whole lot more challenging, and I knew our defense would have to play its part.

"Alright fellas, let's go now," I said to the troops back on the sideline. "We know what we gotta do—whatever's necessary."

Ray, Willie, Dave, Lionel, Herb—all of them were ready, and they all yelled encouragement to each other. We would not lose this game—at least not on the defensive side of the ball.

Matte and the rest of the Colts offense couldn't do anything against us. They simply couldn't move. Anytime they got a drive going, it only lasted for a few plays. They rarely made it to our side of the field, and when they did, it was a few yards at a time. Matte himself looked utterly perplexed. In a move that became immensely popular years later, he had several plays taped to his wristband. Even with the extra help, our defense was just too ferocious, and we frustrated the natural receiver/running back. At day's end, he had completed just five passes as the Colts' offense quickly switched to a reliance on the running game.

Unfortunately, our offense sputtered as the Colts quickly switched up their defense to protect against the run. The philosophy was to force our backup, Zeke, to make some plays. No matter what running back combination Coach tried, the Colts seemed to have an answer. It didn't matter if we tried running inside or applying our famous sweep, the Colts had the personnel and the positioning to stop it. Paul, Jim, Elijah, Tom—all of them came off the field looking madder and madder with each short series.

"Come on," Coach yelled from the sideline after yet another stop, and it sounded almost pleading, something rarely heard from Lombardi.

At the half we trailed 10–0, and his halftime speech sounded just a bit desperate.

"What are you doing out there?" he asked, and nobody had an answer. "You've come so close! How hard do you think it will be to get back here? Do you want to stop now that we're so close?"

Again, words weren't going to satisfy the Old Man. The only thing we could do was go out there and show him we could still play like the Green Bay Packers. As he met with the offense, I pulled our defense together for a last-minute huddle, imploring them to buckle down even more. There was an understanding that giving up any more points, especially before we got a score, might seal up the game and our season.

In the second half, the defense did its job even better than in the first. The feeling from the Colts early on in the half was that they were hoping to simply hang on with their lead, adding to it only if an opportunity came their way. They buckled down on defense, making sure they didn't give up a big play or make a mistake. But as is often the case in important games the mistakes and/or opportunities rarely come from the offense or defense, but rather the special teams.

After a strong defensive stand, the Colts were forced to punt from inside their territory. Lucky for us we got the break we were looking for when the punter fumbled a near-perfect snap and tried to run with it for the first down. We instantly smelled blood and flocked to the punter, who came up well short. Suddenly, we were in business with a first-and-10 inside Baltimore territory at the 35. Soon after, Zeke hit Carroll Dale with a long pass to take us down to the 1-yard line, followed by a quick Paul Hornung plunge to bring the score to 10–7.

The defense watched excitedly on the sideline as the Golden Boy did what he and Jim Taylor had done so many times before. When the crowd roared, we threw up our hands and got ourselves ready to head back out onto the field, more determined than ever to not only stop whatever came our way but to try as hard as we could to create a turnover.

We stood firm as the tide shifted ever so slightly in our direction. Both offenses still moved slowly, but there was a sense that Zeke was getting more comfortable with his short passes and that Jim's toughness on his runs was wearing down their defense. Like the Colts, we played our offense tight, not taking too many chances but always looking for an opportunity.

It came in the fourth quarter when Zeke caught Bill Anderson on a deep hook. It was a blown-coverage play; the defender guessed wrong as to where Bill was going and Zeke recognized it, launching a perfect pass that set up a field goal.

The field goal.

A lot has been written about Don Chandler's infamous field goal, a controversial kick that pushed the league to raise the bars of the goalposts and station two referees underneath instead of one.

Packers and Colts fans from that generation *still* debate whether or not it was good. Film footage of the kick, limited in its quality, has done little to prove either side right. Countless analysts have discussed the science behind the trajectory of the ball's flight, and they still come out on both sides. Fans, coaches, referees, including those that were there, all seem to see something different. As for the players on the field, they are equally divided, as well. Even when I run into members of the Colts and Packers organization now, they still argue.

I'll settle this debate right now. It was good.

It was a standard 22-yard field goal, one Don had hit a number of times in his illustrious career. He said later there was no reason for the kick to be that close. The snap was good, the hold was good, his rhythm and timing were normal. There was no pressure from the defense. The ball just simply drifted on him, shooting to the right.

As soon as it left his leg, it seemed players from both teams turned and craned their necks to see where it was going. Most kickers have a feel as soon as the ball leaves their leg as to whether or not it is going to be good, and Don certainly didn't think so. He instantly hung his head and started shaking it in frustration while Colts players began leaping up and down in celebration. Then the ref raised his arms. Good.

It was our turn to jump up and down as the Colts players who were running off the field stopped in their tracks, confused by the roar of the fans. Both on the field and on the sideline, we could hear Colts players screaming at the official, but we didn't care. The kick was good. Tie ball game 10–10.

It was the right call. I can say that with 100 percent conviction for one reason and one reason alone. I was on the field, protecting our kicker.

I was also lined up on the right side, aligned precisely with the trajectory of the ball. I also didn't have anyone rushing on my side, which meant I didn't have to block. I was essentially able to stand straight up and watch how the ball sailed through the air. I had an excellent view of the kick, and I can say that there was never any doubt in my mind. Yes, it started slicing dramatically to the right as soon as he kicked it, but when it went over the goal post it was still inside, saving the last bit of curl to the right for the very end.

The reason so many players on the field argued it was no good was because by the time they came up from their rush and turned their heads, the ball was already past and was way off to the right. There is no way it would have looked good to them. I saw what the ref saw and what Don would have seen had he not dropped his head. The kick started right, crossed inside the goal post, and then drifted further off. With the technology and camera angles used in the game today, I can positively say that same kick would equal three points for the Green Bay Packers.

In many ways, Don's kick and the feeling that it was a blown call seemed to suck the life out of the Colts. But they were a good team, a professional team with veteran players and a solid coach, and they turned it around quickly. As the game drifted into overtime, the Colts received and quickly turned their opening possession into a drive that reached our 47-yard line. Suddenly, the Colts were close enough to take a shot at a game-winning field goal.

I couldn't bear to watch and only knew it was no good and that we still had a chance when I heard the crowd erupt and saw the Colts players hang their heads once again.

After that initial overtime drive, both defenses played as brutal a brand of football as we could muster. We were not accustomed to overtime games, and I think it's safe to say the defenses on both sides were utterly exhausted. Still, the game was too important, the stakes too high. Nobody wanted to give up an inch, knowing that a field goal meant the end of a season.

For more than 13 minutes of overtime, the offenses struggled, buckling under the intense pressure of both defenses. Many of the players on the field, myself included, considered this one of the toughest games we ever played. We all made significant plays. Although I pressured their quarterback all game long, my biggest contribution came in overtime on a key third down. The Colts had managed to string together a couple of first downs and were approaching our territory once again. On the play, I let my instincts take over and took a huge chance, pushing my rush to the inside rather than the outside where I was supposed to go. It caught the blocker off guard, and I slipped into the backfield and sacked Cuozzo for a loss—and more importantly, a fourth down to end the drive.

In the biggest moments, winners shine.

I can say with extreme pride that the 1965 playoff game was one of my best. I must have made about a dozen individual tackles, and had sacks been recorded at the time, I think the record books would show I had at least five. I also contributed in a number of other tackles and broke up plays, building off the adrenaline of the moment and using my momentum to push myself even further. There is something to be said for momentum and how it can carry you to achieve more than even you thought possible. It's when the momentum is peaking that individuals should set their sights on bigger and better things because their chances for success grow exponentially.

Nobody could stop me on their offensive line. I was quick and strong, and I played with more focus, heart, and determination then I ever had before. I remember at one point saying to myself as I approached the line, *Man, if I could can up whatever I've got today and use it for the rest of the games in my career, I would be among the best.*

On top of that, I seemed to get stronger—as did the rest of the Packers defense—as the game went on, just like Coach had prepared us. He pulled me aside later and give me some of the highest praise of my career.

"Willie, I don't want to spoil you," he said. "But I have to tell you that you played as close to a perfect game as I've ever seen in my coaching."

I never forgot his words. Nor would I forget the tension and power of that particular fight with the Colts, a fight that finally ended when the Colts defense yielded ever so slightly and Don kicked a no-doubt-about-it 25-yard field goal to give us the win and send us to a Championship Game against the Browns.

There are no "less important" big moments.

Of all the Lombardi championships, the one that's written about or remembered the least was our win over the Cleveland Browns, the first of our three straight titles.

It's not a game most historians, fans, former players, or coaches, etc., talk about. It's not that it has been forgotten in the annals of NFL history. It's just that in a decade of dominance by the Packers, as a playoff or Championship Game, it simply doesn't rank up there as one of the most memorable contests. It didn't have the drama of the Ice Bowl, the improbability of the shutout of the Giants, or even the controversy of the playoff game with the Colts. Considering from this point on, the league (and the world) would soon find itself in the shadows of the spectacle that is the Super Bowl, it's also understandable that its significance got lost as professional football looked to the future.

Plus the game itself was very understated and average—for some. For me, it was one of the most satisfying efforts of my career. I found success and was able to prove to the team that traded me that they had made the wrong decision—this time on a national stage. Combined with my performance in the playoff game with the Colts, this game probably went a long way toward finding my place in the Hall of Fame.

While our offense certainly did its part to give us the win and cement Coach Lombardi's place in NFL history, the defense once again made sure our opponent did not get off the ground—literally. We won the championship because we were able to stop one of the most dominating players of all time—my good friend, Jim Brown.

Jim and I had continued to stay in touch ever since my trade from Cleveland, checking in from time to time. I asked about the city of Cleveland and former teammates, and we chatted about a particular game or play. Like most athletes, we liked to compare war stories and talk about what we would have done and how it would have been better.

However, this was championship football and there was no phone call, no conversation, no idle chit chat before this game. My phone didn't ring, and there was no way I was going to call him. For now, we weren't gonna be friendly.

It reminded me of another time we were playing the Browns and I knocked halfback Leroy Kelly on his ass so hard on the sideline that he jumped up and yelled at me.

"Hey man, I thought we were friends!"

"Leroy, we might be friends off the field, but for the next 60 minutes, all my friends are wearing Green and Gold," I said. "If you want to talk to me, it'll have to be after a tackle—from the ground!"

Jim Brown felt the same way.

Because of Jim Brown, Cleveland was heavily favored to win. They had a generally young and remarkable offense that was led by the veteran running back, who once again was having a career year. Sportswriters called the Browns an offensive juggernaut, and it was hard to argue. They had breezed through their conference with unbelievable ease and were ready to come to Green Bay and earn their spot at the top.

Meanwhile, we were coming off one of the toughest games we had ever played, an extra game with a stressful overtime that had taxed the team. We were hungry and well-conditioned, but to think the playoff game against the Colts had no effect would be naïve. All anyone had to do was look at the injury report. Bart Starr was cleared to play but had bruised ribs from the hit in the Colts game. Boyd Dowler had problems with his ankle. Max McGee was fighting aches and pains as was much of the offensive line. Jim Taylor had pulled a groin muscle, and Paul Hornung was experiencing pain in his legs and his arms. Also the entire defense seemed to be nicked up.

We were being called "old," which didn't sit very well with us. We were determined to show the Browns and the country that we weren't old, we were experienced. Still, the injuries made us wonder.

We had the advantage of playing at home in front of a crowd that could once again taste how close we were to glory. They arrived early, as they always have in Green Bay despite the cold, and they cheered us from the moment we came on the field for warm-ups with signs that said "Go Pack Go!" and "All The Way Today!"

There was an unusual fog that hung low over the field for a good portion of the game, helping to dub it the Fog Bowl. And the field, which had been covered in snow all week until a grounds crew removed it, soon turned to mud. Coach Bengtson and Coach Lombardi couldn't have been happier with the conditions because they knew the field would quickly turn to a soggy mess and that would help us in our primary objective of neutralizing and stopping Jim Brown. The idea was that if we could take away the Browns' top weapon, it would force them to try to find another way to beat us, and we could hopefully force them to make some mistakes or at least hold down their offense.

I became obsessed with Jim Brown the week leading up to the game, trying to recall everything I had seen from both playing with him and against him. I replayed practices, drills, games in my head, and I tried talking about everything I remembered with my teammates and coaches. I had a nagging fear. What if, despite all of this, Jim still came out unstoppable?

We worked all week long on a strategy meant to contain Jim. We wanted to keep him out of the alleys where he was most effective. The key to stopping Jim Brown, if you didn't want to rely on an act of God, was to not let him get started. If he built any kind of momentum and found even the smallest of holes, he would be gone. Even if a defender did clog up the hole at the last minute, chances are he would have enough speed and momentum at that point to run them over. We were intent on clogging up the middle and being ready to shift if he tried to break outside. We wanted to keep a balanced line with everyone holding their position so he couldn't find an opening to exploit, which meant that everyone had to fight against their instincts and stay in their lane, with the exception of the outside defenders who were encouraged to get past the line and try to turn in to force Jim into the clogged-up middle. It was a strategy we had used against other top rushers, and it had been proven to work as it covered all bases and allowed us to adjust as needed. But we knew this was championship football, and Jim was hungry. He would come to play, and we would have to be ready for the unexpected.

Luckily, we were able to set the tone early in the game. During their first series they ran a running play, and we had our chance to try to push Jim inside. Even with the muddy field, however, he was still able to break just slightly to the outside, trying to find a gap on the left side that he could squeeze (or barrel) through—which brought him face to face with me.

I was fortunate or maybe prepared enough to see where he was going, at least for this play. I positioned myself to give him a split-second illusion that the gap would be there before taking an inside move on the tackle blocking me. At that point, there was no way either one of us could avoid each other, so we both put our heads down and went at each other with full force.

I hit him hard, and he went down for a minimal gain. With our pride on the line, we both jumped up, not wanting to show each other how the impact had affected us. I don't know how he felt, but I was dealing with the painful reminder of our time together in training camp when I was a young man trying to prove my worth and he was showing me what it meant to be a professional football player. Just like then, every muscle in my body seemed to scream with pain, *excruciating* pain. There was no way I would leave the game, but each muscle seemed to beg me to sit back down, to lie down, and to never do that again! That was when Jim said his only words to me the entire game.

"Hey man," he said. "Good hit."

With that he jogged back to his huddle, seemingly unfazed by my hardest tackle, just like he did all those years ago.

Still, it had accomplished the mission. We hit him a couple times in a row, and the defense sent a message that the middle was not going to open. A few more early hits from the other fellas on the Packers line and we could tell Jim was quickly getting frustrated. Dave, Ray, and everyone seemed to get a hit on him. That, combined with a field that was totally destroyed midway through the first quarter, made the Browns realize they were going to have to beat us through the air—and our secondary wasn't going to let that happen.

Offensively, we opened with Bart throwing a number of short passes combined with short runs to bring the defense up to the line. While the Browns offense was stacked with Jim Brown, a line that included Dick Schafrath, Gene Hickerson, John Wooten, and a Pro Bowl quarterback in Frank Ryan, the defense had its own reputation. Anchored by Paul Wiggin and Jim Houston, the Browns defense was incredibly disciplined and fast. They didn't give up many points, so offenses had to take what they could and hope they could catch them being overly aggressive.

After playing conservatively at the start, Bart was able to catch them creeping up just enough, completing a long touchdown pass to Carroll Dale on a fake that gave us a 7–0 lead.

Ryan and the Browns quickly countered by stepping away from the run and throwing a 30-yard outlet pass to Jim Brown that caught us off guard. Another short pass for a touchdown and the Browns were in business. A missed extra point made the game 7–6, and a long field goal bumped it to 9–7.

Not long after, our offense got back on track by going to the Lombardi basics and truly one of the more beautiful plays we ran that game. Led by Jerry Kramer, the front line opened up a Packer Sweep by Hornung for more than 30 yards, keeping a drive going that eventually put us in field-goal range and gave us a 10–9 lead.

It was just one of several great runs by the same guys the national media had been calling too old to be a factor, the same guys who had literally carried our offense over the years in several big games. Both Paul and Jim Taylor had exceptional games, each rushing for around 100 yards despite their injuries.

The second quarter featured more of the same as our defense recognized the impact we were having on Jim Brown. As the Browns switched completely to an air game, our secondary was ready with Bob Jeter deflecting pass after pass and Willie Wood getting a pick that set up yet another field goal for a 13–9 lead. We felt good about how we were performing on both sides of the ball, but Coach was nervous about our inability to punch the ball into the end zone.

"It's too close," he warned on the sideline, and when Cleveland got another field goal right before half to cut the lead to one point, we realized that despite our dominance, the game was way too close to call.

Once again, there was no big halftime speech. We didn't need one. We had truly experienced an up-and-down season with plenty of drama and close games. There was nothing more Coach could tell us that we didn't already know. We weren't executing like we knew we could, and we had to fix it. It was up to us, the players, and nobody else. If we were going to walk off this field as champions, we would have to simply work harder to impose our will.

So that's what we did in the second half. Our defense gave the Browns nothing, holding Jim Brown to just nine yards. Meanwhile, our offensive line began to get a push and imposed its will. The running game picked up, with Paul and Jim getting 5–10 yards at a time that resulted in a Hornung touchdown to bring the score to 20–12. As the game moved into the fourth quarter and both teams found themselves covered in so much mud they were almost indistinguishable, the Browns got desperate and started to throw long passes we could easily read. After another field goal, Herb snatched an interception from Ryan that sewed up the game, giving us a 23–12 win and a return to glory.

We were champions once again. I had also achieved my personal goal of beating the Browns in an extremely meaningful game, playing as well as I could and frustrating my old friend and nemesis. Again, it was not the most exciting or memorable of the postseason games that defined us in the 1960s, but it was a start of the most dominating run in all of football history and one that will be tough to duplicate. For that reason alone, it will always live in the hearts of Packers fans everywhere.

Chapter 16	# The Million-Dollar Fumble—and Change

With more success comes more competition.

The NFL changed forever before the 1966 season, as the pressure of the competition of the growing American Football League (AFL) became too much to bear. Both leagues were spending more than they wanted on draft choices, shelling out a combined $7 million after the 1966 draft, an enormous sum compared to what athletes were previously paid. Plus the practice of stealing players from the rival league was becoming more commonplace. The battle really came to a head when Oakland Raiders co-owner Al Davis took over as AFL commissioner and aggressively pursued NFL quarterbacks, signing a stunning eight of them. Suddenly, it wasn't just about draft picks or second- and third-string players, the leagues were in a full-blown tug of war over the top talent. It became clear to both parties that some kind of agreement would have to be made.

A deal was quickly arranged in which owners formed a combined league with 24 teams (including the new Atlanta Falcons in the NFL and the Miami Dolphins in the AFL) and four more added over time; the New Orleans Saints (1967), Cincinnati Bengals (1968), Seattle Seahawks (1976), and Tampa Bay Buccaneers (1976). The two leagues agreed to share a combined draft of college players starting in 1967 to curb the costs of bidding. Both leagues agreed to play a championship game with the winners of both leagues to end the season, a game that would soon be-come more than a game but rather an event called the Super Bowl. Finally, the merger was finalized in 1970 when both leagues officially joined under one banner, the National Football League, as the NFC and AFC conferences. Even with all of the changes in the league, our mission as the Packers stayed the same—to win it all again.

Competition just became more fierce. There would be longer, tougher practices. There would be more meetings. There would open competition for starting roles, including with players who had filled those roles for a long time. There would be numerous speeches, from motivating to almost threatening, but all with a singular message—we were the Green Bay Packers, we were the world champions, and we would *stay* world champions.

Such a decree also meant Coach wasn't going to tolerate any type of funny business with the players. There would be stricter rules for what we did on the field, in practice, and even how we conducted ourselves in our free time. There would also be tougher penalties for anyone caught breaking Lombardi's rules. They were non-negotiable. That was going to be tough for some of the players, especially McGee and Hornung. Paul had settled down quite a bit with both age and the experience of having been suspended for a year, but he still did his part to earn his party-boy reputation. Max, who knew he was coming to the tail end of his career, had never slowed down and still carried a work-hard, play-hard approach to his life.

While we were in training camp, we had a strict curfew that Max seemed to take personal pleasure in breaking consistently. At least once or twice a season he'd get caught, and this almost became a Packers tradition. This year, we found out, was not the time to get caught.

The plan was for Paul and Max to sneak out after curfew and hit a popular bar that was almost as friendly to the players as the girls that frequented the place. Before they left, they saw an assistant coach's car pull up and they knew there would be a final bed check. Paul backed out, not wanting to push any buttons and get in trouble. He headed back to the room, but Max wasn't going to be swayed and he headed out anyway for a late night.

I'm not sure how Coach found out, but the next morning as I sat in the cafeteria with Bob Skoronski, we saw Coach stomping in with an extremely red face that let us know something was going on. My heart leapt in my throat when I saw him make his way to our table.

"We have a meeting, immediately after you get done eating, training room, all of you!" was all he said before storming off in a big huff. Everybody had heard.

"Why is he so upset?" Bob asked.

"Well, I bet McGee was probably out last night or something," I said half-joking, fully unaware that was the truth.

Moments later, we all waited nervously in the training room as once again Lombardi rushed in with a vengeance. We could see it in his eyes, as we had seen it before—he was going to make an example out of someone.

"Gentlemen, I have tried to keep you in order. I have tried to explain to you why we have certain rules and why those rules must be followed. Up until now, there have been only slight fees and penalties for breaking those rules, but that's going to change now!"

We all had a sense now of what happened.

"McGee, I am tired of you ignoring the rules, of you putting yourself ahead of this organization," he said, and Max just stared back stunned. He had never been singled out before, not like this. "I know you went out last night after curfew, and this time it's going to cost you $1,000."

We couldn't believe what he just said. Up to that point, nobody had even been fined more than $100 and even that was rare. For us in the mid-1960s, $1,000 was a *huge* sum of money. Coach was serious about the fine and used it to not only make an example of McGee but also to lecture us on the importance of playing football his way alone.

"And let me tell you, McGee, the next time you find something so exciting that's worth $1,000, I'm going to ask you to take me with you!"

With that he left, and we all sat there wondering if he was serious, especially Max. A little more than a week later, when we got our first paychecks, we found out. I found myself in the wrong place at the wrong time, crossing by Coach's office after a practice.

"Willie, did Max pay that fine yet?" Coach yelled at me from behind his desk.

"Uh, I don't know, Coach" I replied, knowing full well he hadn't. Coach could see it in my face as well.

"You go tell him right now that I want him to pay it and pay it now!"

I found Max and relayed the message, and I could see his face get pale.

He obviously hadn't taken the threat seriously.

"Ask him if I can pay it to a charity so I can write it off as a tax deduction," he said and I went to tell Coach, wondering how the hell I became the messenger in this exchange. After I passed on Max's request, my role in this matter was done.

"Hell no!" Coach said. "I want it to cost him!"

The incident wouldn't stop Max from his partying ways and there were still quite a few times when he would sneak out, but he never missed a bed check ever again. I don't think any of us did.

With Coach cracking down, our experienced star players healthy once again, a batch of new young talent, and the motivation to repeat as champions, we were eager to get the season started and looked forward to an opener in Milwaukee against the Colts. This was typically when we would experience our annual first-game collapse when the doubters would come out and Coach would get frustrated, feeling like we hadn't worked hard enough in training camp.

The Colts posted pictures of Don Chandler's famous controversial field goal, using it as a way to motivate them to victory. In Week 1, their offense came out hot, using a blend of Unitas passes and Tony Lorick, Lenny Moore, and Tom Matte runs. Early in the game, they pushed our defense back to our 19-yard line and decided they were going to send a message on fourth down by opting to go for it rather than kick a field goal. They weren't going to try and surprise us. They were going to run straight up the middle, challenging our defensive line head on with their offensive line.

We held.

Next time down, they kicked the field goal, but two touchdowns, both on interception returns by Lee Roy Caffey and Bob Jeter, gave us a 14–3 lead at half. We decided to not let them have anything more on offense, and they didn't. Our offense, however, put together a package of sweeps, short passes to Boyd Dowler, a couple of surprise plays with Paul Hornung throwing and Bart Starr running, and a determined Jim Taylor bruising his way up the middle. At the final gun, we opened the season with a dominating 24–3 victory over one of our oldest rivals. By this point, they seemed to *all* be our rivals.

During the next three weeks, we dismantled Cleveland, the Rams, and Detroit, all in close games and all tests of our fortitude. There was no doubt the Pack was back for more. After a brief hiccup, a close 21–20 loss to our personal thorn in the side, San Francisco, we came back with a manhandling of the Bears 17–0 at Wrigley Field.

That was another significant game for me personally because I played exceptionally well. The Bears young star running back Gale Sayers was held to 29 yards on 15 carries. Stopping Gale was no easy task—ever. If Jim Brown is the greatest running back of all time, Gale Sayers is a close second. He was one of those rare runners who had everything: speed, finesse, power, determination, intelligence, the ability to score and to surprise you with something different each and every time you played him. He was impossible to plan a defense against. It didn't matter what you did—you had to be aware that at some point, he was simply going to make a spectacular play on you. There was nothing to be done about it other than to try and contain him as best you could.

In Week 6, our defense did one of the best jobs anyone ever did in containing him, and I was fortunate to find myself involved in what seemed to be almost every tackle on the future Hall of Famer. Our defense pushed him and forced him to my side all game long, and I often found myself going heads-up with Gale, which was typically the place a defender did not want to be. If he saw he had a one-on-one situation, much like Jim Brown, he would try his best to run you over. He was the kind of running back who made you look for your teammates asking, "Where's the help?" As the momentum of the game got going, I began to see where he was going to go and how I could cut him off. He could never get going, and without Gale, the Bears offense had nothing. My performance earned one of my most revered and favorite Player of the Week honors. Even more special were the compliments of my teammates, as Fuzzy Thurston proclaimed it the greatest game he ever saw played at defensive end by anybody.

If I had a perfect game in Week 6, the entire team had a perfect game in Week 7 against the Atlanta Falcons. To be fair, the Falcons were a brand new team with guys who had just started playing together, and many were castoffs from other teams. Still, beating any professional team by the score of 56–3 is impressive. It was one of those games where absolutely everything worked as planned. The defense gave one of its strongest efforts, giving up hardly any yardage and causing two turnovers for touchdowns. The offense moved through the air and on the ground at will. Even the youngsters, Donny Anderson and Jim Grabowski, who Coach picked up to replace Hornung and Taylor eventually, got their feet wet with Jim running and Donnie returning a punt for 77 yards, helping secure a place where he could contribute in the immediate future. We played so well that Coach had almost nothing to say after the game.

We followed up with another impressive win over the Detroit Lions 31–7 and then a close loss to the Vikings who seemed to always play us tough regardless of their record. Week 10 saw us stop the Bears 13–6 in yet another defensive struggle and a game that meant something special to true Packers fans. This game against the Bears was the last game Paul Hornung played in his professional career.

Paul struggled with a pinched nerve in his neck that also affected his shoulder, limiting his playing time. In the game against the Bears, he was involved in a run when rookie linebacker Doug Buffone hit Paul hard and essentially put him out for the game, for the rest of the season and, little did we know, for good. Paul was always questionable for the rest of the season and I know he wanted to come back, working hard to get his shoulder feeling right, but it never cooperated. A surprising off-season move ended his time in Green Bay, and the same injury forced him to hang up his cleats before he ever took the field again.

Paul had been one of the Packers' greatest contributors, a model for the franchise (for the most part), a dedicated player who had been with Lombardi since the beginning, and he had truly helped turn the Packers into the organization they were and are today. He deserved a hero's sendoff, a final chance to play the game he loved in front of the fans that loved him. Unfortunately, like so many other athletes who have gone before and after him, his career ended too soon and without the fanfare he deserved. But if he had known it was his last game, I'm sure he would have been satisfied with a win against the Bears at Lambeau Field. He also would have made sure we stayed focused on the bigger picture, winning the next two games and putting ourselves in a position to get back to the championship.

We did just that, beating the Vikings and the 49ers. Now the only thing left in our way was a game against the Colts—a very famous game.

The best way to handle a rival is to continue to dominate them.

It's funny they called it the Million-Dollar Fumble because I was about a $10,000 player and I never saw any of that money!

I'm really not sure why they named it that. Granted it was a key play, one that locked up a tight game against one of our oldest and most bothersome rivals, breaking their hearts for the second year in a row and sending us on our way to the title. It's hard to put a price tag on that, but why a million dollars?

Maybe it was reflective of the rising costs and value of professional football. The financials behind the organization and the sport as a whole had skyrocketed in the last couple years, even going so far as to get two rival leagues to merge. Maybe it's because whoever won that game was going to the championship and would draw in millions of viewers and millions in revenue for the league. Or maybe that was the size of the bounty the Colts and my old friend Johnny Unitas put on the Packers for keeping the Colts from the Promised Land again.

As we entered Week 13, we found ourselves just a game ahead of the Colts who seemed to almost always be on our tails our slightly ahead of us in the standings every year I played. Coach Don Shula had his boys, led by Unitas, wide receiver Raymond Berry, and their three-headed running attack poised to give us a good shot at the division despite our opening-day victory against them. We knew that if the Colts won this game and tied up with us, there was a good possibility we would find ourselves playing against them in another playoff game, and we didn't want to push our luck two years in a row.

We were banged up yet again. The defense had all sorts of nicks and bruises. The always dependable Fuzzy Thurston had to sit out; Boyd Dowler was in and out of the game, taking away a key passing threat; and

Bart Starr started to experience back spasms early in the game, which meant we would once again have to rely on Zeke, who had become one of the league's best and most reliable backup quarterbacks.

As the game started, the rain was pouring down at Memorial Stadium, yet another phenomenon that seemed to happen quite a bit when we played in Baltimore. It seemed to always rain there. Soon we could barely tell who was who as everybody on both sides of the ball was covered with mud. As a defender, when that happens, we've got one rule to follow—look for the ball and chase it!

The defense did a solid job of containing Unitas, mixing blitzes with drop-back coverage and doing what we could to confuse him and plug up their running game. However, at halftime we still found ourselves trailing 10–7 and feeling a little nervous. With the weather conditions and both teams trying desperately to hold on, to not give up an inch, there was very little effective offense. That carried into the third quarter, where it seemed both offenses sputtered around midfield on every possession, unable to get within striking range. As we went into the fourth quarter still trailing, the offense knew it had to start taking a few more chances.

Zeke and Coach had opted for focusing on the ground game, using our arsenal of running backs to wear out the Colts' line while mixing in some short passes. Unfortunately, the Colts weren't budging, and they showed no signs of tiring, hungry to take a game and a title hope away from us. With time running down, the decision was made to continue to pound away but to also start looking for a deeper opening. Midway through the fourth, Zeke found a couple and took his chances, hitting receivers and pushing us to the 25-yard line where we were within field-goal range and had a chance to tie it up.

But we weren't quite finished. On first down the Colts blitzed, hoping for a sack that would move us back outside of field-goal range. McGee, the wily veteran, was supposed to run a short route but sensed the blitz and went long. Zeke only had time to look at his one receiver before being crushed by the defenders and he lofted a perfect pass that Max hauled in before getting tackled at the 4-yard line. Two plays later, Elijah punched in the ball, and we had a 14–10 lead. Because of the time, the Colts, finally looking tired and frustrated, were down to a final chance.

Nobody on the Packers sideline or in that defensive huddle felt safe. We all looked at each other in the huddle on the opening play of the Colts' final drive.

"We know what we gotta do," Dave Robinson said.

"Let's go now, let's go," Herb Adderley yelled, clapping his hands.

Everybody had something to say. We were tired, having played tough in the mud all day, but we had to suck it up for one more stop. We were ready to do our job, to take care of business like we had many times before. But Johnny and Raymond and all three of the Colts' running backs had different ideas, and as they marched quickly with a balanced attack into our territory, I could only think of one thing:

Damn, here we go again.

They were getting dangerously close to striking distance with plenty of time left. We knew at this point they were going to be looking to pass first. Johnny was hot, and we worried about not being able to contain him. As we jogged back into the huddle on a critical down, it was my turn to speak up.

"Alright fellas, somebody's gotta make a play," I said, looking at each of them. "We gotta get this ball back. Somebody's gotta make a damn play!"

As we broke, that was all I could think of—making a play. I was in no mood to see Johnny pull off a show at our expense. I knew I had to do what I could to disrupt this drive, just as I trusted all of my teammates to be thinking the same. If we all went for him, if we all tried to force a turnover, I was confident one of us would break through, one of us would find an opportunity.

Fortunately, it came to me, and I was ready.

All game long, the Colts' linemen were pushing me to the outside. Johnny was a quarterback who liked to drop back in the pocket and then step into a throw to his receivers. By pushing me to the outside, it opened up the pocket and gave him a little more time. On this play, I decided to switch it up, to not try and power through the block but to actually take a half second to go with it. As the ball was snapped, I pushed to the outside, giving the impression to the guard that he was overpowering me.

Johnny stepped up in the pocket and I suddenly reversed off my guard and made a move to the inside, which freed me up to pursue the quarterback. With his great instincts, Johnny saw me coming and looked one final time for a receiver, which our secondary had blanketed, before taking off running.

By the time I got to where he was, I was behind him but in close pursuit. At that point, I knew he could no longer see me because he was looking for a place to run upfield. I made up in my mind that no matter what, I was going to get there, I was going to get to him. I turned up the speed. As I got close, I remembered what I had just said in the huddle about making a play. Just tackling Johnny wouldn't be enough. We needed the ball. Right before I got to him, I swung my arm down like a hammer on the tucked ball, hitting him in the back with my body. I felt the ball pop out. As we crumpled to the ground, I looked around for it desperately only to see Dave Robinson pick it up. I let out a yell, knowing we had won and locked up the division!

A week later we beat the Rams to end the regular season, and we were headed to the NFL Championship Game once again. Johnny and I became great friends. Over the course of our careers, we talked a lot both on and off the field about a variety of things, including key football games and key plays we were involved in, even against each other.

I don't think we ever once talked about the Million-Dollar Fumble.

As soon as one big moment ends, chances are there's another one coming up.

The big game that everybody remembers between the Green Bay Packers and the Dallas Cowboys will always be the infamous Ice Bowl, one of the grittiest, toughest, most exciting games in NFL history. No doubt.

But because of the setting, the struggles, the drama, and the folklore quality of that game, as well as the introduction of the Super Bowl, a lot of NFL fans have completely overlooked the first time we played the Cowboys in the postseason, the 1966 NFL Championship Game, which in my opinion still remains one of the most exciting title games in league history.

We finished up one of our most successful seasons in recent history, going 12–2 and putting up incredible numbers on both offense and defense. Bart Starr led the league by completing more than 62 percent of his passes for 2,257 yards and was given a well-deserved MVP Award. We sent eight players to the Pro Bowl, including five on defense—Henry Jordan, Dave Robinson, Herb Adderley, Willie Wood, and myself—we had also developed some new young running backs, getting them comfortable in the Packers system and using them to complement Taylor and Pitts. We hadn't taken nearly as many lumps this season as we had last year in our championship run, and now that we had finally gotten here, we knew we had the tools to repeat.

The Cowboys had proven to the league that they were a team to be reckoned with, as well, especially on offense. They had opened the season by scoring an average of 45 points per game and pushing somewhat unexpectedly to a 10–3–1 record, getting past the heavily favored Cleveland Browns to get to the Championship Game.

The similarities between the two teams were astounding. The Cowboys' Doomsday Defense (which included names like Bob Lilly, George Andrie, Chuck Howley, Cornell Green, and Mel Renfro) had bullied offenses all season, just as the Packers had. Like Bart, the Cowboys also had an experienced, reliable quarterback in "Dandy" Don Meredith and a whole slew of offensive weapons, including split end and "World's Fastest Man," Bob Hayes, an Olympic sprinter who was the key to the Cowboys' passing attack. Finally, the Cowboys also had a veteran coach in Tom Landry with a penchant for perfection, one that Coach Lombardi knew all too well.

Coach Lombardi and Coach Landry had a rivalry that went back to their days of coaching together with the Giants, Lombardi on the offensive side of the ball and Landry on the defensive. They both had a mutual respect for each other, but there was a competitiveness always bubbling under the surface. Coach Lombardi tried to dissect everything he could about how Tom Landry coached, recalling strategies, trends, and tendencies. Coach Landry did the same.

Despite Coach Lombardi's success, including a chance to repeat as champion, Coach Landry was still getting more attention from the press, having turned the Cowboys into a dominating team in a relatively short period of time, much like Lombardi had done when he first arrived in

Green Bay. It almost seemed as if the press was passing the torch in a sense, and that rubbed the Old Man the wrong way.

We could not lose. From the moment we arrived at our training facilities in Tulsa, Coach Lombardi worked us as if we were huge underdogs. He once again emphasized discipline and endurance, the keys to beating a team as talented as the Cowboys. We couldn't make a mistake, and we had to outlast them. The other element was preparation, and both Coach Lombardi and Coach Bengtson worked diligently with us on new game plans designed to take away the Cowboys' strengths.

On the offensive side, we planned to mix up the running game with both sweeps and runs up the middle to create confusion. We didn't want to show them any kind of trends in the running game, which would hopefully keep the Doomsday Defense guessing. As for the passing game, the plan was to frustrate them with short- to medium-length passes, never going long. This was meant to deny the defensive line enough time to get into the backfield.

On the defensive side, the strategy was simple. We were going to take Hayes out of the passing game by using Jeter, Adderley, and Wood to contain and double team him. Other teams had tried stopping Hayes by blitzing Meredith, hoping to throw off the timing, but Hayes was simply too fast. We were confident that we could use our Pro Bowlers to stick with him if they worked together.

On both sides of the ball, we worked on specific plays over and over again, repeating until Coach felt satisfied with the execution.

"This is going to be a game of will!" he said. "It's about the will to win and to endure, and preparation is the only way you can do this."

As we started the 1966 Championship Game, all that hard work and planning seemed to pay off. We started with a solid drive capped off with a 17-yard pass from Starr to Elijah Pitts out of the backfield for a 7–0 lead. On the ensuing kickoff, Jim Grabowski picked up a fumbled return and ran it into the end zone to give us a two-touchdown lead within seconds. Offensively and on special teams, it looked like we were prepared to impose our will.

Our defense didn't start quite as solid. After we did a fairly decent job of shutting down Hayes and frustrating Meredith, the Cowboys switched to an emphasis on the running game, and they were able to push us around and find holes. Dan Reeves found the end zone first on a 3-yard run, and Don Perkins got in not long after from 23 yards to tie the game before the end of the first quarter. We buckled down in the second quarter, only allowing a field goal while our offense put up another score with a 51-yard pass from Starr to Carroll Dale, but we were still frustrated heading into half with a slim lead of 21–17.

We were containing Hayes like we had planned, but we had to find a way to stop the Dallas run while watching Meredith who was throwing with precision. We decided we needed to put a little more pressure on him, trying to disrupt the flow of their offense. It could work to our advantage. It also could be a Dallas trap, one that other teams had been sucked into all year.

In the third quarter, our defense started to get to Meredith and we held them to a field goal. Starr continued his impressive day, throwing a 16-yard touchdown pass to Boyd Dowler and following it up with a 28-yard heave to McGee to put us up 34–20. It would have been 35–20, but Don Chandler had the extra point blocked, a play that added an unnecessary bit of drama to the end of the game.

As confident as we were feeling, we knew the Cowboys had plenty of time and offensive firepower to stage a comeback.

And that's exactly what they did. With just less than 5:00 to go in the game, Meredith threw a 68-yard touchdown pass to tight end Frank Clarke to put them within a touchdown. It was a blown play by our backup safety Tom Brown. Clarke came out running right at Brown, faked to the right, and then turned left. The move twisted Brown right out of position, and Clarke caught a perfect pass from Meredith and glided to the end zone.

Brown came to the sideline completely dejected, but we had little time to comfort him. On our next possession, the Cowboys defense smelled blood and held us to a four-and-out, sacking Bart and stopping Jim Taylor in the backfield. Don Chandler's punt came up short, and the Cowboys had the ball at our 47-yard line with just more than 2:00 left to play—plenty of time to tie up the game.

Perhaps sensing Brown's frustration at having given up the big touchdown, Meredith and Clarke went at him again with the exact same play. We had warned Tom in the huddle to watch for this because it was the kind of cold-blooded move a championship team would do. As Clarke broke straight at Brown, the safety tried to anticipate which way he was going to cut and unfortunately guessed wrong. Once again, Clarke started streaking past him, but this time Tom reached out and grabbed him, making sure he wouldn't get the pass or a wide-open lane to a tie ballgame.

It was an obvious hold and the refs saw it, calling pass interference. First-and-goal for the Cowboys on our 2-yard line.

Next season, at the Ice Bowl, the Packers offense left its mark in history with a great drive capped off by a gutsy play that sent the Cowboys home and propelled the Packers into our second-straight Super Bowl. But this year, against those same Cowboys, it was the defense on this final drive that brought us the title and sent us to the first-ever matchup with the AFL.

These were the moments we played for, the moments where we defined ourselves as professionals, as men, and as champions. Everything was on the line, and it was going to come down to who wanted it more, who was willing to fight just a bit a harder. On first down, the Cowboys tried what most other teams do on their first possession that close to the goal line. They played it safe, trying a run up the middle that we sniffed out and shut down after a gain of only a yard.

On the next play, which we assumed would be a run, Meredith surprised us by dropping back and throwing a quick outlet pass to tight end Pettis Norman, mainly a blocker and not a receiver. In fact, during the season, he had only caught 12 passes. The ball dropped incomplete, but even better, one of their players had jumped early. A false start penalty pushed them back five yards, giving our defense just enough room to breathe. That ended up being a key play. Without the penalty, they still would have had three chances to probably run it in from just a yard out. Keeping a team to no yardage, especially right up the middle and three times in a row, is asking a lot.

They had three downs left and plenty of time—three chances to force us into overtime. On second down, from the 6-yard line, we got lucky. Meredith tossed a quick swing pass to Reeves in the left flat, just away from me as I was trying to push myself inside. Reeves was open and would have been able to score, but he dropped the pass. We avoided that threat, but we knew we had to now watch both the run and the pass equally.

On third down, Meredith again dropped back and looked for Norman, who once again managed to slip by unguarded. Don saw him open and rushed the throw, coming up short. Still, Norman came back to catch the ball around the line of scrimmage and was able to dive ahead for a few yards, getting tackled at the 2-yard line. Again, this was a play the Cowboys could have possibly scored on with a good pass. Meredith took the blame on this play and despite a great career, he is forever remembered for passing short on what Dallas fans thought would have been a surefire touchdown.

The Cowboys had one play left with time running out. They were close enough for a pass or a running play, so we had to be prepared for both. As it was in many big plays, we didn't have to say much to each other in the huddle. We knew what we had to do, and damn if we weren't gonna do it!

As we approached the line, a calm quiet fell over the stadium. This was the play. Don took the snap and as the two lines collided, Dave Robinson saw an opening. It wasn't in his lane and it wasn't where he was supposed to be defending, but he said later that he thought he could get at the quarterback. Going against what we had been taught, he improvised. Dave popped through the hole, and Don had no choice but to get out of his pocket and roll to the outside. There was nowhere for him to go. A split second before Dave got to him, Dandy Don did the only thing he could, saying a prayer and heaving the ball into the end zone and a pile of Packers and Cowboys who clawed and scratched for the ball.

One man came up with it—Tom Brown, the safety who had given up the big score and caused the pass interference. He had his redemption, cradling that ball and falling to the ground, wrapping up yet another Packers NFL championship.

It was one of the best defensive stands and one of the best games we had played together. It was yet another title, but this one felt incomplete. We didn't want to admit it, but we knew it was true. Our work wasn't done yet. We had one more game, the first ever meeting between the best in the NFL and the best in the AFL. Many of us still considered our league the superior league, but now just winning our league wasn't going to be enough. We had to prove we were the best *anywhere*.

| Chapter 17 | Carrying the NFL in Super Bowl I |

Sometimes we play for more than just ourselves.

It seems almost inconceivable now, but the first Super Bowl (back before it was even called a Super Bowl) between the Green Bay Packers and the Kansas City Chiefs was not a sell out. It was affordable to the common fan and attracted only a slightly larger national television audience.

More than 60 million viewers watched the game on television back then, compared to more than 111 million—the largest TV audience ever—for the 2011 Super Bowl between the Packers and Steelers. The highest ticket price for the first Super Bowl was around $12, while the *average* price for the most recent game exceeded $4,500. At the 2011 game itself in Jerry Jones' mammoth stadium, more than 103,000 people crammed in to watch, and the hosts not only added extra seats but unfortunately had to turn away some ticket holders. At the Los Angeles Memorial Coliseum, where the first Big Game was held, only about two-thirds of the stadium was filled, and the players on the field could feel it.

I don't think people were quite sure what to make of the game. By this point, the NFL and AFL were both extremely popular and lucrative and the joining of the two leagues made a lot of sense, but transitions are never simple. Each league, regardless of how long they had been around, was used to its individual Championship Game being the one that determined who wore the crown. Now there was an extra game, and everyone from the fans to the league executives was unsure of its importance.

That's what we thought anyway—until two things happened. One, Coach Lombardi kicked our asses in the practices leading up to the game like he had never done before and two, the phone calls and telegrams from around the NFL started pouring in, all with the same message, "You have to win."

Several of the Packers' players received calls, many from some of their oldest rivals, talking about representing the league. Suddenly, coaches and players who openly and vocally hated the Packers were pledging their support and begging us to win for the NFL, to leave no doubt about which was the better league. We were all told we were playing for more than just this mythical world title, we were playing to make a statement to the AFL that despite the two leagues merging together, the AFL was still clearly inferior.

I got a phone call from Johnny Unitas the week before as we trained in Santa Barbara. He called to remind me who we were as a team, how dominant we were, and how we had to show the new arrivals in town what it meant to play against someone from the NFL.

"Willie, you guys are playing for all of us," he said.

"I know, Johnny," I said. "We know this is an important one."

Then he laughed and told me something that fired me up.

"How about you go out there and give them the kind of shit you always give me!"

"Johnny," I said. "We're going to do what we have to do."

Nobody got more pressure than Coach, and we could tell it affected him. He seemed extra nervous and fired up at practices and meetings, and it looked like he hadn't slept much. His phone was always ringing, and the telegrams were constantly pouring in, almost to the point of it being a distraction. Every coach, owner, and even some of the players called to make sure he was doing everything he could to get his team ready. Coach shared some of the telegrams with us in meetings, emphasizing the magnitude of this game, making sure our priorities were clear.

"You have to win this one to show them all who you really are," he said. "And we *will* win this one."

What started as a game without definition was quickly becoming the most important game of our lives, one that woud clearly show we were the best around—the best team, the best league, and the best football players in the world. Coach killed us at practices, pushing the exercising and running and making us run plays over and over again until there wasn't a single flaw. He imposed major fines for breaking curfews and for being late to meetings, pushing Lombardi Time even earlier. He was intense and tough, yelling at us about anything and everything. He expected nothing less than total focus and concentration. If any of us had assumed Coach Lombardi couldn't possibly be any more of a hardass than he had shown us in the past, we found out that week in Santa Barbara that we were mistaken.

The biggest challenge we faced, however, wasn't the practicing but rather our lack of experience with the Chiefs. And by lack of experience, I mean none. We knew very little about their coaching style, playing style, offensive plays, defensive schemes, or the true talent of their players. All we had was film to watch, and that's exactly what we did. We gathered and watched as much as we could, trying to pick up any clues about what the Chiefs might throw at us and how their style of play might differ from anything we knew. Unable to really form a game plan from experience, Coach took a basic approach to the game, focusing on our strengths and assuming those would overpower whatever the Chiefs brought to the table.

I was both excited and nervous about my individual matchups. I knew I would face multiple guards and tackles on the offensive side of the ball, so I did my best to study all of them, scrutinizing the film to find any place I could take an advantage. I knew most of my research would come from the first few minutes of the game. I made the commitment to go into the game working my speed and staying observant. I also wanted to make sure I was the one who avoided making crucial mistakes.

Surprisingly, Coach Lombardi shared that same approach, especially in his pregame speech. His Green Bay Packers had never been a conservative team. We had always gone out with the philosophy of imposing our will on both sides of the ball. Coach had a killer instinct that he passed along to his players, making us tough and unapologetic. We were the ones who dictated how the game went and, more often than not, that proved overwhelming to our opponents. This time around, things were different. Perhaps it was the pressure that got to Coach. As the week went on, he emphasized more and more the need for us to be careful. He said we were walking into unfamiliar territory and we shouldn't underestimate our enemy.

"I don't want any of you to think they don't have the right to be here," he said. "They've got a good team made up of All-Americans. They're a talented team, and they need to be respected as such."

As he gathered us in the locker room right before game time, he reminded us how good of a team we were, as well, and how we had the talent and discipline to come out victorious. "You should all be proud of your profession," Coach said. For the final time, he reminded us of the game's significance and our place in history. Then he pulled us back, telling us to be careful on the field and to play with a sense of caution.

"I don't want you to go out there and make the big mistake," he said, the words sounding foreign coming from his mouth. "I don't want you to give this team any reason to feel that they can be successful. I propose that if you don't make the big mistakes, you will be successful."

He was right, of course, but it felt strange to us. For the first time in a long time, I walked onto a football field with a sense of caution. With Coach's words ringing in my ears (and my fears of being the guy who made the big mistake), I played reserved football. I ignored my instincts at times, choosing to stay in my lanes at all times. I avoided going hard in pursuit against the Chiefs quarterback, future Hall of Famer Len Dawson, who was a scrambler with an ability to make plays out of the pocket. I rarely rushed inside, afraid of a runner cutting to the outside. All at once, I found myself playing as a calm, structured, reserved Willie Davis. It wasn't working for me.

Truthfully, it wasn't working for *anyone* on defense. The entire defensive front was getting frustrated as they struggled to get any kind of pressure on Dawson. The linebackers found themselves focusing too much on filling the gaps, and dependable guys like Ray Nitschke were missing tackles. Willie Wood dropped a couple of possible interceptions, and the secondary wasn't applying pressure to the receivers. We were clearly a more talented defense than they were an offense, yet we were getting outplayed, focusing too much on not giving up the big play rather than firing on all cylinders.

Luckily our offense, which was also taking a cautious approach, found some early success with a backup veteran who didn't even expect to play.

Most Packers fans have heard some version of the Max McGee Super Bowl story, the aging receiver with a reputation for living the night life and staying out well past curfew the night before, who showed up at the game hungover and not expecting to play, and then he gave a dominating performance despite it all. A lot of what has been passed down through the years is myth, but I can say that the main elements, from what I know, are pretty accurate.

As Max approached the twilight of his storied career and the offense switched its aerial attack to Boyd Dowler, Max's playing time began to shrink. In 1966, Max had just four catches. Fully aware he was no longer a serious part of the Packers offense, Max began to take more risks with Lombardi's rules.

During the week leading up to the Super Bowl, Boyd was suffering from a shoulder injury and was unsure if he could play, so Max made sure he was ready. However, the day before the game, Boyd seemed ready to go. The story goes that Max went out with a few stewardesses he had met in town, sneaking out past curfew alone because nobody would go with him, fearful of Coach Lombardi's new, larger fines. Max wasn't seen until the next morning when Bart Starr saw him coming in as he went down to get breakfast. Max went to his room, napped for a few hours, and got ready to go to the game, allegedly telling Boyd he hoped he was able to play because Max himself wasn't feeling very well.

I asked Max later, after I heard the story, why he had really risked going out, and his response was classic Max. "Well, I knew it was going to be the last game of the year either way," he said. "How much trouble could I get in?"

As he sat on the sideline, nursing an obvious hangover and talking with a sidelined Hornung early in the game, Boyd once again hurt his shoulder and had to come out. A cautious Coach Lombardi wanted an experienced veteran in there in such an important game, and he called out for Max. Completely surprised and unprepared, Max couldn't even find his helmet, so he grabbed a lineman's helmet by the bench and ran in, trying to shake the cobwebs and focus for the first time in the last few days on the game itself.

The rest is history.

After a few plays, Max realized he wasn't being covered and told Bart. "They're leaving me alone, throw it my way."

Not long after, Max slipped by the cornerback for a 37-yard touchdown pass that gave us a 7–0 lead and set the tone. The score helped us breathe a little easier. However, we were still playing conservatively, and in the second quarter the Chiefs began to recognize it. They took advantage, opening up the offense more and gaining more than 10 yards per play during their next possession. Quicker than we could blink, Dawson had thrown a touchdown pass to Curtis McClinton to tie up the game.

We countered with old-school Packers football, relying on our running game, more specifically the Packer Sweep, charging 73 yards in 13 plays and capping it off with a 14-yard Jim Taylor run for a 14–7 lead. But the Chiefs came right back, advancing the ball quickly once again and setting up a 31-yard field goal with about a minute left in the half, cutting our lead to 14–10. As we jogged into the locker room at halftime, one thing was clear.

This Kansas City team came to win, and if we didn't play better, they could do it.

Coach Lombardi knew it, too. More often than not, I stayed in the back of the room during his halftime speech, but for some reason this time I was seated in front when Coach told us to listen up. He started by telling us he was pleased with some aspects of what we were doing and how we had the lead. He then acknowledged we were playing too tight and we had to make some key adjustments, especially on defense. He wanted us to hit harder and put more pressure on the quarterback. I was thinking to myself about how we had wanted to do that all game but felt confined by Coach's fear of us making a mistake.

Then I felt his leg brush up against mine—and the Old Man was shaking.

I looked up into his face, and I could see the fear in his eyes. Despite everything he had preached to us about winning and the importance of this game, we hadn't quite realized the full impact. Coach was terrified the game was this close. He saw both success and failure within reach. He was sweating, his face looked pale, and his eyes looked tired and worried.

But they also looked determined and there was a recognition there as well, something that let me know before he even spoke the words that we were going to come out differently in the second half.

"You've played 30 minutes of football cautiously, not wanting to make the mistakes that could hurt us. You played 30 minutes, by my suggestion, adjusting to the Chiefs and you came out okay," he said. "Now I want them to adjust to you. Let the Chiefs have the burden of trying to stop you. I want you to go out there and play 30 minutes of Green Bay Packer football!"

A leader is willing to change the plan, even if it's his own.

With that change, we suddenly felt free. You could see it in the eyes of the fellas, all of them eager to let it rip and see what happened. This was a confident team, and a confident team doesn't like being restrained. Coach realized he had been a little too hesitant with a team he had trained to be aggressive. It was time to turn us loose.

"Are you the world champion Green Bay Packers?" he asked us as we all roared, eager to get back out there. "Get out on that field and answer me!"

We owned the second half—it was obvious to us, the Chiefs, and the millions of fans who watched across the country. The offense came out firing, taking advantage of the many options they had, including a re-energized Max McGee and Bart's ability to improvise. The defense came out with a hunger, knowing we could now apply the pressure when we saw the opportunities. Every defender came out and looked at his opposite and said, "No more." On the very first play of their possession, I was in Len Dawson's face, and almost every play after that, somebody on the Packers defense did the same. We sacked him, pressured him, hit him, and hurried him. We made him uncomfortable, and when the quarterback's uncomfortable, it's tough for any offense to put up points.

We shut down the Chiefs in the second half, holding them scoreless, starting with a Willie Wood interception early in the half that came off pressure I applied to Dawson on one of their first drives. Willie returned the pick to the 5-yard line and on the very next play, Elijah Pitts ran it in for a score and a 21–10 lead.

The game was essentially over. Bart threw another touchdown pass to McGee, who had recovered from his hangover to have a career day (seven receptions for 138 yards), and Elijah scored another on a run to give us the 35–10 win and the title of the first *true* World Champions.

The significance of that game, what it was and of course what it would become, was lost on us in the aftermath. We knew we had won the first big game between the two leagues, and it was an accomplishment that made us proud. I remember a reporter asked me after the game what it felt like to win.

"It's like ice cream with sugar on it," I said. "It's double sweet!"

The game's true importance came to us little by little in the minutes after the game with the frenzy of the press broadcasting to the world that we were the champions; then a few days later when we returned to a hero's welcome of epic proportions in Green Bay; in the weeks to follow when we got calls once again from all over the NFL congratulating us and even more; and years later when the Super Bowl grew to what it is today.

| The Pressure of Staying
on the Path

**We all want to quit at some point. We all need
someone to remind us why we should stay on course.**

After the 1966 season ended, I almost made a critical mistake that would
have truly affected the rest of my life. Luckily, I had two unbelievable
mentors and the awareness to realize they were smarter than me and
could guide me in what turned out to be a critical life decision.

With all my success in football and a growing role within Schlitz
Brewing, I found myself busier and busier. Super Bowl and Pro Bowl appearances extended an already exhausting season, and the work at the
brewing company was getting more demanding. Plus there were the demands of helping to raise two children. It was getting a little tough to
handle, and my studies at the University of Chicago were suffering.

When I first decided to go to grad school, it was all about security. I
had no idea what kind of success I was going to have in football, and I was
scared about what would happen when the career ended. I also knew
that success on the field might not equal success after football, especially
for a black player in the 1960s. I was lucky to have that kind of foresight.

I was also scared by what I saw with Hall of Famer Marion Motley, the
former fullback with the Browns who was leaving just as I entered the
league. Motley was a dominant offensive weapon who carried the Browns
to four consecutive championships when the team played in the AAFC.
When the Browns joined the NFL, he smoothly made the transition, also
building a reputation as a tough blocker and ferocious linebacker that

earned him a spot as the second black player in the Hall (after Emlen Tunnell). Injuries forced him to retire earlier than he wanted, and Marion approached the Browns soon after, looking for a job and hoping to get into coaching. What he found were more closed doors than open ones. He could no longer be of value as a player, so the organization wanted little to do with him. They essentially asked him if he had tried the hard labor route, and sure enough, here was this amazing player who had given so much and had so much to offer in terms of mentoring, and now he was desperately seeking contractor jobs. The Browns eventually did bring him back for scouting, but the lesson in how big organizations can treat their employees at the ends of their careers stayed with me for quite a while.

Even so, as I found more and more success, I couldn't help but wonder if my situation would be different. When I registered for post-graduate schooling, I had no idea I would be a perennial Pro Bowler and a captain of a multi-championship team with a solid reputation around the league and the country. I began to wonder if that proven success would open up some doors for me after football. I wondered if what I had accomplished on the field might just be enough to create some other opportunities. Of course, I was using that as an excuse.

The truth is I was tired. I was tired from the season, from having to constantly fly back and forth to go to classes, of the studying and the exams, the never-ending scheduling conflicts, and the extra work I had to do to pay for it all. I was tired of the hustle and bustle of my life and school most of all. I wanted to quit.

If I had made back then the kind of money that players make today, I never would have gone back to college in the first place. I wouldn't have found the need to, and quitting would have been much easier. I also knew that if somebody, anybody I respected had told me it was understand-able—that they supported my decision to drop out—I would have done it. So I drove up to Green Bay in the off-season to talk to Coach Lombardi.

"I thought you'd be in classes today," he said when I walked into his office. Coach never missed anything. I had skipped class to come have this talk and how he could remember my school schedule on top of ev-erything else in his life baffled me.

"Coach, I don't know if I can do it anymore," I said to him honestly.

There was no need to be anything other than honest. He would have seen right through me anyway. I told him about my struggles, about balancing my life, the difficulty of the school work, and finding the time to study. I told him I was exhausted. As I was one of the biggest assets on his team, I thought *that* more than anything would convince him to support my decision. I thought he wouldn't want anything to jeopardize my role on his Packers team. I underestimated him.

He sat silently, leaned back in his chair, occasionally fidgeting with his glasses and giving no expression, no insight into what he was thinking. When he was sure I was done, he took his time in speaking, but his words were few.

"It's always tough to suck it up and go harder late in the game when you'd rather quit, isn't it?" he asked.

"Yeah Coach, it is," I said, knowing exactly what he was talking about.

"But often times, that's when the games are won," he said. I sat there silent and he leaned forward to look directly at me, face to face.

"The Willie Davis I know has never quit on anything important," he said. "You've never been a quitter in your life, have you?"

"No sir," I said quietly.

"And you're not going to quit now."

He exchanged a few more words with me, words of encouragement, support, and praise. He told me how proud he was of me, and as was the norm when somebody heard Coach Lombardi speak, I left inspired. He was right. I wasn't a quitter. I had worked hard at everything in my life. I defined success by looking to always do more, to be better, and to accomplish what might at first seem impossible. Those were characteristics I was (and still am) very proud of because those are characteristics of successful people.

He reminded me why I had gone to school in the first place. His simple words reminded me how I wanted to be able to walk into a job interview after football with more than just my name—I wanted a wealth of experience and to be armed with a graduate degree. He reminded me that I was the kind of person who always looked at where I was and where I wanted to go—and then I went.

That being said, I knew I still needed help getting the school work back on track. Luckily I had former U.S. Secretary of Labor, Treasury, and State George P. Shultz as a mentor. Shultz served as the Dean of the University of Chicago's Graduate School of Business while I attended, and he was very supportive of his students, offering guidance when needed. He helped me organize my life. When I talked with him about the struggles of juggling what seemed like an overwhelming number of responsibilities, he was the one who guided me on prioritizing and finding creative ways to make everything work together.

"You need to look at your priorities in terms of a pursuit," he said. "They are not going to be easy to accomplish. There is a process involved. By outlining everything in your life, you can typically come up with the answer of how you're going to accomplish it all. Just know that it's not going to be easy, and it's not supposed to be."

He worked with me on making decisions that reduced the number of conflicts I faced on a daily basis, on balancing my life to the point that I had space and time for everything I wanted to do. With his guidance, I began an important step in my growth as an individual in seeing the bigger picture. He taught me practices I still use in business today, most notably looking at all sides presented before I sort out any answer. I was always someone who tried to jump into any problem and solve it because that seemed the quickest and easiest way to move on.

"There are always multiple sides, several ways to look at things," he said. "Make sure you look at them all, and when you do, the right answer will reveal itself."

I took Coach Lombardi's motivation and Dean Shultz's advice. I also called upon my faith, which often gave me the sense I could accomplish anything, especially when I started to have doubts. I went forward, committed to finishing what I had started, and I did it the only way I knew how—by making the Dean's List and looking to do better by the time I graduated.

Recognize those who came before you and those who helped you achieve success.

The 1967 season started with a proud moment for me and all black players. My old teammate, Emlen Tunnell, received the honor of being the first black player elected to the Pro Football Hall of Fame. It was a well-deserved seat for yet another pioneer in the sport. Beyond being happy for my good friend and former teammate, I was extremely proud of how far both black players and the league had come in such a short time. On the Packers, black or white, I don't know one person who wasn't happy for Emlen, whether they knew him personally or not. That showed where we were headed, as well.

Unfortunately, the beginning of the season also saw a significant change to the Packers franchise, one that was tough for the players, coaches, and fans, and one that marked the beginning of the end of an era. Before the 1967 season, we lost Thunder and Lightning. Losing one would have been a blow enough, but losing both Hornung and Taylor in the same season—leaders on and off the field—made for a tough adjustment.

Jim's departure was expected. He had been very vocal about feeling undervalued, underpaid, and underappreciated in Green Bay in his last season. He talked first publicly and then privately about leaving the team at the end of the season. Several of us disagreed with Jim and wondered if he was just barking or if he was really going to leave. Throughout the off-season, we heard that he continually argued over his contract and a renegotiation with Coach Lombardi, essentially ending any chance he would wear the Green and Gold again. Jim signed with the Saints in the off-season, playing one very average season before retiring.

Paul's leaving was an absolute shock to everybody except Paul himself. With the Saints entering the league, the Packers, along with all the other teams, had to put up 11 players for an expansion draft. Knowing that Paul's numbers had declined significantly during the past two years, Coach Lombardi felt confident that he could put up Paul and he wouldn't get drafted. But he did—by the Saints.

Somehow an expansion team had stolen the two guys who had literally carried Coach Lombardi to success for the past several years, two guys who were important to Coach himself and the Packers franchise as a whole. They were at the end of their careers, but they were crucial locker room leaders and players who reflected the Lombardi era.

Coach was devastated by Paul's steal, but it came out later that Paul had actually been in touch with Saints management who had told him they were pursuing him in the hopes he could sell tickets by his name alone. Paul saw his time coming to an end in Green Bay and hoped for more playing time with a new franchise. Unfortunately, he suffered from neck problems that got worse in training camp and retired before the season started, an unceremonious end to a brilliant career.

Coming into our training camp, we felt their absence, especially on the practice field where they were always two of the hardest workers on the team. By this point, I had been in the league almost a decade and had gotten used to saying both hello and goodbye to players I battled alongside. It's never easy, but it's part of the business. Still, some were harder to see go than others.

Coach felt confident we would replace them in the lineup with Grabowski and Anderson, as well as Ben Wilson, who we got from the Rams, and Travis Williams, a new draft pick out of Arizona State. He was known as "the Roadrunner," and for good reason. He was so incredibly fast—one of the fastest guys I've ever seen. While helping us periodically at running back, he became a dangerous weapon on special teams, breaking all kinds of team and league return records, including returning four kickoffs for touchdowns during his rookie season alone.

There was no way all of these individuals could equal what Paul and Jim had done, but under Coach's guidance, they could and did contribute in a significant way. It was indeed hard to say goodbye, but the best way to move forward is to honor those people who helped you and then replace them with new talent that can help the organization continue to build off what they started. For me, I felt extremely honored to have shared the battlefield with these two phenomenal players, and while they didn't get their proper sendoff from Green Bay, all these years later I wanted to make sure I took a moment to let them know how appreciated they were by me, the Packers, and their fans for all they did.

Even leaders need friends. Contrary to popular belief, they are not isolated individuals.

Lucky for me, I was playing for a Coach who was extremely progressive without being flashy about it. Coach Lombardi was always a risk taker when it came to race issues, and he always seemed one step ahead of the movement. He recruited black players when few other teams were, making them starters and bumping their pay to make it more equal to white players. He named a black captain, and in 1967 he paired up black and white roommates when he assigned me to share a room with Jerry Kramer on road trips.

We weren't the first black and white roommates—that distinction belonged to the legendary friendship between Gale Sayers and Brian Piccolo of the Bears. But I think we might have been the second, and we were definitely the first in Green Bay.

Jerry and I had become close friends on the field and in the locker room, so in a way it made sense. I admittedly was a little nervous about those cultural differences. I wondered how I would relate to Jerry in a roommate situation. The black players all had a certain way we communicated with each other—certain words and phrases we used. There was a comfort level among us, one we used to deal with any tensions we came across in our NFL experience. I wondered how different this would be and if either one of us would be comfortable.

Rooming with Jerry turned out to be one of the best things I experienced while playing football in the NFL.

Jerry is one of the most intelligent and accepting individuals I've ever met. He impresses everyone he meets with stories of his life and his constant ambition. I had always known he was a leader and a game-changer on the field, but I learned that he had so much more to offer when the pads were off. He was incredibly profound, even back in our younger days, and he had an interesting perspective on everything to go along with his acceptance of anybody and everybody. Jerry not only became one of my best friends as we roomed with each other over the next three years, he became someone I knew I could talk to about anything, and he remains so today.

There was no topic off limits, including the racial tensions affecting the country at the time. We could talk about our feelings on the matter and present two very different perspectives with ease and understanding. Growing up in Idaho, Jerry had very little exposure to black people before playing football, and he was open and honest about his thoughts and eager to gain more understanding. I had my own questions about Jerry's experience, and we answered each other with the utmost respect.

We talked mainly at night after lights out. He and I were both fierce competitors, and some nights it was difficult to sleep. We would lie in our cots and talk about issues of the world, Packers football, our opponents, and more philosophical topics like what we were going to do with our lives. We both had ambitions. Jerry was working on a book project, which eventually became *Instant Replay*, one of the most popular sports books of all time. He also talked about business opportunities he wanted to explore. I talked with him about school, Schlitz, getting into business after football, and making a career for myself. At that point, it was still just a fantasy.

"What exactly do you want to do, Wil?" he asked.

"Well Jer, I'm not sure I've exactly figured it out, but I know in order for it to be satisfying to me, it has to be a fulfillment of the things I've come to expect of myself," I replied. "I can't even think of walking away from this game and not having a continuation of success and achieving the things like we have on this football field."

"You and me both, Wil," he said. "You and me both."

Change in your industry or field is going to happen, so be able to adjust.

To mark the constant growth of the ever-expanding league and to prepare for its merger with the AFL, the NFL divided its 16 teams into four divisions playing within the two conferences. We stayed in the Western Conference, playing in the Central Division (to go along with the Capitol, Century, and Coastal divisions) against the Bears, Lions, and Vikings—all our old friends. The move meant we played each team in our division twice and all others in the conference once, along with four games against teams from the Eastern Conference.

Coming off a Super Bowl win, we were still an early favorite despite losing Hornung and Taylor and the fact that several of the team's key players were getting up there in age. Nobody would come right out and say it, but there was a feeling around the league, especially in the national media, that we might be too old to compete against some of the younger, faster teams. Plagued once again by key injuries in training camp and the preseason, especially among the running backs trying to fill the void, certainly didn't help our cause.

Neither did a Week 1 tie with the lowly Lions in our first "divisional" game. In years past, when we came out flat in the opening game, there was a lot of confusion as to why. We always felt prepared, focused, and ready to play—and then suddenly the impossible happened and we lost. In the first game of the 1967 season, there was still a lot of uncertainty and changes and we just weren't ready.

Plus there had been rumors as early as the previous season that Coach Lombardi was going to retire from coaching soon, which ignited constant talk and controversy among everyone, including the players. He assured us he was committed to the season, but that was as far as he would go. The thought lingered in the back of our minds.

Despite the excuses, that Week 1 tie woke us right up. If we were getting older, if we were getting banged up, if we were getting tired, if this was Coach Lombardi's last season, it might also be our last chance to come out on top. We owed it to ourselves to make sure we gave the season 100 percent dedication. We came back the next week, winning a tight one against the Bears 13–10 on a late field goal from Don Chandler. In this game, the defense showed signs of getting itself back on track, but the offense still sputtered. Bart Starr had thrown multiple interceptions in the first two games despite only throwing three the entire season prior. He was dealing with several nagging injuries, and he also looked uncomfortable without Jim and Paul helping him in the backfield.

The next week, Bart went down with the injuries piling up, and we had to rely on Zeke once again to lead us to a 23–0 victory over the Falcons. We were very fortunate to have played the Falcons that week and not a team that would be competing for the title. It allowed us extra time to gel as a team and fix any remaining kinks. We were 2–0–1, which was not a horrible way to start the season, but we all knew it could be better and had to be better if we were going to repeat. There were too many lingering problems, and our team needed a spark.

It's up to the leader to inspire.

I decided before the Week 4 rematch with the Lions, I was going to be the one to give us that spark. It was my job, after all, as defensive captain, and I had gotten used to speaking in front of the group at meetings, practice, and in the locker room. I typically talked to the defense, but this time, before this game, I wanted to talk to all of them. I thought about what I would say all week.

"I've been thinking about what it means to be a committed player," I said to the group minutes before the game as they sat huddled around me, offense and defense, rookie and veteran. "I've been in the league almost 10 years, and I've seen a lot of people stand up here, and I've stood up here and said some things, talked about what needed to be done, what we were gonna do, how we were gonna play, and then go out and play like they didn't mean a word of it. I don't want to be one of those players, not today. No, today I want to go out there and say, 'Whatever's necessary.'"

Several of them started nodding their heads and a few called out, showing their support.

"Fellas, we need this game. This team played us to a tie at our home, and now we need to show them who we are. We need to get on the right track here."

I looked out over my teammates, and they were all focused on me. The black players were shouting their encouragement. Bart watched me intently and I gave him a look, just enough to let him know he was our leader and I would follow him anywhere. I looked at Forrest and thought about how many battles he and I had been in and how I knew I could always count on him. I looked at Jerry and saw nothing but support. They were all listening to what I had to say, not because I was a veteran or a captain but because I was saying something they all knew to be true. We were brothers, and we had fought too hard together to ever let each other down. We were all willing to do whatever was necessary, and we were going to play Packers football.

"If you're willing to give your commitment today, then stand up," I yelled. "If you're not committed to go out there and do whatever's necessary for us to be victorious, then don't stand up. I'm telling you that I'm standing here and I'm prepared to give it my all today and always for this team. I'm committed."

Everybody stood up, yelling and clapping.

"What do you want to do? Who do you want?" I said, getting more and more fired up by the team. "I want Bradshaw! I want Bradshaw!"

Charlie Bradshaw was a 6'6", 260-pound tackle who had just come to the Lions from the Steelers. He was a ferocious blocker with size and strength. He had done a number on me in the first game, frustrating me at every turn, and I was eager to have a second chance at him.

"I want Bradshaw! I want Bradshaw!"

We all ran onto the field, and I can't remember the last time we were so fired up. I couldn't wait to get into the game, to let the Lions have the ball so I could come face to face with Charlie. Sure enough, on the opening possession we lined up and I just stared at him, not saying a word, focused on getting a good hit on him and busting through to their quarterback, establishing how this day was going to go.

On that first play, Charlie absolutely flattened me.

Charlie hit me so hard I could feel it from my head to my toes. My teammates let out a groan, and I couldn't help but struggle to get up, wondering who was driving the truck that just ran over my ass. A couple plays later, as I jogged off the field with the rest of the defense after a stop, still groggy, Jerry passed me by and had something to offer.

"Hey Wil," he said. "I guess Charlie must have been thinking the same thing. I want Davis!"

Jerry didn't let up on me next week, either. Actually, nobody on the team did, replaying the hit over and over again for me and laughing about seeing me get laid out—something I didn't allow to happen very often. In a speech before our next game the following week, this one a little more subdued, Jerry raised his hand with a question.

"Who do you want this week, Wil?"

We all laughed, but the talk had done its job. We beat the Lions 27–17, highlighted by Ray Nitschke picking off a pass and running it back for a touchdown in the fourth quarter. The following week, we struggled offensively and lost to the Vikings, but then we bounced back a week later, destroying the Giants 48–21, including scoring four touchdowns in the fourth quarter. Before that game, we started to hear the "too old" rumors pick up and decided we needed to show what these old timers could do against the Giants in Yankee Stadium.

That game woke up our slumbering offense and further ignited our rapidly improving defense. We were becoming a dominant team yet again, and in Week 7 against the Cardinals we added another element when Travis Williams broke off a 93-yard punt return for a touchdown. It wouldn't be his last big return of the season, and soon teams were adjusting their kicking schemes to keep the ball away from him. Teams started to introduce squib kicks, which gave our offense great starting field position.

Two major injuries hurt our cause the following week in a loss to the Colts when runners Elijah Pitts and Jim Grabowski went out with injuries to their Achilles tendon and knee, respectively. We bounced back the following week against Cleveland, winning 55–7 in our most impressive win of the year. We also took the next three games in a row and found ourselves 9–2–1, feeling youthful, fully confident, superior to our opponents, and poised to take yet another title shot.

We had easily locked up our division, earning a place in the newly introduced playoff system with two weeks left to go. It would be easy to say our season-long dominance and the fact we had guaranteed our spot in the postseason lead to our losing the final two games of the regular season, but that wasn't the case. It didn't matter what was on the line, Coach Lombardi would never allow us to let up and relax. Those of us that had worked with him for so long didn't know how to ease the foot off the pedal. No, we tried to win those games and came up short.

In Los Angeles we were up 24–20 with a minute left when a hungry and desperate Rams team who needed a win to keep pace with the Colts in their division blocked a punt. A few plays later, they ran a fake and a pass play for a touchdown to give them the win. The next week we simply lost our focus, again giving up a win but this time against the Steelers at home.

We were excited to make the postseason once again, and we knew we had a good shot at repeating as champions and maybe finally getting the coveted three in a row. But the last two games had left a bad taste in our mouths and perhaps even allowed some doubt about age and experience to creep in. This was not how we wanted to end the season and now we had to quickly refocus for a rematch against the Rams, this time in an NFL playoff game.

Sometimes it's okay to release the pressure off your team.

If there was one person who surprisingly didn't look nervous at all, it was Coach Lombardi. In fact, beyond showing a large amount of encouragement during practice the week before the game, he was rather quiet. We all found that a bit unusual because of how we had underperformed the last two games of the regular season. We expected to be punished, to be whipped into shape going into the playoffs, but Lombardi was lighter and almost easy on us. Looking back, it was a brilliant move from a man in touch with his team. We were nervous and putting enough pressure on ourselves. Sometimes a good coach knows when to step back and ease off, when to help his team relax just enough to refocus.

It worked. We had an incredible week of practice, all the fears ebbing away as we handled our business. The only thing that threw us off was just how quiet Coach was being. All of us, especially the veterans, knew his strategy was to get us to focus ourselves, but this was almost unsettling. Was he nervous, fuming, excited, checked out? Surely he wasn't satisfied—he rarely was. Coach typically used Wednesdays as his day to provide spiritual motivation, "preachin' the gospel" as only Coach could. But he had nothing for us this week. The last day or two before practice, he hardly had anything to say at all, and we waited to see what was going to happen.

"What's with the Old Man?" my old friend Forrest Gregg finally asked me on the day before the game.

"I honestly don't know," I said. "I don't know what this thing is with him."

Just then, Bob Skoronski came over to us and joined the conversation.

"Hey, do you guys know what's going on with Coach?"

Lombardi also typically talked a lot with his coaches in private, but even that wasn't happening. In fact, the only thing he really said to me the whole week had to do with the Rams All-Pro Deacon Jones.

"Willie, I know the Rams got Deacon, but when you walk off that field, I want the fans to say that Willie Davis is pretty good, too!"

I began to hope he would say something to the team on game day, just to let us know he was involved and knew what he was doing. As usual, he didn't disappoint.

"Gentlemen, listen up," he said, gathering us together in the locker room minutes before we took the field. We were going through our usual pregame paces, some more excitable than others. I sat calmly, focusing on what I needed to do. Bart was reviewing the offensive game plan. Ray was pacing all over the locker room, yelling at anybody who would listen. Boyd was fighting the nerves and sickness he got before big games. Coach took it all in and then went over last-minute game plans with us, talking to us about individual players and reminding us about the importance of this game. Then he got quiet for just a second, but it was enough.

"I know I haven't had a lot to say this week," he said. "I—my one regret as I stand here today is that I'm not going to be able to play in this game."

He stood quietly, reflecting on his thought.

"I'd love to play in this particular game myself, but I can't. No gentlemen, I have to trust that you are going to go out there and do what you need to do. I have to trust you—and I do. If I need to motivate you before a game like this, then you're not the team I believe you to be. But I don't think that's true. I think you know what you need to do, and you're ready to do it. I can tell you, gentlemen, that if I was playing in this game, I would know exactly what the outcome would be."

I don't think I ever felt more energy in the locker room than that moment. Coach rarely opened up to us about his personal feelings as a man, not to the whole team. We all knew that if he had the chance, he would play harder than any of us. We owed it to him to play for him, to play his way, like he would play. There was such a buzz of energy, such an intense feeling in that locker room, that there was no way we weren't going to win this game.

We all stormed into the tunnel, ready to take the field. Back then, the two teams still came out together, which meant they had to wait for introductions in the tunnel side by side.

"Hey Willie, Willie," I heard Charlie Cowan, the offensive tackle from the Rams and an old rival calling to me as we waited in the tunnel. The poor guy was just looking to say hi, but I just shook my head.

"Not now, Charlie," I said. "I can't talk to you now."

Nothing was going to take off this edge.

If anything, we got even more excited when we looked over at what the Rams were wearing. This game was being played at Milwaukee County Stadium just a couple days before Christmas, and L.A. was dressed like, well, like they were playing in L.A. While we were bundled up in hats, long sleeves, gloves, and so on, the Rams players were wearing short sleeves, and most of them looked like they were freezing in the tunnel before we even got onto the field.

We had heard all week about how the Rams said they weren't concerned about the weather up in Wisconsin. They were telling the press that this was "Ram weather." Now we were watching them shivering, listening to players complain about the cold before we even started. We learned later that they didn't even bring winter gear with them and that for most of the game a majority of the players were dealing with cold feet, literally. At halftime, they sent a trainer to a local store to get baggies to wrap around their feet, hoping to insulate them. Instead, their feet started to perspire in the baggies and then freeze on top of it, so they had cold and *wet* feet!

"Ram weather my ass," Jerry Kramer said.

Still, we came out shaky, perhaps a little *too* fired up, especially on offense. The Rams instantly started applying the pressure, with Merlin Olsen, Roger Brown, and Deacon Jones breaking through our protection. Deacon played with such intensity that there was little anyone could do to stop him. He was everywhere, running over anyone who was trying to contain him, and the result was a few sacks and a pick thrown by Bart.

We also fumbled the ball twice, including a crucial one by Carroll Dale around midfield that ended a much-needed Packers drive.

The defense held its own at the beginning, but with good field position the Rams were able to open up the playbook, and Roman Gabriel started picking us apart. From our 30-yard line, the Rams proved they had also done their homework when Bernie Casey took advantage of our corners coming up to help, slipping past Herb Adderley for a touchdown and a 7–0 lead.

But that was all we allowed them to do the rest of the game. There was no panic; there was no doubt. We knew we simply had to make the adjustments and we did—immediately. We saw how they were going to play us, and we made the necessary changes. First things first, we started double-teaming Deacon Jones, making the Rams beat us with someone else. Once we started putting two guys on him, Deacon disappeared from the stat sheet and the game, allowing our offense to get the wheels turning. We started throwing short passes to the outside while blocking Deacon inside. Once he caught on and started pushing to the outside, we'd run the ball up the middle, avoiding him and frustrating him in the process.

After a strong punt return by Tom Brown, Travis Williams was able to carry the ball up the center through a gap for 46 yards and a tying touchdown. Now it was the defense's turn to buckle down, and we did our part. Although the Rams put together a small drive, we held them to a field-goal attempt from long distance. The kick came up way short and Willie Wood, who was hanging out by the goalposts just in case, snatched the ball and ran through tackles all the way to the Rams' 45-yard line. It was a momentum builder that finally opened up our offense to a variety of options. Just a few plays later, Dale made up for his fumble by grabbing a 17-yard touchdown pass from Bart to put us ahead 14–7 at the end of the first half.

The Rams occasionally had their opportunities. After a Starr interception to safety Chuck Lamson, the Rams found themselves on our 10-yard line with a chance to tie the game. In the huddle, we all talked about keeping them to a field goal and Henry Jordan, normally more reserved in the game, spoke up.

"I'll get him," he said.

Just seconds after the ball was snapped, there was Henry in the backfield, sacking Roman and setting up yet another Rams field-goal attempt, which Herb Adderley promptly blocked. Another fumble, this time by Marv Fleming, again gave the Rams the ball in our territory. Again they faced another third down with a chance to push to the end zone. This time it was my turn as I broke outside on the snap and then charged in, hitting Roman in the backfield and forcing them to another field-goal attempt that was blocked!

The Rams couldn't take advantage of any opportunities, and the defense started to shut them down more and more. Meanwhile, the offense looked to involve some of our little-known players, such as Chuck Mercein. Chuck became better known for his role in our next game, but he stepped up here first. A running back/fullback who had been up and down with the Giants, Chuck was brought to Green Bay late in the season by Coach Lombardi to give us some help at the banged-up running back position. He had only played six regular games with us in limited action, but he was the kind of player who was always ready for his moment to contribute. Against the Rams the opportunity came in the second quarter when he ran it in from the 6-yard line for a 21–7 lead that pretty much iced the game. One more run from Travis Williams in the third quarter put us up by three touchdowns, and the game was over.

Yes, the Packers were a little older and banged up. In fact, I was on the sideline when the defense wasn't on the field, grimacing in pain from a couple of shots I took from the Rams line and my old friend Charlie, who didn't take too kindly to my snubbing him in the tunnel. But there was no way I was coming out of the game. There was no way they were going to get the best of me. There was no way they were going to win. We might have been older and more beat up, but there was no team with our dedication, toughness, and discipline. There was no team that had somebody who could inspire a group of warriors like we did. We were champions of the Western Conference. Next up was the NFL championship, again.

In that game, however, we would be fighting against more than just a bitter rival.

| Chapter 19 | # The Ice Bowl, Super Bowl II, and a Legacy |

Sometimes your competition will be the least of your concerns!

It was cold.

So cold.

Just unbelievably, unbearably cold.

Many times moments in history get exaggerated through the years, so much so that they become more myth than truth, more fiction than fact. The details change and grow with each re-telling until, years later, the story is but a shadow of what actually happened.

Not in this case, and not with this game. It was called the Ice Bowl— and it was cold!

There were plenty of other factors for us to focus on coming into the 1967 NFL Championship Game. We were once again facing the Cowboys and Coach Tom Landry, who was hell-bent on getting his revenge for bouncing him from the last year's playoffs. The Cowboys were also a much better team this year than the one we had faced before. Yet again, we had a handful of key injuries, mostly to our running game, including one that happened minutes before kickoff when Jim Grabowski popped his knee during warm-ups. Plus, there was the ever-looming wonder if this would be Coach Lombardi's last game if we lost.

Luckily for us, the main thing on our minds was the bone-chilling cold.

It came as a complete surprise. The night before it had been near the 30s in Green Bay. But overnight, the temperature plummeted and we faced game-time conditions of 13 below zero with a wind chill of 48 below. The field, which had a state-of-the-art heating system, was a disaster. The cold had broken down the system, leaving the field as hard as concrete and slippery in most parts. The makeshift dugouts that were built for players on both sides of the field did little to keep out the wind, just as the sideline heaters did nothing to keep out the cold. It was so cold the referees were having problems using their whistles because the metal was sticking to their lips and ripping off skin.

After warm-ups, we all waited in the locker room, bundling ourselves up as much as possible with long underwear, extra shirts, extra tape, ski masks, anything and everything we could find to stay at least a little warmer. Players were even sneaking on gloves, which Coach Lombardi forbade. He didn't want anyone who handled the ball to wear gloves because he thought they caused more drops and fumbles. It was one of the few times I saw players blatantly ignoring a Lombardi rule and not getting punished for it.

Most of the chatter was about the cold and how none of us had ever experienced anything like it. Several of the players questioned if we would even play the game or if officials were going to call it. Others were trying to get themselves ready. I read later that Fuzzy Thurston told a reporter he drank about 10 vodkas to stay warm during the game. Who knows whether or not he was kidding?

Once it became clear we were going to go forward with the game, everybody shifted their attention. That was one thing I always found amazing about Coach Lombardi's teams. We had an uncanny ability to focus when we needed to despite all outside distractions. The moment we were told we were close to game time, the cold became the No. 2 thing on our minds. The Cowboys were No. 1.

We received some early encouragement from a group of people we knew we could always rely on. As we ran out, we looked around the field to see it jammed with Packers fans screaming and cheering for us. It's why I still think Packers fans are the greatest fans in the world. It doesn't matter what the conditions are—there is nothing that will keep them away from their beloved team. They are the ultimate supporters, the most loyal and dedicated fan base a team could hope for, and their presence always made a difference. Here we were on one of the coldest days of the year, and they had packed the stadium—coats, facemasks, hunting gear, and all—to cheer their team on to another Super Bowl appearance.

Given the importance of the game, there were obviously a lot of nerves on the team to go along with the sharp chills running through our bones. I unwittingly did something that helped a few members of my team calm down before the big game. The captains walked out for the coin toss and despite the freezing cold, I was somehow pouring with sweat. I was just so amped up for the game. As I walked back, I asked one of our staff for a towel to wipe the sweat off my head. That small gesture showed everybody that Willie Davis wasn't concerned with the cold. I was ready to play.

Truthfully, I was a *little* concerned about the cold!

I thought the field would be the worst of it because it was horrible for planting and getting a running start. With the spots iced over and the pockets of pure rock, there would no speed on this field. But that wasn't nearly as difficult as trying to catch our breath. Every breath burned our lungs, and it definitely took away from my concentration.

Still, the absolute worst of it was how brittle it made our bodies. Before the game, Herb Adderley told me about a play he noticed the Cowboys run, a misdirection play where their linemen blocked down and sent the running back, Don Perkins, to the spot where I would be, hoping I would move with the linemen. To defend it, all I had to do was hold my spot. Sure enough, on the Cowboys' opening drive, they ran the play, I held and hit Perkins head on, and I felt pain shoot from my spine up and down my entire body. It wasn't even that hard of a hit, but I soon learned that every hit would have the same effect. It was on all of our minds, offense and defense, and we all took extra looks at the clock throughout slower parts of the action.

As uncomfortable as we were, the Cowboys looked downright miserable. This was weather they couldn't possibly have prepared for in Dallas. The Cowboys players were huddled up with each other, almost fighting for position in front of the heaters. Once the game started, we even saw players giving away what they were going to run based on their reactions to the cold. Bob Hayes, the exceptionally fast wide receiver who we feared in the passing attack, buried his hands in his pants on some plays, signaling to us that he wasn't getting the ball. Our defensive backs picked up on it right away, and we were once again able to take away a key Dallas weapon.

There were some who thought the weather would be an equalizer in the game, but we quickly realized it might give us just a slight edge. Granted, we hadn't played in *this* kind of cold, but we had dealt with winter conditions before and it made a difference.

Our offense got off to a tremendous start with Bart leading them 82 yards downfield, mixing short passes and strong runs and ending in an 8-yard pass to Boyd Dowler for a quick 7–0 lead. The defense was just as strong, putting pressure on Meredith and getting a read on plays, holding them to minimal gains.

The early moments of the second quarter saw Ben Wilson and Travis Williams working the right side of the Cowboys defense, opening up a 46-yard pass to Boyd for a 14–0 lead. The Packers defense followed up with a quick stop, forcing the Cowboys to give us the ball back with about 4:00 left in the half. We were in control and felt good about our execution. The game tilted in our favor, and we knew all we had to do was continue to execute with precision to get the result we wanted.

But football is an interesting game, and there are always things that can turn the momentum.

As we drove the ball deep into our territory for what we hoped would be one last score before halftime, the Cowboys defense suddenly broke through. Bart dropped back for a pass, and the defense figured out what was coming. They sent everybody after the quarterback, and Bart didn't have anywhere to go. Lineman Willie Townes hit Bart, and he fumbled the ball. In a flash, defensive end George Andrie picked it up and ran it in for a touchdown, making it a ballgame once again.

I didn't know what had happened until I heard the crowd groan. The defense was getting ready to either head back to the field or hopefully to the locker room. After the Cowboys forced a quick three-and-out, our defense took the field once again, holding them to nothing. Unfortunately, on the ensuing punt, Willie Wood, owner of two of the most reliable hands on the field, fumbled the ball trying to call for a fair catch. The Cowboys recovered with less than a minute and ended up with a field goal, bringing the score to 14–10 right before the half. It was a swing that stunned the crowd and let us know this game was far from over.

At halftime there were no inspirational speeches. The players just tried to get as warm as they could, some bundling up even more and others trying to keep themselves loose. We focused on adjustments and wondered why we couldn't hear any bands playing outside (we heard later that the halftime show was canceled due to the weather). We pumped each other up, making sure everyone was focused on doing what we had to do in the second half.

But the offense had stalled. The Cowboys had adjusted to the offensive game plan, and they weren't budging. They broke through and sacked Starr more than a half-dozen times in the third quarter, holding us to single digits in total yards gained. It didn't matter what the offense tried, the Cowboys had an answer. Defensively we didn't come out as strong as we could have, but we held.

Early in the quarter, the Cowboys put on a drive with Dan Reeves running the ball and Meredith throwing short passes. They took the ball all the way to our 13-yard line where we finally broke through, forcing Don to scramble. Lee Roy Caffey found him and hit him, causing a key fumble that we recovered. Later in the quarter the Cowboys found a way to move on us with their running game, taking the ball to our 32-yard line. Lee Roy, the hero of the third quarter, broke though the line again and sacked Meredith, holding them to a long field-goal attempt that they missed. At the end of three quarters, despite shaky play, we still maintained our lead—until the first play of the fourth quarter.

The Cowboys, who were known for complicated offensive schemes and surprise plays, had played us pretty straight up. We were prepared for something unusual from Coach Landry, but as the game wore on we let down our defenses just enough and the Cowboys struck. Meredith handed off the ball to Reeves who ran wide to the left. The defense immediately came up to meet him and cut off the run. We never noticed wide receiver Lance Rentzel sneak past the secondary until it was too late. I was in pursuit of Reeves when all of a sudden I saw him purposely slow down and my heart sank. I turned around just in time to see Lance haul in a 50-yard touchdown pass that gave the Cowboys the 17–14 lead.

The defense just stood there stunned for a moment. We couldn't believe we had let something like that happen. We looked at each other, painfully aware that play may have just cost us the ballgame. Our offense was struggling in the second half, the weather was getting worse, the field was becoming unplayable, and we had just given the Cowboys all the momentum in the world. All of a sudden, the reality of losing everything we had worked for was sinking in.

I spent the rest of the quarter and the game encouraging my defense to not give up one more inch—and watching the clock. Suddenly, the cold was the furthest thing from my mind. We made the key mistake. We lost our focus, and the Cowboys were now in command. Now we had to move on, hold our position, and trust our offense to find the right opportunity.

We thought they had on the next possession when Starr was able to force his way down to Cowboys territory, mainly with passes to Boyd. However, they held once we were inside, and Don Chandler came up short on a long field goal. Later in the quarter, as time wound down with increasing speed, the Cowboys tried to run out the clock with Reeves running on almost every down. However, on a pass to tight end Frank Clarke, we were able to once again cause a fumble, giving us decent field position.

Again we were held and forced to punt. Back and forth we went as the clock ticked down to the end of the game, our season, and possibly an era. It was a completely hopeless feeling. We were not used to trailing in big games, and I think even our coaches wondered how we would respond. They found out soon enough.

Leaders trust their instincts.

We started the drive with just less than 5:00 remaining in the game at our own 32-yard line. The defense stood on the sideline, realizing this might just be our last chance to tie the game or take the lead. We stood there encouraging our offense, with Ray Nitschke yelling so loud he was making himself hoarse. The cold was no longer a factor.

The coaches talked with Starr, who looked as calm as ever, a leader who was never rattled by the pressure of the moment. They went over a few last-minute plays and he trotted out, looking completely confident that his offense would do what needed to be done. That was the resolve, the poise under pressure that Coach had trained us to have no matter the situation. He said later that he looked at his offense in the huddle and wondered if he had to say something to encourage them on the drive. One look into his teammates' eyes and he knew conversation wasn't necessary. Bob Skoronski also said later it was the most focused he had ever seen the offense on any drive in all his time with the Packers. Nobody could argue.

Bart went about driving the team as methodically as ever, not worrying about the time on the clock but rather focusing on finding the openings. Four minutes plus was plenty of time for this offense, and he knew it. He went after the Cowboys with short passes to Boyd and runs with Donny Anderson and Chuck Mercein.

The drive almost faltered once we broke into Cowboys territory with a botched running play that dropped us back nine yards. Suddenly, it was second-and-19. But once again, there was no concern, no fear of execution. The offense simply ran its next two plays, knowing it had enough time and downs to pick up what it needed. A 13-yard pass to Anderson, who snuck out into the flat, and then a nine-yard pass and we had the first down and the drive was restored.

With about 1:35 left, we had the ball on the Dallas 30-yard line and the crowd could barely contain itself. Bart knew he had to pick up the pace even though we still had our timeouts. I split my time watching the field and staring at the clock, pacing nervously on the sideline. There is nothing worse for a competitor than to leave the big moments in the hands of someone else, but there was nothing left for us to do. On the next play, Starr dropped back, looking for Boyd and Anderson, who were both covered. Just as the pocket started to close around him, Bart spotted Chuck in the clear. Bart threw a high pass, but Chuck was able to haul it in, slip past the defender, and take it all the way to the Cowboys' 11-yard line.

The next play was critical. It looked like our Packer Sweep with a key difference, something the offense had worked on in practice specifically for this game. It was meant to catch their Pro Bowl defensive tackle Bob Lilly off guard and out of position, taking advantage of his aggressive play. Once Bart took the snap, the left guard pulled and hoped Lilly would go with him, thinking we were running the Sweep. The risk was that if Lilly caught on and didn't pull with the guard, he would meet our running back, who was breaking right to Lilly's spot, head on. Luckily, it worked to perfection, the one and only time we would be able to run that play. Lilly moved and Chuck took the ball nine yards to the Cowboys' 2-yard line. On the next play, Donny Anderson barreled ahead for a yard and a critical first down.

We had less than a minute left in our season, and it all came down to a yard. It often does.

On first down, Bart handed the ball to Donny and the Cowboys line bore down on him, holding him to no gain. On second down, Donny slipped and again gained nothing. Just like that, we found ourselves at third down with 16 seconds left and using our last timeout. We had time for just one more play—one of the greatest plays in Packers history.

During the timeout, Bart trotted over to talk to Coach about what play to run. I stood nearby, overhearing the conversation. The two talked about running a wedge play, where they would pinch the defenders and open up just enough of a hole for Chuck to squeeze through. Coach and Bart had such a strong relationship at this point that Coach often listened to his quarterback, his leader on the field. When Bart suggested the wedge play, Coach only had one response.

"Well, let's run it and get the hell out of here!"

In the huddle, Bart addressed his one fear. He asked Jerry Kramer, who would make the critical block on the play, if he and the other linemen could get their footing on the icy field for one more play. Bart was also worried about Chuck's footing, having just seen Donny slip, but he knew the play started at the line. Jerry assured him, as did the other linemen, that they would clear a path.

Bart said later, that as they approached the line, his fears of Chuck slipping are what made him change his mind and take an enormous but calculated risk. If the field had been less icy, the Sneak would never have happened. It would have been a running play to Chuck, a Packer for half a season, and who knows what the result would have been. Bart thought since he would already have the footing and the momentum from the snap, he had a much better chance of running the ball into the end zone. It was a risk because the quarterback sneak was a play the Packers never ran in practice—and because nobody knew it was going to be run except for Bart!

I never saw the play. I couldn't. I just couldn't watch. I knew the entire season came down to this, and it was too much for me and several other of the defenders to take. We turned our heads, resigned to watch it, good or bad, in replays later.

As Bart snapped the ball, Jerry got the best jump of his career, finding a divot in the ground and shooting his head and body into the chest of Jethro Pugh, pushing him back on his heels. That was all the gap Bart needed to sneak in for a score, a victory, a trip to the Super Bowl, and yet another spot in Packers history. Although I wasn't watching, the roar of the crowd told me everything I needed to know.

The locker room after the game was a frenzy of celebration and players trying to deal with the physical effects of the game. Once the adrenaline started to ebb, the full impact of the cold on our bodies made its presence known. There were a half dozen players or more, including myself, who had severe frostbite.

I wore tape on my hands, but the fingers I used to plant myself in my defensive stance had stuck to the ground multiple times in the game, ripping the skin off my fingertips. They puffed up and filled with fluid, which I had to burst so they would harden and heal. To this day, I still have limited feeling and sensitivity in those fingers on my right hand. I also experienced extreme pain in my legs, which resulted in a discoloration of my feet and ankles, similar to what Ray experienced, circulation problems that came from a combination of the cold and a too tight tape job.

They are unfortunate remnants of a game that will go on in most of our minds as one of the greatest games of all time. I'm not going to say the win was worth the injuries and the scars they left, but—well actually, to those of us who played in that fierce battle, maybe we would say it was worth it after all.

Experience can ease the pressure.

There was *much* less pressure this time around.

That's not to say we didn't respect our opponent for Super Bowl II. We knew very little about the Oakland Raiders, but what we did know was enough to command our attention. They were an aggressive team that hit hard and could get physical and dirty if that's what the game called for—their reputation was established even back then. Once you saw that pirate insignia and the Black and Silver, you knew you had to be ready for anything. They had a ferocious defense called the Angry 11 that ran a tricky style of defense, shifting the linemen and linebackers to confuse the quarterback. On offense, they had a strong line anchored by Gene Upshaw and Jim Otto along with a huge fullback, Hewritt Dixon, and one of the best receivers in football, Fred Biletnikoff. At the helm was a play-action specialist, Daryle Lamonica, who had guided the Raiders to a 13–1 record.

Still, the Raiders came in as the underdog and vocally expressed their respect for what the Packers had accomplished. We felt more confident than ever going into this game, and we didn't have to deal with the pressure of representing the NFL. Not that it would have mattered. If the Ice Bowl had done anything, it had prepared us mentally and physically for anything we would encounter in Super Bowl II.

In just its second year, the game was already taking on a bigger meaning. This one, played in the Orange Bowl, would be broadcast to more than 70 million viewers, more than a third of the total population in the country. Advertisers were starting to realize already what a cultural event this game would become, and the league itself made plans to make the game more than just a game. For the players, we even saw signs of what was to come. Before the game, I met a man who came up to shake my hand and express his feelings for me and the team.

"You know why I love the Packers so much?" he asked. "You guys always cover the spread!"

This game carried extra significance for the Green Bay Packers, and it became much more meaningful than simply a second Super Bowl victory. The rumors about Coach leaving the team after this season were intensifying. Everybody seemed to know someone who had heard something.

Some of the players were convinced this was it, while others, including myself, couldn't accept it. We denied it at every turn, thinking there was no way our immortal coach would pack up and leave. Still, as we tried to focus on winning one more game and completing that three-peat we had coveted for so long, it was a distraction.

Coach Lombardi refused to address it, telling everyone he was focused on this game and this game alone. Still, he wasn't his usual self in practice leading up to the game. He was quiet, more reserved. He was still focused and made damn sure we were focused, but he seemed to be carrying some extra weight, as if his mind had been made up and he was simply trying to savor this one last experience with his men.

At the last practice Friday, he huddled us together and reminded us we would win and bring home the Super Bowl trophy, which had yet to take on his name. He reminded us how hard we would have to work, how proud he was of us, and how lucky we were. Then he said something that should have had more meaning at the time, but caught up in practice and the emotion of the game, many of us missed it.

"You are the finest team in professional football," he said. "It's been a long season, but Sunday might be the last time we're all together, so let's make it a game we can be proud of."

Come game time, he was all business. There was no sentimental goodbye speech before the game. It just wasn't his way. He wanted us to stay focused, to not pay any attention to the rumors or anything that might distract us. There was much more emotion in our speeches to each other.

The Packers always had a tradition before every game where the coaches would leave the room and let the captains and other players address the team. It was a time and place for us to be open with each other, to say what was on our minds and rally each other. Before Super Bowl II, Ray Nitschke pleaded with the team to play with our hearts, Herb Adderley asked us to hit, and Bob Skoronski reminded us that everything we worked for rested on this game.

"I don't know about any of you, but I have no damn intention of losing this game!"

When it was my turn, I reminded them what a challenge we faced once again and how we had overcome many challenges before. I reminded them that this was for a championship, something special that we could do—and I reminded them to have some fun.

"[A win] is recognition, prestige, and money," I said. "Now I know those are three things that will capture the attention of everybody in here."

After we spoke, Coach's words were brief, poignant, a summation of how he felt about us and what we could accomplish. What we *would* accomplish. He went over our assignments, talked about the game plan, warned us about how the Raiders would play us, how they would come out swinging and how we needed to take control of the game early. I recently listened to old recordings of Coach's speeches that were taken by my old friend Jerry Kramer, and Coach's words still give me goosebumps today.

"All the glory, everything you've had, and everything you've won is going to be small in comparison to this one," he said. "You might be the only team in the NFL to have this opportunity to do it twice. If I were you, I would be so proud of that."

And then, one last time, he rallied his troops.

"We've faced it all," he said, his voice booming loudly, almost god-like. "There is nothing they can show you out there that you haven't faced a number of times, right?"

You can't hear the rest because it's covered by the yelling of his team as he led us out onto the field one last time as coach of the Green Bay Packers.

We played a near-flawless game.

The offense moved, the defense hit, the special teams provided points and opportunities, and we once again showed the country how we were the most dominant team in football. After the challenges we had faced over the course of the season, a dominating performance was a welcome relief.

For my part, I had one of my best all-around defensive efforts, pressuring the quarterback and making several key tackles, including some on critical downs. My main rival in the game was tackle Harry Schuh, who had some kind words for me in postgame interviews.

"He's the greatest I ever came against," he said, looking tired and sore. "He taught me a few lessons I won't forget."

The game itself provided little in terms of excitement. Starr moved the offense into field-goal range with relative ease twice in a row, giving us a 6–0 lead on two Don Chandler kicks. The defense countered by stuffing the Raiders offense on both passes and runs. By the second quarter, the Raiders defense got frustrated and started playing tighter on the receivers, hoping to bump them off their routes, while the aggressive line tried to leap into the backfield. It backfired when Boyd Dowler broke free for a 62-yard touchdown pass to give us a 13–0 lead.

If there was one point the outcome was in question, it would have been on the next Raiders drive when Lamonica orchestrated the Raiders' one truly effective offensive attack, mixing in runs from Dixon with short passes. The drive culminated in a touchdown pass to Bill Miller a half second before I hit the quarterback, bringing the score to 13–7. The touchdown sparked the Raiders defense, and they briefly started to get to Starr, pushing us back on our running plays. Still, we caught a lucky break near the end of the half when the Raiders fumbled a punt deep in their own territory and we were able to add another Chandler field goal for a 16–7 lead.

Halftime was business as usual—the various groups broke up into separate corners and discussed adjustments. The only thing different was Jerry Kramer going around to the different players, making sure they understood the extra importance of this game. Jerry had been more convinced than anyone that this was Coach Lombardi's last game and hadn't been afraid to share his beliefs. Now with half the game over and a victory in our clutches, he wanted to make sure we all knew what could be riding on this game. If it was Coach's last game, we had to send him out as a champion. We owed him that much. Although some of us were still skeptical, nobody argued.

The third quarter was more of the same with Donnie Anderson and little-used Ben Wilson out of USC running for steady gains and Bart showing his accuracy on the passing game. After a loft pass to Max McGee, playing along with Fuzzy Thurston in their last game, Anderson scored on a running play to give us a 23–7 lead.

"That put the frosting on the cake," I told a reporter after the game. "Instead of a shaky lead, we had a secure lead. It was the first time we felt we were on easy street."

Don added another field goal, and Herb Adderley returned a pick for 60 yards and a touchdown. The Raiders added a touchdown late, but it didn't matter. We won decisively 33–14, giving us our second straight Super Bowl victory, the coveted three-peat, and our fifth title in just seven years.

When the final gun sounded, I looked over from my position on the field to find Coach, and I saw Jerry Kramer and Forrest Gregg pick him up and put him on their shoulders, carrying him off in victory.

"This is the best way to leave a football field," he told them, and his smile was never bigger.

In the locker room after the game, some of the players expected Coach to announce his retirement, but again there was no way he would distract from the accomplishment. At this moment, he wasn't our departing coach, he was just our coach. He talked about what we had accomplished, what we had won, and even offered up a last bit of criticism about us letting up at times. But there was nothing that could mask his pride.

"This has to be one of the great years," he said. "I think it's something you'll always remember—boys, I'm really proud of you."

As my good friend Jerry said, we didn't want to leave the locker room. If I had known it would be the last time we would be in a locker room with Vince Lombardi as our coach, I don't know if I would have ever left.

Chapter 20 | ## It's Been More Than a Game; It's Been a Way of Life

We have to find a way to continue
when our idols and influences move on.

It came out in the press much later that Coach Lombardi had made his decision to retire from coaching midway through the 1967 season, but as we all thought, he kept it to himself and a few close family members and friends to avoid distracting the team from our goal, his goal, the only goal—winning it all.

After I heard he had retired, by reading about it in a newspaper while I was in Chicago, I thought back to his last few speeches and even some individual conversations he had with me and some of the other players. I suddenly remembered how he seemed to always carry an extra burden on his shoulders, how his speeches were filled with more emotion than normal and even a bit of sentimentality. He seemed to take more time when talking to us, as if he was savoring the experience, especially in our postseason run, knowing each game could be the last. He let us know repeatedly what a privilege it was coaching us, and I thought what a far cry that was from the disciplinarian we could never fully impress or satisfy during my first few seasons with the team.

Coach announced his retirement and his replacement by Phil Bengtson in a simple emotionless press conference after a Packers function. The reason he gave was that his increased duties as general manager made it "impractical" for him to carry on as coach, as well. Nobody could fault him. Though he had managed to juggle both jobs for several years, the expansion of the league, player salaries, and the overall growth in the business of football provided new challenges for management. Still, those of us who played for him had a hard time believing there was anything Coach couldn't handle.

There was also the idea—stuck in the back of my mind—that Coach might have known we were done as a dynasty and saw this as his chance to get out.

If that was the case, I certainly wouldn't have felt any bad feelings about the decision, partially because I found myself thinking along the same lines. After we won the 1967 championship, there was a feeling that regardless of who was coaching us, it would be difficult to get back to the Promised Land. The theory of the team getting older during the past couple years was becoming more fact than fiction. Paul and Jim were gone. Now Max and Fuzzy had retired. We lost several defenders, as well, and the dozen or so of us who had been with the Packers for the better part of the last decade were coming close to the end. The injuries were piling up, the legs were slowing down, and it was getting tougher and tougher to fill the vacant spots.

Coach was one of the smartest men I ever knew, and he was a winner first and foremost. He was not the kind of man who could sit on the sideline and watch this team, this dynamic force he created, slowly fade away. It was something I believe he couldn't bear to be part of, and I think that pushed him to leave more than anything else.

It was still difficult to take. He just seemed immortal, one of those guys who would coach for the next 20 or 30 years. He was not only part of the Green Bay Packers, he *was* the Green Bay Packers. There was no way any of us could comprehend a future without him. He was our leader and just like that he was gone—and things in Green Bay would never be the same.

Coach Lombardi's departure was a tough but valuable lesson for me. It is easy to let our leaders carry us, but we have to realize that one day they will move on. Instead of mourning their departure, we should take what they give us, what they teach us, and use it to prepare ourselves for our journey down our own path. It is easier said than done, but it's necessary for growth. It took me a while to adjust, but when I did I realized that beyond the hurt and loss I felt at Coach Lombardi's retirement, I had a treasure trove of tools, skills, and lessons I got from him that would always lead me to great things in my life, whether he was there or not. More than anything, the leader that was Coach Lombardi had taught me to be a leader myself—and for that I will always be grateful.

Success in one area simply can't last forever.

For as quickly as Coach Lombardi's arrival built a dynasty, his departure began the downfall. The team seemed to struggle all season long with ailments they played through only because the backups were even more hurt. Our top receivers missed games, and Bart Starr missed some game time, as well. Combine the injuries, the lack of a kicking game, the target we had on our backs as three-time champions, and a number of bad breaks, and the season was set up to be disastrous. Still, we had faced problems in the past and persevered. The difference, however, was that we had our leader then, and now he was gone.

It wasn't that Phil Bengtson was a bad coach. He was just a *different* coach. To be fair, he never had a chance. There was no way anyone would be able to fill Coach Lombardi's shoes. No way. Everyone felt bad for Phil, from the players to the writers to the fans. How can you possibly replace somebody as successful, somebody as charismatic, somebody as legendary?

Coach Bengtson's approach was to be the complete opposite. Where Coach Lombardi yelled and did what he could to fire us up, Bengtson was laid back, calm, and methodical. Where Coach Lombardi was emotional, Coach Bengtson at times seemed unaffected and even uninvolved. He was gentle, subtle, even to the point of being monotone. At first, it was a relief, a nice change of pace for us, but we soon found ourselves missing something. We couldn't quite put a finger on it.

Then Coach Lombardi would come down from the offices to watch us practice and we would remember what it was. Just his presence on the field made us focus more and pay attention to the details. It motivated us and pushed us to over-achieve. To his credit, Coach Lombardi never offered his advice to the players or Coach Bengtson (at least in front of us). He respected Phil too much and didn't want to do anything to take away our new coach's voice and power. Still, anyone watching Coach Lombardi's body language, especially as the season got under way and we started losing, could tell he was burning inside. It was killing him to stay silent, to not grab the whistle and the clipboard and get back to work with his team. We could see him pacing, we could see him shaking his head, and then suddenly we didn't see him at all. He stopped coming to practice, perhaps embarrassed by the team's performance or perhaps scared he wouldn't be able to contain himself any longer.

The 1968 season was one of the longer ones of my career.

We finished 6–7–1. We were a lost team, a team that was starting to realize that no matter how much we wanted to fight it, the dream might actually be over.

My last season in the NFL, 1969, was one of the toughest years of my life. I had dreamed of playing professional football. I had worked my way past some obstacles and my own expectations to make it into the league. I had experienced unbelievable success both individually and with the Packers. I had accomplished more than I had ever hoped and had taken advantage of the many opportunities my professional career had brought me. I was doing exactly what I wanted to do.

Now I could feel it coming to an all-too-abrupt end. Actually, it wasn't that sudden, it just feels that way sometimes looking back. One minute I was at the peak of my career, and the next thing I knew my body didn't work like it used to. And even worse, I noticed a change in my drive.

The biggest change we experienced on the Green Bay Packers before that 1969 season had to be the shocking news that Vince Lombardi was leaving the organization to go back to coaching, this time with the Washington Redskins. As outraged as folks around Green Bay were, the move made perfect sense for Coach. The Redskins had wooed him for a while and could offer him more money, as well as a piece of ownership of the team and more influence. He also saw some young talent that needed molding like the Packers had when he first joined. He also had help in veteran quarterback Sonny Jurgensen, whom he had always respected for his accuracy and leadership—much like Bart.

It stung me greatly, as it did many of the other players and fans in Green Bay. Although he had stepped away from coaching the year before, there had been at least some comfort from the knowledge that he was still around and involved with the team he had built. We didn't see him or hear from him every day, but with a presence as large as Coach Lombardi's, you felt it everywhere. Now it was gone, and there was no doubt about the size of the void we all felt in Green Bay coming into that season.

For as much as it hurt, I saw it coming. I had an experience with Coach during one of the last practices we had as a team in the 1968 season. He had come down to watch the team that had brought him so much joy and success. Instead he saw a shadow of what they once were, and he saw himself reflected in that.

"How you doin', Coach?" I asked as I jogged to the sideline.

"Willie, there is only one place in this game for me," he said, looking at the field pensively. "And that's out here coaching."

I had seen that look of determination and resolve many times in my career, and I knew he would be gone soon. He couldn't come back and take over coaching at Green Bay again because it would upstage Coach Bengtson and ruffle some feathers. It wouldn't have been fair to Phil, and Coach Lombardi knew that. Plus with all the teams looking for coaches to turn around their programs, I knew Coach, despite bleeding Green and Gold, would look for another actual opportunity where he could build another legacy.

Beyond the psychological and emotional loss in losing Coach Lombardi to another franchise, there was something else many of the veterans felt coming into my last season, something we hadn't really felt before despite what others liked to say about us.

We felt old. I know I did. I had always been willing to push through the pain and do whatever it took to get the job done. I was hopeful about our team and ready to give it my all, but my body wasn't always cooperating. I woke up with many more aches and pains, especially in my legs. I was shorter of breath, more easily tired. They weren't big changes, but they were enough that I noticed. I even found myself dreading certain drills and exercises in practice, something I never would have complained about a few years prior. Now those drills were almost as much of a struggle as the recovery after.

For the first time in my life, I felt that football was no longer exciting. Halfway through the year, I told my coaches and my teammates I was going to retire at the end of the season.

If you know you're leaving, soak up that last day.

My last professional football game, as it is for many professional athletes, was a surreal mix of sadness, relief, excitement, and so many other emotions.

There is no way to fully prepare for an experience like that, and I had no idea what I was in for. Once word had gotten out to the local press that I was retiring, the last home game against the St. Louis Cardinals suddenly took on a certain level of importance for the fans in a season that had been lost way too early, and I was very happy to be part of that.

Governor Warren Knowles declared December 21, 1969, to be Willie Davis Day, and the crowd was there to cheer on their beloved Packers one last time for the 1969 season, to let them know they were still behind them, that they would always be behind them no matter what. But they were also there to give me a special send off, to say thank you in a way only a crowd of Packers fans could.

As an interesting end to my career, we had lost to the Browns two weeks prior in Cleveland, giving me an opportunity to say farewell there, as well. Then we went into Chicago one last time and took care of business. Mixed in with the boos we always experienced in Chicago were also quite a few cheers from the fans who had respected my effort over the years despite their hatred for the uniform. But nothing could possibly come close to ending my career at home, at Lambeau Field, in front of these fans on the field that had provided so much for me.

As I trotted out of the locker room and heard the roar of the crowd, I knew instantly I would miss this forever—and I was right. I took a moment to look around and take it all in, my last time coming out onto the field as a player. Within weeks after I retired, I started fielding offers from other teams to return to play for them, but it would never happen. I know that moment of looking out over the Green Bay crowd helped my decision. I would never be able to wear another uniform ever again. I was a Green Bay Packer. I am a Green Bay Packer, and the Green and Gold will be my colors forever.

For me personally, the game took a back seat. I do remember that our developing quarterback, Don Horn, threw for five touchdowns, and we routed the Cardinals 45–28. I also remember that I struggled mightily that day—as if I needed yet another reminder that my time had come and gone.

The Cardinals had a huge right tackle by the name of Ernie McMillan, a Pro Bowl player at 6'6" and 260 pounds. He was a monster who had always given me trouble in my prime and not the kind of guy I necessarily wanted to end my career against. I really wanted to end with a dynamite performance, one that I could savor. I even told Ernie as much when I first walked onto the field.

"Now you know this is my game, this is my day," I said laughing.

"I know that Willie," he said, laughing right back.

"Now, I'm gonna need you to do somethin' for me," I said.

"Oh yeah, what's that?"

"I don't know, get out of the way or somethin' when I come at ya!"

We both laughed, and he just shook his head. He wouldn't go easy on me, and I wouldn't have had it any other way. We battled back and forth, and I can say I did get the jump on him a few times and made a couple of key tackles, remnants of how I had played at my prime. But admittedly Ernie got the better of me that day. Still, when Coach Bengtson pulled me late in the fourth quarter, one of the first things I saw was Ernie, along with several other Cardinal players, giving me a huge round of applause. That respect warmed my heart almost as much as the standing ovation from the crowd.

The officials stopped the game and actually brought out a microphone for me as I made my exit. I had a hunch this might happen, but I also knew if I talked real long I would start sobbing. Between the handshakes from my teammates, the roar of the crowd, the respect from the Cardinal players and coaches, and the overwhelming power of the moment, I didn't know how much I could take.

"I'd just like to say it's been a great time for me the last 10 years playing for the Green Bay Packers. I'm surely indebted to my teammates, the Packer organization, but most of all to you, the fans. I'd just like to say it's been more than a game; it's been a way of life. Thank you."

With that, I jogged off the field, shaking hands and starting my goodbyes. I had practiced my speech, knowing full well I would be emotional. I wanted to make sure to get out my words, to let everyone know how important it was to me to be a Packer. I looked up into the crowd and I could see people crying, and the full impact of their love for me and for this team surprised me yet again. I suddenly realized I would no longer play another down as a Green Bay Packer. I tried to collect myself and wrap my head around the idea. Luckily I was distracted by everybody coming to talk to me.

"Hey man, you had a great career," Dave Robinson said. "I don't know what it's gonna be like without you, Doctor! It's not gonna be the same."

"Well," I said. "It ain't gonna be the same for the Doctor neither!"

There was my old friend Forrest reminiscing about meeting me in the army and about all we had been through together, how we helped each other grow as players and as men.

"A lot of huddles and a lot of good times, isn't it Will?"

There was the whole defense huddled around me, their captain, one last time looking for any final words of advice.

"Well, you guys got it now," I said. "You gotta carve your own niche now. You gotta meet the challenge."

And then, caught on video as I looked out onto the field for the last seconds of action, I had some final words to anyone who was listening, but mostly to myself.

"This game moves on," I said. "There is no person or no group bigger than the game."

When the game ended, I congratulated the players on the field and jogged like I had always done to the locker room, making sure to look around one last time and take it all in. I was aware enough to savor the moment, the sights, the sounds, the feeling, and the energy that came from wearing the uniform on that field in front of those fans. I embraced all of it.

I was tired, drained, ready to move on to the next challenge. More than that, I was appreciative, honored, and truly grateful for everything. I had lived my dream, and I knew even then it would be the first of many. I just needed to figure out what was next.

I took extra long to take off my pads and uniform that final day. As I did, I looked at the number on my jersey, No. 87. I looked at my teammates, my fellow warriors, celebrating after ending the season on a win. I looked at the spot where Coach Lombardi used to stand to deliver the speeches that changed my life. I looked at my hands, bruised and battered from a career spent punishing opponents. And I looked one last time at the uniform—and to this day, I have never felt such pride as I did in that moment.

Yes sir, I am a Green Bay Packer.

| Chapter 21 | The End of an Era |

Never forget.

After I retired, I had several offers from various teams to come back as a player as well as coaching offers in both college and the pros. But I felt my football career was done. It felt like the end of an era for me, and that was confirmed on September 3, 1970, when Coach Vince Lombardi passed away.

Beyond being one of the saddest moments in my life, it was also *the* most shocking. In my final season when he left to coach the Redskins, we said our goodbyes to each other and then lost touch. He had to focus on turning around his new organization, and I was still dedicated to the Packers and my new coach while also contemplating my future. During that season, I kept my eye on Washington, tracking how they were doing and wondering like the rest of the league if Lombardi's magic would be able to rub off on another organization. I also wondered if I would ever have the opportunity to play against him and a different team and how I would feel about it. That chance never came.

I had no indication he was sick. From what I heard, he was gearing up for another season of coaching. In the aftermath of his passing, I suddenly learned about all of his ailments. Coach had experienced digestive problems for the last few years of his life. A tough man, he wasn't the kind to regularly go to the doctor, and his stubbornness could have contributed to his early passing. When the pain finally became too much to bear and things started to feel wrong, he went to the hospital where he was diagnosed with a vicious and rapid form of cancer. Just like that, this legendary man's days were numbered.

Over the next few weeks, as he fought the disease from a hospital bed, everyone from his past and present came to visit, including clergy, family, and friends. He got calls from celebrities and politicians, including President Nixon, who wanted to let him know the whole country was pulling for him. Coach responded by saying he would fight to the very end. He didn't know any other way.

Several Packers made the trek, including Willie Wood, Jim Taylor, Jerry, Fuzzy, Skoronski, Zeke, and of course Bart and Paul. They all showed up not knowing what to expect and left in disbelief. This couldn't happen to a man like Lombardi. He was immortal, he was legendary, he was far too young. What would football be like without him? What would this world be like without him?

I found out he was sick when I visited San Diego to see a preseason game between the Giants and Chargers. Giants owner Wellington Mara pulled me aside and told me Coach was in bad shape and might not make it through the weekend. I couldn't believe what he was saying. I didn't even know he was sick, and now suddenly he was going to die any day. I drove back to L.A. that day and caught a red eye flight to Washington D.C. to get there the next morning.

I met Marie, Coach Lombardi's wife, outside the hospital room, and there was more than a look of concern on the strong woman's face. She knew her husband well and knew it was difficult for him to have his players see him in a weakened state. Balancing her husband's need to hang on to his dignity alongside his players' need to say goodbye was easier said than done.

When I walked into his room, I saw why. It didn't even seem real. I didn't realize until that moment how bad it was, until I saw it for myself. He was never a physically imposing man, but his presence commanded attention and respect. Now here was this small, skinny man attached to a number of machines, barely strong enough to keep his eyes open to look at me. This wasn't my Coach. It couldn't be. But then I saw him force a smile at me, and I knew.

"Hey Coach," I said, my voice wavering as I tried to muster the strength to hold myself together. "I came here to make a deal with ya. You're going to get better and come back to coaching, and I'm going to come out of retirement to play for ya."

That might have been the one time I actually would have.

Coach chuckled painfully and patted my hand. He struggled a bit to talk but still had his wits about him. We were able to exchange some small talk and even chat about football, a distraction he needed now more than ever. Then as the conversation started to slow, he did what he always did, what he still continues to do even in death. He caught my attention and told me something that not only moved me but touched my heart for the rest of my life.

"Willie, you are the best deal I ever made."

He then told me a few other things that I just can't bring myself to share, some things who I need to keep private for myself and to honor and respect the man that meant so much to me. I had trouble holding back the tears, and he could see it in my eyes. He asked me to pray for him, and I told him I would.

"Alright Willie," he said, flashing that smile once again. "Now I need you to get out of here."

He was my Coach, and I had built a pretty good career based on doing what he told me to do. So I got up and left, walking out with more pain and sadness in my heart than I thought possible. I ran into Mrs. Lombardi one more time, who made a point of telling me that while everybody who visited Coach while he was in the hospital meant a lot to him, nobody lit up his eyes like his former Packers.

Just more than a week later, Coach Lombardi passed away. There was a beautiful funeral in New York at the St. Patrick Cathedral. There were more than 1,500 mourners lined up to watch the procession and an enormous service full of people there to pay their respects, including players from the Packers, Giants, and Redskins, former college teammates, coaches, Commissioner Pete Rozelle, and other luminaries Coach had associated with through the years. There were also people he hadn't really talked with, people who had just been inspired by what he had done and the man himself. I had the honor of being a pallbearer along with Bart Starr, and we both helped each other get through the pain of the service.

One part I remember most was the reading of Coach's favorite quote from the scriptures. It's from Saint Paul's Letter to the Corinthians.

"Do you not know that the runners in the stadium all run in the race, but only one wins the prize? Run so as to win. Every athlete exercises discipline in every way. They do it to win a perishable crown but we an imperishable one. Thus I do not run aimlessly; I do not fight as if I were shadowboxing. No, I drive my body and train it for fear that, after having preached to others, I myself should be disqualified."

It was a great quote for a great man whose focus was that winning is the only thing. The service was over before we knew it, and Coach was buried in a beautiful cemetery. Articles were written that celebrated his life and his legend. People in and out of football began to realize how special Coach was if they hadn't already known. The trophy given to the winner of the Super Bowl was now named the Lombardi Trophy to honor him. All over the country, fans mourned and moved on, living better for hearing about and following the wisdom of Coach Vince Lombardi.

But for those who knew him intimately, we got something much greater. We were able to touch greatness because of this man, and it went far beyond the football field. As I was writing this book, I talked with my old teammate, Herb Adderley, and he told me he still hears Coach's words each and every day. He lives his life by what Coach would want and expect from him. He's not alone. Those who knew Coach Lombardi continue to pursue greatness and excellence today because as he said, "Winning is not a sometime thing; it's an all-the-time thing."

As I've mentioned, he is the man responsible for all the success I have achieved in my life. As I continue to heed the words and wisdom of Coach Lombardi, I can't help but think of perhaps my favorite of all his quotes and how he could affect us with his words, and how lucky I am to have known him.

"I don't say these things because I believe in the brute nature of man or that men must be brutalized to be combative. I believe in God, and I believe in human decency. But I firmly believe that any man's finest hour, the greatest fulfillment of all that he holds dear, is that moment when he has worked his heart out in a good cause and lies exhausted on the field of battle—victorious."

Chapter 22	Talkin' Football

Find a way to continue to do what you love.

Even if you can't make it your life's work, if you can't necessarily make a living doing it, find a way to involve your passion in your life because it will bring you joy.

Although I could no longer play professional football and I wanted to pursue other business opportunities that kept me out of coaching, I knew I couldn't just give up my involvement with football. It had meant too much to me for too long, and it was still in many ways my obsession. I had to do something to help ease into my retirement, something that would keep me involved in the NFL. So I did what many former players do. I became a TV analyst, working for seven years covering games for NBC alongside the great Ross Porter. It wasn't my main source of income, but it provided me with a chance to stay involved, easing the pain of having to walk away from the game.

I wasn't approached to be an analyst. I pursued it, making a call to Chet Simmons, the former commissioner of the United States Football League, who at the time was the president of NBC Sports. I was able to talk him into letting me on the air, saying I could provide key analysis, which is what *all* former players turned analysts have to offer. I still wonder if he wasn't just doing me a favor when he said yes.

I was not the best on-air personality the network had. Lucky for me (and them), they paired me with Porter, who quickly built a reputation as a play-by-play legend covering both football and NCAA basketball before spending 28 years broadcasting Los Angeles Dodgers baseball games. Though he was just starting out, he had the habits of a true professional who had been in the business a while. He was a meticulous personality who was almost religious in his preparation. He approached his job with a serious sense of professionalism, studying players, working assignments, and making sure he was familiar with everything we would cover in the game. He also expected the same from everyone else.

We covered both preseason and regular season games, mainly teams on the West Coast. It was an interesting challenge for me, something a lot more than just talking football on the air. I jumped into it not knowing what to expect and still found myself surprised by the amount of work that went into each and every game. We received our assignments a week in advance and did what we could to collect as much information as possible about the two teams. That information on personnel, records, trends, history, etc., wasn't as readily available as it is today, nor was access to coaches and players for pregame interviews quite so easy. We'd fly out to the hosting city on Friday and try to get what we could from the teams. We'd also meet with the crew to go over coverage plans, laying out the various segments we'd show during the game, sharing the information we gathered, and preparing as best we could for the inevitable surprises.

My main contribution, especially the first couple years, was my insight on players I had played against, coaches I had faced, and the defensive and offensive schemes. That part of the broadcast I had down, and whatever I didn't know I relied on the players to help me with by preparing me beforehand.

"Come on man, give me something I can use on the air," I asked players who were afraid of spilling any information that would get them in trouble with their coaches. Most of them were willing to offer something small as long as I didn't attribute it to them. They would give me a play they would run in a certain situation, a plan of attack for a particular quarterback, etc. Like any analyst, I would then take that information and make it look like I had some extra keen insight into the minute details of not just the game but that particular team.

"Well Ross, I wouldn't be surprised if on this play we see them do..."

I truly wasn't the best color analyst.

My other fear was covering Packers games. I was very clear with my employers at NBC that I had a bias, and I didn't know if I'd be able to completely hide that bias. An announcer can get in trouble really quickly in this business by saying the wrong thing, by showing favoritism to one side. There are phone calls, letters, or much worse. I knew I could try my best to be fair, but it was tough to contain my true thoughts and emotions when it came to the Green and Gold. And God help me if they were losing!

Luckily, I only had to cover a few in my career, and they were mostly preseason games where I wasn't as invested as a fan or former player. I apparently did a pretty decent job of holding in my bias. In fact, I did such a good job I actually got letters from Packers fans saying I was now *against* the team!

The broadcasting experience served multiple purposes for me. It paid me well enough to help me rid myself of some debt that came with launching my other business venture. It gave me some experience in a completely new arena, which I found exciting and challenging. More than anything, though, it kept me involved in the game I loved and helped make the transition out of football less painful. It made me realize that even if we aren't involved in our passions the way we necessarily expected, we can still always find a way to participate and leave our mark.

| Chapter 23 | # Business Is a Lot Like Football: From Worst to First |

Loyalty will eventually bring opportunities.

While the NFL analyst job provided a bit of comfort and joy, the beer business and all the work I had done with Schlitz over the course of my football career provided me with a future.

I was fortunate enough to have a number of options in front of me when I left football. My advanced degree had brought a number of job offers in a variety of industries, including multiple beer and beverage companies. Not wanting to rule anything out, I chose about a dozen of the best ones and explored the opportunities, even visiting firms in New York and Chicago.

But there was nobody who provided me with the opportunity, the encouragement, and the belief in me as a future business leader like Schlitz Brewing, and I did feel a sense of loyalty to them for all they had done. It was Schlitz who offered me more than just the typical promotional off-season work that many star athletes had. They offered me chances to learn about the business and get more involved, fully aware of what I wanted to do with my future. Schlitz also helped me pay for some of my schooling, further showing its support. As I worked more and more with the company, they not only assigned me to various jobs but started to ask my opinion, reminding me that if I wanted it, I had a future with the company.

When I was close to retiring from football, I was sent out by Schlitz as part of a task force that studied the company's various distributorship branches around the country, including California. One that stuck out was the company's South Central L.A. branch, which had struggled mightily but still had quite a bit of potential, especially with the products we offered and the community. When I came back and made my presentation, I threw out an offhand comment that I initially meant as nothing more than a joke.

"Well I'll tell ya, if South Central is ever for sale, I'm interested."

It wasn't long after I announced my retirement that I got a call from Schlitz's vice president of marketing Fred Haviland, asking me if I was serious about wanting the distributorship. At first I didn't even know what he was talking about, but when he reminded me of my presentation, I suddenly realized we were talking about something bigger and more challenging than I could even imagine.

"How about you come to town this week and stop by the office?" Fred said. "I think there are some people who want to talk to you."

When I told the execs at Schlitz I wanted to be more than just the promotions guy, this wasn't exactly what I had in mind. I didn't feel nearly qualified yet to run a branch, but I had to at least listen to what they had to say about such a unique opportunity. I met with several executives at the company, men who would soon become key mentors in my life, and they all expressed an interest in my taking over the distributorship. Nothing was offered or agreed to, but I was told to think seriously about it and about all it would mean.

This was a completely new adventure with its own risks. I had always wanted to eventually own my own business, but I hadn't expected even the possibility of doing it so early in my post-football career. Despite my drive and my work ethic, I had a lot less experience than most others in the field, and now I was talking about an entrepreneurship and all the risks, pressures, long hours, and opportunities to fail that come with such a venture.

I worried about company support. I worried about whether or not I was qualified. I worried about the investment of time and money. I even worried about the product itself. I hadn't necessarily envisioned myself involved in an alcohol company. It wasn't that I was opposed to the product or even to drinking alcohol, but I knew careers in those industries sometimes came with negative connotations from people who didn't necessarily share the same views. In fact, at one point in my business career, I was sent a letter from a fan, a sweet old woman, who admonished me for my involvement with Schlitz, saying she "couldn't understand why, with all that I had achieved, had I chosen the beer business." I actually kept that letter for a long time, just as a reminder to keep my perspective on the thoughts and opinions people had about the industry.

I also worried about the location. Although I had seen potential, it would require quite a bit of work. Schlitz had 13 distributors in the area, and 12 of them were doing well. One wasn't, and that one would be mine. My warehouse covered the L.A. area that had just experienced the Watts Riots. When I went to visit, I could still see torch marks on the sides of buildings and other damage that had been done. It was not a pleasant place to live or work, and it was a struggling business that had all but been forgotten.

It was also an opportunity. I couldn't help but see the potential there, not just for the distributorship and the company but also for myself and my career. I had an opportunity, just like I had in football, to be a trailblazer for the black community. I had an opportunity to be the first black person to own a distribution company with a major brewery. Within a few years, every company would have one, but in 1970, I had the chance to be the first, and that was something that filled me with pride. In fact, at an early meeting with the company, somebody asked me if I ever thought I would have the chance to own a company with my own building and trucks.

"When I was growing up," I said. "I didn't even think I'd be able to *drive* a truck!"

There was also the money to consider. In the pros, I had never made more than $50,000 as a base salary. When the company's financial advisor asked what I wanted for a reasonable salary while I set up the distributorship, I had no idea. He said he would put me down for $125,000, and I nearly jumped three feet in the air.

"Uh yeah, that sounds good!"

All that aside, the real reason I decided to take the leap and work for Schlitz was that I felt a sense of loyalty to a company that had believed in me so much. I knew they were taking a chance on someone as unproven as me. They had been there every step of the way to help and sure enough, as I expected, they called with an offer. They wanted me to take over.

I decided to trust in and repay a company that had been so dedicated to me and my future with my own loyalty. I purchased the distributorship with all my savings left over from football, about $150,000, and I took out a $500,000 bank loan. Just like that, I had incurred more debt than I ever thought possible as well as a wholesaler company I knew very little about in a region of the country I knew even less about. I was in way over my head, and I was terrified and excited.

"Willie, don't worry," Fred said. "We'll be there to help you every step of the way."

I made sure to hold him to that.

There is almost always someone who knows something more than you do.

When I first launched Willie Davis Distributing Company, I knew there were a whole lot of people who were willing to lend me a helping hand, and I was more than appreciative for their advice.

On the football field, we not only had the veterans who had been around the game to guide us through the jitters or explain how the flow of the game worked—we also had coaches who made sure we were performing at our highest potential. Since high school, I had been blessed with some of the best. Tricky Jones, Eddie Robinson, Paul Brown, and Vince Lombardi had all been there to teach me the game of football, to help me excel well beyond my expectations. Through my experience on the football field, I learned the value of humility and working closely with those who could see the bigger picture a little clearer than I could. It's no different in the beverage industry, or any industry, for that matter. There are always mentors if we're smart enough to find them and listen to them.

I had three men at Schlitz who guided me in my first year and beyond. What made each of them great in terms of mentoring was how they balanced when to give me advice and when to leave me to grow on my own. This is easier said than done, a skill learned only with practice and experience, and I was fortunate to have three masters.

Robert Uihlein Jr., the company's president and chairman when I took over the distributorship, was as encouraging as any man I ever knew. Bob was a tall, skinny man who could intimidate the hell out of me. Born into the family that founded Schlitz, becoming chairman was his destiny, and he had worked his way up through the ranks. He was an authoritative figure who would have been extremely imposing if he wasn't so helpful and supportive. He also demanded excellence, as was proven by the record sales numbers the company put up while he was in charge.

When I got involved with the company, I told Bob about my fears of how much of my own money I had invested and how afraid I was of failing.

"I'm telling you Bob, if this doesn't work you're gonna see me jumping off a building," I said jokingly.

"No, no, we don't want you doing that," he said. "I'll tell you what. You go out there and work that business for two years. If you don't like it, we'll buy it back from you and you can just come work for us again."

I don't think he was serious. I'll never know. He didn't let me fail. He was there every step of the way, calling to see how I was doing, offering his advice whenever I asked for it, and encouraging me to perform. As I was with Coach Lombardi, I was in awe of Bob at times and did whatever I could to prove to him that he had made the right call in giving me the franchise.

Fred Haviland taught me the intricacies of the beer business and the secrets to working sales in a particularly tricky industry. A friendly man who believed in me, Fred was the one who gave me the advice I needed to get comfortable in the beverage business—advice I adapted to other industries.

Fred told me to always do what I could to avoid conflict, especially with customers. He told me where to focus my efforts to help me sell more product. He taught me how to work with my own sales crew, how to communicate with my drivers, and how to balance every aspect of the industry to make sure nobody felt neglected from employee to customer. He also gave me the single greatest piece of advice when it came to working with customers.

"Make sure you know the person your sales people are working with closely," he said. "And then make sure you know the person *above* the sales people you're working with."

If Fred taught me the beer business, my friend Ben Barkin taught me how to be an entrepreneur. Ben is a local legend around the state of Wisconsin, a true "doer" in every sense of the word. He was a PR and marketing guru who worked for Schlitz (one of his many clients). With the backing of a major brewery, Ben was able to not only grow the company name but also use its influence to launch other initiatives around the state.

Most notably, he helped found (along with circus historian Chappie Fox) the Great Circus Parade, a throwback to the early part of the 20th century when kids and adults lined up to watch the circus come marching into town. The parade attracted thousands each year, and it quickly became one of the state's premiere events. It was one of Ben's great passions, and each year he miraculously generated thousands of dollars in contributions from the state's elite to keep the parade going.

Ben and I worked together on a number of projects over the years. He was the one man I can say who may actually have been busier than me. He was a true "make it happen" kind of guy. After seeing Ernest Borgnine tell Johnny Carson he had always wanted to be a clown, Ben somehow got him Ernest be the lead clown, walking in the parade down the streets of Milwaukee. Ben also somehow always got me to participate, often riding in a vintage car dressed in a full top hat and tails. He could talk anybody into anything.

Ben was an extremely passionate guy who taught me how each and every client was vitally important to the business, all equally, regardless of size. Schlitz was one of Ben's major accounts, but he had several others and he gave each of them the time and attention they deserved. He always put the customer first and was a believer in taking care of the customer so they take care of you. He also taught me about passion for business, charisma, and the drive I needed to succeed. He was a brilliant man and I idolized him.

Of course, I had one other mentor who helped me in starting my business. It was a voice I had heard for many years, a man whose words transcended more than just football. Although he was gone, I still relied on

Coach Lombardi as a mentor, a man who would help me succeed and help me rile up my employees and get them to perform at their very best.

It became clear right away how closely matched football and business were. When I first went into football, coaches were talking about how successful companies like AT&T, IBM, and General Motors were working and how teams could use them as a model for success. When I first got into business, everyone was talking about modeling their companies like the Yankees, the Celtics, and yes, the Green Bay Packers.

The language was all the same—talk about winning, facing challenges, creating the right attitude, meeting expectations, making a statement, coming out victorious. These were phrases I understood intimately, and I used them to inspire and drive my employees. The similarities helped me feel more comfortable about leading and established what needed to be said and what I needed to expect from my employees to achieve the success I so desired. For that, I recalled the words of my great coach.

Winning is the only thing.

In my first meeting with my new crew at the distributorship—the drivers, the sales people, the staff—I gave a short speech, one of many I delivered to them to let them know who I was and what I expected. It was short and to the point with no room for any confusion, and it set the stage for what we were about to accomplish.

"As many of you know, I have never been a wholesaler before. This is all rather new to me. I've worked with the company for a while now and I have an understanding about the business, but I still have some things to learn. I'll admit that I am going into this with no proven track record but only goals and expectations. And the biggest expectation is this—we will not fail."

I looked around at the employees, trying to read their reactions to see if they believed in what I was saying or if they thought I was full of it. I saw both reactions.

"I'm not sure how we will gauge our success or just how much we will accomplish, but we will not fail. That's where we're going to start. That's the new commitment."

I have used a variation of those words with every one of my business ventures. It's pure Lombardi. I didn't know any other way. I couldn't accept failure because I couldn't comprehend it, and I didn't want anyone in my company to entertain any notion of it.

Later in my business career, I used an analogy about how all the NFL teams start out the season with hopes and expectations of winning the Super Bowl but only one team actually takes the prize. I would analyze what that team had beyond the talent and the coaching, what other factors set the team apart and led them to do something great. I learned many of those things playing for Coach Lombardi's Packers, and I learned many more as I pushed further and further into my business career, intent on succeeding everywhere I went. I always found one thing most interesting. It started with the commitment Coach preached about. It started with the commitment to pursue greatness.

Very early on in my business career, I realized just how much more Coach Lombardi had to teach me beyond the game of football.

There were several basic but vital tips I learned and applied in my first year (and beyond) that helped me achieve success in the beverage industry, setting the stage for all my future accomplishments in business.

You need to be tough to survive and even tougher to win.

In football, we talk about not just physical strength but also mental toughness, a psychological fortitude that comes from being emotionally invested in what you're doing. That's what sets apart the winners. It's the same way in life. There will always be challenges as well as opportunities, and only those who are physically prepared, mentally tough, and spiritually focused will be able to overcome or take advantage of the moment.

When I first started the business, I was truly overwhelmed by everything that needed to be done. But I knew if I could get my footing, I could make it work. I prioritized and tackled one challenge at a time, making sure I conjured up the strength to take on each and every task. I started out surviving and quickly moved to achieving—and the business grew.

Learn everything you possibly can about what you're doing.

It will help you always stay one step ahead of any competitor. When I first got into the business, I had several years' worth of knowledge and experience that came with working promotions for the company. I used that as my base to learn more about how beverage distribution worked, from balancing all the products that Schlitz carried to how to work with each individual customer to marketing and so on, just like how I used to scout teams in football.

When I came into the business, I worked solely with Schlitz, carrying about 30 beer brands in all sorts of packages (cases, 12-packs, 16 oz. cans, etc.) as well as a line of wines and some malt liquor. The longer I stayed in the business, the more common it became for distributors to carry competing brands to widen their product line, which led me to carry Hamm's, Olympic, Coors, some Mexican beers, and one from Kenya called Tusker Lager by the time I finished. I read, researched, and learned everything I could about each and every product, how it sold, where it sold, who bought it. I looked for any kind of trends, however minute in detail, to give me an edge. I also trained my sales people and route drivers to do the same. There is no such thing as non-valuable information, and I started my career in business as a collector of data, reports, and whatever I could find to give me an edge.

I'd also be more than willing to share that information with potential customers. I told my salesmen to walk into a liquor store or convenience mart and check the competitors' displays to see if they had been sitting there a while. A great way to do this was to make a small mark on a can or package and come back a few weeks later. If that package was still there, we'd tell the manager the product wasn't moving. We guarantee to give him a product that would move itself through at least two or three times in the same amount of time. We made sure we could make some pretty imposing arguments for rotating products that could get them the best sales—and it started with information gathering.

Acknowledge your fears and deal with them quickly.

There is nothing that can hold you back from accomplishing your goals like fear. Unfortunately, fear is unavoidable, especially when tackling a new venture. There are so many opportunities for failure, so many ways you can lose before you even start. It's difficult to balance all of it, especially at the beginning. Whether it's a business venture, training camp, or a new job, there is a lot to be afraid of and a lot to overcome.

My biggest fear was competition and how I could beat them. It was the same when I played football. Just as I would lay awake at night both nervous and excited about how to play an opponent, I would now lay awake thinking of other distributors and how I could beat them in my market. I would think of the bigger players like Budweiser and how they could storm into a city with a tremendous marketing machine behind them and oust several other smaller competitors. I would think of how I could not only leave my imprint but dominate. That was what I was used to from my Packers days, and that was all I could accept.

Competition is just one fear of entering a new business as anyone who has done it will attest. There's worry about the quality of the product, if the customers are happy, what would happen if the employees left, making payroll, and so on. My approach has always been to let in those fears and find ways to either resolve them or prepare for them as quickly as possible. The more we acknowledge and fix the potential hitches, the easier we can breathe and the more we can focus on doing what we need to do to grow.

Be willing to work, and don't ask anyone to do something you won't do.

This is where the old adage "lead by example" comes in. I am a firm believer in it. I truly think the greatest leaders are also the best ones at the job. They are willing to get their hands dirty and do whatever is necessary with no concerns of status. They might be the boss, but they don't see themselves as higher up than the people who work for them. If the business needs them to do the work, they need to do the work. It's an unselfish attitude that does wonders to build a bond and a legacy among teams.

I can't say how many times I loaded the delivery trucks to make sure my product got out to the stores on time. If a driver got sick or had an emergency and couldn't find a replacement, then it was up to me to make sure the customer got what they needed. There were even a few times when all the trucks were out and a customer called on a Friday saying he didn't have enough product to get through the weekend. We'd load up cases in pickup trucks and the trunks of cars and I'd drive it over myself, making sure the customer knew that if he or she ever needed anything, I was just a phone call away.

I also made sure I went on the routes with the salesmen to random stops and not just their top customers. I listened to the owners as well as the customers. I made sure the message of top-quality service was consistent wherever we went and that they knew I was personally involved. While at one stop, I overheard a group of girls talking about buying a six-pack of Schlitz, so I told them to get two and then I paid for them both. When I delivered to a bar, I made sure to tell the patrons the first round was on me—as long as they kept drinking Schlitz.

There were many times I thought of sleeping in or skipping work. I was the boss after all. But I would remember something Coach Lombardi said about how compromising was the road to demise. I also thought about all the reasons he made me a team captain, so each and every morning I got up and went to work ready to lead—at least 15 minutes early.

Take advantage of your strengths.

I was the first African American to have his own distributorship, and in a predominantly black area like South Central, black success stories can go a long way. I made sure to spread the word about the new man in town, introducing myself to customers and organizations that I knew would have a sense of pride in my opportunity.

I also realized the name Willie Davis carried a bit of weight, as it does with all athletes. Right or wrong, I was smart enough to know people would associate the product with me as a player, and as promotions and marketing have shown through the years, having a spokesman with some notoriety helps. I launched a series of 250-plus billboards around Los Angeles that showed me holding a Schlitz malt liquor can and the phrase, "Tackle this one!" Pretty soon, Schlitz began its reputation in that area as Willie Beer.

We all have an asset, something to give us an advantage, and there is absolutely nothing wrong with using it to get a leg up.

People don't always care who you were.

On one of my first sales calls, I was very quickly reminded that my name alone was not going to carry me in this business.

I stopped at one of our better accounts to meet the manager, and he couldn't stop raving about how much he loved me as a player. He told me he had been a Packers fan for years, and I was one of his favorites. Then he got real serious.

"Mr. Davis, you are absolutely one of the best ever as far as I'm concerned," he said, giving me a stern look. "But if I don't get my beer on Friday afternoon when it's supposed to be here, you ain't gonna be nothin' but a son of a bitch!"

I made sure he always had his beer on Friday.

Always focus on the customer.

In Green Bay, I took great pride in playing for the fans. I felt a sense of loyalty and obligation to these people who forked over much more than just their hard-earned cash. When I took the field on Sundays, I made sure I didn't do anything to let them down.

When I got into business, my focus was on the customer. I did whatever I could to make sure they stayed happy, especially the ones who showed loyalty to me and my product. But customer service goes even further than keeping the happy ones happy. The real challenge is turning the ones that are a little unsure in your favor.

There was a bowling alley in Inglewood that was a large account. We could never get our product in there, mainly because the owner already had a partnership with a beer company that had Frank Sinatra as a key investor. They had a long history with the company and didn't want to change their deal. I contacted them a few times until finally I decided to stop by.

After giving him my pitch and being met again with a "no," I handed him my business card with my home phone number written on the back of it. I told him if there was ever an occasion where he didn't get his product on time, he should call me day or night, weekend or holiday, and I would be over there to stock his shelves. About a month later, I got a phone call from him saying his partner had missed a delivery.

"I was thinking, you gave me your card and here you are, talking to me on the phone," he said. "I don't know if I'd be able to reach Frank Sinatra. You're here, ready to work with me. That's the kind of guy I want to do business with."

Make sure your staff is prepared for anything.

It's one thing to have all the strategies running through your head, but you have to make sure your people are just as prepared for everything—and maybe even more. They need to know the approach, the philosophy, the challenges, the opportunities, the backup plans, anything and everything they need to make the business thrive.

One of the first things I did was go on the routes with the truck drivers, making sure they took me to both the top accounts as well as the struggling ones. I wanted them to be prepared to talk about all of them, including their strengths and weaknesses. I worked with the drivers on how to do the job, how we could improve the areas where we struggled and keep improving on the ones where we had success. It's about having everyone on the same page, moving forward together as a unit to a shared vision, and using shared strategies.

Never stop working.

Successful people are busy people. They don't take too long of a break. They are always looking for ways they can improve even when they're at the top of their game. When we won a title in Green Bay, we immediately looked to repeat. When I made a key play, I couldn't wait to make the next one. For successful people, there is no such word as "enough."

When I first got started in the beverage business, I had Willie Beer in more than 85 percent of my market, a significant step up from where Schlitz was before I got there, around 25 percent. I had more than tripled it, but I wanted at least 95 percent. Not long after that, I had it in 98 percent.

I looked for 99 percent next.

Celebrate your success.

The result of all these philosophies was an astounding jump in the South Central Schlitz distributor known as Willie Davis Distributing Co.

When I started, I had 1,200 accounts. I doubled that in my first year, and by the time I exited the beverage business, I had 4,600 accounts. After my first year, Schlitz did a survey and saw that of all the beer products sold in California, Schlitz owned 18 percent. In my area, Schlitz owned 48 percent.

We went from the lowest of the 13 area branches to the highest in terms of sales. Worst to first is a crowning achievement for a first-time businessman. For a little boy with business dreams, it was just as exciting as holding that championship trophy or going to the Pro Bowl. It was the first of many accomplishments I experienced as I continued to grow my beer business, gain national attention, and lay the groundwork for my next ventures.

We congratulated ourselves on a job well done and then celebrated by looking forward to what was next. For me, that meant in the beer business and beyond.

| Chapter 24 | Never Too Late to Discover a New Passion |

Don't be afraid to jump.

There is no success without at least a little risk. Granted, really success-ful people often take very calculated risks—others simply find them-selves in a position of having to make a quick choice that could signifi-cantly change their future. Sometimes we just have to jump. We might fail, but if we apply personal principles, we'll recover. We might also find unbelievable success and even a new life calling.

After about six years or so in the beverage business, I was looking to diversify. I continued to raise profits and awareness of Willie Davis Distributing Co., launching my division into one of the company's elite. We were making a lot of money, not just for the company but also for myself. I had been invited to join the company's board, I took part in local orga-nizations, and I established myself as an influential local business leader.

I was also still getting my football fix working for NBC. That's how I first heard about the radio industry. My colleague, the great Curt Gowdy, who worked as part of the NBC football broadcasting team, first suggest-ed it to me. The "broadcaster of everything," as he was known due to his diversity in the sports he covered, Gowdy cornered me during a network corporate meeting in New York where we were running over industry changes for the season.

"I understand you're doing really well with your beer business," he said I told him in fact I was, but I was also looking for other opportuni-ties. "Have you ever thought about radio?"

I told him I hadn't as it was perhaps the furthest thing from the beer industry. I had absolutely no clue about radio other than I liked to listen to it. I lived with the radio growing up in Texarkana, like so many other kids from my generation. It was southern radio that introduced me to the blues, pop, jazz, and soul. I loved listening to the raw pain and power of Bobby "Blue" Bland, B.B. King, Muddy Waters, and John Lee Hooker. I followed the Motown wave with Smokey Robinson and Stevie Wonder and even developed a love for jazz with Duke Ellington and Ella Fitzgerald. Then, of course, the radio also gave me the chance to follow all the ballgames.

While I had an affection for radio, Curt was big on the economic benefits. He owned several profitable stations in Florida and parts of Boston, where he called most Red Sox games before he was hired by NBC.

"Well, all I know is that the FCC is currently working more and more with minorities to open up opportunities and encourage them to get into the business," Gowdy said. I found out he was absolutely right. At the time, there were just a handful of black owners and hardly any of diverse nationalities. The same was true for women. The FCC made a very public mission to encourage diversity, trying to catch up to changing trends in the business landscape. "If you want, I can make some calls and put the word out for you."

I said sure, not really thinking anything of it. A few weeks later I got a phone call from an aggressive and brilliant radio engineer by the name of Cliff Gill, a USC grad who was an expert on the technical side of radio as well as a broker for businessmen looking to buy and sell radio stations. He was in possession of a radio station in Southern California that was broke and facing a bankruptcy judge. Cliff was trying to save the station, seeing a potential for profit and trying to find the right partner who could invest in the station and turn it around. He had managed to persuade the judge to give him more time to find a partner and actually had an alleged deal in the works with actor and comedian Redd Foxx. Unfortunately, they were approaching the judge's deadline, and there was a hitch.

Cliff couldn't reach Redd or anybody associated with him. This was on a Friday, and the judge had given him one last extension—to Monday.

After a series of desperate calls, Cliff realized the Redd Foxx deal was dead in the water, so he tried to find someone else who could swoop in. The one catch was that he needed a minority owner because he had made that promise to the judge. So he called the Los Angeles Urban League, which I was chairman of at the time, leaving a message asking if they had anyone they could recommend. Two members called him back and gave him my name. He wasted no time in calling me.

After he laid out his story about the station, he went through a long dialogue about the benefits of radio and how this station just needed a push to re-launch itself.

"Yeah, but Cliff," I said when he gave me a moment to speak. "You're telling a first-time radio buyer to rescue a station out of bankruptcy. How does this make for a good opportunity for me?"

Cliff told me how the previous owner had gotten caught up in other assets that didn't go well so they collapsed his radio business. Cliff's point was that there was nothing wrong with the station itself, just the last owner. A strong business leader could turn it around.

He intrigued me, but it wasn't something I wanted to rush into, and he didn't have the time to wait. I told him I needed to think about it, and unfortunately I had to take off to go to a national Urban League meeting in Boston that weekend. He asked if he could call on Saturday to see what I thought, and I agreed. On the flight, I talked myself out of it, afraid of the risk of jumping into something new and something that looked like it might require a lot of time and money. He said the new buyer had to give $10,000 to the bankruptcy court just to save it, and I wasn't excited about having to fork over that extra money on top of buying the station itself. Knowing how aggressive Cliff was, how badly he needed me to take the deal, and how convincing he could be, I stayed out of my hotel room as much as possible, hoping to avoid his phone call. He caught me in the lobby.

"Mr. Davis, you have a phone call."

I should have known it would be Cliff. I got on the phone and told him how worried I was about the whole deal. I also tried to use the excuse that I was in Boston and couldn't possibly get back in time to give him the money for the court even if I was interested.

"Willie, you tell me you're interested and give me your word that you'll do this and I'll put in the $10,000 for you," he said. "That's how much I believe in you."

I was stunned. He completely just took a leap of faith on me, a $10,000 risk because he believed, just like Coach Lombardi did the moment I came to Green Bay.

"This can work, Willie, this is going to be a great opportunity for you."

"Cliff, I don't know anything about the business, though. I wouldn't even know where to start rebuilding," I said.

"If you buy it, I'll come help you rebuild it."

I jumped. There was something about his persistence, faith, and his promise to stay by my side that gave me a sense of confidence about taking the risk. There was something else gnawing at me, as well and I think, it was intrigue. I was looking for something more, something exciting, and maybe taking a shot on a new venture was the thrill I needed.

"Alright, Cliff. You got yourself a deal."

I didn't sleep much on that trip. I had just bought a damn radio station! And I had bought it off a phone call alone, with no real research. Now what? It would be the first of many sleepless nights in the next six months as I worked to rebuild the station while also keeping my beer business going strong. While Cliff fronted the $10,000, I had to come up with $225,000 to buy the station, the equipment, and the license.

In 1976, All-Pro Broadcasting was born.

Cliff and I worked to rebuild the station. We brought back some of the personnel who were there under the previous owner for their experience, as well as some new sales people who were on top of their game. We got a waiver, at Cliff's request, to move the station's offices to my warehouse and office complex in Watts so I could keep a foot in both my radio and beer business (and save a lot of money on rent). While I didn't have radio experience, I had *business* experience, and I went to work learning about radio and working with my staff to develop a plan for success. We worked hard and quickly to get everything lined up and to get the station profitable as quickly as possible.

I bought the station in August 1976. On March 11, 1977, KAGB-FM went on the air. We had hoped to turn a profit in 11 months after the launch date, well ahead of what other similar stations had done coming out of a bankruptcy. Instead, we did it in six months. Even more important, because I took the jump, I ended up finding something that brought me even more opportunities, success, and a whole lot of joy in my life.

There shouldn't be anything fun about losing.

In six years at the distributorship, I had learned a lot about building a winning business. One of the first and most important lessons I had learned was making sure everybody in my organization was on the same page, that I spoke my message loud and clear.

When I launched the radio station, I was fortunate to have a professional general manager with a lot of radio experience, Bill Shearer. Anyone working in business can attest, the general manager is the most crucial hire an owner makes. Bill was a pro who was also highly motivated and very likeable. If I had one concern going into the business with Bill, and with everybody I saw working for me who had experience in radio, it was their more laid-back approach they maintained than I was used to in football or my other company.

"Willie, radio isn't like beer," Bill said. "It's a lot of fun!"

I'd hear this from other employees, too. They'd talk about the on-air personalities, the promotions, the partnerships with local businesses, giving away tickets, and so on. What I didn't hear enough of was the desire to be the best, to accomplish some rather ambitious goals that I had laid out. Fun was important, but I had my own way to find the *fun* in my work—and I needed to make sure they all knew it and felt it themselves.

I called the entire staff together for a meeting right before we launched to have a talk I knew might be tough. As a boss, the tough stuff is part of the job. After Bill introduced me to those who still didn't know me, and I thanked everybody for their hard work in putting this station back together, I got right to it.

"I've been hearing from a lot of you about how much fun radio is, and I really hope that's right because I love to have fun," I said. "But I gotta tell you, we're not gonna be having any fun if we're losing. If we're not making money, if we're not meeting our goals, if we're looking at failure, there shouldn't be any fun. Winning is what's fun for me."

I made sure to drive the point home.

"Coach Lombardi had a favorite expression," I said. "He used to tell us that we wouldn't continue to lose with the same faces. We'll find the people to get the job done."

It was probably a little harsh right out the gate, and I'm sure it wasn't exactly what they had in mind for an introduction speech, but I wanted the message to be clear for everyone. The room got very quiet and very serious, going from an energy of sheer excitement to quiet reserve. What thrilled me, however, was how many of them were looking at me straight in the eye and nodding their heads. Those who were checking their shoe shine ended up not being with us very long. A majority of the staff agreed with me and got excited about my drive to succeed, knowing we would all benefit in the end.

"There is no laughter in losing, no parties if we're not winning, so let's do what we gotta do to win."

We talked about my approach to business. We talked about how the sales managers were going to tackle the area and re-introduce us as a community radio station. We talked about programming and how important it was to make ours stand out. We talked to the jockeys about putting in the best four hours of their day when they're on the air and how we were going to offer our listeners more quality programming than any of our competing stations. It was like working with the offense, defense, and special teams to make sure we were all ready. We all knew what the game plan was, and we were ready to go execute.

"So let's have some fun," I said. "I want to have some fun with you. Let's get out there and do the best we can do. Let's win."

Stick with what works.

It doesn't matter where you're going in your life. If you've had some rules, philosophies, or guidelines that have helped you achieve your goals and brought you success, why change them? Stay consistent and keep doing what works—that's how you win.

As I started to learn more and more about the radio business, I couldn't believe how much easier it was than the beverage industry, especially when it came to operations and the product. I was so used to juggling a number of different products with beer that coming to a business where we were really selling only one commodity simplified things tremendously.

The structure also made things more compact and efficient. We had a sales staff who worked with local businesses to sell as much advertising as possible to make the station its money. We helped them develop promotions and programs to reach out to the community with one goal— sell air time. We had our administrative people who handled the business. We had the technical people who kept the station running, and we had the programming side who determined what went on the air. All of it was overseen by the general manager who reported to me. It all ran so smoothly compared to the more chaotic beverage industry.

My role was to develop the culture of a successful business. That's what I knew. I relied on the principles that had made me successful on the field and in the beer business. I tried to carry the excitement and the feeling of success we had at Willie Davis Distributing Co. into All-Pro Broadcasting by applying the same ideas.

I made sure I had the right personnel—people who believed in what I was trying to do combined with the experience they needed to get us over the hump. We started at a disadvantage because we had the reputation of a station that had failed. We needed to overcome that, and we were only going to be able to do it with the right people. I hired the old sales manager and some others who had leadership positions in the company. They taught me all they could about the industry, and I also left them alone to take care of their various divisions.

Everyone had the training they needed, whether it was consultations, seminars, etc. I also worked with people individually to make sure they had what they needed. I looked for consistency in my staff, creativity, and efficiency in how they went about doing their jobs. Mostly, I looked for them to be knowledgeable about the job, the business, our station, and the approach from the jockeys to the sales staff and beyond.

Everyone also understood the old Lombardi philosophies of coming prepared to meetings, showing up at least 15 minutes early, and working as long as it took to get the job done. I worked with them on staying organized and disciplined in our approach, constantly resorting back to examples from my playing days and explaining why these good habits would lead to more success for them as individuals and for us as a station.

I also showed them I was willing to do anything I asked them to do. Just like the beer business, I took it on myself to work as much as I possibly could in all facets of the company. I went out on sales calls and met with customers. I attended sales training. I sat in on programming meetings and brainstormed with the staff on creative promotions. When we held events, I was there to work with the community, putting myself to work doing whatever was necessary. I didn't take time off when we were rebuilding, choosing to show my team how I was willing to be as dedicated as I was asking them to be and how I would stay there until the job was done.

I tried to show my loyalty to them while I asked for theirs in return. I rewarded that loyalty with respect, and I showed it to them by taking care of them the way a manager should, mainly financially. As a result, I can proudly say I have several employees who have been with me for more than 20 years and even a few who have been with me for more than 40 years!

As I continued to reinforce my philosophies, show my dedication, and work with my staff, something wonderful happened. It's something that happens in successful organizations—it's the "thing" that really makes them work. I experienced it in Green Bay several times and with my beer company, and I couldn't be more excited that it was happening here, as well. We very quickly became a team.

We developed a close bond, a mutual understanding of not only how this whole radio thing should work but that it could work. We got confident that we could leave a mark in the community and make a difference, and it fueled us to push ourselves even harder. Nobody talked about "I" or "me" it was all about "we" or "us." There was a level of trust and dedication that hadn't been there before, a level we all committed to individually.

"Individual commitment to a group effort—that is what makes a team work, a company work, a society work, a civilization work," Coach Lombardi once said. We were living proof.

We started to celebrate each other's individual victories as well as those of the company. When someone made a key sale, we made a note of it. When the company turned a profit, we had a party. We all made sure we left work every day knowing that we had put all of our effort into what we were doing.

Suddenly, we were having fun and making a difference at the same time.

Know when (and how) to get in and when (and how) to get out.

After my first two years in the business, my L.A. radio station was doing very well, as was my beer business, and I found myself in the position of looking to expand once again. Where Green Bay gave me the chance for success in football, Milwaukee gave me the opportunity in radio. Cliff Gill continued to work as my radio broker, checking for struggling stations with huge potential, and the first place he looked was in a state where my name carried some weight. I purchased WAWA-AM and WAWA-FM from Suburbanaire Broadcasting Co. in 1979.

It was exactly the situation I needed. The owner was looking to sell a station that had experienced both high and low moments, a station with all the potential in the world masked only by mismanagement problems and a lack of leadership. As I had proven with the beer business and my L.A. station, it was perfect for me. My challenge would be building trust and showing both the staff and the community that I was the guy for the job, especially since I was essentially an outsider in the world of radio.

Radio is an interesting industry in that the community typically demands that its stations are run by local guys who know the market. Because it is such a community-based medium, providing a specific group of listeners, news, and information along with entertainment, the audience wants to know it has someone who understands their specific needs at the helm. While I had a reputation in Milwaukee as a Packer, I hadn't worked any real business there. I had to prove I knew not only the market but that I knew radio.

I explored the needs of the community, what they didn't have and what they were looking for in a radio station. I broke down each aspect of how we worked and what we targeted and made sure we were filling those needs. I also went on a campaign to introduce myself to the public, talking about my business accomplishments and sharing my successes to help listeners feel at ease. I also looked at ways we could build the base—and that started with cleaning up and changing the station itself.

One of the big problems was mismanagement. Most alarming, the AM station had a bad reputation among local businesses and the industry itself, mainly with charges that some of the sales execs and even the on-air personalities were taking kickbacks from ad sales. I quickly found the people involved and made sure that stopped immediately. I was never able to prove these things were happening, but those who were accused were simply told that regardless of what had happened in the past, this would not be the way the station was run anymore. Any hint of such activity would be met with severe consequences.

Another problem was what to do with the programming and the stations themselves. The FM station had a small following, not really sure of its place in the community. It essentially held space on the dial, its main listeners tuning in only when the AM station (which operated only during the day) switched over its programming to FM in the evening. Upon gathering feedback from the community and the advice of other radio experts, people who at the time knew a lot more than I did about running a station, we made some significant changes.

First, we split up the stations, giving the FM station the new call letters WLUM-FM, which stood for "We Love U Milwaukee." It was an effort to show Milwaukee there was a station that focused on serving the needs of the community, one that wouldn't treat them like a second-class market. The FM station had been a bit of a joke in the area, and we wanted to really build a niche. We re-launched the programming on Valentine's Day and played off the "station with heart" theme, trying to show the community of listeners that they now had a more personal option.

Ironically enough, we had several leaders in the community complain about how we changed the format from being a predominantly "black music" station to one that featured more contemporary hits. It wasn't a complete switch, rather it was a new version of an existing format, which was dubbed "churban," contemporary hit radio for an urban listener. Still, the few followers left over from the WAWA days worried about taking away from the already limited urban options in the city. As such, we kept WAWA-AM as it was, only increasing the signal to give us all day and night programming. This way we could keep the station's hard-core followers while also expanding our place in the community and hopefully picking up new listeners.

By cleaning up the problems, listening to our customer base, re-enforcing the strengths of the station, expanding, and providing more targeted service, we grew in Milwaukee as we grew in L.A. Both stations have gone through even more changes over the years as the listener's needs have changed. WLUM 102.1 is now a successful alternative station, while WAWA moved down the dial to 1290 in the mid-1980s and briefly became WMVP, a rhythm and blues station, before switching once more to WMCS, Milwaukee's Community Station in the 1990s, servicing the city's African American community. Both stations continue to thrive.

◆ ◆ ◆

But I wanted even more. Radio was addictive, and I wanted other opportunities. The trick was finding the right ones.

There are some rules for finding the right opportunities, but a lot of it comes down to factors beyond our control. There are a lot of things that need to go right in order for any kind of opportunity to work out. Our job is to work as hard as we can and prepare as much as possible to put our investment in a place where we have the best chance at success. That means scrutinizing each opportunity and learning everything we can about the investment, including what's not on paper. We have to learn about the customer base—or in the case of radio, the listeners. We have to make sure we have something to contribute to the investment. We need the right people—employees who have a shared vision and know exactly what needs to be done to turn around the investment. We need a plan, working with experts to formalize both the overall business philosophy and the specifics on how we're going to execute that approach.

Finally, we need to know when to get in and when to get out, when it's working and when its time is done. We need to set parameters and make sure we stick to them. It becomes very easy to want to throw all we have into an investment, as we do get invested. There have been many entrepreneurs who don't know when to say, "That's enough." It doesn't matter how big or small, any project we put our time and effort into leaves an imprint on us. That's why it's so crucial to go in with a plan, a strategy, and an idea of what we want to accomplish and what we're willing to sacrifice.

I have been fortunate to keep my L.A. and Milwaukee stations thriving for the better part of four decades. But I did have some other shorter investments. One of the advantages of experiencing success in the business world, or really anything, is that it breeds other opportunities. After growing stations in two markets, others opened up opportunities for me. In 1982, I bought a station in Houston for $1 million and sold it for $2.5 million. In 1984, I bought a station in Seattle for $700,000 and later sold it for $3.5 million. In 1988, I bought a Denver station for $5 million and sold it not long after for essentially what I paid for it, my least successful investment.

Sometimes we even have to put the parameters on our first love. In the 1990s, I focused mainly on my Milwaukee and L.A. stations. In 1992, I bought KBON-FM in San Bernardino to improve the signal in the highly competitive L.A. market. I was admittedly struggling to compete with the larger publicly owned companies who were operating with seemingly unlimited funds in the same area. My hope was that strengthening the signal would give us a chance to compete, a chance to say, "We covered L.A. from the ocean to the upper desert."

Unfortunately, it wasn't enough, and when Cox Broadcasting came along with an enormous offer in the mid-1990s, I had to sell the Inglewood operation, my first venture into radio. While financially I made a significant profit, it was a blow to my business ego. I was never one to quit on anything, and the competitor in me viewed the sale as giving up. Of course, over time, I've grown better at making the distinction between giving up or not giving my all into an investment versus doing all I can and finding the right opportunity to walk away.

I was able to keep the San Bernardino signal, which I changed to KCXX-FM, an alternative rock station I still run today along with its sister station KATY-FM. I sometimes question if there was more I could have done with my original station or any of the other radio investments I've made over the years. Over the years, though, my tremendous success in L.A. and Milwaukee has shown me I've actually learned how to run a radio station, and maybe I can finally actually trust my own instincts when it comes to successful investing.

| Chapter 25 | Mom, It's a Long Way from Texarkana |

Be humble and appreciative, especially in the face of grand success.

In 1981, I became the first player from an all-black college to be inducted into the Pro Football Hall of Fame, an honor I never dreamed possible. After all, I was a poor black kid who was extremely lucky to land a scholarship with a small college that nobody in the country knew about. I just happened to get drafted and eventually landed on a team that won some championships. I definitely did my part, but the idea of the Hall of Fame was not one I truly entertained—while playing, anyway.

I figured my best chance at making the Hall of Fame would come immediately after my career. According to NFL rules, a player has to be retired for at least five years before being considered by the prestigious Board of Selectors, which would have put my first year of eligibility at 1975. When no announcement came that year or the next five, I began to seriously doubt it would ever happen. History has proven that as time goes on in a player's eligibility, the longer they're not selected, the more likely they'll be kept out for good.

Something working against me was the number of Packers that had been inducted in the five years prior to my induction year. Jim Taylor received his invitation in 1976, Forrest Gregg and Bart Starr in 1977, Ray Nitschke in 1978, and Herb Adderley in 1980. There were rumblings around the league at the number of Packers being inducted and those still to come. Paul Hornung, Willie Wood, and Henry Jordan received their calls after me, while other deserving players like Jerry Kramer,

Dave Robinson, Carroll Dale, and Boyd Dowler would have to wait (and they still are). There was a sense the committee would back off from some of Lombardi's players, at least for a few seasons. Still, before the 1981 Super Bowl, the whispers about how the committee might finally be ready to call my name began to intensify.

When I heard the announcement, my heart swelled. I was fully aware that I had just received one of the greatest honors that existed in all of professional sports. It wasn't so much the prestige or recognition that came with it. For me, it was more of a confirmation that I had truly accomplished what I had wanted to achieve. I had the defensive captain title. I had the Pro Bowl appearances. I had the championship rings—all things I'm sure contributed to my eventual induction. The Hall of Fame was the pinnacle. My induction was the final confirmation that I had done what I sought to do and people had noticed. For me, that was the biggest honor of all, and I was overwhelmed.

I was inducted along with quarterback/kicker George Blanda, old-timer Red Badgro, and my former teammate, Jim Ringo, who was just as thrilled and humbled to be there as me. The entire event was a celebration in our honor, and I can honestly say there is no organization that takes care of its members like the Hall of Fame. Over the course of a weekend, there are dinners and luncheons, a parade, congratulations, and mixers with other members, constant recognition, etc. It felt like a dream to me, a celebration that made me feel so special, so blessed, that I couldn't help but wonder, "Why me?" It was an experience I will remember for the rest of my life, and it culminated in the speech officially inducting me.

If Coach Lombardi was alive, it would have been tough to ask anyone other than him to introduce me on that special day. As he was so instrumental in my growth and much of my success, it would have been only fitting. However, I was fortunate enough to stay in contact with one of the first major influences in my life, Coach Eddie Robinson, and I asked him if he would consider speaking on my behalf.

"Willie," he said in his always parental voice, "it would be an honor."

I heard Coach Robinson, a dynamic speaker, share stories of recruiting me and my playing days at Grambling. He talked about following me through the pros and how he watched me grow into a man, how he was proud of my being the first player from an all-black college inducted and how he knew my other coaches would be just as proud.

I actually didn't listen too much as I was too busy focusing on what I was going to say. Plus I was trying to think about what could possibly make me cry and how to avoid it. Each year at the ceremony, there are running bets among the other inductees past and present on how far into a speech a player can go without breaking down. Very few make it all the way through without shedding at least a single tear. I couldn't for the life of me think of anything that would move me to tears, but I started to worry.

Coach Robinson introduced me, and for the first time in a long time, I felt nervous. I suddenly felt all the people looking at me, and I worried about losing it. Just as I had in big game moments, I found my sense of calm and composure. I focused and went through my prepared speech, which was really just scraps of notes I had put together. I thanked Coach Robinson and all my coaches, taking a little extra time to talk about Coach Lombardi. I thanked my Packers teammates, especially Forrest Gregg, who I attributed to helping me get to the Hall. The more I spoke, the more confident I felt and the more I was able to take it all in. I suddenly realized the significance of it all, how I had gone from someone just lucky enough to play to an elite group of people who were considered the best of the best. I couldn't believe it was happening to me.

That's when I looked down and saw my mother sitting in the crowd on the edge of her seat, hanging on my every word. She was spellbound, and I couldn't help but think in that moment of just how important and influential she had been to my entire life. While I had played for some of the greatest coaches of all time, it was my mother who had left the first and arguably the biggest impression on me. I stared at her for a long second or two and had to say something.

"Mom, it's a long way from Texarkana, and nobody ever said the road would lead here."

She broke down instantly, her eyes swelling with pride. As soon as I saw the first tear fall, I thought to myself, "Well, here we go." Within seconds, I was a blubbering mess—and it was wonderful.

My Hall of Fame induction proved to be a culmination for my mother, as well, a chance for her to realize that she had raised her son to be the best he could be. It was the last significant event in my life that she saw and one she bragged about in her later years. It was the one I know she enjoyed the most, and I am so happy I was able to share that with her.

The Hall of Fame still carries that magic for me today. I am very active with the Hall, going back almost every year to take part in the festivities. It's more than what they do for their members—it's just a special place to have that once-a-year reminder of what I accomplished, how lucky I was, and how appreciative I should be for all the success I've experienced.

Always remember those who were there for you, and be open to forgiving those who weren't.

A few years after she witnessed her baby boy honored with entry into the Hall of Fame, my mother passed away. It was sudden and tragic. She had traveled to visit my sister for a Thanksgiving celebration and came back complaining she wasn't feeling well. She had chest pains and shortness of breath and a general feeling that something wasn't right. But my mother was always tough, and she figured it would pass. She had a heart attack on the way home and another at the hospital.

I was busy traveling with work, trying to juggle my now-chaotic life of running multiple businesses and even working for some boards of directors. When I heard from my sister, I instantly made plans to go see my mother, but as she often did, my mother called me to lay down the law.

"Don't you be coming down here if you got things to do," she said. "I'll be fine. I *am* fine."

Every time I tried to argue with her, she cut me off.

"Willie, I don't want you worrying. The doctor says I'm recovering, and I'll be out of here soon enough. You just take care of yourself."

She had been admitted to the hospital on a Sunday. After trying to find a middle ground between my responsibilities, her request, and my desire to see her, I decided to go visit her on the following Friday.

She passed away suddenly after another heart attack on Thursday.

The fact that I didn't get to see my mother in her dying moments, the person I have always loved the most, the person truly responsible for making me the man and the success I am today, crushes me still. I am not a man with many regrets, but this is my biggest. It still serves as a constant reminder of another lesson I adhere to each and every day—never put off anything important.

Since her passing, I have made sure to stick by that rule. If I could go back, I would have dropped everything else I was doing to go be with the one person who meant more to me than anything. Everything else could have waited, could have been set aside. If I could go back, I would have been there by her side the entire time.

But I can't. Instead, what I can do is honor her by not only remembering everything she did to raise, support, and mold me but also making sure I continue to live up to her expectations. I can honor her and her memory by always continuing to be the best man I can be. I truly feel I have done that to the best of my ability.

I have showed her toughness in dealing with various issues and obstacles that have popped up in my life, always remembering what she had to go through to raise me and my siblings from the moment she ran with me through the woods to escape the Southern sharecroppers. I have made sure to appreciate each and every accomplishment to its fullest, showing her humility and remembering the opportunities she never had and how proud she was of each of mine. I have been as kind, loving, and protective as I can be with the people most important to me, remembering how she was willing to sacrifice for me regardless of the situation. I have also tried to show as much compassion for others and for life as a whole as she had, which led me to a relationship with my father, despite years of anger, bitterness, and resentment.

I had reconnected with my father in college and kept in touch with him through my football days and beyond. It was never more than the occasional phone call or visit, but it was enough to maintain a relationship of sorts. He even attended my Hall of Fame induction with my mother, who softened up on him in her later years. Perhaps it was my mother's compassion, perhaps it was my curiosity about the man, or perhaps it was an ever-present need to have a father. Whatever the case, later in his life, I hired my dad to come work for my beverage business.

He was actually an incredibly helpful and hard-working employee. He helped with organization around the office and also ran deliveries and other errands, essentially doing whatever I needed him to do to keep the operation running smoothly. He was desperate to continue a relationship with me, and he dedicated himself to working as hard as he could for me. At first, it was unusual to have my father working for me, but we soon found a groove and a relationship that worked for us—even when problems arose.

In fact, it was after a confrontation between my father and me in the office that we changed a company policy, one I still adhere to today in my business. There had been miscommunication about a delivery, and a top client didn't get the product he needed. He wasn't happy, and from where I was sitting, it looked like it was my father's fault. I told him so.

"Let me tell you, I am committed to running this business," I told him after calling him into my office. "I have over 100 people working for me, and I expect each of them to carry out their responsibilities. If they don't, I don't care who they are, they're in trouble with me."

He told me he never got the information and that somewhere down the line some wires had gotten crossed. I had a different story from the people in the office.

"Well, I'm just telling you what is and isn't acceptable to me," I said to him. "And if this happens again, you're outta here."

He took a second before standing up.

"We'll never have this conversation again," he said and exited the office. As soon as he was outside my office doors, he yelled to anyone in the office who was listening, "From now on, if anybody wants me to do something, write it down!"

We never had a problem again.

In fact, despite my constant apprehension to him and our relationship, we actually developed a bond of sorts. We never really discussed his leaving or the years he spent away from us while my mother struggled. We also didn't address the lingering tension, content to have a civil working relationship—until he was on his deathbed.

A year after my mother passed, my father got sick and deteriorated quickly. He spent the last days of his life in a hospital bed, which I made sure to visit each and every day. I did feel a sense of urgency to handle the problems we had left unresolved, but I never knew when or how. I also didn't know if I really wanted to since I had carried the burden of this bitterness toward him. We were now on speaking and even working terms, but there was still a lot of pain. It took my father facing death to finally bring it to the surface.

I went to visit him on one of his last days, and he immediately called me to his bedside. It was clear he had something to say, and I was eager to hear it. I realized later there was a part of me relying on him to bring this up, to step up and address our tension and what he had done. I was eager for him to finally be my father.

"Son, I want to apologize to you for not being a good father," he said. And just like that, it was out there. "I'm sorry I wasn't there for you and that you all had to struggle without me."

He grabbed my hand and wouldn't let me speak. He wanted to get this off his chest. He told me again why he had left, how he thought at the time he was doing the right thing, how much it had hurt him, and how he regretted his decision for most of his adult life. He told me what a failure of a father he had felt like before he left and how the feeling got worse after he left. He acknowledged my feelings and the tension that existed and took the responsibility and the blame on himself.

"I don't know how you feel about me now," he said with tears in his eyes. "But I want to tell you that what I respect more than anything about you is what you've done to succeed in your life."

I could feel all of my pain boiling to the surface. I stayed quiet, not knowing how to express everything I was feeling.

"I'm sorry I wasn't there for you," he said again. "And I'm just hoping you can find it in your heart to forgive me."

Even though there were no words that could possibly ease the pain of what he had put us through, I had a very powerful feeling rise within me. I *did* want to forgive him. I don't know why, but I did. I wanted to embrace him just once, possibly for the last time, as my father. And I did just that.

We embraced, both of us crying for about 15 minutes, letting all those years of anger and resentment wash away. It wasn't easy, but now I look back on that moment as yet another step on my path to growing as an individual—this time, for once, with a man helping me like...a father.

| Chapter 26 | # Welcome to the Board Room |

If the opportunity arises, be the first. Be ground-breaking.

During the past 30 years, I have served (or am serving) on the board of directors for some of the country's top companies, including, Dow Chemical Co., Metro-Goldwyn-Mayer (MGM) Mirage, Sara Lee Corp., Mattel Toys, Fidelity National Financial, Johnson Controls Inc., Alliance Bank, Strong Capital Management, K-Mart, L.A. Gear, Manpower Inc., Rally's Inc., WICOR Inc., Wisconsin Energy Corp., and of course, Schlitz Brewing.

I have also worked in a leadership position with a number of other organizations, including the Ewing Marion Kauffman Center for Entrepreneurial Leadership, Marquette University, Occidental College, the University of Chicago, and the Green Bay Packers.

In all of those companies, I was the first or one of the first African Americans to serve.

It was not something I sought out. I never really thought about working as a director in the business world. I always envisioned running my own companies and building my reputation as an entrepreneur and maybe one day a full-fledged business mogul, but not a collection of board positions. I absolutely did not seek out the opportunity to be among the first black directors at these companies. It really never occurred to me, and making the effort to break new ground was just not something I focused on.

But when the opportunity arose, I said yes. Then I made sure I was ready to do the job well. If I was going to be a representative of not just the business world but also the black community, I made absolutely sure I was a strong enough example to open doors for those who came after me. I made sure—through my performance—that other opportunities would be provided for black business leaders. I didn't have to be a trailblazer. I didn't have to seek out that kind of glory or attention or life mission. But if I was asked and the opportunity arose, yes, I would take the lead.

As recently as the 1980s, corporate America was still lacking in terms of minorities in upper management positions. As each new board opportunity presented itself, I found myself continually surprised that I was the first black director the company had. I also found it fascinating how intrigued and sometimes even uncomfortable certain board members were in terms of dealing with a black director. I can say truthfully that I never once encountered any kind of blatant racism or even really any bad feelings toward me and my involvement. Instead it was more of an uncomfortable adjustment at times for companies that had been so used to doing things a certain way. They wanted to change, they wanted to broaden their world perspectives, especially when it came to issues related to minorities, who were becoming a much larger customer base with each passing year. It was like anything else at the beginning. It was sometimes awkward as they took those first steps.

I am still admittedly stunned at the number of opportunities I've received over the course of my business career. There were many times that I found myself in these board rooms, looking at some of the multi-millionaires and even *billionaires* sitting across from me and hanging on my words of advice, and I almost couldn't believe it. If I stepped back and thought of how instrumental I was in terms of deciding where these businesses would go and how they would grow, it would be overwhelming. I didn't have fear. I had the sense I could live up to everything that was asked of me. As flattered as I was, I also believed enough in myself to know I had been asked for a reason.

I was also going to make sure that everyone else felt the same. I would be humble. I would be outspoken. I would be educated and informed. I would make good choices. I would be the best director I possibly could. The result was continued success and growth in my business career and some of the most amazing experiences of my life.

The first board I served on was Fireman's Fund Insurance Co. when it was owned by American Express. I was invited in a rather unusual way, which made me wonder just how these boards actually do come together. I think we all have visions of special ceremonies where a certain individual is scrutinized by his peers before he is deemed worthy enough to serve. In truth, while some formality exists, the invites themselves are a lot more casual.

I was invited to join Fireman's by James Robinson III, then the CEO of American Express. I got to know Jim at the Super Bowl. As a gift to his employees and key clients, Jim obtained tickets to the Super Bowl each year, and as part of the festivities, he invited me and a few other former players to make an appearance and mingle with his group. I was invited for five years in a row and got to know Jim rather well. At one of the events, we were discussing my business successes and my MBA from the University of Chicago, and I could see his wheels turning. Of course at the time, I couldn't even dream that he was thinking of offering me a board position, but I did think a job offer might be coming my way.

When he did offer the board position, I was completely thrown but also excited. I knew what a chance he was taking on me. As these publicly traded companies looked to infuse more minorities in their leadership positions, including even the upper echelons of the board of directors, they had to make sure they had the right people for the job. We minorities would be trailblazers and would only encourage more diversity by showing we were qualified for the job. I knew what I was capable of, how I could make a contribution. I knew I could convince others I had something to offer. Just as I had on the football field, I knew I could leave an impression and make people see me as something more.

I also knew what kind of an opportunity this could be not just for the black community but also for me as an individual business leader. This hadn't been part of the plan, but it was a welcome surprise. Part of being successful is having a willingness to deviate from the path if a different situation arises that will eventually help achieve your overall goals in the long run. A board of directors invitation for a top insurance company was unexpected, but I saw the potential.

Thirty plus years, 17 boards, and countless organizations and awards later, as well as an enormous rise in the number of minority business leaders among Fortune 500 companies, I feel taking advantage of that opportunity has paid off.

Be patient and know certain things take time.

Like most industries, the corporate world of directors works mainly on a referral-based system. If you do well on one board and make a contribution, more often than not you'll get a call or a recommendation. I take great pride in the fact I never once sought out a board position with any company but was asked to join each board.

While serving with Fireman's I was asked next to join the board of directors with Mattel and from there I was given the opportunity to go to the Schlitz board. I immediately jumped at the opportunity to join these two and hoped for more. Just like success in football, the more I got, the more I wanted.

As with Fireman's, I was the first black director on both Mattel and Schlitz. Serving on these first few boards, I learned many valuable lessons, but one of the biggest was to have patience. I had to accept that these were changing times, and change *takes* time. I remember sitting in a board meeting with Schlitz talking about how we could target minority markets and build workforces that mirrored those markets as a way to help the community feel more involved. I learned from my own personal experience that the more minority employees (especially truck drivers) that people saw working in their community, the more loyalty they displayed to the brand. At one point, one of the directors tried to ask about the attitude in minority communities and where perceptions came from.

"I never understood why those negras..." he said and tried to stop himself, fumbling over the words and making it sound like an even worse N word. The room went quiet, all eyes on me.

"I think its pronounced 'Negroes,'" somebody said, trying innocently to help.

"Yeah, I always have trouble with that word," the director said, and I prayed we could just move on. It became very clear early on that the transition of working with minority directors and being perhaps a little more self-conscious of what they said and how they said it would take some time. It would also take some patience on my part.

With each of these initial boards, I was at times met with some attitude. I could tell many of my peers wondered why I was in the room, why I was qualified to be a director. I was perceived as a black former athlete who had some success with a minor beverage distribution company and some small radio stations. Even worse, I felt in many cases, I was perceived as an experiment, a token minority meant only to make the board look more diverse and progressive.

That wasn't easy for me to take, but I vowed to remain calm and patient. Even when I was openly asked why I was there, I chose to be humble, responding that I wasn't sure but I knew I could make a contribution. Then I made sure I made a contribution! I believed I was asked to join each board for a reason, and I let that propel me forward. I compared my accomplishments with those of other directors, and more often than not, they were comparable or I had done more. I didn't let any confusion, judgment, or misperceptions get under my skin. I accepted the fact that things had been done a certain way for quite a while, and people needed time to adjust. I didn't defend myself or promote my qualifications. Rather, I focused on my job and showed through my actions just how valuable I was and how I could contribute.

That in itself was enough for me to concentrate on, especially as the various offers started to pour in. When I joined Mattel's board, I suddenly found myself with a foot in beer, a foot in radio, a hand in insurance, and now a hand in the toy business, which I admittedly knew absolutely nothing about.

I told people my only real experience with toys was as a child, looking at all the ones we couldn't afford! I was clearly brought in to help as the company looked to revitalize its struggling business by exploring opportunities to target a widening customer base. One of the most interesting problems Mattel faced at the time was with its line of Barbie dolls, the most popular toy of all time. The company looked to target younger minorities by offering Barbies of different colors and cultures, but the minority kids, who had grown up with the white Barbie, didn't appear to be interested. While I was no toy expert, I did have experience in marketing and working with a minority clientele. The more I accepted that was my strength, the more I realized I could contribute to whatever board opportunity came my way.

This was another area where my sports background helped me considerably. I was involved in four very distinct businesses, each with their own issues and needs. Sports had provided a great arena for rapid change. It taught me to keep on my toes and be ready to handle whatever came my way, even switching direction at a moment's notice. Most importantly, sports taught me to handle the pressure, no matter what. Juggling four types of businesses (and much more later on) wasn't easy, but I knew I was capable of handling the stress.

Patience was the key. I had to take the time to prepare myself, to learn all I could about the company, its strengths and weaknesses, the problems at hand, and all pitched and proposed solutions. I prided myself on my prep time, often averaging at least three hours or more of reading and analyzing before every meeting. I was ready to answer any question thrown my way and to offer my personal opinion and solution on any problem. I was relevant, and I contributed. I listened to what everybody had to say before sharing my thoughts. I went in with 10–15 good questions that gave me all I needed to know, and I took the time to soak it all in. In the many board meetings I've experienced, I am always surprised by the number of people who both show up unprepared and love to hear themselves talk without listening to others. Nothing gets done that way. I was patient, waiting for my moment to make my play, my contribution.

With the combination of my success as a business owner, my reputation as a prepared and effective director, my notoriety as a Hall of Famer, and my drive and desire, I suddenly found myself with more offers than I could possible take. However, I did take some of them, and they led me to some of the most fascinating places in the world where I met some of the most interesting people—which to this day is still pretty amazing to a poor black boy from Texarkana.

Chapter 27 | **Letting Go and Moving Forward**

We all need support in a variety of ways.

After almost 20 years of being together, Ann and I separated in the early 1980s and officially got divorced about eight years later. It was an amicable split and one without any true hard feelings—at least on the surface. She told me later, right before she passed away after a battle with an aggressive cancer, that she always struggled being my wife because she felt like she had lost her identity.

"When we met, you were Willie and I was Ann," she said. "After a while, in our marriage, you were still Willie, but I was just Mrs. Willie Davis."

As an independent person, I understood the feelings that must have caused. Ann always had her own ambitions, and that title might have gotten in her way. I also know I wasn't always the most supportive husband, wrapped up in my own ambitions and taking on a whole slew of career-advancing opportunities. I'm sure it wasn't easy, and I give her credit for standing by my side for as long as she did and for helping raise our two beautiful children, Duane and Lori. Even though we didn't work out as a married couple, I still have a place in my heart for Ann and all she helped me with and supported me through.

Several years after Ann and I separated, I met another amazing woman, Andrea, a PR maverick who ran her own advertising agency that worked with my Milwaukee radio stations. She was a feisty, ambitious business leader and fellow adventurer who identified not only with me but also with my field of business. I soon discovered that she was both sweet and aggressive.

I met Andrea at a popular club on Milwaukee's east side. She told me later that she approached me first as a potential business opportunity, a chance to talk to a radio station owner, which could open even more doors for her young company. But the conversation quickly turned flirty, and soon we were making plans to go out on the first of several dates. I was impressed with Andrea from the moment I met her, and that has never changed despite how our relationship has changed over the years. We formed a very deep connection right from the start, and we quickly began seeing each other socially.

Andrea and I dated for almost eight years long distance while I worked out of Los Angeles and she worked out of Milwaukee. Truthfully, it was a convenient relationship for me. I was extremely busy at the time, trying to juggle my many careers, and I was hesitant to jump into anything serious again because of my separation from Ann. This was enough for now, I thought, and suddenly eight years had passed. Andrea was extremely patient, but as time went on she wanted a bigger commitment and rightfully so. Still, I didn't really know what I could give or even what I really wanted.

And then I got prostate cancer in 1995, and it scared the living daylights out of me. I had spent the majority of my adult life pursuing all of these goals, of trying to constantly close the gap and get from Point A to Point B with as much success as possible. I was lying awake at night with a life-threatening disease wondering what the end was going to look like.

Although I was able to take the necessary steps to clear myself of the cancer more quickly than expected, it was enough to make me really think about where I was going and what I needed for the rest of my life. It made me want to take action to ensure I had what I needed to continue a life I now approached with even more clarity. I wanted a partner, a person with a career who would understand me and who would be easy for me to live with and share experiences. I wanted someone I could care for and someone who could care for me. I wanted someone happy, energetic, and supportive. Andrea encompassed everything I was looking for at the time, and it had taken me too long to realize it.

Because of my lack of commitment, Andrea and I had started to drift apart, and I heard rumors she was dating some other guy. I wasn't used to losing, and those competitive juices started flowing in me again. So I kidnapped her on a business trip, took her to Las Vegas, presented her with a ring, told her exactly how I felt, and married her. That's how we started our married life together, a very meaningful relationship that saw a lot of great memories.

Andrea was there with me for a lot of my work with both the radio stations and the many boards I served on, standing by my side. She is somebody who knows me better than most, a special lady and a great friend, someone who has always accepted me for who I am. Even later on in the relationship when we faced our own troubles, mainly because of my hectic lifestyle and an admittedly extreme commitment to my various businesses, she didn't hold it against me. She supported who I was and what I wanted to do. She still does as we maintain a great friendship built on respect and caring for one another. It is Andrea who encouraged me for years to finally do this book, and for that I am extremely grateful.

We all need people who support us, and we should be grateful for the ones we have in our lives.

We also need to let go to move forward.

In 1988, I sold my beverage distribution company. In some ways, it was a tough call for me to make personally, but from a business perspective, it was time. I had moved on to other things, bigger things, and I had to let go of the place that started it all for me.

Honestly, there wasn't much more I could do with it. I had gone from 13,000 accounts to 45,000 accounts stretching from Manhattan Beach to Malibu. Along the way, I had purchased four other wholesale operations and changed the name of the company to West Coast Beverage Co. to reflect its growth. I began to carry more brands, including some that weren't from Schlitz, to compete. I had made an enormous profit off my initial investment in the company, and I had an even bigger offer from a competitor, an aggressive wholesaler who was initially aligned with me and now wanted the business for himself.

When the offer came, my first instinct was to fight it, to say no. This was my baby, after all, and despite the problems that seemed to constantly arise with running a beer business and my new interest in my other ventures, I had a deep commitment to my first enterprise. I didn't want to let go of something I had poured so much of my heart and soul into and just let it disappear.

When I got over my emotions about the offer and really looked at my situation practically, it made sense. While it was still making money for me, it wasn't making nearly as much as other ventures. In fact, in my last year in the industry, I did $6 million in radio and $39 million in beer and made several times more profit in radio. I was really getting more and more excited about growing and expanding my radio business. Radio had a lot more of a team mentality, and it had a better energy to match its increasing profits. The beverage industry had problems with the truck drivers, the constant coddling of customers, and it was a lot of work with shrinking rewards. While I had my heart in my beverage company, I did not have it in the beverage *industry* any longer.

Plus I was tired. I was juggling too much with the radio, the boards, and all my other community involvement. The beer business was a giant step on that path to success, an important one, a wonderful one. I had absolutely no regrets about my time in the beverage industry, and I appreciated what Schlitz had done for me in terms of opening up doors. But now I needed to move forward, and in order to do that I had to say goodbye.

| Chapter 28 | Commissioner Davis? |

Never put yourself in the position to wonder, "What if?"

In 1989, I was a frontrunner in line for a chance to take over as commissioner of the National Football League. It was not a job I asked for and one I went back and forth on whether I even really wanted, but I knew it was an enormous opportunity that at the very least was worth exploring. I went about it the only way I knew how—as honestly and aggressively as I could, never wanting to look in the mirror and ask, "What if?"

The person who stepped into the role had big shoes to fill, as he was going to replace Pete Rozelle, the league's commissioner for nearly 30 years and, in my opinion, the best the league ever had. Pete was a driven, focused guy who helped turn an average league with a handful of teams, a mediocre fan base, and very few outside partnerships and media contracts into one of the most successful sports leagues in the entire world.

"Good luck replacing him," I said to myself when he announced his retirement because of declining health.

Next thing I knew, I was being considered. The funny thing is, I didn't know I was being considered until I got a call from the league's commissioner search committee and asking if I would come down to Dallas to meet with the league's owners for an interview.

What?!

The way the search process worked was that a representative from each team was asked to throw a name in the ring for the committee to consider and then the list was pared down to just a few names for the owners to vote on. At first, in an attempt to expedite the process, the committee only submitted one name for approval, Jim Finks, who was the president and general manager of the Saints. However, the owners protested, choosing to unanimously abstain with their vote until the committee provided more options.

Not long after, I heard I was being considered along with Finks, J. Patrick Barrett (the New York state republican party chairman), and a Washington-based lawyer who had represented the league in cases since the late 1960s, Paul Tagliabue. Needless to say, with no warning that my name had even been submitted, I was stunned.

Because of Rozelle's work to improve the league into a true entertainment monster, the commissioner's job had become a prized position. I could remember back when I was a player how much respect we had for the commissioner, and that had only grown with time and the league's prosperity. For as much pressure as there was for the next man in charge to take the lead, there was also quite a bit of prestige and notoriety that came with the position. Anyone would be flattered to even be considered.

By this time I was deeply involved with a number of corporate boards, which led to some national prominence and a large amount of success for me in the business world. I had a reputation of being a big-time player in the business world and a man who could get things done as much off the field as I had on the field. It was a reputation I owned with pride. I had also kept myself involved with the league, both with the Packers and other league initiatives and outreach programs, lending my help wherever I could.

Yet, I seemed like a long shot. My first thought was that I might have just been considered to have a minority in the mix. In the late 1980s, the league was making a serious push to encourage more minority involvement in coaching, front office positions, and even ownership. Having a successful black business leader considered certainly looked good for the search committee. However, even if that was the case, I thought there surely were others out there more qualified than me.

My next thought was whether or not I would even want the job. It was a fair question. Being commissioner, despite the honor of such a position, was not something I was striving for or something I felt a great deal of passion about. For one thing, there were increasing tensions between players and management that would lead to bigger headaches and league problems in the near future. The job would by no means be easy. Also, I had a good thing going at the time. My radio business was booming, the board work was booming, and I felt comfortable with where I was headed on my path. A commissioner position meant much more than packing up and moving from L.A. to New York. It meant having to quit the boards and possibly even step back from radio. While it was a tremendous opportunity, I wasn't sure I was ready to sacrifice all I had worked for to take on the role.

Still, I couldn't pass up the chance to at least try to see where it would lead. Successful people explore their options. It doesn't mean they necessarily have to drop everything else and take each and every opportunity. But if one looks good, it's at least worth exploring. I decided I would work for the position without the pressure of needing to succeed and see what happened. I would be honest and hard-working, and if at the end of the day the owners wanted me—well, I would deal with that when I got there.

Suddenly I found myself all over the news, talking to Larry King, doing countless interviews, and being scrutinized by sports and business editors all over the country on whether or not I was qualified. I wasn't alone. Each of the candidates seemed to endure the press process as much as the search committee process, especially Paul Tagliabue, who many dubbed the favorite.

Paul is an extremely bright and interesting man who also did a fairly decent job in continuing the league's growth. When I met him, he was by far the most eager and hungriest for the job. He seemed always ready to list his qualifications to anyone who was listening, how long he had worked in the league offices, how familiar he was personally with some of the issues the league faced, and how he had groomed himself to take over.

"How important is the job to you?" he even asked me on one occasion, almost like he was sizing up his competition. I evaded directly answering him, not wanting to give anything away. If there was one of us who was campaigning the hardest, it was Paul.

All of the candidates were called to Dallas to meet with the owners in an hour-long individual interview. For some, that might have been intimidating, but I was used to long board meetings with prominent people. I was used to preparing what I was going to say and preparing for what I might possibly be asked. I was used to doing my homework and walking in calm and collected, not necessarily looking to charm or impress but rather to show them why I belonged there.

The room had an intensity about it. These owners rarely all met together for anything, and there was quite a buzz. They knew the implications of picking the right man for the job, what it meant not just for the league but also for their individual teams, and they were going to make sure they got the answers they were looking for and the candidate they wanted.

It was quite a collection of personalities, as well. There were the old-timers like Al Davis, who had seen the league through the good times and bad and wanted to see what I would do to make sure the league stayed on track. There were some friendly faces like Ralph Wilson from Buffalo and Bud Adams from what was then the Houston Oilers, who were more pleasant in their questioning and visually supportive of my responses. Then there were the rising stars, the owners who clearly wanted to take charge of the interview, none more so than Jerry Jones. There has always been a sense for anyone who has ever met Jerry that he would be successful in whatever he did. He is an aggressive business leader who knew what he wanted and how to get it. Back then he wasn't quite the mogul he is now, but you could see he was well on his path to gaining power, prestige, and a voice in the NFL.

This was a group that had done their homework, as well, so there was little need to go over what I had accomplished. Instead, we talked about the issues the league faced and what I would do as commissioner. They each asked pointed questions, asking for specifics on how I would handle certain situations. We talked about how to continue growing television contracts, how I thought the league should go about expanding, scheduling, and division alignments, how I thought free agency could work in the league, and how I would work with the NCAA to come up with parameters for college players wanting to leave early and come play in the pros. The college plan was the focal point of my pitch because it was a growing problem with more kids leaving early and jumping to the pros with little to no restrictions. My plan was met with a lot of positive nods (and later, the plans the league did implement had a number of similarities).

One of the last questions I got was one of the only ones that threw me off for half a second, and it came from Jerry Jones.

"Do you realize the magnitude of this job?" he asked after we had been talking for about an hour.

"Well, yes sir, I do," I said with a hearty laugh that broke any remaining tension in the room.

I left Dallas feeling as good as I could about how I had done. I walked out of that meeting saying, "Well, I'm not sure I got the job, but I do know one thing—they learned that Willie Davis was more than just a player today."

I went back to my businesses and tried to forget about it. If I was offered the job, great. If not, no big deal. I was glad I followed through with it, if for nothing else than the process alone and the attention it brought to me and my businesses. I thought of a funny story I heard where somebody said they submitted their resume for the job of president of General Motors when the job opened up, even though they weren't really qualified.

"Why'd you do that?" somebody asked.

"So I could say 'was considered' on my resume!"

I wasn't surprised or even disappointed to see Paul get the job. I thought he was a good fit and would do well. Meanwhile, I went back to doing what I did well—working my businesses, continuing to grow as a business leader, and looking for new opportunities wherever I could find them.

Chapter 29	**There Will Always Be a Game to Play**

Sometimes you just have to find a way to win.

The biggest obstacle I have ever faced in my years in the business world is the Telecommunications Act of 1996.

It was my biggest hurdle, the biggest obstacle on my continuing path to success, my Bears, Vikings, Cowboys, Eagles, and Rams all wrapped up into one shocking government act.

Prior to the act, almost anybody could own a radio station. Assuming you could raise the capital, put together a functioning staff, and offer programming that attracted listeners, you could operate a station and even make money doing it. It was truly an example of American capitalism in action. The airwaves belonged to the public, and the public was encouraged to use them for what they needed and wanted. That was the whole point of the Federal Communications Commission—to ensure individual operators a fair and open market where they could run and compete with each other to offer the public a wide variety of listening options. It was a tremendous industry for small business owners to build a business and set themselves on their path to being an entrepreneur. It was an industry that celebrated the American Dream.

There had been a previous act that essentially capped the number of stations an entity could own and operate, holding back conglomerates from coming in and taking over a market or several markets. When the act was passed, those caps went away and what happened was the monopolization of the airwaves, which, in its defense, did create some rather large pay days for solo operators looking to sell their stations. However, for the rest of us who still wanted to run the businesses we had worked so hard to build, it simply made it easier for these larger corporations to swoop in, buy up our competitors, put together a super chain of stations we couldn't compete with, and ultimately force us out.

What's ironic is that the act was designed to do just the opposite. The framers wanted to get rid of any regulations or barriers that stood in the way of an open market where several entities could compete. They wanted to make sure that anyone who wanted to purchase a station in a market had the ability to do so. What they didn't anticipate was how valuable a commodity the airwaves were and how eager major conglomerates like Clear Channel and Saga Communications were to come in and gobble up as many operators as possible to own the market. Consolidation had always been present in the radio industry, but the number of "major media companies" went from about 50 in the early 1980s to just 10 in the aftermath of the act. Today, there are maybe five or six that fit the criteria. The 1996 Telecommunications Act practically killed smaller operators by taking away the only protection they had.

Everyone in the industry was stunned, especially with how much government had done to encourage new business owners in the industry, most notably minorities and women. Suddenly, the government threw up a major roadblock in front of the very people they were claiming to help.

The way these conglomerates got rid of their competition was brutal. First, they came into a market, starting with the most popular, and offered to buy out an owner. If the owner said yes, they got a decent pay day. If they said no, these conglomerates implemented a series of strategies, all perfectly legal and now protected by the act, to force the owner to sell or fold. They put competing programming on the air with the much stronger signal they got from combining stations and airwaves in a market, essentially drowning out the smaller station. If you ran a country station, they launched a country station sometimes just for the sole purpose of running your business into the ground.

While radio stations run on local advertising, these conglomerates offered the same type of advertising and promotions for a lot less, backed by the parent company's financial wealth. Plus they offered a wider signal range and more listeners, leaving the smaller operator with few incentives to offer—so the advertising dollars dried up. With no advertising revenue, there is no station. Once they eliminated smaller competitors and owned the market, they jacked the prices back up, now in full control of the industry. When they finished with the top markets, they moved on to the mid-sized markets and so on.

It was a bleak situation for operators like me and for the public, as well. Away went community-based programming with public service announcements, community news, and talk shows that the listeners of that region wanted to hear, and in came cookie-cutter programming that could be heard anywhere in the country. There was little anyone could do about it—except merge themselves.

I was determined to not fall victim to the act. In a sense, I saw the writing on the wall after losing my first L.A. station. But I was not going to lose Milwaukee where I offered two growing stations that the community had come to love and rely on for their programming. We were true-blue community-oriented stations, and our listeners needed us. At least that's how I felt, and listener feedback convinced me I was right.

As Milwaukee was not a top market, I had some time to form a strategy, and the best thing I could think of was to grow my own entity to compete with what I was sure would be an onslaught from the major competitors. It was only a matter of time. With two profitable, successful, and immensely popular stations with a proven track record under my belt, I felt like I didn't need much more to compete. In fact, one more big station should give me the security I needed.

I approached Shamrock Communications with an offer to buy one of Milwaukee's hottest rock stations, WQFM, 93.3 FM. The company's owner, Bill Lynette, an easy-going Irishman who was always ready to crack a joke, didn't want to sell. He knew he had a powerful station as well, despite a lagging listener base that was switching to other rock stations in a rock-heavy market. Although he was reluctant to sell, Bill was a deceptively crafty businessman who knew something had to be done to protect ourselves from the inevitable invasion of major communications companies.

So the Milwaukee Radio Alliance was born.

We simply merged our two companies and took a 50/50 split on everything related to our three stations, WLUM, WMCS, and WQFM, which we flipped into a jazz station and gave the new call letters WJZI. With the popularity of those three stations and the reputation of its two owners, we had our own version of a mini-conglomerate built not for gobbling up competitors, but for protecting what we had built.

Suddenly, our listener base went from the thousands to more than a million. And we vowed to maintain a business strategy that focused on offering those listeners what they needed and expected. It was back to business basics, providing for the customer. We not only continued community-based programming, we offered more of it, listening to the requests of our base and making sure we were adjusting to what they needed and what they couldn't get anywhere else. Announcements, community news, music requests—you name it, we offered it. We still do.

We also focused on working closely with advertisers, aware we couldn't necessarily compete with the deals our larger competitors could throw their way. However, we could show them how integral we were to the market, to the local community, and how their business wouldn't get lost. We offered sponsorship opportunities, and we took part in local events with our advertisers backing us. We offered unique promotions, scholarships, giveaways—whatever we needed to do to stay relevant, to keep our listeners and advertisers happy, and to keep the conglomerates far, far away.

We were a throwback to old-fashioned radio, a group of stations that relied on professionalism, community involvement, affordability, and credibility. As we said, we offered a "Main Street product in a Wall Street world." As a business, we applied almost everything I've written about over the last several chapters on our path to not just surviving but thriving—and people responded.

Today, more than 15 years later, we still have three of the most vibrant, popular, and successful stations in Milwaukee. We are an active member of the community, going far beyond what we offer on the air. We help hold charity events, and we organize community leaders in forums both on the air and in live events to talk about the issues surrounding our listeners. We offer scholarships to promising students—more than $50,000 a year. We have won awards in our industry, and we continue to practice the same business philosophies and principles today, a true testament to what can be achieved if the path to success is followed.

Thriving in the aftermath of the 1996 Telecommunications Act is one of my crowning achievements, on par with my Super Bowl victories and my entry into the Hall of Fame. Even with all the individual success I achieved in business, there is nothing that gives me more satisfaction and pride than looking at where my radio stations are today and how we got there.

Chapter 30 | Final Lessons

Pass on what you've learned.

I truly believe that the more people who succeed in general, the better off we are as a society. The more we can do, the more we can help each other, the more we can thrive, the better off we'll be now and in the future. I believe in sharing what we've learned on our individual paths, especially the formulas for success.

I think back to all my mentors, from my mother through my various coaches and even into business school and beyond. They were all willing to share their philosophies with me, their approaches to sports, business, and life in general. I could never have achieved all that I did without their words of wisdom, their encouragement, and their belief in passing on what they had learned.

My mother was always there for me with words of wisdom, reminding me how much strength I needed and how much I had. To this day Coach Tricky Jones and his Board of Education get me going in the morning. Coach Eddie Robinson and I kept in touch well after my college and pro football days when I was struggling to get my business going. While he couldn't help me with the specifics of business, he could tell me a lot about hanging in there and pushing through to success. The lessons of Coach Paul Brown consistently tested my will to win. Coach Lombardi's voice still echoes through every single decision I make each day, as do the lessons I've learned from some of the great business leaders I've had the fortune to watch and work alongside.

I would never have gotten anywhere without them. For that reason, I have taken it upon myself to pass on what I've learned wherever and whenever I can. For several years now, really ever since my playing days, I have traveled all over the country and even parts of the world to speak about my Packers days, my upbringing, my life in business, and my approach to being successful.

I have talked to businesses large and small, professional sports teams, college graduates, community organizations, high school students, politicians, and even Boy Scouts. I don't get paid for these speeches, and even the few that have insisted I do have later found a surprisingly similar donation made to their school or organization.

I have always felt a need to give back as a way to repay my incredible good fortune. Sometimes that has meant charitable donations or involvement in certain events. I have been extremely active in a number of organizations whose mission it is to provide opportunities for people and their communities. I have taken part in outreach committees with my various boards. I have worked with several colleges, including Marquette University, Occidental College, Milwaukee School of Engineering, and of course, Grambling. I have also worked with more than 20 groups, such as the NAACP, the Urban League, the Boy Scouts of America, and the Kauffman Foundation, which gives financial awards to entrepreneurs. My radio stations continue to donate to their respective communities with events, scholarships, food drives, etc. I have proudly received multiple awards for my contributions, including NFL Man of the Year (1987), the first ever Vince Lombardi Varsity Scout Award, Walter Camp Man of the Year, the Byron "Whizzer" White Award, NAACP Man of the Year, the March of Dimes Lifetime Achievement Award, and an honorary appointment by President Ronald Reagan to the President's Commission of Executive Exchange.

But more often than not, my contribution has meant delivering all-too-important messages to eager minds looking for that bit of help, that piece of advice than can jumpstart their own travels down the path to success. Believing that I can help with that is thrilling to me.

The topics always vary, but they have quite a few similarities in theme since they almost always follow some of my most basic (and advanced) business and life philosophies. They are universal lessons that can apply to anyone of any age, helping them achieve success in whatever they're doing. I've learned them all from the mentors in my life and even some of my own life experiences.

- We are all looking for leaders, and we are all capable of leading. We all have within us the mindset, the energy, the drive to do great things and lead others to great things. Often all we need is the motivation.
- We need to make good judgments as often as we can. That comes with patience and making sure we're always seeing the bigger picture. It also helps to have people we trust who can help with these major decisions.
- We will never get anywhere without a team, a support group that shares our beliefs and wants to accomplish the same goals. That team will only ever be as strong as its weakest link.
- We must always be as clear as possible in how we communicate with each other, whether it's discussing goals, discussing a process, or discussing problems. We must be clear.
- We have to set ambitious but realistic goals that should always grow with each success. Failure can't be an option. We won't give up. If we do fail, we will come back and come back better than we were before. We will also celebrate our successes because those successes will fuel us to want more.
- We will be calm, casual, and courteous. We won't seek the unnecessary attention, the glory without substance. We won't waste our time. We'll believe in working for success and believe that glory and all its rewards will find us.
- We need to live life to the fullest and make sure we always keep our sense of humor—even as we get serious about accomplishing our goals.
- We will develop good habits.
- We will remember the words of those who inspire us, that an early start beats fast running, and that winning is the only thing. We will hold those words in our hearts and carry them with us each and every day as they lead us to where we want to go.
- We will remember the key elements to success in everything we do: dedication, discipline, commitment, and pride. If we have all four of those things, we absolutely cannot fail.

One of the most memorable moments I ever had in regard to my speeches came in the early 1980s when I went to visit the Packers during training camp. As I walked around on the practice field, one of their up-and-coming stars, James Lofton, ran up to me and shook my hand.

"Mr. Davis, I just had to tell you something really quick," he said. "A few years ago, when I was in high school, you came and spoke to us. I'm gonna tell you something—when you spoke, you truly inspired me. In fact, you motivated me to do what I had to do in high school so I could go to college. You motivated me to all the success I have today."

James went to Stanford, became a football star, was drafted by the Packers, and became an even bigger star receiver, earning himself an election to the Hall of Fame, a broadcasting career, and a coaching career.

There are few moments for me more rewarding than that one.

Epilogue

Close the gap.

Know where you want to go and get there. You might not always know how or where your path will take you. I can assure you it will not be achieved in just a few big steps but rather a series of small steps along the way. But figure out what you want to do, what you want to achieve, and then do the work to get there. It is possible.

As I have been writing this book and looking back on my life, it's almost unreal to me. I talk about all of these things I've been part of, all that I've done, all that I've achieved, and I am so humbled by not only how fortunate I've been but by how much work I put into getting here. I am blessed to be someone who truly has very few regrets. Instead, I'm someone who has a lot of great memories, accomplishments, and a legacy to leave behind.

I couldn't have asked for anything more. As I look at where I am right now, I realize I am exactly where I always hoped I would be. I am a member of the Pro Football Hall of Fame. I am a business leader with a number of accomplishments under my belt. All-Pro Broadcasting continues to thrive as do the companies whose boards I still serve on. I am still an active member of the Green Bay Packers organization and several other organizations. I am still able to travel and speak to a wide variety of groups about my experience. I can tell you honestly that I have no interest in slowing down.

I am close with my children, and I have four wonderful grandchildren, David, Wyatt, Harley, and Haden. I also have an incredible wife, Carol, who understands me and loves me for who I am. She has been there for me during the past few years, in good times and bad, always lending her support. She has cared for me, even acting as a nurse at times when my health has suffered. She is a beautiful and amazing woman, someone whom I'm excited and content to share my remaining days alongside, the perfect person to have at my side for this point in my life. I live in a wonderful home with her overlooking the ocean in Southern California. And each Sunday in the fall, I get to watch my Packers, who named me an honorary captain in their march to a Super Bowl victory while I worked on this book.

Life couldn't be better.

I've worked hard to close that gap. I set out when I was a young kid, knowing at an early age that I wanted to be a businessman and then a few years later that I wanted to be a football player. For most of us, the answer to "What do you want to do with your life?" doesn't come that quickly or easily. One thing we do share is that we all want to achieve success. Even if the path isn't crystal clear, we can all do things along the way to help us get there. Remember, it's a series of steps, not any giant leaps. This book has reminded me of all the steps I took, the people who have helped me along the way, the successes and failures that happened, and how I was able to stay on the path.

I don't say it to brag. I'm just extremely proud, and as I reach my older years, there is something extremely satisfying about looking back on your life when there are few if any mountains left to climb, and realizing that you did it. From humble beginnings to being the first in my family to go to college, from working hard for a pro football career to championships, business school, the Hall of Fame, and a business career that far exceeded even my expectations—I, with the help and advice of several people along the way, have closed the gap.

I want to sign off with what I guess is my last piece of advice. I said that closing the gap means finding a way to get from Point A to Point B. For most of us, that means from getting where we are now to achieving success. I always knew what I wanted to do, but I had no idea how I was going to get there—and I realize there's a lesson in that.

We're not necessarily supposed to know, at least not all the time.

It's enough to have your dream and know what you want to get started. If you apply all the right principles, if you are determined and willing to work, if you practice good habits and stay ambitious and humble, if you always keep your eye on the overall prize, then an amazing thing will happen. Opportunities will arise along your path that will help you take the next step—and you will be ready for them.

That's truly the key to success. As I look back on my life, I realize that absolutely everything led to something else—something that could either further my attempt to achieve my goals or hinder me and throw me off course. In Texarkana, my upbringing led me to part-time jobs, high school led me to football, which led me to college, which led me to the pros, which led me to championships and notoriety, which opened up the opportunity for business school, which led me to the beer business, which led me to radio, which led me to the boards, and so on. Along the way, there were key moments at each stage, key opportunities that, when I took full advantage of them, propelled me to the next level. I had some slip-ups along the way, but when it mattered, when it was important, I stepped up, practiced what I believed, took the advice of those I respected, and went for it with everything I could give.

That's how I succeeded in football, business, and beyond. That's what leaves me satisfied and fulfilled today, looking back at my life with a smile. That's the legacy I want to leave—that's how I closed the gap.

Appendix 1

Closing the Gap: A List of Lessons

Good planning builds success.

Appreciate those early influences and what they've done for you.

Find your motivation and take on the work.

Sometimes we need confrontation to achieve what we want.

Your actions, behaviors, and conduct will show that you are professionals.

Work is characterized by a result, and if you set out with an intended objective that you don't reach, then you haven't done the work.

An early start beats fast running.

Have an appreciation for achievement at all levels.

Work to instill the spirit of teamwork.

Play like you practice.

Be both prepared and grateful for opportunities.

Be the bigger man. Win the battle. Do what you know you can do.

It's okay to be obsessed with what you love to do.

Always aim to be a leader.

A little taste of success goes a long way when it comes to building self-confidence.

If you play well, they'll find ya.

If you work hard, you will eventually be given a chance.

We can teach you and we can show you, but we can't do it for you.

There is a lot you can learn by watching the greatest.

Find the opportunity to leave an impression.

Savor every first moment.

Sometimes the best opportunities are tough to see at first.

While it's good to be skeptical, also be open.

Learn from your mentors and pass on their words and influence.

How you play this game is a reflection of how you will live the rest of your life.

Good or bad, habits will soon become the natural thing to do.

Success is not a gift, it's earned.

There is often a simple formula to building a winning team.

Find someone to help you where you're weakest.

Be careful in making assumptions.

Be proactive, especially when it comes to relationships.

A leader must have a clear mission, inspiration, and rules.

Practice will make us as close to perfect as we can be.

A team of focused, like-minded individuals is unstoppable.

Ask yourself, what if this is the *only* shot I get?

Don't let a bumpy start throw you off course.

Rivals should make you step up your game. We all need rivals.

Being the favorite to win rarely means anything.

A team is only as strong as *every* individual component.

Never give up on a moment because it may be the crucial moment.

Replace missing pieces to help you achieve even more.

There is nothing wrong about seeking redemption.

Be patient and be ready when the time comes.

Relish in perfection.

There are many different kinds of toughness, and they all have a benefit.

Don't let success kill your hunger to do more.

Be willing to give an unknown a break.

Don't let success go to your head—stay focused!

Study your competition, know them inside and out, and you will have
an advantage.

Take calculated risks, even when you don't necessarily need to.

There will always be interesting characters in your life.

Adversity is inevitable, especially with continued success.

Sometimes fixing a problem means staying the course.

Have perspective on what's truly important.

It's never too late to pursue your real passion.

Sometimes things simply don't go the way they should.

Being a leader means sometimes taking one for the team.

Achieving success rarely comes easily.

When you have the chance to step up and lead, do it!

Winning isn't everything; it's the only thing.

Being a great coach or leader also requires having a very special skill—
awareness.

A great team will both face and overcome adversity.

Success requires you to keep working even as the work piles itself on.

In the biggest moments, winners shine.

There are no "less important" big moments.

With more success comes more competition.

The best way to handle a rival is to continue to dominate them!

As soon as one big moment ends, chances are there's another one coming up.

Sometimes we play for more than just ourselves.

A leader is willing to change the plan, even if it's his own.

We all want to quit at some point. We all need someone to remind us why we should stay on course.

Recognize those who came before you and those who helped you achieve success.

Even leaders need friends. Contrary to popular belief, they are not isolated individuals.

Change in your industry or field is going to happen, be able to adjust.

It's up to the leader to inspire.

Sometimes it's okay to release the pressure off your team.

Sometimes your competition will be the least of your concerns!

Leaders trust their instincts.

Experience can ease the pressure.

We have to find a way to continue when our idols and influences move on.

Success in one area simply can't last forever.

If you know you're leaving, soak up that last day.

Never forget.

Find a way to continue to do what you love.

Loyalty will eventually bring opportunities.

There is almost always someone who knows something more than you do.

You need to be tough to survive and even tougher to win.

Learn everything you possibly can about what you're doing.

Acknowledge your fears and deal with them quickly.

Be willing to work, and don't ask anyone to do something you won't do.

Take advantage of your strengths.

People don't always care who you were.

Always focus on the customer.

Make sure your staff is prepared for anything.

Never stop working.

Celebrate your success.

Don't be afraid to jump.

There shouldn't be anything fun about losing.

Stick with what works.

Know when (and how) to get in and when (and how) to get out.

Be humble and appreciative, especially in the face of grand success.

Always remember those who were there for you—and be open to forgiving those who weren't.

If the opportunity arises, be the first. Be ground-breaking.

Be patient and know certain things take time.

We all need support in a variety of ways.

We also need to let go to move forward.

Never put yourself in the position to wonder, "What if?"

Sometimes you just have to find a way to win.

Pass on what you've learned.

Close the gap.

Appendix 2

Pledges for Success

- We are all looking for leaders, and we are all capable of leading. We all have within us the mindset, the energy, and the drive to do great things and lead others to great things. Often all we need is the motivation.
- We need to make good judgments as often as we can. That comes with patience and making sure we're always seeing the bigger picture. It also helps to have people we trust who can help with these major decisions.
- We will never get anywhere without a team, a support group that shares our beliefs and wants to accomplish the same goals. That team will only ever be as strong as its weakest link.
- We must always be as clear as possible in how we communicate with each other, whether it's discussing goals, discussing a process, or discussing problems. We must be clear.
- We have to set ambitious but realistic goals that should always grow with each success. Failure can't be an option. We won't give up. If we do fail, we will come back and come back better than we were before. We will also celebrate our successes because those will fuel us to want more.
- We will be calm, casual, and courteous. We won't seek the unnecessary attention, the glory without substance. We won't waste our time. We'll believe in working for success and believing that glory and all its rewards will find us.
- We need to live life to the fullest and make sure we always keep our sense of humor—even as we get serious about accomplishing our goals.
- We will develop good habits.
- We will remember the words of those who inspire us, that an early start beats fast running and that winning is the only thing. We will hold those words in our hearts and carry them with us each and every day as they lead us to where we want to go.
- We will remember the key elements to success in everything we do: dedication, discipline, commitment, and pride. If we have all four of those things, we absolutely cannot fail.

Appendix 3

Willie Davis Bio

Willie D Davis

No. 77: Cleveland Browns: 1958–59

No. 87: Green Bay Packers: 1960–69

Games Played: 162 (including 138 consecutive regular season)

Fumbles Recovered: 21

Fumbles Returned for Touchdown: 1

Interceptions: 2

*Sacks were not officially counted and recorded until 1982, but historians estimate Willie easily had more than 100, which would make him the team's all-time leader in that category.

All Pro Selection: 5 (1962, 1964, 1965, 1966, 1967)

Pro Bowl Selection: 5 (1963, 1964, 1965, 1966, 1967)

World Championship Appearances: 6 (1960, 1961, 1962, 1965, 1966, 1967)

World Titles: 5 (1961, 1962, 1965, 1966, 1967)

Ranked No. 69 on *The Sporting News* 1999 list of the top 100 Greatest Football Players

NAIA College Hall of Fame Inductee

NCAA Silver Anniversary Team

U.S. Army All Service Football Team

Green Bay Packers Hall of Fame Inductee

Pro Football Hall of Fame Inductee

Appendix 4

Professional Football Season Records

1958: Cleveland Browns: 9–3: Eastern Conference Playoff

1959: Cleveland Browns: 7–5

1960: Green Bay Packers: 8–4: League Champions

1961: Green Bay Packers: 11–3: League Champions

1962: Green Bay Packers: 13–1: League Champions

1963: Green Bay Packers: 11–2–1

1964: Green Bay Packers: 8–5–1

1965: Green Bay Packers: 10–3–1: League Champions

1966: Green Bay Packers: 12–2: Super Bowl Champions

1967: Green Bay Packers: 9–4–1: Super Bowl Champions

1968: Green Bay Packers: 6–7–1

1969: Green Bay Packers: 8–6

Appendix 5

Business Service

Here is a list of professional organizations where Willie Davis has served:

Alliance Bancshares California
Bassett Furniture Industries Inc.
Checkers Drive In Restaurants Inc.
Dow Chemical Co.
Ewing Marion Kauffman Center for Entrepreneurial Leadership
Fidelity National Financial Inc.
Fireman's Fund Insurance Cos.
Findley Adhesives
Grambling State University
Green Bay Packers Inc.
Johnson Controls Inc.
K-Mart Corp.
L.A. Gear Inc.
Los Angeles Olympic Committee
Manpower Inc.
Mattel Inc.
Marquette University
Metro-Goldwyn-Mayer Inc./United Artists
MGM Grand Inc.
Milwaukee School of Engineering
Occidental College
Rally's Hamburgers Inc.
Sara Lee Corp.
Schlitz Brewing Co.
Strong Capital Management Fund
University of Chicago
Wisconsin Energy Corp.

Appendix 6

About Willie Davis

Al Davis, Younger Brother, Radio Entrepreneur:
It was tough to follow in his footsteps sometimes. He was a great football player who built a reputation at Grambling. When I followed him there, it was tough to live up to his name because of all he accomplished. Still, he was always supportive—always protective and supportive. I followed him into the beer business and then into radio, working for his business until I left to work at my own station in Texarkana. We had a great time working together all those years, and more important was how much I learned from him.

I saw determination and perseverance. Once he gets on the path, he stays with it until he finishes. That's something I've picked up from him. Same with his work ethic. I've had to walk in his footsteps over the years, and in doing so I learned things from him that I now pass on to my son, lessons we should all live by.

Alexis Herman, Former U.S. Secretary of Labor:
Willie Davis is one of those people you meet in your life that has a great spirit and a great presence, someone just as large in life as he is on television. I got to know him very well from being on the board of MGM together. Willie was my coach on the board, just helping me understand the "players" and the "plays." He used his football knowledge to teach me about the members on the board and the challenges they had faced in the past. He was a true mentor.

One thing about Willie—when Willie's ready to go, Willie's ready to go! I learned that the hard way in Detroit when Willie took the company car immediately after a board meeting, stranding some of his fellow passengers downtown. It was an accident, of course. Willie didn't know we were still all riding together, and he was eager to move on to his next piece of business. I still tease him about that today.

Allan H. "Bud" Selig, Commissioner of Baseball:
Willie and I became friends around 1961, and we've been through a lot together, especially in working with local organizations like Athletes for Youth. His success is obvious, but what might not be is that he is the nicest human being you would ever want to meet. He's also one of the most interesting people I've ever known. He stands as one of the great success stories and great human interest stories.

We also have had a lot of fun with each other. For as good of a football player as Willie was, he kind of lacked baseball skills, despite what he'll tell you, and I used to have a good time teasing him about that. He really isn't as good at baseball, and he'd like people to believe he is. As Willie does, he would just argue for a little bit and then let out one of those deep, signature laughs.

When he was a player, he had incredible loyalty to Coach Lombardi. I remember once when he came down to Milwaukee, I met up with him and he told me he had to get a haircut. Even back then, Willie didn't really have any hair, and what he did have was already cut short.

"I don't know what you're going to get cut," I told him.

"I don't know either," he said, "but Coach will get mad if I don't get it cut!"

Later on in his career, Willie was a guest of mine at a baseball game. After the Braves left and before the Brewers were in Milwaukee, we would bring the White Sox up from Chicago to play some home games in the late 1960s. The year before Mickey Mantle retired, the Yankees came to play the White Sox and we had the game up in Milwaukee, which brought a sell-out crowd for the festivities of what was going to be a retirement tour for Mantle. Willie and I were standing in front of the loge section, and the announcer told the crowd Willie was there. When he was introduced, he got a big ovation from the fans. That was all Willie needed to convince himself that the sellout was for him and not Mickey Mantle!

Still, later, I would hear him talk about that game when he and Mantle made an appearance together—followed by that signature laugh once again.

Andrea Erickson Davis, founder Phantasia Ad Inc.,
Former All-Pro Broadcasting Corporate V.P., Former Wife
When Willie Davis makes up his mind, there is no stopping him. After an eight-year courtship, Willie literally kidnapped me, swept me off my feet, and whisked me away to a whirlwind wedding at the MGM Grand chapel in Las Vegas. Our deep friendship has flourished now for more than two decades. Both in business and in life, traveling with Willie Davis has been an incredible adventure and profound learning experience in diversity and closing the gap.

Here are a few fun memories from my front-row seat as Mrs. #87.

Living on Lombardi Time: The clocks were always set on Lombardi time, or earlier. From stovetop to dashboard, it was difficult to know what time it really was because no clocks were ever set on the current time!

Willie had special skills in the kitchen, not just from watching his mom seasoning and preparing food, but also as a result of his playing days. Frostbite from the Ice Bowl has given his right hand heat-resistant fingers with little to no feeling. His big paws doubled as oven mitts, so when something needed to be quickly moved off a stovetop burner, Willie was the man. It surprised me how Willie could tell me with a straight face he was lucky he had no injuries. I'd point out his lost teeth, cracked ribs, bad knees, replaced hips, and those frost-bitten fingers and toes! After all that punishment, I asked him, would you still do it all over again? Without a pause to consider, Willie answered, "In a nanosecond."

A True Football Addict: If football is an addiction, then Willie is incurably, irredeemably hooked. Just how bad is his habit? Before the picture-in-picture feature on TV, Willie would stack television sets on top of each other in his bedroom and the main den so he could watch multiple games at once.

Willie balanced church with football Sunday and gained a reputation for being especially devout at the Brentwood Presbyterian Church in California. Willie was so intent on attending the earliest service at BPC, he would insist we leave the house almost as soon as I woke up. No shower, no shave, wearing yesterday's clothes, and leaving so early every Sunday morning, there wasn't even traffic on the infamous L.A. six-lane highways. We'd get there and still have an entire half hour before the church doors opened, so we'd listen to Willie's friend Stevie Wonder's radio station, KJLH (Kindness, Joy, Love, and Happiness) while we waited. It played church sermons and songs only on Sundays, much like Willie's urban AM station did in Milwaukee.

Considered the most conservative of all the services, 8:00 AM was the earliest. The midday game, because of the time-zone difference in California, started at 10:00 AM. Pushing me through the clog of well-wishers in the aisle at the end of the service, Willie skipped fellowship and practically lifted me over the crowd, smiling and waving a somewhat hasty goodbye to the Reverend as we left. We always made it back home well before kick-off.

Two things are sacred to Willie on a Sunday morning—going to church and watching football. He made sure he did both.

Always prepared and ready to adjust the game plan: I've never seen anyone as happy to get up and go to work as Willie Davis. He worked out first thing each morning, and I think it was his mental preparation time, as well. His Willie-sized briefcase carried reports from boards, the radio stations, community activities, the Packers organization, and more. But Willie really mainly relied on notes he kept in just one spiral-bound, three-hole college-ruled dimestore notebook. Willie would open that notebook and start at the top. With his handsome fluid handwriting, Willie would number a list of things to do, people to meet, projects to complete, checking off the items as they were taken care of. Dates, names, numbers, and notes—it was simplicity.

When the University of Chicago asked Willie if he would talk to its business school minority students, Willie said yes, absolutely. This was Willie's alma mater. He wasn't being paid to speak, and he was committed as always to prepare something that was meaningful to tell these future leaders. Willie carefully copied long-hand the speech notes for more than a day, even mouthing parts as he read and re-read. He was still rehearsing at the Formica-covered breakfast table in Chicago the morning of the speech. The back of a three-folded letter from the university was used again to list his main bullet points.

Before he was introduced, as he waited on the sideline, Willie heard something from the previous speaker that he, too, wanted to talk about. I listened as he went to the podium and used not one word of his original speech. Without any notes, Willie changed his entire presentation to fit the new topic. Passionate and inspiring, Willie was so well-received, he got an enthusiastic standing ovation.

Man on the Move: To this day, Willie rarely ever sits still. He is and always was a man on the move. I would tease Willie about never being in one place long enough for a party, so newly married—and working off a long holiday-card list of important people I'd heard of but hadn't yet met—I made Willie a Surprise Birthday Party in a Book, asking everyone to please send wishes with a story. While not letting Willie know what I was up to all those nights on the computer, I researched and replaced stories, magazines, and various items that were destroyed years earlier by an attic fire in Texarkana. The Party in Print has served as an inspiration and a template for this book.

No. 1 Fan: Every day there were letters from fans, often forwarded from the Hall of Fame or Green Bay. East Coast to West Coast, often with handmade Green Bay Packers Green and Gold stationary, fans sent photos to sign (or to keep) and asked him if he could share a story or memory, as well. Willie read all the mail, signed pictures, and sent an autograph, even when his hands cramped from all the requests. Although Willie didn't have time to write answers to all the questions about his life lessons and experiences, he always added a personal word. I was lucky enough to hear stories from Willie that no one had ever heard before, not even his children or best friends. Willie loves his fans as much as they love him, and I always knew a book about this inspirational, amazing man needed to be shared with everyone. Like so many others, I also count myself as Willie Davis' No. 1 Fan.

Andrew Liveris, President, CEO and Chairman of Dow Chemical:
Willie was on the board for Dow for a long time, someone I noticed when I was presenting to the board in my early management responsibilities. He was someone who impressed me greatly, especially with how he reached out to young up-and-comers. There is no question in my mind that during the CEO selection process, all my prior exposure to Willie and his investment in meeting and working with me earlier in my career paid dividends.

He's got a human touch, asking questions that are always on point but not pointed. He doesn't want to jab you but rather get you thinking. He also has the ability to see business in wide angles, looking at all sides. It was a sad day when we had to bid him farewell at his retirement.

Although we have no need to stay in touch professionally, we continue a personal relationship today. He's an individual who sticks with you through thick and thin. He continues to call and his opening line is always, "How are you?" It's sincere, and that's a special attribute. He'll read something in the paper and, good or bad, he's not asking about the topic. He's just checking in with you. He likes to keep in touch, keeping a strong affinity for the company and his friends. He's impacted all of us by being good professionally and caring enough to understand us personally.

Barbara Franklin, Former U.S. Secretary of Commerce:
I met Willie on the Dow board a long time ago, but one thing that I remember most about him and see it even today is that everybody likes Willie—and that's a very good quality to have, especially in business. He can persuade people to do something for him, to work with him. He can get a board full of directors from different backgrounds to work together as a group, and that's the only way anything gets done. He's a facilitator, the person who keeps things going. It's great to have that quality, to be the catalyst.

Belinda Hamilton, Corporate Business Manager, All-Pro Broadcasting:
Willie runs his business like a family. It doesn't matter what the situation is, he is like the head, the father. He has an open-door policy with everyone. I've been working for him since 1985, and he treats me like I'm his daughter. He is just so open and warm-hearted. If you talk to his other employees, they'll tell you the same. He is our patriarch.

Bill Hurwitz, General Manager, All-Pro Broadcasting:
Of course, I grew up watching Willie Davis play football and always admired him. Later on, I got to know him as a radio owner. I was working with a competitor and when I met Mr. Davis, I knew he was a man I wanted to work for instantly. I got that opportunity five years later when he offered me a job.

"I need guys like you to come here and make a difference in business," he said. And 24 hours later, we were working together.

Willie Davis knows how to run a business. He knows how to get involved and when to walk away and let people do their job. He knows that's part of leadership, knowing when to walk away. We might fly, or we might crash. But he leaves it up to us and gives us the chance. If we do crash, he'll be there to pick us up. And we know he's there, that he's only one phone call away or one flight away. He'll step in if he needs to, and it's comforting to both know he's there and know that we have his trust.

We also have a great deal of admiration for him and how he didn't sell out to Wall Street after the 1996 Telecommunications Act. When the act passed, there was a proliferation of Wall Street corporations buying radio stations like Willie's. If he had sold, he could have made millions. He chose to not only keep his assets but to fight for them.

Today there are five major players in the Milwaukee radio market; Clear Channel, Journal Communications, Entercom, Saga—and then Willie Davis. He had a vision to keep his assets, and he's never looked back.

Bill McNulty, General Manager, All-Pro Broadcasting:

In the 31 years I've worked with him, I would say that if Willie Davis has any one fault, it's that he's too giving. I have seen people take advantage of his good nature time and time again. People will hit him up for sometimes self-serving financial interests, and he often acquiesces and helps them out. He is an incredibly smart man and knows exactly what he's doing. It's not that anyone's fooling him—he's just very generous and caring. And if that's his big fault, then God bless him!

Bob Skoronski, Former Tackle, Green Bay Packers:

The thing that sticks out most in my mind is his ability to speak to the guys and get them ready for a big game. As captains, we were responsible for talking to the guys before the games, to get them focused on what we had to do. He was better than anyone—the way he talked, the excitement in his voice, the focus in his eyes. He could deliver on the things he said we had to do to win. When he told you he could do something, you could go to the bank with it.

That was what made him special. He didn't expect anybody to do something he couldn't, wouldn't, or didn't do! There are lots who talk the talk but don't walk the walk. Not him. He was dominating. I believe one year, back before they recorded sacks, he must have had about 27 or so. I remember a game against Minnesota where he must have had seven in that one game. Between Willie and Henry Jordan, that year they must have had close to 50. They had more than most teams have now in a season! He was so quick. There are a lot of defensive [players] who can rush the passer, but they can't stop the run and vice versa. He could do it all.

He could also respond to any challenges. If he heard an opponent was making some kind of comment about him, he'd respond to that challenge. He was intense on the field, but he was also a huge joker off the field. He would talk to the other guys about his experiences growing up and would have them roaring.

We even saw Coach Lombardi roaring on occasion. We also saw how Coach respected Willie. At the Thursday practice after a game, Coach would give out game awards—he got plenty. They were a big deal among the teammates, and very few of us could argue when Willie got his.

He was and still is the ultimate Packer. He is very concerned about the image and well-being of the organization. He's a great representative of the team in every way. He's one of my best friends and just an outstanding person. He's always there, never a "no show" guy. Just like he was on the field, if you need him to do something, he'll do it and you can take that to the bank!

Carol Davis, Founder of Market Design,
I.T. Project Management Consultant, Wife:
I have never in my life ever met anyone quite like Willie Davis, and I doubt I ever will. God must have thrown away the mold he used for Willie. Maybe I am just blinded by my husband's talents and persona, but I don't think so.

Willie is sensitive and compassionate. I will never forget being in Milwaukee a few years ago when he received a very early morning phone call from his friend, Ralph Stayer, owner of Johnsonville Sausage. Ralph had a friend who was in the hospital and was not expected to live through the day. The dying man had a wish to talk to Willie. Ralph gave Willie the contact information to call, and no sooner did Willie disconnect the call from Ralph, he dialed the hospital. Willie never before had such a request. I couldn't listen because I felt that it was just too personal for both of them. But later I had to ask.

"Willie, what did you say to this man?"

He told me that he thanked this person for all his support and that he told him the Packers never would have been as successful as they were had it not been for people like him.

Packers fans are like veins for the Packers' bodies. They are the end-all reason why the players play their hearts out to achieve victory. And the fans love all the Packers' players old and young. Of course, they are always quick to tell Willie how much they admire the Lombardi-era players. They tell him how tough he was and how he was one of the best that ever played the game (he is one of the football pioneers that set the standard for future players). And you have to know that Willie just *loves* hearing all this. His chest pokes out, and if it is possible to have someone's head actually swell because of pride, Willie's head would burst!

A few years ago when the Packers were in a slump, Coach Mike McCarthy asked Willie to talk with the team. I was thrilled to sit in the back of the room that day when Willie talked to the guys. It was incredible to see how the team listened to him. All eyes were on Willie. Afterward, most players came up individually to thank Willie for his time. And yes, they won that game and went to the playoffs that year. Naturally, Willie will take absolutely no credit for the team's turnaround, but to me he was the hero who saved the day.

One more thing about Willie, just a funny little thing. One day I was talking to Doris, his office manager in Milwaukee, about his generosity. During that time something came up about someone that needed some kind of help. Doris started chanting a little song teasing Willie. It went, "Willie can't say no," in a playfully mocking tone. Over time, this chant has spread throughout all management personnel at his radio stations. I can't tell you how many times he has heard it. With a look of pride and a hearty laugh, Willie takes it as a compliment.

Willie is a very special person. He is all that is good in this world. He is blessed, and I feel blessed to be part of his life. He has made many people, including myself, better people just because we have the pleasure of his company and the inside scoop to his secret of life.

Dave Robinson, Former Linebacker, Green Bay Packers:
Willie and I never had a team run the same play successfully against us twice in the same game or in the same year.

Willie and I would analyze what the teams were doing, before the game and during the game, and we would do what we had to do to shut it down—always. We had an understanding of, "You do this, and I'll do that." We talked to each other, the coaches, the rest of the defense, and we promised that if they tried to run the same play again, we'd shut it down.

He was the smartest, most intelligent player I ever played with. He was also so strong with his strong upper body. And he was fast with those teeny tiny little legs of his. I mean it, he had the smallest legs! He was always worried about someone taking his legs out. He always wanted me to make sure the tight end wouldn't crack back and block on those little legs. Yeah, well, we rode those legs to championship after championship.

He was also the kind of guy who led by example, even off the field. Coach was ahead of his time when he named Willie captain. But he knew the time was coming and that Willie would make a great leader. Everyone knew how hard Willie would play on the field, but off the field he was just as disciplined. He didn't act a fool. The first time I saw Willie have any kind of drink, it was a beer right before he retired—and I think it was just one. I'm not saying he was a saint, but he never made a fool of himself. He never did anything that would show he wasn't a great leader.

And he knew his football. If I ever had any questions about anything, I'd go to Willie first and then I'd go to Coach Bengtson. Phil even once said that Willie was right 99 percent of the time anyway.

The greatest time in my whole football career was when I played next to Willie Davis. I remember when he retired because my whole life changed. I always felt bad for Clarence Williams from Texas who we got to replace Willie because there ain't no way he was ever going to be as good. In my opinion, nobody would have been.

We worked together perfectly, reading offenses, switching up the holes like it was the natural thing to do, and helping each other and everyone else on the defense with our weaknesses. We confused coaches all over the league, and we loved it. We gave them fits.

Dick Strong, Founder of Strong Financial Corp.:

Willie is the perfect example of how, if you have the ability and desire and you're willing to work, miracles can happen. He is blessed with natural ability, smarts, and a shrewd business sense while also being very likeable. He genuinely cares about people, and everyone he meets genuinely cares about him. He treats everyone the same and is so warm and giving to people. He truly feels that if he helps others be successful, *he'll* be successful. If he can make others more successful, then what he's trying to accomplish will take care of itself. He has that "juice" that special people have, and it's paid off.

He has always treated me the same from the moment I met him, through both good and rough times. Along the way, I've learned a lot by being his friend.

I met Willie when I needed a guest speaker for a Christmas party. My close friend, Ben Barkin from Schlitz, recommended Willie.

"No, he's probably too big," I said. "He wouldn't do it."

Sure enough, he did, and he gave a great speech. We hit it off and developed a relationship. Not long after, in the early 1990s, he joined our mutual fund board and proved to be one of the hardest working and most informed directors we had.

When my company went through a rough time, Willie stood by me. I remember an article in the *Wall Street Journal* that had other company's executives poking fun at my firm at Willie's expense. One of them said, "Well, we don't have any ex-football players serving our shareholders."

It was a cheap, uneducated shot, but Willie never said a word about it, at least to me. What he did do was call me at least once a week for the next several months just to check in and see how I was doing.

"Hang in there, it will all be over soon," he said again and again, and it gave me hope. I felt like I was being unfairly targeted and I was so low, battling depression. Willie's calls helped me overcome it, and for that I will always be indebted.

There is a story that I think shows the true Willie Davis. When Willie was on our board, I had to go on a business trip to Hong Kong. Always curious to learn more about the business, Willie asked me to take him along so I agreed. We talked on a Friday and made plans for my plane to pick Willie up in L.A. on Sunday morning.

When I saw him on the plane, I noticed he was out of breath and pouring with sweat. He also looked extremely tired. I asked him if he was okay, and he told me he was fine. I would find out later (from someone else because he wouldn't tell me) exactly what had happened.

After our phone call, he had discovered that his passport was expired and there was no place open on the weekend to renew it on a rush except for a place in Washington D.C. Willie had committed to me to make the trip and didn't want to cancel. So he left Friday night on a flight from Milwaukee to L.A. to get some proper forms he needed, then from L.A. to Boston, a shuttle down to D.C. and a flight from D.C. back to L.A. by Sunday to make it in time to get on the Hong Kong flight.

All of that to honor his word.

On that trip, we met with several CEOs and other major business people, many of them asking if Willie was my bodyguard. He had gotten used to this by now with his various board work and found it easier just to say "yup" and smile. One of the leaders we met was a CEO who had gone to the University of Minnesota for a business degree. He told us he was a *huge* Minnesota Vikings fan. In fact, he was such a fan he had the games taped and air-shipped overnight so he could watch them

"You hear that, Willie?" I said. "Vikings fan."

Willie just smiled as the many looked at his broad frame.

I looked at the man and pointed to Willie.

"Green Bay Packer."

"Oh, I *hate* the Packers!" he said, and we all laughed. Sure enough, next thing I knew Willie is pulling out his Super Bowl rings and this billionaire is calling the company photographer to take pictures, acting like an excited child as Willie lets him hold the ring.

The point is, it doesn't matter who you are, Packers fan or not, Willie Davis will treat you with the same kindness, and that's a lesson we all could learn. Willie's full of those lessons. He is willing to work. He believes in leaving a legacy. That's what motivates him. He has a desire to succeed and excel at everything he does, and he does it the right way.

I always wonder how much better would our society be, how robust, if we all contributed like Willie Davis.

Don Newcombe, Pitcher, Brooklyn Dodgers:

I first met Willie back when he was at Grambling. I went to visit the school as part of an outreach program to black colleges with other baseball players Larry Doby and Roy Campanella. Willie was playing football there at the time for Coach Eddie Robinson. Coach Robinson introduced us to Willie and said something that stood out in my mind for quite some time.

"You watch," he said. "This young man will be one of the greats in football."

Willie smiled but kept quiet. Later we heard that Willie went to the pros, and we watched him do what Coach Robinson said. Over the years, I got to know Willie more by going to watch him play, whether he was with the Browns or the Packers, whenever they came to New York. I knew all the guards at the gates of Yankee Stadium, and they'd always let us sneak in for the game, sitting on the visiting team's sideline.

We kept in touch over the years, and when he launched his radio business, I actually worked for Willie for a while, doing commercials for his stations. We became really good friends and still are today.

In fact, we had a chance to get married to our brides in a joint ceremony. I had been married twice before and didn't think I would again. I used to tell people that three strikes and you're out in my business. But I met a wonderful woman and decided to try again. When I told Willie, he told me he was getting married as well, so I suggested we do it together.

"Hey big fella," he said. "That's a great idea."

We talked to our girls to see what the bottom line was, and they went along with it. I was glad to have him there. He's a great friend of mine. I admire what he does and how he does it. He's one of the finest men I have ever met.

Doris Hantke, Business Manager, All-Pro Broadcasting:

He's just somebody you want to work for, and he's incredibly loyal. I had been working for him for quite some time when I suddenly left to pursue another job in Houston in 1983. After a short amount of time, Willie asked what it would take to get me back to All Pro—and not long after, I came back. I've been with him ever since, and I couldn't be happier.

Duane Davis, Operations Manager, All-Pro Broadcasting; Son:

What resonates with me most about my father is passion.

Passion has always been one of the most important things in his life. He has always stressed to me that passion is something you absolutely need to accomplish any goal, and everything that's important to you should be approached with passion.

It's that passion that drove my father to a lot of his success in life. And it's funny, sometimes it's hard for him to understand people that don't have it. There have been times he's talked about people he's worked with and he wonders why they lack the passion he has for success. My father has no sympathy or tolerance for any sense of entitlement. He expects people to work for their success and pursue their goals with drive and desire.

It's a philosophy that both he and my mother shared. They both said they'd rather have us kids be a failure at something we pursued with passion than not pursue anything. And what we learned most of all from watching them was how successful we could be when we did pursue with that passion.

Edna Garnet, Assistant for more than 40 Years:

I was working for Schlitz and I guess he inherited me. I think that's how I started working for him—it's been so long.

He was more or less sent to us by Schlitz when we were struggling. All of us who were working there heard that the company had sold the distributorship to the big athlete Willie Davis. Well, I thought they were talking about the former Dodgers baseball player! The Dodgers had just won the World Series recently, and the players were in the news quite a bit. My first thought was, *What does this baseball player know about beer?*

I was on vacation when they introduced Willie Davis and didn't meet him until I got back. When I came back, I see this big hunk of a man, and I mean that literally, come up to introduce himself and I'm thinking, *That's not Willie Davis!* I was expecting to see this little guy from the Dodgers. It was very weird to see this tree of a man walking over to me.

I soon learned a lot about football.

I got comfortable working for him, and I guess I was satisfied because I've never had the need to look anywhere else. He's easy to work for, not very demanding but still expects everyone to work hard. He's also very fair, and he's caring. I'll never forget when I was sick with cancer, he was more than generous with the time off he gave me. But beyond that, he called me every day to see how I was doing. Even when I came back, he allowed me to work part-time and pretty much did whatever he could to help me. Yes, he's a very loyal person.

Forrest Gregg, Former Tackle, Green Bay Packers:

I'm sure he already told you about how we met in the army at Ft. Carson and played together under Coach Dickey. I remember coming back from leave after practicing for a few weeks in this beat-up pair of shoulder pads and I'm looking to the equipment guy, asking where are those pads I asked for? All of a sudden, I see this big guy in the locker room wearing this brand-new pair—so I thought I should introduce myself and let him know he was wearing my pair. Well, they got me another one.

I'll tell ya, it was obvious from the beginning that he was a heck of an athlete. He must have weighed about 235, 240, but he could run like a deer. I always thought I was fast for a lineman, but he could outrun me.

We became good friends in the army and played well together until he got his early release in 1958. I told him, "I'll see you somewhere along the line." He went to Cleveland and I eventually went back to Green Bay, but I kept track of him. There were only 12 teams at the time, so you kind of knew everyone.

Then a couple years later, in the off-season before 1960, I got a call from Jack Vainisi telling me we got this defensive lineman from Cleveland. That got my attention.

"What's his name?"

"Willie Davis," Jack said. "You played with him. What kind of guy is he?"

I told Jack that he was a good guy, great football player.

"He can help us right away," I said. "But I think he should be defensive end."

Willie had played both offense and defense in the army, but it was clear he was stronger on defense. Jack agreed and said that's where they were looking at him.

Our first Packers training camp together, we got caught up on everything and immediately started to compete with each other. He was an outstanding football player, and he was trying to impress the coaches and make the team. In those days, there were no guarantees. It only mattered what you did in training camp. And he came ready to play.

Playing against Willie every day in training camp and later every day in practice helped me become a better football player. For as much as we liked each other, Willie and I always went at each other at full speed—or at least close to it.

In training camp we did this drill called the Nutcracker. This was Lombardi's baby. My job was to get Willie out of the way. Willie's was to keep me moving and make the tackle. We dreaded it every year. But when we did it, we did it with everything we had. We didn't leave anything on the field. So one year, we got to talking and we decided we would both move down the line so we could each go against someone else and not each other once we lined up for drills. We maneuvered around the line so Willie got stacked up against a rookie tackle and I got matched with a young defensive back who was a quick kid but not real strong.

We only got through the round once before Lombardi yelled.

"What the hell is going on here? Gregg, Davis, get the hell up here! I wanna see you two go at each other!"

He knew what we were doing. We resigned ourselves to the fact that we were going to have to go against each other anyway so we might as well go hard. Sometimes he'd win, sometimes I'd win, but I can say that we both learned a lot from each other as players, both in those drills as well as all the years we spent practicing and playing with each other.

Frank Popoff, Chairman, Chemical Financial; Former Chairman, Dow Chemical: Boards can be a little prone to fly at about 40,000 feet. At Dow, Willie always brought us down to tree-top level. He made sure we thought of everything. He would ask the good questions at the right time for the right reason. Outside of the board room, he would visit the plants and get to know the people. Everybody knew him and loved him, and he was both a teacher and a learner. Willie took the time and got involved, and that's why he was so good as a director.

Herb Adderley, Former Cornerback, Green Bay Packers: When I was a rookie, I didn't know what to expect when I went to Green Bay. I knew they only had about four or five black players there, and the city didn't have a very big black population. I really had two players that helped me out. Emlen Tunnell was a guy I had a tremendous amount of respect for in terms of what he did in the league, and he really helped me when I switched from offense to defense. And then I lived with Willie Davis, and he helped me understand both how to carry myself off the field and what it takes to play in the NFL.

Even though he was still young, he was one of the best players the Packers had at the time. I watched him give 100 percent effort on every play, even special teams. That's what it was all about. He never gave up on any play; he set the pace.

Off the field, he taught me to be polite to everyone. Green Bay was a small town, and it was important how you treated the fans. Willie taught me that. It wasn't about hanging out in the bars and drinking and smoking. It was about being in Green Bay as a professional player and conducting ourselves in a certain manner at all times. He wanted to set an example, especially for the black players. For as fierce as he was on the field, he carried himself as a gentleman off the field.

He was also someone I could talk to about anything. Even after we stopped rooming together, we talked on the phone every day. We'd talk about football and just life itself. We'd talk about playing in the NFL and how fortunate we felt. We'd talk about the city and how surprised we were that we didn't really encounter any kind of racism and how the fans loved our team and accepted all of us. We'd also talk about world affairs, the Civil Rights struggle that was going on at the time, everything.

During his career, I watched him develop into a leader. He was a natural leader, doing everything a leader does for his team, especially in terms of effort. He was one of the few guys who could chase down any kind of play. Between me, him, and Dave Robinson, we shut down that left side. It didn't matter who we played. We shut it down.

Jack McKeithan, Former Chairman, Schlitz Brewing Co.:
One thing I know for sure, every board Willie Davis was invited to join, including Schlitz, he wasn't brought on for diversity or for his color. They brought him on for his knowledge of business.

Jim Murren, Chairman and CEO, MGM Resorts International:
I joined the board in 1998, and Willie was already a director. I honestly didn't know what to expect. I knew him as a football player, though growing up in Connecticut I was a Giants fan, and bizarrely enough a Chargers fan, as well. I also knew he had some business success after football, but I knew very little about him as a person or director.

When I joined, I was the most junior member by far in terms of experience and age. I was awestruck by the power and presence of these people on the board, including Willie. One thing I noticed in that meeting and almost every meeting after was that Willie almost always sat right next to Kirk Kerkorian. Kirk, who pretty much helped launch Vegas, one of the most powerful and influential men in the world, and here was Willie sitting right next to him, by Kirk's request! I always thought that was pretty telling about Willie's value to the board.

As I progressed in the company, I saw Willie in action and learned myself how valuable he is to the board. He has an extraordinarily calming, stable influence for me and the rest of the board, and that's something we've needed. He's actually at his best when we're facing a crisis. Recently, we've worked on building the largest green project in the world, privately funded in the U.S. in the middle of a recession. You can imagine how difficult that's been. The board meetings got to be highly intense with passions and emotions getting inflamed.

Willie always remains calm. He digests all the information and isn't quick to judge. He tries to look at all the information with different perspectives. When he speaks, it's because he has something to say. He doesn't speak to hear himself talk. He is direct, he doesn't beat around the bush or mince words. He is fearless when it comes to expressing his point of view regardless of who's in the room and what they have to say. Yet he is very open. He has a commanding presence that has helped our board time and time again.

Which is why I make sure he sits right next to me at those meetings now.

Jim Robinson, Former CEO and President, American Express:
When I was CEO at Amex, we were a sponsor of the Super Bowl. We would always host a big corporate party and typically invite some current and former players—Fran Tarkenton, Deacon Jones, and of course, Willie Davis—to mingle with our guests and talk a little football.

I got to know Willie during those events, and he always had a big smile and a twinkle in his eye. He was a great networker. All the guests enjoyed being with Willie. I also discovered he was serious about pursuing business opportunities. We were looking for board members for a subsidiary called the Fireman's Fund, and I instantly thought of Willie in that capacity.

He had an established record well beyond football. He had good common sense, and he was very likeable. I reached out to him as a person who had depth and who could contribute. He was also very, very different than the profiles of others on the board, and he could bring a unique experience and point of view. He quickly became a contributing, thoughtful director who listened, did his homework, and worked as hard as he could.

He has also had (and has) incredible humility despite his success. When I asked him to join, he asked, "Why me?"

"Because you're a unique individual who's been successful," I said.

He just laughed. I still don't know if he was seriously asking me or if it was just Willie being Willie. Whatever the case, that low-key personality was very contagious.

John Bergstrom, Chairman and CEO, Bergstrom Corp.:
I've worked with Willie on three boards and have always been amazed at the combination of wisdom and experience he brings as well as his business intuition.

At a break once at a Wisconsin Energy board meeting, I asked him what the most important business lesson he ever learned was. He smiled and said, "You probably think it would come from a winning season as a Green Bay Packer. Actually, it comes from a game we lost," he said.

He went on to describe a close game they played down to the wire. With just a few minutes left, the Packers kicked off and one of their special teams players made a mistake and went out of his lane, giving up a big play that set up a game-winning score. He said the Packers weren't able to accomplish their goal because one fella didn't do his job.

"The lesson I learned is that every single person on a team is important, and each of them must do their job," he said.

John Wooten, Former Guard, Cleveland Browns:
I played one year with Willie in Cleveland but saw more in that one year, especially in terms of competitiveness, than I saw from a lot of other guys in my career. It was clear he was going to be a great player.

I was actually with Willie when he found out he had been traded to Green Bay. It wasn't very surprising to me. With the situation at our ballclub, he wasn't being given the opportunity to play a lot. I knew he had excellent ability, and I think the coaches did too, they just didn't know where to put him—on offense or on defense. And he knew he wasn't getting the opportunity he needed.

Still, when he got traded, he was devastated. Green Bay at the time was way down on the list. They were not a winning team. Meanwhile, Cleveland was one of the top teams. He looked at it almost like a punishment. Plus he had a life in Cleveland with his off-season teaching job, his wife, and ties into the social scene in Cleveland.

I know he took some convincing, but those of us who knew him knew he would make the best of it eventually. And that's what he did. He was able to pull himself up because of his character, integrity, and values and make himself say, "Hey, I'm going to go take advantage of the situation and be the best I can be."

That's the Willie Davis I knew, and that's why he's had so much success.

Kirk Kerkorian, President and CEO, Tracinda Corp.; Founder, MGM Resorts:
Willie's smart as a whip and just the most pleasant person you could know. That's why I always sat next to him at those board meetings. I thought so well of him and what he could bring to the board but he was just such a kind person.

I remember when the former chairman of MGM, Fred Benninger, passed away a few years ago. Fred and I were very close, and it was an extremely tough loss for me. I was sitting there next to Willie at this memorial, and as people spoke about Fred, I got very choked up and started crying a bit. The whole thing was just so sad and a little overwhelming. So the tears were flowing. All of a sudden, I feel this big hand on my shoulder and patting me on the back. It was Willie Davis making sure I was okay and letting me know he was here for me.

I never forgot that moment, a kind gesture from a kind man.

Lori Davis, Attorney; Daughter:
It was weird growing up with my dad sometimes, especially in Green Bay, because he was such an icon and a public figure. Going out in public with him could bother me sometimes because we could never just have dinner without someone approaching for an autograph or wanting to trade war stories.

My father is more quiet and low key, but you'd never know it. In public, he's gracious and obliging. He'll always stop and talk, and that's one reason why so many people love him.

I remember watching him on TV when I was younger. I don't remember much from his playing days because I was so young, but I remember watching this game on TV with my mom. He got hit in the game. He didn't get too hurt, but he was slow getting up and they showed him on the bench bleeding.

Now at the time, I didn't realize that my father was far more inclined to put the hurt on someone rather than get hurt. So I flipped out. "Mom, we have to go get him! He's hurt! They're hurting him!" My mother tried to calm me down, but I was really upset.

When I talked to my father later that night on the phone, I told him I didn't want him to play anymore.

"Well, that's my job," he said, trying to explain it to me. "That's just part of my job, and I have to go to work."

Then he laughed that big laugh of his and told me not to worry about it.

"I'm Superman!" he said, and I must have taken it to heart because when a reporter did an interview with us a few months later, I told him and everyone watching that my dad was "as tall as a light post and as strong as Superman!"

But what I got from that and what has followed me my whole life was my father's commitment. When you have a job to do, you have an obligation. If you have pain, you deal with it and go to work. That's something I learned from him. That's my dad. He's one of the toughest men I know.

Lurenia Bratton, Sister:

He's always been very protective of us, his family—especially me. I knew that no matter what happened, I could count on him to get me out of trouble. It's always been like that. When we were small, our mother worked so he would have to baby-sit. Even though he was still pretty young himself, he learned how to make us ham and tuna sandwiches. He'd be cleaning at home, washing the dishes, whatever. If I didn't feel well, he'd even take care of my chores. He'd also work all the time to help my mother pay for food and the bills. He was very much a father figure in a lot of ways. He had to be, and in some ways, he still is. If I have a problem, I know he'll be there for me.

Mark Murphy, President and CEO, Green Bay Packers:

There's a reason why we invited him to be our honorary captain against the Chicago Bears in our championship run during the 2010 season. Willie has stayed very active with the Packers, and he continues to inspire the guys on our team today.

It was pretty interesting to see how many of our players knew all about him and what he meant to the game and the organization. He's a tremendous role model for the current players, and I think his presence is very inspiring. It's also great for these young players to see what he's done with his life after football, the success he's achieved off the field. We need more examples like that for to-day's young athletes.

Mike McCarthy, Head Coach, Green Bay Packers:

He and Bart Starr were two of the first players to reach out and welcome me to Green Bay, and that's something that has always meant a lot. Willie is a big part of the Packers family and a great representative of the organization, and he wears that title with pride. I've always appreciated his enthusiasm and his support.

I've had him come talk to the team during training camp, the regular season, and even in the postseason because of what he brings to the table. He's a dynamic individual who speaks from the heart, and our guys need to see that. It's good for a coach to have people like Willie Davis that you can call on.

Paul Oreffice, Former President, CEO and Chairman of Dow Chemical:

In the entire time I worked with him, if you went to anybody, from secretaries and staff to executives and other board members and asked who was the most popular and well-liked member of the Dow Company, every single person would say Willie Davis.

Polly Williams, Former Member, Wisconsin State Assembly:

I've known Willie for over 20 years, since I started leasing office space from his radio station. I also used to run a program on his station where a group of us discussed issues from a black woman's perspective, a program that Willie supported as something that could impact the community.

Willie is very involved in the community, and that's something I've always admired. When he brought his radio station back to a format to serve the black community, he didn't have to do it. But he responded to a need we had. He was receptive and open to what we needed in that community, and many people are grateful for him. Without 1290, our community went into a bit of a depression. When we got it back, we knew it was because of Mr. Willie Davis.

Steve Roell, CEO, Johnson Controls Inc.:

Willie is the kind of man who will bring all his experiences with him in everything he does and every decision he makes. Lucky for anyone who knows him—he has a *lot* of experiences to draw from.

Sources

Organizations

The Green Bay Packers
The Cleveland Browns
Grambling State University
The National Football League
NFL Films
The Pro Football Hall of Fame
The Green Bay Packers Hall of Fame
NFL Alumni Association
All Pro Broadcasting
MGM International
University of Chicago

Newspapers/Media

The Green Bay Gazette
Green Bay News-Chronicle
The Milwaukee Journal Sentinel
The Los Angeles Times
Los Angeles Sentinel
The Milwaukee Times
The Milwaukee Community Journal
Investor's Business Daily
Midland Daily News
The Daily Breeze
Texarkana Gazette
Parade Magazine
Fast Track Magazine
The Urban Network
Databasefootball.com
Jerry Kramer's Inside the Locker Room: The Lost Tapes of His 1967 Championship. Audio CD. Kramer & Company, 2005.

Books

Bengtson, Phil, with Todd Hunt. *Packer Dynasty: The Saga of the Championship Green Bay Teams.* New York: Doubleday & Company, 1969.

Kramer, Jerry, and Dick Schaap. *Instant Replay: The Green Bay Diary of Jerry Kramer.* Norwell, MA: Anchor Press, 2011.

Lombardi, Vince, with W.C. Heinz. *Run to Daylight.* New York: Prentice Hall, 1963.

Maraniss, David. *When Pride Still Mattered: Lombardi.* New York: Simon & Schuster, 2010.

Index